MW01155936

INTRODUCTION TO COMPARATIVE POLITICS

This stimulating and accessible introduction to comparative politics offers a fresh perspective on the fundamentals of political science. Its central theme is the enduring political significance of the modern state despite severe challenges to its sovereignty. There are three main sections to the book. The first traces the origins and meaning of the state and proceeds to explore its relationship to the practice of politics. The second examines how states are governed and compares patterns of governance found in the two major regime types in the world today: democracy and authoritarianism. The last section discusses several contemporary challenges – globalization, ethnic nationalism, terrorism, and organized crime – to state sovereignty. Designed to appeal to students and professors alike, this lively text engages readers as it traces states' struggles against the mutually reinforcing pressures of global economic and political interdependence, fragmented identities and secessionism, transnational criminal networks, and terrorism.

Robert Hislope is Associate Professor in the Department of Political Science at Union College.

Anthony Mughan is Professor of Political Science and Director of International Studies at The Ohio State University.

"Comparativists hoping to teach their craft to undergraduates have oscillated between staid country-by-country approaches and abstract frameworks. Introduction to Comparative Politics: The State and Its Challenges strikes the perfect balance. Hislope and Mughan join accessibility with rigor, helping students learn the nuts and bolts of comparative politics through an engaging tour of the state in its modern variants. Their book efficiently covers a large amount of material while keeping readers engaged with tight prose and vivid examples. Five chapters teach students what the state is and how its operations vary across democratic and authoritarian governments. A quartet of chapters addresses the forces shearing at the twenty-first-century state: globalization, ethnic nationalism, terrorism, and organized crime. During an age of 'hybrid regimes' and a 'global democratic recession,' Introduction to Comparative Politics will help students and educators understand politics across regime types. This is a world-class gateway to the field's most important findings and insights. I strongly recommend it."

– Jason Brownlee, The University of Texas at Austin

"Hislope and Mughan have written a superb book – full of fresh insights, lively writing, and good sense. They introduce traditional theories and concepts in comparative politics with skill and economy, but also highlight contemporary issues of great interest to today's students such as globalization, terrorism, and organized crime. Moreover, by including an extended discussion of autocratic regimes and ethnic nationalism, they offer an important corrective to the Euro-centrism of many textbooks. An ideal introduction to comparative politics."

– Timothy Frye, Marshall D. Shulman Professor of Post-Soviet Foreign Policy and Director, Harriman Institute, Columbia University

"The political scientists Hislope and Mughan have written a timely and impressive introduction to the study of comparative politics. Drawing upon and expanding the best recent research in the subject, they explain how the modern state provides a powerful pathway to understanding key differences across political systems and political institutions such as legislatures, elections, administrative bureaucracies, levels of political violence, and provision of government services. The book is genuinely comparative as the authors examine states in all sorts of political systems, some highly democratic, others less so, and some undemocratic, whether authoritarian or totalitarian. This pedagogical exercise is undertaken with a carefully defined concept of the modern state and with a powerful explanation of the value of comparative analysis. In the second half of the book the two scholars demonstrate how the study of comparative politics centered on the role of the modern state is indispensable for understanding four key trends pressing in on them: the effects of globalization, ethnic-based nationalism across boundaries, non-state-based terrorism, and transnational criminal activities. The result is an outstanding book now available for students and scholars of comparative politics that I recommend highly."

– Desmond King, University of Oxford

"In a complex world, modern states face major challenges from issues as diverse as globalization, democratization, ethnic nationalism, terrorism, and organized crime. In this stimulating, accessible, and thoughtful book, Hislope and Mughan provide an essential overview of these issues and much more, giving readers a well-organized and comprehensive introduction to comparative politics. The book will provide a first-class guide for undergraduates and for all readers interested in understanding the role and limits of the state."

– Pippa Norris, John F. Kennedy School of Government, Harvard University

Introduction to Comparative Politics

THE STATE AND ITS CHALLENGES

Robert Hislope
Union College

Anthony Mughan
The Ohio State University

CAMBRIDGE
UNIVERSITY PRESS

CAMBRIDGE UNIVERSITY PRESS
Cambridge, New York, Melbourne, Madrid, Cape Town,
Singapore, São Paulo, Delhi, Mexico City

Cambridge University Press
32 Avenue of the Americas, New York, NY 10013-2473, USA

www.cambridge.org
Information on this title: www.cambridge.org/9780521758383

First published 2012

Printed in the United States of America

A catalog record for this publication is available from the British Library.

Library of Congress Cataloging in Publication data

Hislope, Robert.
Introduction to comparative politics : the state and its challenges / Robert Hislope,
Union College, Anthony Mughan, Ohio State University.
    p. cm.
Includes bibliographical references and index.
ISBN 978-0-521-76516-9 (hardback) – ISBN 978-0-521-75838-3 (paperback)
1. Comparative government.   2. State, The.   I. Mughan, Anthony.   II. Title.
JF51.H427   2012
320.3–dc23   2012004348

ISBN 978-0-521-76516-9 Hardback
ISBN 978-0-521-75838-3 Paperback

Robert Hislope: *To my wife, Ann-Marie Rajhmundhani.*

Anthony Mughan: *To my parents, Frank and Norah, who made everything possible.*

CONTENTS

LIST OF TABLES

ACKNOWLEDGMENTS

Both authors wish to thank our many students who over the years have provided a wonderful intellectual laboratory for the generation of critical ideas about comparative politics. We especially thank the following Union College students – Andrew Davis, Georgia Swan-Ambrose, Shanique Kerr, Jennifer Ramirez, Lorraine Ater, Sean Mulkerne, and Trevor Flike – who read early versions of the text and whose comments made a substantial contribution to the final product. We thank Cambridge University Press, the book's editors (Robert Dreesen and Ed Parsons), the external reviewers who commented on the manuscript during its various stages, and the copy editor, all of whom offered valuable advice. Also, both authors thank their respective institutions, Union College and The Ohio State University, for creating a rich intellectual climate within which to work.

Robert Hislope offers special thanks to his parents, Bob and Joyce Hislope, and his grandfather, Leroy "Chic" Farrow, Jr. I thank my mates in distant lands – Nenad Marković, Ivan Damjanovski, Dane Taleski, Vladimir Božinovski, Zoran Ilievski, and Aleksandar Kostovski in Macedonia; Kerry Ravello and Riaad George in Trinidad; Michael Frontani at Elon University; and Andy Cumberbatch in transit. I thank President Gjorge Ivanov of the Republic of Macedonia for his friendship and support during years of visits to his country. I offer a most grateful thanks to Tony Mughan, for being an inspiring teacher and an equally inspiring coauthor, and for inviting me on this book journey. Most of all, I thank Ann-Marie Rajhmundhani for her friendship, wisdom, support, and love.

Anthony Mughan offers special thanks to his children, Siân and Tomos, and to his brothers and sister for the richness they have brought to his life. Various colleagues, too many to mention individually, at Cardiff University, The Australian National University, and The Ohio State University also deserve special mention for their friendship and their influence on his thinking about the nature of comparative politics. Lastly, I could not have had a better coauthor; he has been superb in all respects.

1 *The Modern State*

*T*his book is about states and the challenges to sovereignty they face in the contemporary world. We address this issue by systematically comparing states around the globe. As such, this book represents a contribution to comparative politics, which is a core subfield within the academic discipline of political science. The other subfields include international relations, political theory, and American politics. The object of study of comparative politics is to understand similarities and differences in the domestic, or internal, politics of states. Specifically, the goal is to explain why countries are sometimes similar and sometimes different in their domestic political processes and outcomes. A typical political process question is why some governments are popularly elected by their nation's citizenry and why others come to power through violent upheaval, such as revolution. A typical political-outcomes question is why some states provide more generous welfare provision for their citizens than others do. Thus, a "comparativist" is one who observes similarities and differences in the domestic politics of states, develops theoretical explanations for them, and then seeks to test these explanations against new cases.

The state is central to the study of domestic politics because it defines the territorial framework and institutional landscape within which these politics unfold. India, Switzerland, and South Africa, for example, all have political parties to organize and aggregate the various and competing political interests in society. But exactly how these parties function, how they represent their supporters, how they raise and spend money, how they gain power, and even how many parties exist are all strongly shaped by the values, ideas, myths, and practices embedded in the state, as well as by the institutional rules of governance set forth in the state's founding documents (such as the constitution). In other words, there is a "statist" context to politics, and by that we mean that states are among the primary causal elements that shape, frame, and condition the how, what, when, and why of domestic politics. Of course, states are not static entities immune from, and impervious to, the impact and pressure of external forces. On the contrary, the history of the modern state is marked by adjustments and adaptations, and occasionally by revolutionary transformations, which are prompted by powerful social forces such as war, mass movements, technological change, and economic crisis. In the pages that follow, we raise the overarching question of how a number of contemporary global forces – globalization, ethnic nationalism, terrorism, and organized crime – are challenging the sovereignty of modern-day states. As an important step toward solving this puzzle, this chapter establishes a foundation for analysis by providing answers to three specific questions: (1) How significant is the modern state in the contemporary world? (2) What is the state and what are its constituent elements? And (3) from what historical circumstances did the state arise and develop? In addition, we close this chapter with a few brief thoughts on the purpose and role of comparison in the study of the domestic politics of states.

THE SIGNIFICANCE OF THE MODERN STATE

The modern state has a looming presence in the lives of each and every one of us. There are very few people who live outside the reach of a state, and there is very little valuable land on the planet that is not claimed by one or several states. Around the globe, the state is the normal and prevailing mode of political organization, and state-to-state interaction is the cornerstone of international relations. Most of us live under state authority. It was not always this way. Before the nineteenth century, for example, it was still possible to escape the reach of a state. At that time, states had little control over their borders, limited knowledge of their populations, and a low capacity to enforce laws uniformly across their territories. All this has now changed.

Today, the state touches our lives, in one way or another, from cradle to grave. Typically, our first encounter with the modern state begins with compulsory registration at birth, followed by the legal obligation to attend a public (or state-certified) school, a requirement historically referred to as "compulsory education," and which sometimes involves a daily public pledge of allegiance to the state. Over the course of our lives, we encounter representatives of the state in a variety of settings – the policeman, the mailman, the bureaucrat, the judge, the elected official, and of the course, the most difficult to evade, the taxman. As these examples indicate, the state is a special institution in society. It makes unique authority claims and has the power to enforce them. That is, unlike other institutions in society, such as the business corporation, the trade union, or the church, the state claims the preeminent right to rule and regulate the affairs of all. And unlike all other institutions in society, the state alone possesses a preponderance of the means of deadly violence that it can deploy for purposes it alone sees fit. For these two reasons, the state is *the* central political institution in modern society.

The reach of the modern state is both deep and wide. It is deep in the manner in which it can reach into the pockets of its citizens for taxes, mobilize its youth for war, and the way in which it regulates the universals of human existence: reproduction, education, work, health, sex, marriage, and death. Of course, we may not be surprised when nondemocratic states overburden their citizens with onerous invasions and violations of personal freedoms. But consider, for a moment, the omnipresent types of regulations that occur in modern Western democracies, which govern everything from the disposal of yard waste to the building of tree houses in backyards, the zoning of land, the consumption of alcohol, tobacco, pharmaceuticals, and recreational drugs, the appropriate type of public clothing ("no shirt, no shoes, no service"), and the wearing of seat belts and motorcycle helmets. In the U.S. state of Illinois, there are even legal limits on the distance (no more than one-half mile) that one may drive an automobile in the left passing lane! The prominent political scientist Giovanni Sartori had in mind such micromanagement when he wondered "how posterity will be able to cope with the hundreds of thousands of laws that increase, at times, at the rates of thousands per legislature" (Sartori 1987, 325).

Modern states have also proved adept at consuming an ever-larger share of the nation's wealth, or gross domestic product (GDP). For instance, at the beginning of the twentieth century, state budgets amounted to only 10 percent of GDP in Western Europe and the United States. By the end of the century, however, the average was close to 50 percent, with some northern European countries, like Sweden, reaching 70 percent. In sum, the power of the modern state runs deep in society and shows no sign of abating. In light of such trends, the historian Eric Hobsbawm makes the rather sobering and frightening observation that the modern state's "powers are immense – far greater, even in liberal democracies, than those of the greatest and most despotic empires before the eighteenth century" (Hobsbawm 2000: 14).

The reach of the state is wide too, in the sense that the state as a model of political organization has been replicated around the globe, trumping and subordinating all other authority structures. The growth of the state, in fact, has been nothing short of spectacular. Since the 1700s, states have spread across the globe, displacing empire, city-state, feudal order, tribe, and village commune as alternative forms of political organization. Today in the world, there are 193 states that enjoy international recognition and therefore membership in the United Nations (UN). Another eighteen entities are potential states, such as the former Yugoslav province of Kosovo, but they lack international recognition. When the UN was founded at the end of World War II in 1945, it had a membership base of only fifty-one states. By 1975 (a mere thirty years later), this number had grown to 144 member states. Another way to look at this is through participation in the International Olympic Summer Games. The ancient Greek games were revived in 1896, with the number of attending states growing from 22 at the 1908 London Games, to 46 at the Games in Amsterdam in 1928, to 112 at the 1968 Games in Mexico City, and most recently to a record 191 states, plus 13 non-state territories, at the 2008 Beijing Games. From where did all these new states come?

The short answer is the end of colonialism. Of the fifty-four sovereign states that define Africa today, only two were independent prior to the 1950s: Ethiopia and Liberia. The modern state system first developed in Europe between the seventeenth and nineteenth century, and the economic and military advantages offered by this mode of organization facilitated the European conquest of the rest of the globe during this time. Between 1880 and 1914, Europe began a "scramble for Africa" that ended with the subjugation of virtually the entire continent. All the major European powers had colonies in Africa: Great Britain had present-day Nigeria, Ghana, Egypt, Sudan, Uganda, Kenya, Zambia, Zimbabwe, and South Africa; France controlled most of western Africa plus the island of Madagascar; Spain held a portion of Morocco and the western Sahara; Belgium controlled the Congo; Portugal possessed Angola and Mozambique; Italy had Somalia, Eritrea, and Libya; and Germany, a relative latecomer to colonialism, was able nonetheless to grab Namibia and Tanzania for a brief period. It was not until the 1960s that most of Africa finally achieved independent statehood.

The two decades following World War II thus witnessed a remarkable expansion in the number of states, for the story just told about Africa could also be repeated for much of the Caribbean, Asia, and the Middle East. (Latin America, in contrast, won its independence from European colonialism during the early nineteenth century.) Major shakeups in the international order, including world wars, political and economic crises, and dramatic shifts in power, such as the end of colonialism, often create new opportunities for aggrieved groups to press for statehood and political control of their own destiny. World War II is an excellent example of this phenomenon, but so is the aftermath of World War I (1914–1918).

At the end of World War I, the principle sites of state construction were Eastern Europe and the Middle East. U.S. President Woodrow Wilson diagnosed the causes of the war to have been the nondemocratic, multinational empires of Germany, Austria-Hungry, Ottoman Turkey, and Czarist Russia. These great powers matched their domestic authoritarianism with an external belligerence that Wilson and others at the time described as militarism. Wilson's famous "Fourteen Points," written to guide the postwar settlement, called for the dismantling of such empires and the liberation of their subject peoples on the grounds of national self-determination and democracy. Consequently, in the 1919 Treaty of Versailles, Poland regained the sovereignty it had lost to Germany and Russia, Hungary became independent of Austria, the small and diverse peoples of the Balkans were grouped into a new state called Yugoslavia, the Baltic peoples of Estonia, Latvia, and Lithuania were freed from Russia (as was Finland), and the Czechs and the Slovaks of Central Europe merged into a new state bearing a synthesis of their names. All in all, a total of nine new states were added to the map of Europe.

In the Middle East, the dissolution of the Ottoman Empire also led to the formation of several new states in the 1920s and 1930s, such as Egypt, Saudi Arabia, and Iraq. The League of Nations gave "mandates" to both Britain and France to govern temporarily many of the other Middle Eastern states with which we are familiar today, such as Jordan, Lebanon, Syria, and Palestine/Israel. Statehood would come to these mandates only after World War II.

The collapse of one-party communist rule in Eastern Europe and the Soviet Union in the late 1980s–early 1990s brought about a third and final wave of new state creation in the twentieth century. Like the authoritarian empires of the past, communism failed to satisfy the political demands of ethnic groups for cultural expression and political self-rule. And like the new opportunities created for national self-determination that occurred at the time of the two world wars, the postcommunist transition produced the political space for dissatisfied groups to free themselves from the rule of others. When the dust settled from the crumbling of the Soviet bloc, three multinational states had disappeared – the Soviet Union, Yugoslavia,

| TABLE 1.1 | The global diffusion of the state in the twentieth century |

Time period	Regions	Number of new states
Post–World War I (1918–1935)	Eastern Europe and the Middle East	14
Post–World War II (1945–1965)	Africa, the Caribbean, Asia, and the Middle East	54
Post–Cold War (1989–1993)	Eastern Europe and Eurasia	23

and Czechoslovakia – leaving twenty-three new states in their wake. Fifteen of those newly independent countries came from the Soviet Union, six from Yugoslavia, and two from Czechoslovakia. This veritable boom in new state construction compelled Warren Christopher to declare, during his 1993 Senate confirmation hearings for the position of U.S. Secretary of State: "If we don't find some way that the different ethnic groups can live together in a country, how many countries will we have? We'll have 5,000 countries rather than the hundred plus we have now" (Binder and Crossette 1993). Table 1.1 presents the number of states that were established in specific geographic regions during critical junctures in the international order.

Secretary Christopher's fears may be exaggerated, but even so, the rapid duplication of the state around the globe and the regulatory extension of state authority into the most intimate details of the private life of citizens lead one to conclude that the state stands as the central political institution of modernity. All politically organized groups and activists hope to either run the state or influence its policy. Political parties aim to win public office and thereby set state policy; interest groups, lobbyists, and social movements seek to reinforce or change the direction of state policy; and anti-system radicals seek to overthrow the state so that they and like-minded others can reorganize it and run it according to their own principles. Around the globe, the aspiration for statehood has led to the mobilization of mass movements, riots, civil wars, terrorism, genocides, and state partitions. The magnetic power of modern statehood is no better exemplified than during the postcolonial periods in Asia, Africa, the Caribbean, Latin America, and the Middle East. In many of these cases, the generation of national elites at the time of independence rejected variously capitalism, Western culture, democracy, and/or alliances with Western powers, but none rejected the model of the modern state first forged in Europe between the seventeenth and nineteenth century. Let us now turn to a closer examination of that model.

▩ WHAT IS THE STATE?

The state can be a difficult concept to grasp intellectually. It is closely associated with other concepts that are often used interchangeably with it, such as government and regime, but it is distinct from both. Furthermore, different cultures conceive of the state in different ways. The Anglo-American political tradition, defined by the classical liberal philosophy of John Locke (1632–1704), Adam Smith (1723–1790), and Thomas Jefferson (1743–1826), leans toward an empirically grounded conception of the state as the "government." In this view, the government constitutes the day-to-day officeholders and permanent bureaucrats who decide on and carry out the activities of the state. It is the government that acts on behalf of the state, and it is those elected to government offices that are held accountable for its actions by the citizenry.

The continental European tradition, in contrast, frames the state in more abstract terms, often capitalizing the concept ("the State") to emphasize its role as a unitary and autonomous actor with interests distinct from society. Continental European thinkers like Jean-Jacques Rousseau (1712–1778) and G.W.F. Hegel (1770–1831) argued that the state was a special moral agent that was greater than the sum of its individual parts and capable of transforming and elevating humankind. As Rousseau wrote, the architects of a state are "in a position to change human nature, to transform each individual . . . into a part of a larger whole; to alter man's constitution in order to strengthen it;" and to provide a "moral existence for the physical and independent existence we have all received from nature" (Rousseau 1983: 39). A grand conception of the State such as this cannot be meaningfully captured by the rather ordinary concept of government.

When studying the state, most political scientists take as their starting point the German sociologist Max Weber's (1864–1920) classic definition, whereby the state is a "human community that (successfully) claims the monopoly of the legitimate use of physical force within a given territory" (Gerth and Mills 1946: 78). Each constituent part of this definition – *community, legitimacy, monopoly of force,* and *territory* – is crucial and therefore must be considered separately and in greater detail.

Nationalism and the Nation-State

First of all, states are based on human communities. Populations that share a sense of national identity and unity are an indispensable condition of states. Without a sense of collective identity, a belief in "we the people," a state cannot exist. Such a belief is not automatic or even natural, however. How then does it come to be that millions of different people hold a common identity? How is this possible when "members of even the smallest nation will never know most of their fellow-members, meet them, or even hear of them, yet in the minds of each lives the image of their communion" (Anderson 1983: 15)? This is partly explained by the fact that states use ideological tools, like patriotism and religion (the combination of which Rousseau called a "civil religion"), to generate a common identity and encourage an overriding loyalty to the whole. One of the most powerful political doctrines used to accomplish this goal in the modern world is nationalism.

Nationalism is a political doctrine that demands a vertical and horizontal congruence between nation and state (Gellner 1983). In vertical terms, nationalists insist that political leaders be of the same national composition as the general population. Foreign or alien rule is no longer politically acceptable in the way it was in European history before the nineteenth century. Before the age of nationalism (the 1800s), there was the age of absolutism (1700s), in which monarchical families, whose territory and peoples were determined by conquest, compensation, inheritance, purchase, and marriage, ruled Europe. Thus, the Romanov dynasty (a Russian-German family) ruled Russians, Tatars, Germans, Armenians, and Finns from 1613 to 1917; the House of Hapsburg (originally a Swiss family) ruled Hungarians, Croats, Czechs, Slovaks, Italians, Portuguese, and Austrians for 600 years; rival factions of the House of Bourbon (a French-Spanish family) ruled France, Spain, and Luxembourg; and the Hanoverians (a German dynasty) became the royal family ruling Scots, Irish, English, and Welsh from 1714 onward.

The modern nation-state is built on the contrary premise that leaders and masses must share a common culture and national background. So powerful is the sense of nationalism in the world today that the English philosopher Isaiah Berlin expects that most people, if given a choice, would "consciously prefer" rule by domestic authoritarians rather than foreign democrats (Berlin 2000, 196). The overwhelming public opposition in Iraq to America's occupation is an example. In a January 2006 poll, 71 percent of Iraqis demanded that U.S. forces withdraw from their country within a year, while 79 percent felt that the U.S. military had a negative influence on internal conditions (WorldPublicOpinion.Org, 2006).

In horizontal terms, nationalism demands that the state's territorial boundaries encompass all members of the nation as well as the land on which they reside. The Italian nationalist Giuseppe Mazzini (1805–1872) offered a like-minded formula of nationalism: "every nation a state, only one state for the entire nation." Prior to the 1700s, there was no attempt by European monarchs, princes, or lords to promote a common culture based on a single language or ethnic makeup. Elites and masses were segmented into distinct groups. The aristocratic class was linked by culture, marriage, and language, speaking Latin during the Middle Ages (from the twelfth to the seventeenth century) and French in the eighteenth century. The masses spoke their local dialects and associated identity variously with place of origin, craft, or faith. Nineteenth-century "national awakeners," like Mazzini, transformed this situation by persuading masses to broaden their identities from a parochial to national level (Hroch 2000). Promoting the idea of statehood for nations, nationalism contributed to the state-building process. Once established, states find nationalism useful as a unifying force and encourage it by way of centralized education, the promotion of a single language, and the cultivation of patriotism. In European history, the building of nations and states were mutually reinforcing processes. As another Italian nationalist and statesman Massimo d'Azeglio (1798–1866) declared, "we have made Italy, now we have to make Italians" (Hobsbawm 1990, 44).

The nation-state idea became an attractive model for replication on the heels of the French revolution (1789–1815). French radicals declared the "universal rights of man and citizen." The forces of nationalism were harnessed in the new republic to spur the state-building process. A new national flag was adopted, a new national anthem (*La Marseilleise*) was written, a new calendar was invented, and the term *citoyen* (or citizen) became the standard form of greeting. Napoleon himself is responsible for a number of crucial innovations. He was the first leader of Europe to mobilize the mass of peasants into a formidable national army. He promulgated the "Code Napoléon," which was a system of uniform laws aimed at annulling and overriding the myriad relics of feudal authority. And he created a massive bureaucracy whose role was to ensure the national laws were implemented effectively at the local level. Armed with these innovations, the French exported their revolution across central Europe, knocking down feudal privileges and archaic forms of authority everywhere. It was this progressive impact that led the German philosopher Hegel to proclaim Napoleon the "world spirit on horseback." Overall,

TABLE 1.2 The state and moral terms of discourse

Concept	Definition
Sovereignty	Indicates possession of supreme authority over a given territory such that no other entities – whether domestic or international – may interfere with the exercise of that authority.
Authority	The moral right to rule coupled with the obligation of the ruled to obey.
Legitimacy	Indicates that compliance in an authority relationship is acceptable and given voluntarily.
Power	The use of coercion to get someone to do something he or she would not otherwise do.
Hegemony	Masses provide consent (and therefore legitimacy) to a system of authority that exploits them.

the French revolution demonstrated the power of patriotic symbols and national unity, and this was a lesson that ricocheted across Europe, leading to the rise of nationalism as a major political force in the nineteenth century and in the rest of the world in the twentieth century. It remains a critical ingredient in the continuation of the organizational supremacy of the state to this day.

Moral Foundations of the State

At this point, we need to pause and clarify a few fundamental terms of political discourse and examine how they relate to one another. In Weber's definition, he mentions the idea of the "*legitimate* use of physical force." What is legitimacy? And how does it permit the use of physical force? To answer this question appropriately requires that one inspect a range of concepts in the same semantic field as legitimacy, such as sovereignty, authority, power, and hegemony. Table 1.2 provides a summary of the terms discussed in this section. Let us start with sovereignty.

Sovereignty conveys the idea that states reign supreme within their own borders and enjoy legal equality internationally. The concept underpins the international system of states we have in the world today. One of the earliest thinkers on the issue of sovereignty was Jean Bodin (1530–1596), who wrote at a time of extreme political rivalry between Catholics and Protestants in France, and whose goal was to reinvigorate the French monarchy so that it could stave off rivals and establish order. In his *Six Books on the State*, published in 1576, he defined sovereignty as "the absolute and perpetual power of the state, that is, the greatest power to command" (Bodin 1955).

The Peace of Westphalia in 1648 is often cited as the "big bang" that began the modern state system. This was the peace treaty that ended the Thirty Years' War – a conflict between Catholics and Protestants that engulfed most of Europe. Traditionally, political scientists have deemed Westphalia to be the critical juncture at which Europe moved away from the Holy Roman Empire and set out on the path of modern statehood. Recent scholarship, however, has subjected this view to considerable criticism, arguing that Westphalia had less to do with establishing sovereign states than previously imagined and was, more than anything, a new constitution for the Holy Roman Empire (Krasner 1993; Osiander 2001). There is no doubt that the sovereign state as we know it developed gradually between the 1600s and 1800s and had not taken anywhere near final shape by 1648. That it is still common to read phrases in the political science literature like the "Westphalian state" or "Westphalian sovereignty" points more to its value as a summary statement of the way the international state system evolved rather than as an accurate description of a watershed change that took place at a single point in time. As an iconic phrase, Westphalian sovereignty communicates two principles: (1) that each state unit has absolute authority (i.e., is sovereign) within its territorial boundaries, and (2) that all states have legal equality and therefore none can interfere in the domestic affairs of the other (called the principle of nonintervention).

Authority is the moral right to rule and, reciprocally, the duty of the governed (citizens or subjects) who accept that right to obey (Wolff 1970). In modern democratic states, authority rests on the consent of the governed. It is this consent that grants authority figures the *moral* right to rule and imposes on all the *obligation* of obedience. Another way to say this is that popular consent in a democracy makes authority legitimate. Legitimacy, in turn, means that compliance in an authority relationship is acceptable and given voluntarily. It follows that authority and legitimacy are closely interconnected concepts.

What happens if authority is deprived of legitimacy? This is certainly a possibility, and history offers many examples of authority figures overstepping the bounds of what is politically acceptable and thereby inducing mass rebellion. The revolt of the American colonies against Great Britain in the eighteenth century is a case in point. As Thomas Jefferson wrote in the *Declaration of Independence*, when the people suffer from a "long train of abuses and usurpations," all of which point to the onset of "absolute Despotism, it is their right, it is their duty, to throw off such Government and provide new Guards for their security." The American colonists had many complaints against the English crown, with one of the more noteworthy irritations being the imposition of burdensome taxes without first seeking consent; hence the famous phrase used to justify American revolutionary action – "no taxation without representation." The gap between elite demands and mass expectations can often grow so wide that dangerous conditions are set for intense conflict between the state and society. When legitimacy is subtracted from authority, only power remains to sustain the hierarchical relationship between the governors and the governed.

Power is the use of coercion to get someone to do something he or she would not otherwise do. The reduction of authority to power has real political consequences, in that authority is a relatively cheap and efficient form of rule. If citizens regard authority figures as legitimate, then mass compliance is relatively easy to secure. All that is needed is knowledge of what authority figures want. In the words of the scholar Charles Lindblom, authority is a "method of control that often works with extraordinary simplicity. Sometimes not even a word is needed; in an authority relation a docile person knows what is wanted of him and does it without being told" (Lindblom 1977, 18). A good example of this is U.S. Senator John F. Kennedy's call to young people to engage in voluntary international service during his 1960 presidential campaign. The appeal was so effective that in the weeks following the speech, 30,000 letters flooded into his campaign office expressing support for the creation of a "peace corps" (Vestal 2001).

Power, in contrast, is not so cost-effective. It requires the use of coercive instruments – police and military action, surveillance, imprisonment, monetary fines – to extract compliance. This can be very costly in two senses: (1) state resources are consumed and therefore must be replenished; and (2) repressive action may backfire and encourage an even more serious rebellion than the state initially faced. Now, in the real world of politics, power and authority are often intermingled, and any given state will usually employ both methods of control, the balance between them depending on the issue and subgroups involved. For example, the U.S. government uses its authority to persuade people, via media campaigns, not to use what it defines as illicit drugs. For those that fail to comply, the full force of the state's punitive power is employed in what it calls, tellingly, the "*war* on drugs." In short, authority "appeals" whereas power "orders" (Sartori 1987, 188).

On what principle is the modern state founded: power or authority? As in most things political, the answer depends on who you ask. The classical liberal philosophers in the Anglo-American tradition employed the idea of a "social contract" to account for the origins of the state. In the stories told by thinkers such as Thomas Hobbes (1588–1679) and John Locke, free people in a state of nature find they lack security and are readily open to attack by others. To ensure the safety and liberty of each, individuals willingly and rationally consent to the creation of a state that is charged with protecting all. To quote again Jefferson's famous lines: "We hold these truths to be self-evident, that all men are created equal, that they are endowed by their Creator with certain unalienable Rights, that among these are Life, Liberty and the pursuit of Happiness. – That to Secure these rights, Governments are instituted among Men, deriving their just consent from the governed." Thus, in the Anglo-American liberal tradition, authority is created when the social contract is signed and remains legitimate unless or until state authorities gravely violate the terms of the compact.

Critics of classical liberalism contend just the opposite; to wit, the founding of the state is based on violence, usurpation, and conquest. The French philosopher Jean-Jacques Rousseau was part of the social contract tradition, but what stood out clearly to him was how flawed and unequal relations were at the original signing. "Man is born free, but everywhere he is in chains," he famously wrote. The rich and powerful in the state of nature were responsible for this unhappy outcome, for it was they who "invented specious reasons" that equated their narrow interests with that of the common people. Driven by the "hidden desire to profit at the expense of someone else," the rich donned a "mask of benevolence" and were thus able to fool average people into believing that liberty would be theirs, when in fact "they all ran to chain themselves" (Rousseau 1983, 17, 148–50). Rousseau thus began an antiliberal tradition that paved the way for the development of two powerful anti-system ideologies in the nineteenth century: socialism and anarchism. For these radical traditions of thought, it is power, not authority, that underlies the modern state.

This brings us to a final concept to consider, which is hegemony. This term has become increasingly popular among students of politics over the past few decades. At the same time, it takes on different shades of meaning depending on whether one is applying it to domestic or international politics. In international relations, hegemony is defined as a condition in which one state has clear political, military, and economic supremacy over all others. The "hegemon" is the leading state in the international system, and it uses its power to promote and preserve the established world order. Although the hegemonic state certainly has a preponderance of power, it will typically employ measures that Joseph Nye (2008) characterizes as "soft power," such as diplomacy, ideology, economics, and cultural resources (movies, music, etc.), to realize its goals, rather than the "hard power" of brute force. In this way, hegemons are distinguished from empires, which rely much more on violence and the threat of violence to secure their interests. This particular use of hegemony has Greek origins and was originally used by Thucydides (460 B.C.–395 B.C.) and other ancient contemporaries to describe the shifting fortunes of Athens and Sparta, as well as the types of alliances they constructed to battle external threats (Lentner 2005). Today, it is common to hear the United States described as the hegemon of the international order.

It is in the domestic setting that hegemony takes on critical overtones and directly challenges the notion of legitimate authority. The historical roots of this application of the term are found in the writings of the Italian Marxist, Antonio Gramsci (1891–1937). Marxism in general argues that the profit-oriented, free-market economic system of capitalism is inherently oppressive and exploitative. The Marxist aim is to mobilize the working class to overthrow capitalism and replace it with a more egalitarian, fairer economic system, typically called socialism.

Hegemony is an important concept for Marxists and other critics of capitalism because it explains why and how the working class is loyal to a social, economic, and political system – capitalism – that institutionalizes inequality and exploitation. This issue held particular relevance for Gramsci who, like all European Marxists of the time, expected a left-wing socialist revolution in western Europe between the two world wars (1920s–1930s) and instead witnessed, and suffered under, the rise of right-wing fascism. There is often a very high price to pay for political miscalculations, and Gramsci spent the last eleven years of his life incarcerated in a fascist prison reflecting on his party's errors. It was here that he developed the concept of hegemony.

For Gramsci, hegemony is a form of capitalist rule in which popular consent is accorded to the ruling class for the general direction of social life. It is much like the concept of authority in the sense that the governed provide their consent, and therefore the state can rely more on persuasion and influence, and less on coercion, to attain compliance. Unlike authority, however, hegemony conveys the suspicion that the original contract between elites and masses to establish a system of authority was a bad contract, and that the populace was less than fully informed when it provided consent. Specifically, Gramsci and his followers explored how the state uses institutions in society – schools, churches, the media – to convince the working class that its interests are best served by the capitalist class. The French Marxist Louis Althusser (1918–1990) characterized these institutions as "ideological state apparatuses" whose primary function is to persuade the working class that capitalism is a part of the natural order of things, an unchangeable "given" that must simply be accepted (Carnoy 1984). In this way, workers provide their "consent" and come to embrace a system that is in reality antithetical to their interests.

WAIT A MINUTE. **CONSIDER THIS**. Hegemony is an important concept because it offers a critical and suspicious view of established authority. Whether one chooses to use the term "authority" or "hegemony" to describe the conceptual and moral foundations of the contemporary state is a function of intellectual reasoning and political allegiances. Which term – "authority" or "hegemony" – do you think is most fitting to describe the moral foundations of the modern democratic state?

Monopoly of the Means of Violence

A third pillar associated with the state, according to Max Weber, is the "successful claim on the monopoly of the legitimate use of physical force." States control the legal means of coercion and violence, such as the military, customs agents, the secret services, and the entire penal system (police, prisons, and parole). It is this monopoly that distinguishes the modern state from other institutions in society, none of which – the business corporation, the trade union, the church, the interest group, the political party – are permitted to amass similar weaponry or to use violence to challenge the state or punish its individual members. Just what exactly is entailed by the monopoly of the means of violence is no better appreciated than by anarchists, who steadfastly oppose state authority. In the following quote, the French anarchist Pierre Joseph Proudhon (1809–1865) conveys, with full rhetorical force, what states are capable of doing with all that concentrated means of violence at their disposal:

> To be GOVERNED is to be watched, inspected, spied upon, directed, law – driven, numbered, regulated, enrolled, indoctrinated, preached at, controlled, checked, estimated, valued, censured, commanded, by creatures who have neither the right nor the wisdom nor the virtue to do so. To be GOVERNED is to be at every operation, at every

transaction noted, registered, counted, taxed, stamped, measured, numbered, assessed, licensed, authorized, admonished, prevented, forbidden, reformed, corrected, punished. It is, under pretext of public utility, and in the name of the general interest, to be placed under contribution, drilled, fleeced, exploited, monopolized, extorted from, squeezed, hoaxed, robbed; then, at the slightest resistance, the first word of complaint, to be repressed, fined, vilified, harassed, hunted down, abused, clubbed, disarmed, bound, choked, imprisoned, judged, condemned, shot, deported, sacrificed, sold, betrayed; and to crown all, mocked, ridiculed, derided, outraged, dishonored. That is government; that is its justice; that is its morality (Proudhon 1923, 293–94).

The monopoly of the means of violence not only distinguishes the state from other institutions in society, but also distinguishes the state historically. Medieval Europe, circa 1500, for example, was a place where rival claims of authority between competing kings, lords, princes, and the church were matched by the possession and use of organized force on all sides. In this setting of political fragmentation, overlapping authority claims, and the proliferation of competing armed groups, life was, as the English philosopher Thomas Hobbes famously said, "nasty, brutish, and short" (Hobbes 1958, 107).

Early American history, and particularly the process of westward expansion, offers another interesting example of an incomplete central authority competing with other forms of organized, lethal resistance, such as local settler militias, vigilante squads, gangs of outlaws and bandits, and Native Americans. American culture is populated by notorious figures (Billy the Kid, John Wesley Hardin, the Great Depression exploits of Bonnie Parker and Clyde Barrow) and infamous gangs (the Jesse James–Cole Younger gang of western Missouri [1866–1882], the Doolin–Dalton gang of the Oklahoma Territory [1892–1896]), all of which not only robbed and murdered at will, but also garnered substantial popular support in the process. By targeting institutions perceived to exploit the common man, such as banks and railroad companies, and by fighting and killing predatory representatives of the state – tax collectors, federal Reconstruction agents, Pinkerton guards, and U.S. Marshals – these otherwise common criminals became champions of the people.

The popularizing of criminals in the American past speaks to a time when state authority was not universally considered legitimate and the consolidation of the state was incomplete. But far from being a product of American exceptionalism, this situation is a near-universal of the state-building process. Thus, in the nineteenth century, Spain, Italy, Greece, Macedonia, Serbia, and Brazil all experienced notable periods in which banditry was dressed up, and in many respects legitimized, by an anti-state/anti-authority posture. In an 1872 letter to the *Kansas City Times*, Jesse James spoke of the fine line that separates outlaws from those who write the laws: "Some editors call us thieves. We are not thieves – we are bold robbers. I am proud of the name, for Alexander the Great was a bold robber, and Julius Caesar, and Napoleon Bonaparte. Just let a party of men commit a bold robbery, and the cry is to hang them, but [General Ulysses] Grant and his party can steal millions, and it is all right.... They rob the poor and rich, and we rob the rich and give to the poor" (McPherson 2003, 21–22; Hobsbawm 2000; White 1981).

By the twentieth century, the state in Western Europe and North America had developed sufficiently to eliminate banditry as both a social phenomenon and a challenge to central authority. Technological advances in information, communications, and transportation were employed by the state to gain greater control over its borders and to amass knowledge on the movements and activities of its citizens. The bureaucracy accumulated and used ever more details about the population to, for example, levy taxes, while the police forces became professionalized and effectively exerted control over the entire territory of the state. The process by which the state came to monopolize possession of the means of violence was not an easy or automatic task. It often entailed coercively suppressing renegade regions, imposing martial law, executing oppositional leaders, and sometimes offering amnesty for those willing to turn in their guns. The political scientist John Sidel calls this process "primitive political accumulation," by which he means the state's expropriation of the means of coercion from autonomous and private powerholders in society (Sidel 1999, 18).

Now, we must consider a very inconvenient and perhaps astonishing fact: The modern state does not technically hold a monopoly of the means of violence. Civilians around the world actually own more firearms than military and law enforcement agencies combined! There are approximately 875 million factory-made firearms in the world, with civilians possessing 650 million of them, or 75 percent. This far exceeds that held by the military (200 million; approximately 22 percent) and policing agencies (26 million, or 3 percent). The incomparable scale of private gun ownership in the United States does work to skew these figures. Americans are only 5 percent of the world's population, and yet they possess somewhere between 35 percent and 50 percent of the world's firearms.

In 2007, a study estimated that for every 100 people in America, nearly 89 had a gun; on the other end of the spectrum are European countries like England and the Netherlands, where the matching figures are 6.2 and 3.9, respectively. Still, if one were to eliminate the American case from the equation, civilian ownership of firearms around the world would continue to eclipse that held by the state, albeit by a lesser margin. Thus, the preponderance of civilian ownership would fall from a ratio of three or five civilian guns for every military/police gun to two or three to one (Small Arms Survey 2007).

The caveat to all this is that weaponry held by the state is more sophisticated and deadly than that found in the general population. The 1960s marked a turning point for military forces, which began to use more automatic weaponry, and this was matched by the transformation of law enforcement in the 1980s, when it turned to semiautomatic pistols as standard issue. In the U.S. alone, the number of local police forces adopting SWAT (special weapons and tactics) units increased by 1,500 percent in the last two decades (Baker 2011). Furthermore, states everywhere possess forms of deadly force usually not found in the general population, such as tanks, armored vehicles, grenades, machine guns, rocket launchers, helicopters, and so on. In the final analysis, therefore, the balance of firepower is in the hands of the state. The uneven and random holdings of firearms in the population at large, no matter the quantity, remain no match for the concentrated and easily mobilizable instruments of coercion at the beck and call of state authorities. Furthermore, most states place constraints on citizens' access to, and use of, firearms. Japan is an extreme example in forbidding not only the possession of firearms in the general public, but hunting guns as well. Accordingly, for every 100 people in Japan, only .6 has a gun (Small Arms Survey 2007).

Thus, what states really possess is an *effective*, rather than an *absolute*, monopoly of the means of violence. Of course, many states around the world fail to measure up even to this standard. Pakistan is a case in point. Its borderlands with Afghanistan, particularly the districts of North and South Waziristan, are heavily militarized areas that lie outside the control of the central government in Islamabad. Recent estimates suggest the region is home to 2,000 armed Islamic fighters, the recruits being drawn from local Pakistani tribes, Afghans, Arabs, Uzbeks, and other Central Asian nations. The Pakistan military has tried on different occasions to establish control over the region, described as a Taliban "mini-state," but has not been successful (Gall and Khan 2006; International Crisis Group 2006).

Situations comparable to Pakistan are replicated around the globe. Mexico, for example, is currently in the throes of a vicious drug war in which organized crime groups target police, politicians, and judges (McKinley 2008). Colombia has been enmeshed in a guerrilla war with the Revolutionary Armed Forces in Colombia (FARC), a group that has controlled between 15 percent and 20 percent of Colombia's territory for forty years. When the Yugoslav state began to unravel politically in the early 1990s, the new political parties that emerged in Croatia, Bosnia, and Serbia all quickly rushed to create armed wings. The same is true in Lebanon. During its civil war (1975–1991), forty different armies, representing Lebanon's dense and deeply divided religious communities, as well as neighboring states, fought for political control. Although Lebanon is now relatively stable and peaceful, one of the most powerful political parties in the country, Hezbollah, maintains a private army of 3,000 soldiers. A final example comes from Macedonia where, in February 2001, ethnic Macedonian police entered a remote Albanian village bordering Kosovo. The shooting spree that followed triggered a six-month conflict between the Macedonian military and Albanian paramilitaries that had organized during Kosovo's war with Serbia two years earlier (Hislope 2004).

In short, states that have yet to secure an effective monopoly of the means of violence tend to experience a dizzying proliferation of militarized groups including party militias, private mercenaries, insurgent armies, jihadist/terrorist fighters, right-wing death squads, and mafia drug cartels. In these states, armed militias are often de facto rulers of entire regions of states, law enforcement is absent or corrupt, the judiciary is compromised or intimidated, and the legal infrastructure is underdeveloped. In a word, the historical task of primitive political accumulation remains an unfinished business in many parts of the world. The states that experience such conditions are commensurately weak.

Territory

We have now come to Weber's last element of the state, which is territory. Without territory, states do not exist. Revolutions and internal upheaval can compel governments to go into exile (from where they may plot their return), but when states lose their territory, they disappear. This was the unhappy fate of Poland for 123 years, as it was divided between Prussia (later Germany) and Russia in 1795. Geography is destiny for states, for in the absence of a definite territory over which it is sovereign, one cannot properly speak of a state. Apart from international recognition, which bestows formal sovereignty, control over territory is the most tangible confirmation of statehood. In fact, territory is more fundamental, for without it, recognition does not make sense. As the sales pitch of the real estate agent suggests, God is not creating any more land. It is for this reason that states are extremely reluctant to cede any part of their territory to other states or to allow rebellious regions within the state to break away. Take away a state's zip code, and you take away the state.

The territory of the modern state serves to demarcate the jurisdiction within which claims of authority and the monopoly of the means of violence are applied. If a state were to apply authority claims and coercive measures outside its recognized territory, other states would likely treat such maneuvers as acts of war for such behavior threatens their own sovereignty. Within the territorial jurisdiction of the state, normal politics can commence. In other words, by providing a secure political environment, competing interests in society can safely press their claims and jockey for political office and power. The territorial state can be described, therefore, as providing the fundamental framework for domestic politics.

Furthermore, the rights that citizens enjoy in the world today are attached to territory. International travelers know full well that when they are visiting another country, they must abide by the laws of that state. Rights and liberties are not geographically mobile. This contrasts with the empires of the past, where rights were often attached to people and not place. For example, the Ottoman Empire recognized the rights of distinct confessional communities, and these rights were guaranteed wherever members of those communities moved within the empire. Thus, Muslims, Jews, Catholics, and Orthodox Christians each had specific (and very different) rights and obligations that were to be honored irrespective of location (Glenny 2000). In medieval Europe as well, one can find monarchs claiming to be "King of the Franks" or "King of the English." Later, these titles were transformed into "King of France" and "King of England" as monarchs became rulers of a precise geography (Spruyt 2002).

Most of the planet has been appropriated and carved up by states, but the impact of global warming has created a new and unexpected rush for territory in the Arctic, where Canada, Russia, Denmark, and the United States are currently in the throes of conflicting ownership claims. Since 2000, the polar ice cap covering the Arctic has shrunk by 700,000 square miles. The consequence is that is it now becoming easier for ships to cross the Northwest Passage sea lane (previously only navigable for a brief period each year) and to search for exploitable natural resources. In August 2007, Russia caused an international stir when it sent a team of scientists to plant a Russian flag on the Arctic seabed. According to Russian authorities, this act entitles Russia to ownership of half of the Arctic ocean floor. Canada, for its part, has been busy furbishing its claims by ordering its military to undertake "sovereignty patrols" and staking out the parameters of its borders. The prime minister of Canada, Stephen Harper, has popularized the phrase "use it or lose it" in reference to Arctic sovereignty. "Make no mistake about it, this national government intends to use it," he insists (Broad 2008; Krauss 2004).

If the history of territorial disputes is any indication, the Arctic issue will not be easy to resolve. Territory, like private property, is a form of exclusion. The only way I can own something is if you do not. This makes territory a zero-sum game and explains why so many wars have been fought over territorial rights. In fact, conflicts over territory constitute the single most significant cause of interstate wars, the frequency of such wars, and their intensity (Zacher 2001). The discussion of territory brings us full circle with our definition of a state. Territory determines the human community over whom states exercise authority and against whom the state may apply violence.

ORIGINS AND DEVELOPMENT OF THE MODERN STATE

Thus far, we have examined the definition of the state and fleshed out its meaning with reference to history and contemporary politics. What we now need to address is how and why the state has become the central political institution in modern society. To answer the "how" questions, we must turn to history in order to reconstruct the sequence of events that connect the past to the present. The "why" questions, in contrast, compel us to look for underlying causal forces that drive and steer history in the direction it takes. In what follows we will investigate the historical evolution of the state, with particular attention paid to identifying the causal mechanisms that spurred its development and expansion.

The Middle Ages (600–1500) was a period of political turmoil and general insecurity. The successor institutions of the Roman Empire were the Rome-based Christian Church and the German-based Holy Roman Empire, the latter founded in 962 A.D. Underneath this superstructure of authority was a number of competing power centers whose mutual antagonism locked Europe into a period of near-constant warfare. In the words of the scholar Charles Tilly, "early in the state-making process, many parties shared the right to use violence. . . . The continuum ran from bandits and pirates to kings via tax collectors, regional power holders, and professional soldiers" (Tilly 1985: 173). Furthermore, lords and nobles owned great estates and enjoyed the right to raise armies and to maintain fortresses in return for their obedience to the imperial authorities. But possession of organized violence offers opportunities for resistance as well as compliance, so that powerful nobles, controlling peasant labor and having their own private armies, often clashed with each other as well as with the emperor and church officials. The monarchs that eventually emerged from these general political struggles and physical elimination contests were the more successful princes who were able to subdue rivals and extend their rule over more and more territory.

Thus, generally speaking, the expansion and consolidation of states in Europe was a process of a core authority establishing itself and then subduing and dominating peripheral authorities and incorporating adjacent territory. By the eighteenth century, the capacity for violence held by European monarchs began to surpass that of competing princes and lords (Tilly 1985: 174). This marks the beginning of the process of *primitive political accumulation* in Europe and ends with centralized states gaining an effective monopoly of violence within their borders.

The first monarchical states were established in England, Spain, and France in the late fifteenth century. Absolutism, a political doctrine advocating unchecked centralized rule, was defended by leading thinkers of the time, the most prominent being Jean Bodin and Thomas Hobbes. Bodin and Hobbes argued for the moral and political need to concentrate absolute power in the person of the monarch. Unrestrained by civil laws, legislatures, or public opinion, the sovereign would provide what was most lacking at the time: domestic peace and political stability. Hobbes even invoked the biblical image of the Leviathan, an all-powerful creature, for the title of the political treatise he wrote defending absolutism. His intention was to argue that the sovereign should possess a capacity for ferocity that immediately inspires awe and submission in subjects. In the seventeenth and eighteenth centuries, political theories of absolutism flourished in the form of the doctrine of the divine right of kings, which holds that monarchs rule by the benevolence and intent of God, and are answerable only to God, not to their subjects. The French king, Louis XIV (1643–1715), exemplifies the spirit of absolutism. As a child he was tutored to believe in the divine-right theory. Upon accession to the crown, he became known as the "Sun King" on the grounds that just as the sun is the center of the universe, so the king is the center of France. His most famous declaration – "*l'état c'est moi*" (I am the state) – perfectly reflects the absolutist view. The state, in this conception, is obviously not rule *by* the people; neither is it *of* nor even *for* the people, to complete U.S. President Abraham Lincoln's famous phrase. Rather, it is the private possession of the monarch.

Absolutism and the divine right of kings functioned as ideologies that transformed raw power into authority. Apart from England, where monarchical power was curtailed in the 1688 Glorious Revolution, absolutism prevailed in Europe for most of the 1700s and was treated as an unquestioned given of political life. Whereas this may invoke thoughts of tyranny and despotism in the modern mind, the state's ability to penetrate the daily lives of citizens in the 1700s was minimal. To be sure, monarchs did attempt to determine the religious allegiances of their subjects, and grotesque forms of punishment could be inflicted on dissenters, but generally, the capacity of the absolutist state to control its subjects was limited because of the generally undeveloped nature of both state institutions and technologies of control. Moreover, some monarchs were influenced by the humanist and rationalist philosophies of their day and accordingly pursued progressive reforms. Historians use the term "enlightened despots" to describe such rulers and typically include in this category Frederick the Great (1740–1786) of Prussia, Maria Theresa (1740–1780) and Joseph II (1780–1790) of Austria, and Catherine the Great (1762–1796) of Russia.

What is most important about the absolutist state for our concerns is that it first put the core elements of state rule into place. For instance, in France, the Hundred Years' War compelled monarchs to develop a standing army and a system of national taxation by 1450. In Prussia, Frederick William I (1688–1740) introduced conscription and developed the bureaucracy to augment Prussian power. His successor, Frederick the Great, "made Prussia in many ways the best governed state in Europe, abolishing torture of accused criminals and bribery of judges, establishing elementary schools, and promoting the prosperity of industry and agriculture" (Burns et al. 1982, 680). In short, these and other monarchs laid the institutional foundations for the modern state. Basic features of the state – territory, taxation, professional armies, bureaucracies for the administration of domestic and foreign policy, a judicial and penal system, the regulation of economic transactions, and even, in the case of Prussia, welfare – took shape under the rule of absolutist monarchs.

What then changed was not the nature of the state, but the source of its legitimacy. It took the republican-inspired revolutions in the 1700s and nationalist-inspired movements and revolutions in the 1800s to transform the principle of dynastic sovereignty into a new doctrine of popular sovereignty and thereby complete the construction of the modern democratic state. To be sure, even today, absolute monarchy continues to thrive in many parts of the world, most notably the Middle East where monarchs with substantial power – absolutist or constitutional – control nearly half (seven of eighteen) of the states in the region. Elsewhere, monarchies have continued to dwindle in both number and power. Where they persist, such as in many European and Asian countries, their political function has been largely reduced to a ceremonial role.

Now that we have examined some historical features of the absolutist state, let us consider more broadly the causal forces in European history that contributed to the emergence and success of the modern state. A major causal factor is the near-constant state of war during the European Middle Ages. The imperative to defend against rivals placed a premium on the ability of princes to extract resources – principally taxes – from the population and to raise armies. Those who successfully secured regularized access to revenue were better placed to organize large military forces and thereby enjoy structural advantages in the competitive process of dynastic aggrandizement and state formation. By the late fifteenth century, England, France, and Spain had all experienced an increase in both their revenues and the size of their standing armies (Bean 1973).

A second force behind the rise of the territorial state is found in the capitalist, commercial revolution Europe experienced between 1450 and 1800. The impact of the discovery of the "new world" of the Americas was a powerful economic stimulus for Europe. The injection of new wealth encouraged manufacturing industries, the expansion of markets, and improvements in banking. A new middle class began to grow as cities increased in size as well. This general expansion of economic activity facilitated the development of the state by enabling monarchs to pay for increasing administrative and security costs.

In circular fashion, state activity promoted economic development, which, in turn, facilitated the success of the modern state. A mutually reinforcing relationship developed between state making and capitalist accumulation. Very simply, states protected capitalists and provided a secure environment for their economic activities, while taxes on capitalist profits strengthened the state by allowing it to invest more in military and/or economic development. On the business side of things, by reducing the risks, and thereby lowering the cost, of commerce, state protection allowed trade to expand (Lane 1979). As Karl Marx observed in his economic treatise, *Capital* (1867), the genesis of capitalism depended on the "power of the State, the concentrated and organized force of society, to hasten, hot-house fashion, the process of transformation" (Marx 1967, 703).

Another reason that the state has proved so critical for the development of capitalism in Europe is that private property and the market – the twin pillars of capitalism – cannot work well outside a state-sanctioned legal framework. Private property is a right of exclusion. It assigns to owners the exclusive right to use the property and to profit from it. Without a state to enforce and protect property rights, ownership would be uncertain, vulnerable, and subject to violent disputation. In the same way, a market relies on the integrity of contracts. But what happens if some traders are opportunistic and refuse to honor their commitments in the marketplace? As long as there is a state to monitor contracts, adjudicate disputes, and punish transgressors, such transaction costs (or the costs of doing business) are lowered and economic activity can flourish. It is ironic, but a free market requires an effective state.

In sum, state making in Europe was the product of the interactive effects of constant war-making, the regularization and institutionalization of taxation, and the growth of capitalism. During the Middle Ages, there were many wielders of violence. It was often difficult to tell the difference between a bandit and a state agent, not the least reason being that princes often hired bandits to fight their enemies and/or conduct outrages against their own rebellious subjects (Tilly 1985). The scholar Mancur Olson employs the concept "stationary bandit" to highlight the thin line between criminals and early state builders and to describe the logic behind state formation. According to Olson, once a bandit recognizes that theft by regularized taxation is more lucrative and steady than theft from roving banditry, incentives are provided to reduce anarchy and monopolize extractive rights from the population. In the words of Olson, this marks "'the first blessings of the invisible hand': the rational, self-interested leader of a band of roving bandits, is led, as though by an invisible hand, to settle down, wear a crown, and replace anarchy with government. The gigantic increase in output that normally arises from the provision of a peaceful order and other public goods gives the stationary bandit a far larger take than he could obtain without providing government" (Olson 1993, 568).

WHY COMPARE?

Unlike other fields in the social sciences, comparative politics offers a method for studying and explaining a phenomenon of interest in its very nomenclature, namely comparison. Good comparative work begins with a research puzzle or basic question on an important topic. We may, for example, ask why some multiethnic states descend into violence whereas others do not. The questions we raise determine the cases (or units of analysis) we research. In this case, the unit of analysis is the multiethnic state; studies of voting behavior, in contrast, might focus on individuals, with the goal being to explain why they choose to vote for a particular party. Once an intriguing research question is articulated and a set of cases identified for investigation, a scholar endeavors to explain similarities, patterns, and generalities, as well as contrasts, anomalies, and unique events and outcomes that the cases manifest. Given the inability of political science (and the social sciences in general) to conduct highly controlled laboratory experiments as the natural sciences (like chemistry, biology, and physics) do, comparison represents a vital method for generating explanations of politics.

As a matter of fact, comparison is vital not only for the social sciences, but for all human knowledge. From early childhood on, human beings compare and contrast empirical phenomena. It is only by comparing that we come, first, to appreciate the rich diversity in both the natural and social worlds, and second, begin to ponder on how that diversity might be explained. Many of us have probably heard the old adage, "you can't compare apples and oranges." Ironically, the only way one can reach this conclusion is by a prior comparison whereby the different shape, color, texture, and taste of an apple as opposed to an orange become familiar. In short, comparison is an inevitable and indispensable method by which people organize and explain the complexity of the world; it is, according to the authors Mattei Dogan and Dominique Pelassy (1984, 8), "the engine of knowledge."

The direct comparison of a number of cases is not the only approach used by students of comparative politics. The investigation of a puzzle by means of a single case, such as the cause of ethnic war in Bosnia-Herzegovina, offers potentially important contributions to the quest for understanding and explanation. By focusing one's intellectual energy on a single case, a deep understanding of local conditions can be achieved. At the same time, however, case studies pose problems of reliability and generalizability. In other words, if we study only a single case, how much confidence can we have in the wider applicability of our conclusions? If it can be established to general satisfaction that nationalist elites were to blame for the outbreak of ethnic war in Bosnia-Herzegovina, how can we be sure that the same phenomenon plays a more or less equally important role in the explanation of other incidences of the outbreak of ethnic war? The case study provides us with the "apple" but not with the contrasting "orange" that clarifies both the differences and similarities between the two cases, or fruits.

Comparing states offers the advantage of putting research questions to a more rigorous empirical test. By systematically checking the conclusions of one case against another, we are better positioned to assess whether a potential cause like nationalist elites is a general cause of ethnic war, or if it is confined to certain cases under certain conditions, or if it in fact has any causal power at all in a general explanation of the outbreak of ethnic war. A good way to test our proposition on Bosnia, for example, might be to compare this case with the former Soviet republic of Georgia and the current Russian republic of Chechnya. In all these cases, interethnic war occurred during the postcommunist transition. If nationalist elites can be linked to violent outcomes in each case, then the initial proposition gains plausibility. An additional round of comparison should include multiethnic states like Slovakia and Romania where interethnic violence did not occur during their postcommunist transitions. If they too had aggressive nationalist elites during this period, then such elites cannot be concluded to be essential to the outbreak of ethnic war. If, by contrast, they did not have them during the transition, then the case for their importance in explaining ethnic war is strengthened. Thus, comparing both similar and different cases offer opportunities to test, amend, gain confidence in, and falsify potential answers to the compelling political puzzles of our time.

Many thinkers in the western tradition argue for, or demonstrate by their work, the virtues of comparison as a foundation for knowledge claims. John Stuart Mill (1806–1873), Auguste Comte (1798–1857), and Emile Durkheim (1858–1917) all contributed to the development of the social sciences as we know them today, and all were champions of the comparative method. The German philosopher G. W. F. Hegel contributes an important insight on the value of comparison when he writes "what is familiar is not known." Similarly, the English writer Rudyard Kipling (1865–1936) poetically asks, "and what should they know of

England who only England know?" Both Hegel and Kipling realized that human beings tend to take for granted that which is familiar, and that such familiarity gets in the way of genuine knowledge seeking. For example, if someone has never traveled much outside of his hometown, let alone outside of his state, then how well can he really know the strengths and weaknesses, vices and virtues of either his own hometown or the larger country of which it is a part? There is a powerful tendency for people to accept the familiar as natural and normal when in fact a little comparative work may demonstrate how abnormal it is and bring them to understand how and why it is abnormal. It is no accident that outsiders and foreigners often see what locals do not. Hence, it was the Frenchman Alexis de Tocqueville (1805–1859) who noticed the curious potential for "majority tyranny" as he traveled America in 1831 and studied its developing democracy (de Tocqueville 1990). Likewise, it was the German intellectual Werner Sombart (1863–1941), accustomed as he was to socialist militancy in his home country, who wrote an important text on American exceptionalism in 1906, entitled *Why Is There No Socialism in the United States?* (Sombart 1976).

Essentially, comparison helps us see beyond what our society considers normal; it helps us break down ethnocentrism (or the view that our society or our group is always right); it helps us rigorously check our knowledge claims; and it helps us discover deeper truths about the organization and conduct of politics (and other types of human behavior) on a global scale.

LOOKING BACK AND FORWARD

This book is organized around the theme of contemporary challenges to the modern state, which we argue is the preeminent political actor in modern domestic and international politics. This chapter started by exploring what the state is, why it enjoys the political importance that it does, and where it came from. In other words, this chapter sets the background for the remainder of the book.

In the next chapter we explore various meanings of politics and how those meanings are related to the notion of the state. In addition, we contrast democratic, authoritarian, and totalitarian regimes and compare strong, weak, and failing states. Chapters 3, 4, and 5 examine the rules and structures by which states are governed as well as the major political institutions whose operation makes their governance possible. The final four

chapters examine contemporary challenges to the fundamental characteristic of states, which is their sovereignty, or monopoly of decision-making
power within the territory they control. These challenges are: (1) globalization; (2) ethnic nationalism; (3) terrorism; and (4) transnational crime.
Let us now turn our attention to meanings of politics in the contemporary
world.

2 | *States and Politics*

States, then, provide a framework or container for the practice of politics. The task of this chapter must therefore be to address the question: What is politics? Is it a dignified and noble activity that involves serving the public good? Politicians often speak this way, lauding colleagues or other officials for their public service. Or is politics a negative, corrupting, and perhaps evil form of human behavior? Common people often speak like this, painting the politician as a crook or depicting a government's loss of an election as "throwing the rascals out." Philosophers in the Western tradition are divided on this question, and some have even constructed in their writings ideal worlds without politics, but human history has yet to record the existence of such a community.

What is your conception of politics? Is it a dignified vocation or a sordid game involving corruption, power, and greed? This is not an easy question to answer, because how one addresses it invariably reflects prior political values. Politics as a concept is a contentious term involving competing traditions of political thought. One cannot simply offer a definition of it and thereafter remain politically neutral. Rather, defining it requires one to "take sides" in some key philosophical disputes.

In the next section of this chapter, we explore three different approaches to the meaning of politics and link those approaches to the concept of the state. We then turn our discussion to the governance of states, specifically the analytical distinction between the state, regime, and government with a particular focus on the differences among democratic, authoritarian, and totalitarian regime types. The third and final section of the chapter compares strong, weak, and failed states while highlighting how different conflict management strategies – the minimal liberal model and the more interventionist social democratic model – shape the scope and strength of the state.

WHAT IS POLITICS?

Everyone has opinions about politics. From the high school student to the CEO of a corporation, we all have political views, whether fully developed or not. But how does one go about defining the very term *politics*? What is meant by this term? How does political activity differ from other forms of human interaction, such as art, religion, or economics? More fundamentally, why is it important to articulate a definition of politics? Why can we not just move on and discuss the issues, actors, and events of the political world?

A major reason why conceptual analysis must precede the study of the real world is that we cannot make sense of this reality without concepts. In a world without concepts, humans would be overwhelmed by sensory impressions and therefore unable to identify what is significant about them. They would, in effect, feel the "great blooming, buzzing confusion" that the American psychologist and pragmatist, William James (1842–1910), famously ascribes to the cognitive experiences of a newborn baby (James 1931). In this sense, concepts are like filters for the senses in that they screen out noise and prevent sensory overload. It is our concepts that delineate the world, carve it up, and determine that politics is this, economics is that, and sociology is this other thing. As such, concepts are basic analytical ordering devices that make knowledge possible. Concepts furnish the social sciences generally with basic terms of discourse. They provide the means to observe, interpret, and communicate about the empirical world and they are the building blocks of the theories that explain political phenomena of interest to us, such as, for example, different levels of welfare provision from one state to the next. The formulation of theory is the ultimate goal of students of comparative politics, and concepts are at the heart of this endeavor because they serve as "data containers" – they help us lump together similar phenomena and differentiate what *is* from what is *not* (Sartori 1970).

Comparative politics is a subfield of political science, and science demands that there be rigor and discipline in concept construction. Definitions cannot be arbitrary or just whatever strikes the fancy of the researcher. If this were the case, then no science or systematically organized body of knowledge would be possible, because researchers would forever speak "past" rather than "to" each other. At the same time, however, a major problem for political science is that its most basic terms of discourse are essentially contested. For example, everybody wants justice, but the problem is that not everyone has the same view of what justice is.

The same could be said for other basic terms, like freedom, equality, and democracy. It is this fundamental disagreement over ideas and ideals that makes politics such a contentious and conflict-prone human activity. As Marx observed, when an antinomy exists, a "right against a right," then "force decides" (Marx 1967, 225).

By the same token, even in the case of essentially contested concepts, like politics, some minimal agreement among researchers must be present if the accumulation of knowledge is to take place. The concepts that populate the field of politics, including the concept of politics itself, are what the scholar Giovanni Sartori describes as "experience carriers." In other words, every concept has its own unique history. Terms like the state, democracy, freedom, authoritarianism, and the like are shaped by experience and reflect historical struggles of the past as well as desired visions of the future. Social groups mobilize on the basis of competing concepts, and it is in their competitive struggle that concepts are formulated, analyzed, criticized, adjusted, applied, and then criticized again. Over time, the meanings of such concepts become "stabilized by an endless trial and error process" (Sartori 1987, 265–66).

Thus, when we survey the history of political thought, we find that what counts as political is highly variable. What was political to the ancient Greeks differs in important ways from the modern conception. In the ancient Greek world, for example, there was no line drawn, as there is in modern democratic states, between the private life of the individual and the public life of the citizen. Again, to quote Sartori: "[P]olitical life and the things political were not perceived by the Greeks as a part or a single aspect of life; they were its essence and totality" (Sartori 1973, 7). However, despite the great differences in context between the Athenian polis (or political community) and the modern centralized state, there are common themes across western history that enable one to categorize philosophical perspectives on the meaning of politics into three main traditions. They are (1) politics-as-war, (2) politics-as-process, and (3) politics-as-participation. Each provides a distinct perspective on the nature of politics and the role of the state. Let us examine each in turn.

Politics-as-War

The phrase "politics-as-war" conveys the idea that politics is a struggle for power among antagonistic groups and individuals. Power, in this tradition, is the most important good to be secured, for its possession is the key to accumulating all other desirable goods, including wealth, status, and reputation. Political opponents are perceived as mortal enemies who threaten one's ability to amass or maintain power; therefore, they must be either dominated or eliminated. Although politicians and public officials may express fidelity to principles such as honor and morality, such assertions should be treated suspiciously, for underneath all lofty public rhetoric stands one unchangeable principle: "might makes right."

Among the first in the Western tradition to espouse this position was the character of Thrasymachus in Plato's *Republic*, who proclaimed "justice is nothing else than the interest of the stronger" (Plato 1982: 19). Niccolò Machiavelli (1469–1527) is another famous advocate of this position. In his *Prince*, Machiavelli provides a primer to the rulers of his day on how to perpetuate their hold on power. He recommends, for example, that it is better for princes to be feared than loved, that princes should never feel bound by their promises, and that "it is necessary to know how to disguise this [cunning] nature well and to be a great hypocrite and liar" (Machiavelli 1979: 134). Historically, both the political left and the political right have adopted this politics-as-war viewpoint. An example on the right is Carl Schmitt (1888–1985), the Nazi jurist and ideologist, who "defines 'the political' as the eternal propensity of . . . collectivities to identify each other as 'enemies,' that is, as concrete embodiments of 'different and alien' ways of life with whom mortal combat is a constant possibility and frequent reality" (McCormick 2007, 317). On the political left, our example is Vladimir Lenin, the leader of the communist revolution in Russia in 1917, who quoted approvingly the formula of the military theorist and Prussian general Karl von Clausewitz (1780–1831): "[W]ar is the continuation of politics by other means" (Clausewitz 1943). In other words, war and politics are two sides of the same coin. In both, the main objective is to defeat one's enemies.

Thomas Hobbes is another central figure in this tradition. His description of the state of nature as a "war of all against all" leads him to argue that only an all-powerful state – the Leviathan – can generate a sufficient level of "fear and awe" to produce peace in society. Not surprisingly, there is very little room in this perspective for the use of soft-power instruments like diplomacy and compromise. Because "men are a sorry lot," as Machiavelli frequently wrote, the hard-power instruments of coercion, sanctions, and violence will always be necessary tools for rulers. In the field of international relations, the doctrine of realism falls within the politics-as-war paradigm. Realism holds that all states pursue, and should pursue, their national interest by maximizing their power and maximizing their advantages over other, competitor states. Because there is no centralized international authority to police state behavior, anarchy is a permanent condition of international relations. War, therefore, is an ever-present possibility. Thinkers in the realist tradition include scholars like Hans Morgenthau (1904–1980) and public officials like Henry Kissinger.

Politics-as-Process

Like realists, liberals maintain that human beings are prone to conflict in their relations with each other. Citizens in civil society have different interests, so the clash of those interests is inevitable. Unlike realism, however, liberalism maintains that such clashing interests are best constrained not by an all-powerful state, but instead by an effective set of political institutions that limit the state's power over individuals. James Madison (1751–1836), a founding father of the United States and its fourth president, represents the position of political liberalism well. In his *Federalist Paper* #51, he writes, "[I]f men were angels, then no government would be necessary.... In framing a government of men over men, the great difficulty lies in this: you must first enable the government to control the governed; and in the next place oblige it to control itself" (Ketcham 1958: 64).

The solution to political conflict, according to political liberalism, is constitutionalism. Constitutions are sets of procedures that regulate citizen-government relations and internal government practices, specifying the procedures, relations, and functions of the various branches of government. The *New York Times* writer Thomas Friedman likes to use the metaphor "gulliverize" to describe the role of constitutions and institutions that set the frameworks for governing (Friedman 1997). Like the fictional Gulliver (in Jonathan Swift's *Gulliver's Travels* [1726]) who awoke from a shipwreck to find himself tied down by the Lilliputians, a people one-twelfth his size, constitutions limit and regulate government by tying it down with rules, standards, laws, and other means of accountability and scrutiny. By emphasizing the rule of law in place of the rule of men, political liberalism espouses a procedural view of politics, or what we label politics-as-process.

A wide variety of thinkers adhere to this procedural view of politics. The eminent political scientist Harold Lasswell described politics as "who gets what, when and how" (Lasswell 1936). Likewise, David Easton offered the view of politics as the "authoritative allocation of values" (Easton 1965). Both thinkers shaped the orientation of political science from the 1940s to the 1960s, and both definitions of politics bring to our attention the procedures and processes by which offices, power, and goods are distributed and winners and losers created. This understanding of politics has also influenced contemporary theories of democracy in the Western world, which are described by many political scientists as "procedural" or "formal" democracies (Kaldor and Vejvoda 1997). By this term they mean that a democracy is a set of procedures, such as the regular election of political officeholders, offices open to all, a competitive party system, universal suffrage, and so on. Democracy is thus akin to a game in which all can play if they abide by the rules. If we combine the rule-based character of contemporary democracy with the practice of free elections, we can summarize the essence of democracy with the formula "certain rules, uncertain outcomes" (Bunce 1990: 400). The rules of a democracy are certain – regular elections, the right to free speech and assembly, the right to petition government, and so on – and cannot be compromised if democracy is to be maintained. But the outcomes are uncertain precisely because they are the product of the operation of open, free, and competitive elections. As long as political actors faithfully adhere to the rules of democracy, the losers of today's election can always rebound and win the next one. This equal opportunity to win public office no doubt helps explain the great appeal that democracy has in the world today.

The state in this conception is a neutral umpire, adjudicating disputes and providing a framework for government according to the rule of law and with the consent of the governed. Sometimes referred to as the "night watchman state," the purpose of government for the liberal democrat is to maintain domestic order so that civil society and the free market may flourish. The citizen is free in a liberal-democratic state because laws are in effect that protect all against the arbitrary exercise of power by government. America's Founding Fathers, for example, clearly saw the dangers of civil society slipping into a politics-as-war mode. Rather than trying to change human nature, their political strategy was to curb its baser impulses by establishing constitutional mechanisms, like the separation of powers, checks and balances, the Senate filibuster, and the Electoral College, designed to prevent any one faction in the republic from dominating the others (see Chapter 4).

Politics-as-Participation

Radicals have never been content with the political formula of liberalism, or its description of democracy as nothing but a set of procedures or methods. For them, the great social, economic, and political inequalities that market societies generate inevitably overwhelm the democratic process, subverting its rules and biasing its outcomes in favor of the rich and powerful. Furthermore, to reduce democracy to the procedures by which it operates is to deprive it of its aspirations, its heart and soul. The word "democracy" is Greek in origins and invokes the Athenian practice of the full participation of citizens in decision making. The etymology of the word reveals its literal meaning: *demos* means people and *kratos* means authority; hence the phrase "rule by the people." If democracy is to have not merely a "formal" existence but instead a "substantive" realization, then all citizens must have real decision-making power over the issues that affect their lives.

There are many thinkers in the history of Western thought who accept the perspective we label politics-as-participation. Despite their vast philosophical and political differences, Aristotle, Jean-Jacques Rousseau, John Stuart Mill, Karl Marx, and anarchists like Mikhail Bakunin all identify full participation in the public life of society as the key to human freedom, progress, and fulfillment. Anything less is enslavement to others, a condition known as heteronomy. For these thinkers, freedom is made manifest when the individual obeys laws he/she participated in making. Politics, in this tradition, is understood as the "deliberate efforts [of free citizens] to order, direct, and control collective affairs and activities; to set up ends for society; and to implement and evaluate those ends" (Sibley 1970: 1).

Aristotle's understanding of politics exemplifies this paradigm perfectly. Man, for Aristotle, is uniquely a creature of *logos*, or reasoning capacity. Whereas animals know how to live by nature, "man alone of the animals is furnished with the faculty of language," which "serves to declare what is just and what is unjust." The polis offers human beings the widest forum to direct social life collectively. It furnishes the arena in which conceptions of justice may be advanced and the human community elevated. It affords individual citizens the opportunity to develop their highest and noblest capacities. Political participation, in short, is the key to both a healthy community and healthy individuals. Without it, man is reduced to a "poor sort of being." It is in this context that Aristotle famously calls man a "political animal" (Aristotle 1958: 4–7).

John Stuart Mill is another philosopher whose work falls in this tradition. For Mill, politics serves an educative function for citizens. In his words, participation in politics contributes to the citizens' "advancement in intellect, in virtue, and in practical activity and efficiency" (Mill 1910: 195). How, we may ask? According to Mill, when citizens take part in the political process, a sense of responsibility for the direction of society develops in them. Confronted with issues and problems that affect all, individuals are compelled by public participation to broaden their horizons beyond their narrow self-interests and consider what is in the common good. As a result, citizens exercise both self-reflection and self-restraint.

The state in this approach is reconceptualized as a forum for public deliberation. The demand for participation extends to all key institutions of society, such as the workplace, schools, and the local community. Political institutions are to be built on the principles of horizontal (as opposed to vertical, or hierarchical) relations, cooperation, and consensus. All power is to be decentralized as much as possible.

*W*AIT A MINUTE. **CONSIDER THIS.** While ideas about politics-as-participation are certainly ennobling and do appear profoundly democratic, what if man is, as the Russian Marxist Leon Trotsky (1879–1940) quipped, a "lazy animal"? Is it possible that this model of politics makes unrealistic demands on average people, specifically concerning their willingness to invest the time and energy it takes to sustain a participatory political system?

Some political thinkers, dismissing the prospects for human freedom within the framework of the state, argue either for the complete abolition of the state (in the case of anarchists) or for its gradual withering-away once the class differences that produce social conflict are mitigated (in the case of Marxists). This is so because Marxists and anarchists see the state as an inherently oppressive entity whose function is to keep a ruling class in power. Thus, for humankind to be free, the state must go. As Lenin wrote on the eve of the Bolshevik Revolution: "Where the state exists, there is no freedom. Where there is freedom, there is no state" (Lenin 1932, 79). Of course, the state never did wither away in communist Russia. The practical need to govern a large society, as well as the seduction of power for holders reluctant to relinquish it, ensured that the communists proved to be no more willing than other rulers to renounce control over the state or to diminish its capacity. As far as the anarchists are concerned, no large-scale application of their program has ever occurred. Perhaps this points to the infeasibility of their ideas.

The End of Politics?

Another group of philosophers takes this disdain for the state a step further by advocating an end to politics altogether, but this disposition is

linked to some very unpleasant political outcomes. The desire to eliminate politics because it is an evil component of human nature can be
traced back to Plato, who argued that only "philosopher-kings" – that
is, the wisest – should rule. Nineteenth-century French positivists like
Auguste Comte (1798–1857) and Henri Saint-Simon (1760–1825) were
enamored with science and felt that in a rational polity, only scientists
should rule. It was Saint-Simon who coined the phrase, later adopted by
Marxists, that in utopia, the "government of men will be replaced by the
administration of things" (Fay 1975). Religious zealots as well, from the
Protestant John Calvin (1509–1564) to Iran's Ayatollah Khomeini (1902–
1989), have sought to wipe out politics by enforcing doctrinal uniformity
and intolerance toward those of different creeds.

By most accounts, however, politics is impossible to abolish. As long
as societies are burdened with scarce resources, conflicts over their distribution among competing social groups are inevitable. Even if we could
imagine a society (as Marx did for his communist utopia) with material
abundance, in which no trade-offs were necessary between investments
and consumption, or between guns (military spending) and butter (consumer goods), it is still difficult to see how politics could be superfluous.
Would not people still get old, sick, and depressed? Would not jealously
and strife also spring from genetic inequalities (assuming social inequalities have been resolved)? Would gender, or race, or cultural or regional
differences cease to animate politics if all enjoyed prosperity? There are
strong indications from history that humankind has no difficulty discov-
ering new ways to practice politics-as-war. Politics, in short, is here to
stay.

> **W**AIT A MINUTE. **CONSIDER THIS.** Let us return to the opening
> question: What is politics? Earlier we have noted the essentially
> contested nature of this term and responded by using the labora-
> tory of Western political thought and history to identify three broad
> approaches to it: politics-as-war, politics-as-process, and politics-as-
> participation. Which one do you find convincing? Is it the most con-
> vincing under all circumstances? In Table 2.1, we provide a summary
> of the approaches to facilitate critical reflection.

Although the authors do not wish to impose any single approach on
readers, it is necessary to note that the question this book raises concerns
challenges to the modern state. Thus, our understanding of politics is
necessarily restricted to politics in which the state is involved. We

TABLE 2.1 The three approaches to politics

Politics as . . .	View of politics	View of the state	Key proponents
War	the struggle for power among antagonistic groups and individuals	institution of coercion that seeks to maximize power	Thomas Hobbes Machiavelli Carl Schmitt Vladimir Lenin realists
Process	"who gets what, when, and how" "the authoritative allocation of values"	state as a neutral umpire; the rule of law state that is constrained by a constitution	James Madison Harold Lasswell David Easton liberals
Participation	citizen involvement in decisions that affect the public interest	state conceived as a noncoercive forum for public deliberation	Aristotle J. S. Mill communist and anarchist thinkers

acknowledge, along with many theories such as feminism and postmodernism, that politics can be conceived as being present in all human relations and activities, from the bedroom to the boardroom, and from the amusement park to the mental asylum. However, the questions we raise and regard as significant in this work are connected to the state, and therefore our understanding of politics must be duly focused on its statist context.

Now that we have discussed the various meanings of politics, let us consider the conceptual distinctions between the principal arenas of political activity, states, regimes, and governments.

STATES, REGIMES, AND GOVERNMENTS

In Chapter 1, we discussed in detail the main characteristics of the modern state. Two other concepts closely related to the notion of the state are regime and government. All three terms are used in everyday discourse, and sometimes interchangeably. This is confusing, and the aim of this section is to draw a sharp analytical distinction between them and to sustain this distinction in the remainder of the book.

Of the three terms, the government is the least contested and easiest to define. Simply enough, the government comprises the day-to-day officeholders – that is, those in authority positions who are charged with routinely devising, implementing, and enforcing public policy. The government essentially runs the state. Regimes are a trickier concept to define because there is commonly a contradiction between the popular and scholarly uses of the term. In popular discourse, as seen in newspapers and television news programs, regime usually takes on a negative connotation. For instance, we often hear of the "Mugabe regime" of Zimbabwe or the "Castro regime" of Cuba. In both cases, regime becomes synonymous with entrenched authoritarian or despotic rule. In the comparative politics literature, in contrast, regimes are understood more neutrally as the constitutional values, rules, and procedures found within states. Democratic regimes, for example, can be represented by a written constitution or by an unwritten one that reflects tacit but widespread conventions, agreements, and understandings adhered to by politically significant actors. Whereas the popular understanding equates regimes with authoritarianism, scholars in comparative politics treat authoritarianism as but one of several types of regime, the other basic types being democracy and totalitarianism. Thus it is important to keep the popular and political science versions of regime in mind when using the concept.

If the specific empirical referents of regimes are constitutional values and the rules of the political game, and that of governments the office-holders of the day, then what are the precise political institutions that embody the state? They are the more permanent institutions exercising authority in society, namely the bureaucracy, the military, and the penal system (police, courts, prisons). In the modern world, all political actors employ these institutions, whether they are democrats, communists, fascists, or Islamists. No matter the regime type or government in power, all use bureaucracies, police, prisons, secret services, intelligence agencies, military forces, and judicial systems to help manage conflict in society and maintain domestic order.

Regime, government, and state are suggestive of the different types of change and instability political systems may experience. For example, governments regularly change in democratic systems. Elections often bring about peaceful transfers of government power, and when this occurs, the state and the regime most often remain unaffected. Regimes can change as a result of internal popular revolutions, external invasions, coups d'état (the sudden, violent, and illegal seizure of power), and even reform. In these instances, governments almost always change along with the nature of the regime, but states can remain the same. States also can undergo profound political change. They can expand (as the United States did over time), contract (as Hungary did when punished by the Allies of World War II for its alliance with Nazi Germany), or disappear (as did the USSR, Yugoslavia, and Czechoslovakia during the postcommunist transition).

The tumultuous political histories of Italy and France offer interesting examples of the interrelationships between government, regime, and state. Since the inception of Italy's post–World War II democracy, its governments have epitomized instability, or rapid turnover. Apart from the French Fourth Republic (1946–1958), in which the average life of a government was eight months, Italy's modern-day democracy has the record in Europe for the shortest-lived governments. Between 1945 and 1998 – a period of fifty-three years – Italy had fifty-six governments. Giulio Andreotti, a member of the Christian Democratic Party, represents well the experiences of Italy's political class. In a career that lasted from 1947 to 1992, Andreotti held ministerial positions in thirty-six governments, serving as prime minister seven times (Mershon 1996: 541). Amid this profound government instability, the Italian state and its democratic regime remained intact, but the story has been very different in modern France. Whereas Italy's governments come and go while its state and regime persist, France's political history is one of ever-changing regimes. From the year 1791 to the present day, France has had fifteen different constitutions and an assortment of regimes, including five republics, three monarchical restorations, two emperors (Napoleon Bonaparte [1804–1815] and Louis Bonaparte [1851–1870]), and one fascist regime (the Nazi puppet state, known as the Vichy regime, from 1940 to 1944). France's turbulent political history at the regime level has been matched by consensus at the state level. In other words, the idea of France as a state deserving its place (and a special one at that) among the community of nations has rarely been challenged in modern French history.

Thus, states, regimes, and governments point to distinct authority dimensions in political systems. Among them, the state is the most fundamental. The architects of a new political system must always first address the question: Who are the people? Fortunate are the states where the answer is self-evident and incontestable. If a community of people is unanimous about the need to live together in a common state, and if the territorial boundaries of the community are acceptable to neighboring communities, then the "stateness problem" (Linz and Stepan 1996) can be considered solved and the political architects (or founding fathers and mothers, if you will) are able to move on to resolve regime and government issues. Problems arise when distinct subgroups within a community challenge the notion of a common state. In such cases, democracy is completely incapable of providing a solution and violence is difficult to avoid.

The postcommunist experience of Bosnia-Herzegovina is a case in point. From the moment of its first democratic election in 1990, the three ethnic communities residing in Bosnia – Muslims (44 percent of the population), Serbs (36 percent), and Croats (17 percent) – were dead-locked as to whether Bosnia should secede from the state of Yugoslavia or remain within it. No amount of democratic consultation was sufficient to resolve the issue, because the question was not the acceptability of democracy, but rather the territorial extent of its application. Bosnia's Muslim and Croat communities, intent on seceding from Yugoslavia, demanded a national referendum so that the entire republic could decide its collective fate. Its Serbian population, in contrast, desired to remain part of Yugoslavia and therefore called for each ethnic group to hold its own national referendum to determine the fate of only that community. In this way, Serbs could avoid being "outvoted" by Muslim and Croat interests. The lesson from Bosnia is that the democratic method cannot make right a state that is perceived to be illegitimate by significant subgroups in its population. In this sense, the state question of "we the people" logically precedes the normative choices of regime type and government structure.

In the comparative politics literature, democracy, authoritarianism, and totalitarianism constitute the three main regime types. The following section explores each in turn.

Regime Types: Democracy

Scholars, activists, and politicians who subscribe to the politics-as-process perspective offer a view of democracy distinct from the advocates of politics-as-participation. In the case of the former, democracy is understood in procedural terms. In other words, democracy is a set of rules and processes encompassing key features like competitive elections, a free press, multiple parties, offices open to all, the right to petition government, the right to assembly, the right of habeas corpus (i.e., the right, if arrested, to see a judge and to be informed of the lawful grounds for detention), and so on. "Certain rules, uncertain outcomes" is perhaps the most succinct formulation of democracy possible. On the other side of the aisle are the champions of "participatory democracy." Largely left-wing in orientation, participatory democrats argue that any democracy worth the name must meet three criteria: (1) provide for real political equality among its citizens; (2) involve the entire citizenry in collective decision making; and (3) produce real benefits for the *demos* (or people). Which perspective is best suited for the comparative study of politics?

Because comparative politics is an empirical enterprise that seeks to describe and explain the real world of politics, we argue that procedural democracy (sometimes called "formal democracy") is the most serviceable definition to use. By providing a checklist of precise criteria by which to measure the "democraticness" of a regime, procedural democracy offers a straightforward and uncomplicated way to compare the character of regimes around the globe. This is not so with participatory democracy. The reasons are many. First of all, there are not enough real-world examples of participatory democracy from which to build any kind of comparative science of politics. Secondly, it is too cumbersome and difficult to use participatory criteria. Exactly how much mass participation is needed before one deems a regime democratic? By the same token, how much equality is required and how many *demo*-benefits must be generated for a regime to meet this standard? None of these questions have clear answers. This is not to say that participatory democracy is a useless conception. On the contrary, political activists often find it a constructive ideal that can be harnessed by social movements to press governments to become more responsive to their peoples. But since the goal of comparative politics is not to create political change but rather to advance scientific explanations, it is simply more sensible to identify democracies on the basis of tangible procedures as opposed to more philosophical, less easily measured standards like equality and participation.

Since the nineteenth century, three waves of democratization have spread around the globe in the following time periods: (1) 1828–1920; (2) 1945–1965; and (3) 1975–1992 (Diamond 1996; Huntington 1997). The first of them was concentrated in the Western world and Eastern Europe. Between 1828 and 1920, a total of thirty countries adopted representative institutions including at least universal male suffrage, and therefore acquired at least some of the criteria of procedural democracy. Among them were Britain (universal male suffrage was achieved in 1919), France (in 1875, its Third Republic with universal male suffrage was established), Germany (which had a democratically elected parliament in 1871 and a full-fledged parliamentary democracy by 1919 with the Weimar Republic), Sweden (which instituted universal male suffrage in 1907), and Spain (where the Second Spanish Republic was declared in 1931). Eastern Europe was a concentrated laboratory for democracy at this time as parliaments, competitive elections, independent parties, free press, and civil society freedoms were instituted in all of the newly independent states – Yugoslavia, Czechoslovakia, Hungary, Poland, Romania, Bulgaria, Albania, Estonia, Latvia, and Lithuania – that emerged from the ashes of the Ottoman, Austro-Hungarian, German, and Russian empires. In the United States, the early adoption of representative institutions was strengthened by the attainment in 1828 of universal white male suffrage and in 1920 of white female suffrage.

The phenomenon we are describing is called democratization. Democratization is a power transition from a regime in which political power is in the hands of elites who are not accountable to their populations for their exercise of that power (i.e., authoritarianism) to a regime with the characteristics of procedural democracy. It is important to note, however, that just because a regime has become more democratic does not mean that it is a consolidated procedural democracy. In comparative politics, one must never take a regime's democraticness for granted, no matter how much government actors may assert their democratic values and credentials. Furthermore, history suggests that regimes embarking on a democratic path often find themselves taking a non-democratic detour along the way. This in fact happened in Europe in the 1920s and 1930s, as one democratic regime after another fell to fascism. Nazi military invasions toppled many European democratic states (for example, Czechoslovakia), but in many others, such as Germany, Italy, Spain, Poland, Hungary, Bulgaria, Albania, and Yugoslavia, democracy failed because of a combination of deep-seated internal cleavages, economic depression, institutional dysfunctions, and/or the presence of violent anti-democratic opposition movements. In some places, fascism was popular and supported by right-wing mass movements, such as the National Socialists in Germany, the Iron Guard in Romania, the Arrow Cross in Hungary, and the *Ustaša* (Insurgent) in Croatia. The *zeitgeist* (spirit of the times) was that democracy was failing, and that political salvation could be found only in transformative, totalitarian ideologies like fascism, ultranationalism, or communism (Rothschild 1974). This "reverse wave" of democratic breakdown highlights the fact that democracy is a fragile system of governance. Until *all* politically significant actors in a polity support democratic values both verbally and in practice, a democratic regime cannot be considered consolidated. Until this point is reached, nascent democracies remain vulnerable to authoritarian reversals.

The next democratic wave came after the end of World War II. Between 1945 and 1965, a number of democratic advances were made around the globe. The successful Allied defeat of the Axis powers (Germany, Italy, and Japan) meant that democratic institutions would be imposed on these societies and their cultures de-Nazified (in the case of

Germany) and de-deified (in the case of Japan's cult of the emperor). The postwar period brought independence from mainly British and French colonial rule for many new states in Asia, Africa, the Middle East, and the Caribbean. The new political class in these states more often than not exuberantly embraced the democratic rhetoric and institutions bequeathed by departing colonial powers, but by the mid-1960s, the enormous problems in the way of their economic development coupled with issues of ethnic diversity and weak functioning institutions led to another global retreat from democracy. The good news from the 1960s is that popular pressure from below compelled incomplete democratic regimes in the Western world to deepen and expand popular sovereignty by adopting important reforms, such as the Civil Rights Act (1964) and the Voting Rights Act (1965) in the United States, which ensured African Americans' right to vote. Around the globe, the late 1960s (the high-water mark was 1968) witnessed a participation explosion as new social movements such as youth, feminists, peace groups, ethnic groups, environmentalists, and others mobilized to press governments for progressive change.

The third democratic wave dates from the 1970s, with the end of authoritarianism in the southern European countries of Portugal (1974), Greece (1974), and Spain (1976). This is followed in the 1980s by the breakdown of authoritarian rule in Latin America and its movement toward democratic practices. At this point, a new political theory was launched known as the "democratic transition paradigm." Scholars such as Guillermo O'Donnell, Philippe Schmitter, and Laurence Whitehead (1986) introduced it by identifying the typical patterns, anomalies, elite strategies, and dynamics of democratization in southern Europe and Latin America. When communism collapsed in Eastern Europe in 1989, and then again when the Soviet Union disintegrated in 1991, there was a tremendous expansion of new regimes all touting democratic values. Popular, oppositional movements began to demonstrate the weakness of communist regimes in Eastern Europe in 1989, and one by one, each regime tumbled in a remarkable case of regional contagion (or domino effect). Democracy on the march was the new *zeitgeist*.

There are many reasons why authoritarian regimes broke down and the process of democratization began. As we will clarify in the next section, there are many subtypes of authoritarianism, each having its own key players, alliances, dynamics, and social bases of rule. It should not, therefore, be surprising that different subtypes of authoritarian regime fall for different reasons and at different rates. Despite this variation, one of the most common reasons given for their disintegration (except for oil-rich regimes, also known as "petrostates") is economic crisis. So confirmed is this thesis that it is treated as a major "stylized fact" of the regime transition literature (Geddes 1999; Smith 2006). A second reason for collapse is the emergence of divisions in the ruling elite. When the political class begins to fragment into hard-liners and soft-liners, opportunities for reform become possible. According to Barbara Geddes (1999), internal elite divisions are especially likely to cause military regimes to fall apart.

International factors constitute a third major force that can promote regime transition. It is often the case, as Adam Przeworski (1986) argues, that authoritarian regimes are durable because the subject population sees no acceptable alternative to the status quo, but this docile resignation can be jolted by exogenous shocks. This was certainly the case in the fall of communism in Eastern Europe. Gorbachev's enunciation of the "Sinatra Doctrine" ("I did it my way") in December 1988 was a signal to both hard-liners and soft-liners in the communist hierarchy throughout the Soviet bloc that each country would have to find its own way to reform, or what Gorbachev called *perestroika* ("restructuring"). After Gorbachev made this announcement, the independent trade union movement in Poland, Solidarity, was emboldened and pushed for "roundtable talks" with the communist elite. These were held in April 1989, and free elections took place in June. The regime vulnerabilities exposed in Poland encouraged popular mobilization elsewhere. Hungary was next in line, as popular forces compelled communists to hold roundtable talks in October 1989. When the barbed wire separating Hungary from Austria came down, thousands of citizens of the German Democratic Republic on "holiday" in Hungary and Czechoslovakia decided, in September, to flee to West Germany. This set off a crisis in several states at once, ultimately culminating in the fall of the Berlin Wall on November 9 and the end of the communist political monopoly in Czechoslovakia on November 29 (Oberschall 1996). Powerful regional demonstration effects were evident here as each movement learned from the other.

Linz and Stepan (1996) argue that the *zeitgeist* matters, and that during the 1980s and early 1990s, Soviet-styled communism appeared a sterile and bankrupt system. Conversely, the ideals of globalization, market liberalization, and Western-style democracy were ascendant and appeared to meet with no ideological resistance. This is precisely the time when the noted scholar Francis Fukuyama wrote his (in)famous book, *The End of History?* (1989). In it, he argued that liberal democracy and capitalism had achieved universal victory because all significant alternatives to them – namely fascism and communism – had been discredited.

Rather than an "end to history," however, this brief discussion of the three waves of democratization demonstrates that movements toward democracy ebb and flow, as is evident in the already noted authoritarian reversals in interwar Europe and the developing world in the 1960s. It should come as no surprise, therefore, that the third wave of democratization began to contract in the 1990s. Authoritarian regimes do not so much increase in number at this time as the gap between "electoral" democracies (i.e., those who hold regular elections but offer little in the way of political rights) and real procedural democracy begins to grow in "new" democracies. The scholar Barbara Geddes collected information on eighty-five countries that underwent a democratic transition between 1974 and 1999 and found that fifty-five experienced some type of retrograde movement in the direction of authoritarianism (Geddes 1999). This poor record has led thinkers like Thomas Carothers to argue that the third wave is over, and along with it the transition paradigm that supported it (Carothers 2002). He argues that most of the 100 transitional regimes have entered a "political gray zone" somewhere between authoritarianism and democracy. To appreciate the interpretive and conceptual issues raised in this debate, let us now turn to authoritarianism and define it more explicitly.

Regime Types: Authoritarianism

Authoritarian regimes in the modern world are tremendously varied in the political characteristics they display. Under the general label of authoritarianism, one may group states as diverse as Syria, Zimbabwe, Belarus, Pakistan, Myanmar, and Saudi Arabia. The common thread among all regimes that fit the authoritarian mantle is the denial of political freedoms to citizens. In authoritarian systems, a politically organized group (such as a party, a military, or an extended family) controls the state and the government and manipulates its institutions to serve its own ends. The political participation of competing groups is either not permitted or substantially restricted. If democracies can be logically reduced to the phrase "certain rules, uncertain outcomes," then authoritarian regimes are the opposite: "uncertain rules, certain outcomes." The rules are uncertain in such regimes because their interpretation and enforcement is at the whim of the ruling group. But political outcomes are known in advance – namely, the ruling group generally does and gets what it wants.

The comparative study of authoritarian regimes has yielded a rich semantic field of concepts to describe the proliferation of different authoritarian practices and institutions around the globe. For example, there are monarchies, family dynasties, and patrimonial regimes (in which the state is the private property of the ruling family); various types of personal rule, often described as tyrannies or dictatorships, or in some cases as sultanistic regimes; and theocracies, or regimes in which religion dictates political life. Military regimes have comprised a large proportion of the authoritarian systems around the world. In the 1970s, many scholars who studied underdevelopment in Latin America attributed it to "bureaucratic authoritarianism" (or the self-serving alliance between the military and the bureaucracy). When armed insurgents successfully toppled governments in the region, such as Castro's movement in Cuba in 1959, or the Sandinistas in Nicaragua in 1979, or the New Jewel Movement in Grenada in 1979, they brought a military-like mobilizational strategy to government and were therefore called "mobilization regimes" or even "rebel regimes." Sometimes authoritarian regimes are so saturated with corruption and organized crime that they are described variously as "kleptocracies," "shakedown states," "narco-states" and, in the case of oil-rich countries like Nigeria, Russia, Venezuela, and Saudi Arabia, "petrostates."

There also exists a growing variety of authoritarian regimes that incorporate a veneer of democratic practice, such as partly free elections and limited press freedoms, but regularly violate democratic rules (e.g., Serbia under Slobodan Milošević and Peru under Alberto Fujimori, both in the 1990s). Such regimes have been labeled as "electoral" or "competitive authoritarianism" with a further distinction turning on whether and how many political parties are allowed to operate effectively. Thus, electoral authoritarianism may involve "no party" regimes (in which candidates, but not parties, compete for office), "single party" regimes, or "limited multiparty" regimes. As a final addition to this already dense category of concepts, one must include the mixing of distinct subtypes into hybrid forms, such as a military/single-party regime, or a monarchy/theocracy combination, the latter of which characterizes many Middle Eastern Arab countries (Hadenius and Teorell 2007; Levitsky and Way 2002).

WAIT A MINUTE. **CONSIDER THIS.** The expansion of authoritarian subtypes means that the boundaries separating them are often blurry so that the decision what to call any particular instance of authoritarianism becomes a difficult interpretive act. For instance, how may we best describe Saddam Hussein's regime in Iraq? Was it a case of personal dictatorship, or was this a one-party regime run by the Sunni-dominated Baath party? How may one classify the rule of Hugo Chavez in Venezuela or Vladimir Putin in Russia? Both were popularly elected to the presidency, and yet both control the press and routinely violate the political rights of opponents. Are these regimes examples of "electoral authoritarianism," or is it preferable to describe them as electoral democracies (i.e., regimes which practice regular, competitive elections but lack key civil and political rights), or even "illiberal democracies"?

Accurately matching a concept to an empirical case is a critical step in comparative political science. Nothing good can come out of misreading authoritarians as democrats (and vice versa). If we are careless in the application of concepts to reality, we lose our ability not only to describe our world scientifically, but also to evaluate it politically and perhaps even morally. In this sense, bad concepts make for bad explanations, bad theories, and – insofar as the social sciences have an influence on public policy – bad domestic and foreign policies. Thus, it is of no small consequence to which side of the line separating authoritarianism and democracy we assign a given regime.

The task facing students of comparative politics is to choose concepts that faithfully capture local specificities but are not so parochial as to prohibit comparison with other countries. Concept choice must balance what the respected anthropologist Clifford Geertz (1987, 134–35) defined as "experience-near" and "experience-distant" considerations. In the first case, concepts must correctly describe the domestic character of politics, which may include ideas and practices that are culturally unique. In the second case, an experience-distant concept must be "one that specialists of one sort or another . . . employ to forward their scientific, philosophical or practical aims." Within the comparative-politics discipline, there is often tension between scholars who seek to highlight the local, the unique, and the anomalous (such scholars are sometimes called "area specialists") and those who seek cross-national comparisons and general rules about political behaviors and outcomes (sometimes called "comparativists").

If the main problem of the area specialist is thick description and little comparison, then comparativists sometimes commit the opposite error by forcing concepts (like democracy) to cover more institutional and geographic terrain than is warranted by the evidence – a problem Giovanni Sartori labels "concept stretching" (Sartori 1970). Returning to the

TABLE 2.2   Freedom in the world, selected years

Year	Total countries	Free countries number (%)	Partly free number (%)	Not free number (%)
2011	193	86 (45)	60 (31)	47 (24)
2008	193	89 (46)	62 (32)	42 (22)
2000	192	86 (45)	58 (30)	48 (25)
1992	186	75 (40)	73 (39)	38 (21)
1990	165	65 (40)	50 (30)	50 (30)
1988/89	167	61 (37)	44 (26)	62 (37)
1987/88	167	60 (36)	39 (23)	68 (41)
1981/82	165	54 (33)	47 (28)	64 (39)
1972	151	44 (29)	38 (25)	69 (46)

Source: Freedom House, "Freedom in the World, Country Ratings," <www.freedomhouse.org>.

earlier example, is the use of electoral methods by Chavez in Venezuela and Putin in Russia sufficient to bestow on their regimes the vaunted term "democracy," even if qualified as "electoral"? Or is it more empirically accurate and comparatively useful to describe such regimes as some variant of authoritarianism? The scholar Larry Diamond, for one, draws the line between authoritarianism and what he calls "pseudodemocracies" on the grounds of whether opposition parties are tolerated (Diamond 1996, 25). When they are, a regime tips into the democratic category for him, because independent opposition parties lay the seeds for future democratic development.

Whereas what to call any given regime can be a contentious issue, the political trends of authoritarianism are both clear and encouraging for those who support the march of freedom. Based on data gathered by Freedom House (an independent, nongovernmental organization that monitors elections, political rights, and liberties around the globe), authoritarian regimes outnumbered all other types in the 1970s. Since then, however, far-reaching changes have occurred. The collapse of communism in the late 1980s and early 1990s ushered in a great expansion in the number of regimes employing elections to choose leaders and transform power into authority. As a result, authoritarianism fell to a historically low figure of 21 percent of all regime types in 1992. At the same time, the number of "free countries" (i.e., democracies) and "partly free" ones (mixes of democracy and authoritarianism) countries has grown exponentially (see Table 2.2).

Within the universe of authoritarian regimes, military regimes were among the most common in the 1970s and 1980s. Latin America and Africa have witnessed more military regimes than any other region since

1945, although places like Greece, Pakistan, Portugal, Thailand, Myanmar, Indonesia, and Egypt have also had their share of military rule. Militaries typically seize power during periods of profound unrest and justify their takeover as an attempt to save the nation from domestic and/or foreign enemies, sometimes real and sometimes imagined. In 1973, General Augusto Pinochet and the top military elites of Chile forcibly overthrew the democratically elected, leftist government of Salvador Allende and subsequently carried out a fifteen-year reign of terror against left-wing parties, political activists, union leaders, professors, and students. In Brazil, all its presidents were generals between 1964 and 1985. It is Bolivia, however, that undoubtedly holds the world's record for the most military coups. In the 187 years of its existence as a state (Bolivia was founded in 1825), the military has attempted 150 military coups (Nash 1992). The frequency of coups d'état in Africa is equally startling. Between 1952 and 2000 thirty-three states (out of fifty-three on the continent) experienced a total of eighty-five military coups (Kieh and Agbese 2004, 44–45).

Although the popular impression may be that military coups are a right-wing phenomenon, occasionally they come from the political left. In Portugal, for instance, a left-wing movement within the military staged a bloodless coup in 1974 and put an end to Europe's longest-running dictatorship. The declared goal of the army officers was the establishment of a democracy, and this was eventually realized in 1982 with free elections. In Turkey, although the armed forces cannot be regarded as left-oriented, the nation's constitution does enshrine the military as the official guardian of both the republic and securalism. Since the end of World War II, the Turkish army has been responsible for four coups (1960, 1971, 1980, and 1997), sometimes to prevent Islamist parties from taking hold of the reins of government after winning democratic elections. In this sense, the Turkish military enjoys what some scholars describe as "reserve domains" of power – that is, the concentration of decision-making power beyond the scope of democratic accountability (Linz and Stepan 1996). Whenever a military has such privileged veto points, the "democracy" label becomes a less appropriate term to describe the regime in question.

Since the 1970s, monarchies have been remarkably resilient. There were fifteen of them in 1972 and thirteen in 2003. Ruling monarchies (as opposed to purely ceremonial ones, like that in the United Kingdom and other European countries) in fact have the best record for persistence among all authoritarian regime types (Hadenius and Teorell 2007). The Middle East is home to the largest number of hereditary monarchies in the world. Bahrain, Jordan, Kuwait, Oman, Qatar, Saudi Arabia, and the

United Emirates are all ruled by family dynasties. In all of these cases, religion serves as a powerful ideological justification for monarchical rule. At the same time, it is possible to find examples that distinguish clearly between theocracies on the one hand and monarchies on the other. Since the 1979 Islamic revolution, religious elites have ruled Iran according to Islamic principle and law, making that country an example of theocracy. In contrast, Asian countries like Cambodia and Thailand are monarchies that do not depend for their perpetuation on the same degree of religious sanction as in the Middle East.

Single-party regimes were the most numerous type of authoritarianism in the 1970s and 1980s, with more than eighty countries falling into this category. In single-party regimes, a political party monopolizes power by either banning all political competition or by severely restricting its opponent's ability to organize and campaign. The ruling party merges itself with both the state and the government, controlling the distribution of perks, positions, and patronage. This was the experience of Mexico's Institutional Revolutionary Party (PRI), which came to power in 1929 and ruled unchallenged for the next seventy-one years. The rule of such parties is often comparable to what was referred in early American history as "political machines." Such machines utilize patron-client networks, which may be defined as asymmetric relations of reciprocity in which clients "sell" their support, usually in the form of their vote, to patrons in exchange for social and economic favors and/or political preferment. In other words, they represent exchange relationships between political unequals. The patron controls access to resources and offices desired by clients. To secure access to critical goods (like medical care, education, licenses, jobs, and security), clients are expected to offer patrons something in return, be it a vote for the ruling party in a rigged election, free labor for a state-sponsored economic project, or even silence in the face of government misdeeds.

Beginning in the 1990s, limited multiparty regimes have become the most common type of authoritarian regime. Given the spread of democracy in the wake of the demise of communism, coupled with the desire of many authoritarian rulers to hold on to power, it stands to reason that some type of competitive or electoral authoritarianism would gain an edge over military and one-party rule. It also makes sense that limited multiparty regimes are the most fragile of authoritarian systems, having an average life span of only nine years (Hadenius and Teorell 2007). When a populace is afforded some liberties, and political parties are able to organize and mobilize on a limited basis, it becomes more difficult for the ruling political class to maintain its monopoly of power and, consequently, its control over society. It is often the case that limited reforms turn the "rising expectations" of a population for greater freedom into "rising frustrations" with the status quo (Huntington 1968). Eventually, a tipping point is reached at which the authoritarian government can no longer contain the political momentum for full and complete democracy.

Regime Types: Totalitarianism

As long as the communist bloc was intact, comparativists advanced a third type of regime, namely totalitarianism. The essential differentiating characteristic of totalitarian regimes is that they seek the total penetration of society by the state. They are not content with the political acquiescence and docility of the population, as authoritarian regimes are. On the contrary, totalitarian regimes demand the total mobilization of society in pursuit of objectives established by the ideology of the ruling party. The goal of Hitler's regime was the creation of a new Aryan race of supposedly superior people; both Stalin and Mao hoped to create "new communist men and women" who would be selfless, moral, and socially active. In such regimes, the entire population is left no choice but to participate in public displays of loyalty, such as parades, elections in which only the ruling party has a candidate, paramilitary exercises, and the completion of enormous economic projects. Under the leadership of Chairman Mao Zedong, the whole of China was forced to study the "Little Red Book," which was a collection of Mao's political thought. Everyone was compelled to engage in public self-criticism, and even intellectuals had to "learn from the peasants" by working in the fields, a practice known as *xia fang*. In contrast, authoritarian regimes demobilize and depoliticize society. They recognize, like democracies, a separation between the public and private spheres of life, allowing citizens some freedom in the social and economic spheres of their lives, but not in politics. Whereas authoritarians can repeat what the French King Louis XIV said of himself, *"l'état cést moi"* (I am the State), totalitarians can rightfully adopt what Trotsky disapprovingly said of Stalin, *"La Societé cést moi"* (I am Society).

The concept of totalitarianism as a regime model was constructed by post–World War II intellectuals on the basis of Nazi rule in Germany and Stalin's rule in the USSR. The difference between totalitarian and authoritarian regimes became politically salient during the Cold War. Jeanne Kirkpatrick, the Reagan-appointed U.S. Ambassador to the United Nations, made much of this distinction, arguing that it was morally and politically acceptable for U.S. foreign policy to aid and befriend authoritarian regimes, but not totalitarian ones. Consequently, the Reagan administration attempted to overthrow left-leaning governments like the Sandinistas of Nicaragua and vigorously supported right-wing governments such as the authoritarian regime in El Salvador despite its systematic abuse of human rights (most notably, the murder of four American nuns and the Catholic archbishop of the country). Since the downfall of communism, however, North Korea stands alone as the sole remaining totalitarian regime. Thus, the use of totalitarianism as a concept in comparative research has declined precipitously.

Nonetheless, the term remains useful at the conceptual level, for it reminds us of the fluid boundaries between regime types. For example, while we have just clarified the differences between authoritarian and totalitarian regimes, does the line ever become blurry between democratic and totalitarian systems? Have democracies ever exhibited a "totalitarian temptation"? Well, it is useful to keep in mind that the Nazi party did achieve, prior to their outright seizure of power, a plurality of the vote in the 1932 legislative elections in Germany. This is what led to Hitler's appointment as chancellor and the emergence of the Nazi regime. It is possible, in other words, for democracies to slip into totalitarianism. The Marxist thinker Herbert Marcuse even goes so far as to label the United States totalitarian in his seminal book, *One-Dimensional Man* (1964). Marcuse reasons that American citizens are so completely bombarded with capitalist ideology that they have effectively been shaped into one-dimensional, self-absorbed consumers who have lost their capacity for critical thought. Others, in contrast, sternly condemn Marcuse's argument as a textbook example of concept stretching – that is, irresponsibly inflating a concept beyond its original meaning (Sartori 1987).

> **W**AIT A MINUTE. **CONSIDER THIS.** Conduct a test of Marcuse's argument. Name all the ways in which consumerist habits are promoted in American culture. Is Marcuse stretching and obfuscating the concept of totalitarianism by applying it to the American capitalist system and its consumerist culture, or is he advancing a plausible and promising insight into the nature of power in the modern American state?

▓ COMPARING STRONG, WEAK, AND FAILED STATES

An implicit factor distinguishing democratic, authoritarian, and totalitarian regimes is the degree of power the state exercises effectively over society. Another way to view this distinction is to utilize the typology of strong, weak, and failed states. Not all states are equal in their capacity to penetrate, regulate, and coordinate society. Some states are highly effective, enjoy widespread legitimacy, and are capable of exercising sufficient autonomy to address difficult social problems. Other states do not have these capacities. In this final section of Chapter 2, we seek to explore and explain variations in state strength.

There are many indicators that may be used to measure the relative strength of states. Does the state possess the capacity to plan, execute, and enforce policies? Is the bureaucracy organized efficiently and does it respect the will of its elected political masters? Are the decisions of officeholders transparent and subject to review and accountability, or has the state become captured by corrupt agents and practices? To what extent are state actors autonomous from the pressures and interests of subgroups in society? Comparative scholars have developed a threefold typology to categorize distinct levels of state power. Strong states are those that have: (1) popular legitimacy, administrative efficiency, and effectiveness; (2) the capacity to mobilize and extract resources (such as taxes) from the population; and (3) the ability to establish and preserve law and order. On the other side of the continuum are failed states in which legitimate authority has crumbled, bureaucracies are starved of resources, government programs are poorly coordinated, punitive institutions (such as the police) fail to uphold the law and instead act in a predatory manner toward the population, and armed paramilitaries proliferate because the state's monopoly of the means of violence has been broken. Weak states can be found somewhere between these two poles.

One instructive way to compare state power around the globe is to examine the World Bank's study of governance indicators. The "Worldwide Governance Indicators Project" maps the relative standing of 213 countries and territories across six dimensions: (1) voice and accountability, (2) political stability and absence of violence, (3) government effectiveness, (4) regulatory quality, (5) rule of law, and (6) the control of corruption (for an interactive analysis of these indicators, go to http://info.worldbank.org/governance/wgi/index.asp). If we take an indicator like regulatory quality and apply it to a selective set of European

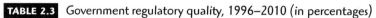

TABLE 2.3 Government regulatory quality, 1996–2010 (in percentages)

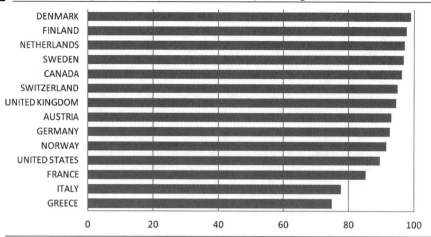

and North American countries, we see right away that there is a range of state capacities within the Western world (see Table 2.3).

Based on Table 2.3, it is clear that many West European countries and Canada rank above the United States when it comes to enacting regulations that govern economic activity effectively. The United States has a similar ranking on all the remaining dimensions. Thus, based on the same group of fourteen countries, the United States ranks twelfth for political stability, twelfth for government effectiveness, twelfth for voice and accountability, eleventh for the rule of law, and twelfth for the control of corruption.

What is it that enables countries like Sweden, Finland, Denmark, Norway, Canada, and Germany to consistently outperform the United States on such tests of state strength? One critical factor that weighs heavily on this issue is the ideology that guides the state's approach to conflict management. Western Europe's modern history has been shaped significantly by the presence of left-wing movements, powerful labor unions, and governments run by socialist and social democratic political parties as well as by conservative and Christian democratic parties, all of whom support, in varying degrees, a strong role for the state in the regulation of the economy and society. This orientation is called the "social democratic model." According to its proponents, unregulated capitalism produces an array of disturbing and unacceptable societal outcomes. Inequality, unemployment, poverty, environmental damage, and uncontrollable boom-bust economic cycles are just a few of the free-market vices that social democrats aim to ameliorate when in office. As opposed to both the "invisible hand" of free-market economies and the "clenched fist" of communist rule, the social democratic model offers a "visible hand" that pushes and pulls the levers of a capitalist economy to produce outcomes that are fair, rational, and beneficial to the great majority in society. "Capitalism with a human face" is how many describe this approach.

It is important, at this juncture, to note that socialism is a capacious term meaning different things to different people. Our use of the term is meant to cover all socialist-oriented parties of Western Europe that accept democracy and play the game of politics by its rules. In other words, Leninist and Maoist versions of socialism (which are more appropriately referred to as communism) stand outside this framework. West European parties that are committed to socialism go by different names and follow slightly distinct social policies. For example, the Socialist Party of France has traditionally focused on state ownership of key industries and has sought to steer and direct capital investments into sectors it deems important. The Social Democratic Party of Sweden is dedicated to full-employment policies and concentrates on retraining workers who are displaced by the market. The Labour Party of the United Kingdom has historically favored state ownership of basic industries like utilities, transportation, and mining. And the Social Democratic Party of Germany regulates what it calls the "social market," focusing on worker's rights at the workplace and providing an extensive, generous welfare system for the downtrodden of capitalism. Since the end of World War II, there has been a strong commitment across Western Europe to provide its citizens with a social safety net below which no one should fall. This commitment takes concrete form in the shape of universal health care systems, public housing, free education, progressive income taxes (in which the rich pay proportionately more than the poor), unemployment benefits, and support for families having children. For example, in Sweden, pregnant female workers are entitled to sixty-four weeks off work at two-thirds of their salary; in Portugal, women get three months off with full pay. In terms of unemployment benefits, a single, childless 40-year-old in Denmark receives 90 percent of gross wages for a period of four years; in Germany, the figure is 57.4 percent of gross salary for twelve months (Judt 2005; Landler 2005).

The bottom line across all these subtle variations is that government intervention in the economy is the primary tool by which social democrats hope to improve the lives of all the citizens in their state. It is small wonder, therefore, that most of the countries of Western Europe consistently outrank America on issues like regulatory quality and government effectiveness.

In contradistinction to Europe, the United States has tended to follow a "minimal liberal model," and particularly so since the "Reagan

Revolution" of the 1980s. As Ronald Reagan himself was fond of saying during his 1980 campaign for the presidency, the scariest sentence he ever heard in his life was "I'm from the government and I'm here to help you." American political culture has always been strongly shaped by an anti-state bias in favor of the free operation of the market. The reasoning behind this position comes largely from Adam Smith, who argued in his *Wealth of Nations* (1776) that a completely unregulated, *laissez-faire* economy transforms the greedy and self-interested behavior of individuals into socially beneficial outcomes. This transformation is possible because the only way a single individual can realize his/her interests (such as making a lot of money) is to discover and deliver what others want. Therefore, if everyone is allowed the unfettered pursuit of selfishness, all will actually benefit. Smith likened this process to being directed by a higher being, which he summarized as the "invisible hand" of Divine Providence (Smith 1976: 477). But today economists generally ascribe this beneficent guidance of the operation of a free market to the role that prices play in it.

When markets are truly unregulated, prices will reflect the ratios between the scarcity of a commodity and the consumer demand for it. Consequently, free-market prices provide three critical functions that turn the apparent disorder of capitalism into a well-ordered machine. Those three functions are: (1) the transmission of information concerning scarcity and demand; (2) the provision of incentives for capitalists to either enter or exit a particular economic activity; and (3) the distribution of income, as markets reward those who succeed and punish failure (Friedman and Friedman 1980). The beauty and attraction of the minimal liberal state model to many is that as long as governments do not intervene and impose arbitrary prices on labor (such as the minimum wage), high taxation on the rich (which is tantamount to punishing success), and elaborate welfare systems that cushion failure and reward losers, then capitalism is self-regulating, self-correcting, and will, as Adam Smith promised, create unimaginable wealth for the national collectivity. Adherence to this minimal liberal state model is what leads many scholars to deem the United States a "weak state" – that is, one with weak regulatory capacity (Gonzalez and King 2004).

This conclusion, of course, is not meant to convey that the American state is weak on every political capability dimension. Currently, it enjoys unquestioned military dominance in the world. With approximately 40 full-scale military bases and more than 700 military installations in 132 countries around the world, no state on the planet can project power like America (Mann 2003; *Democracy Now!* 2008). The United States also excels at law enforcement, as evidenced by the fact that it has the largest prison population (in both absolute and relative terms) in the world. Currently, American prisons hold 2.3 million prisoners, which means there are 751 prisoners for every 100,000 people in the country. China is in second place, with 1.6 million behind bars. In relative terms, America's incarceration rates exceed all others. Russia, for example, has 627 prisoners for every 100,000 people; England has 151, Germany 88, and Japan 63 (Liptak 2008). All of this is meant to show that whereas a state may be weak in some fields of activity, it can be very strong in others. In short, state capacity is distributed unevenly across, as well as within, states (Fukuyama 2004).

If we turn our attention away from the Western world and consider the distribution of weak and failed states in the south and the east, we find that Africa is home to the largest number of unstable, failing states. Since 2005 the journal *Foreign Policy* and the Fund for Peace research institute have collaborated to compose an annual list of states deemed vulnerable to collapse (*The Failed States Index*, 2011). African states consistently comprise more than half of the twenty most vulnerable states each year. There are many reasons for the dire condition of the African state. The legacy of colonialism continues to echo in the contemporary period. European colonial powers drew borders irrespective of ethnic and linguistic frontiers. As Robert Kaplan observes, the "horizontal" distribution of population belts does not match the "vertical" organization of postcolonial states (Kaplan 1994). Compounding this problem was the tendency of colonials to privilege some native groups over others, as the Belgians favored the Tutsis over the Hutus in Rwanda. The resulting political inequality produced resentment among Hutus and set in place a lethal and destructive dynamic for political dominance after independence. A second problem plaguing Africa is that the ruling political class in many states has failed to broaden its legitimacy beyond the ethnic group or clan from which it springs. In other words, the state is captured by specific, narrow interests and is thus unable to rule impartially for the common good (Fatton 1988). As a result, Africa is littered with incomplete, weak states that are ethnically prejudicial, corrupt, incompetent, and illegitimate in the eyes of significant portions of their populations. It is for such reasons that the scholar Robert Jackson uses terms like "quasi-states" and "juridical statehood" to describe many African countries – while they may have a UN seat and thus an aura of sovereignty, the existence of a functioning state on the ground is largely fictional (Jackson 1990; Jackson and Rosberg 1982).

The good news is that weak states are neither permanently locked into this condition nor are they doomed to fail. Russia's postcommunist trajectory is a case in point. The Russian state fell from its superpower status during the Cold War period to an almost quasi- or juridical existence for much of the 1990s. While communists always promised that the state would wither away, Russia's condition in the 1990s was not exactly what they had in mind. With the state unable to protect property, enforce contracts, or provide for law and order, criminal groups arose in response to new opportunities and acted as an ersatz authority and guarantor of last resort for private market transactions. By the late 1990s, however, Vladimir Putin had emerged as a strong leader who was able to regain control of the legal means of violence and reassert state power (Volkov 2002).

CONCLUSION

In this chapter, we have explored three approaches to the question of what is politics. Politics-as-war, politics-as-process, and politics-as-participation speak to distinct philosophical traditions in the history of Western thought. Each one captures important aspects of the way in which people interpret, evaluate, and interact in the political world. Whereas the proponents of each perspective naturally uphold their vision as an exclusively true reflection of reality, it is reasonable to conclude that all three are needed to appreciate the complex political world we inhabit.

A second major theme of this chapter centers on how the discipline of comparative politics defines and employs the concepts of the state, regime, and government. It is important to keep in mind that the way politicians, activists, and the media utilize these key terms, particularly regimes, is different from their treatment in political science. Comparative political scientists identify three fundamental regime types: democracy, authoritarianism, and totalitarianism. In principle, these regime types are mutually exclusive and turn largely on the accountability of governments and the degree of power the state exercises over society. Although clear definitions can certainly be provided for each, in the real world it is sometimes a challenge to determine if a specific states fall into one regime category or another. Occasionally a single government can combine both democratic and authoritarian practices (or any combination of the three types) and this makes classifying it in a single regime category a difficult interpretive act. The lesson is that subjective interpretations and personal value judgments can never be completely excised from scientific work. In other words, political science is irreducibly both scientific *and* political.

The third and final section of this chapter involves a comparative examination of strong, weak, and failed states. Apart from their status in international law, not all states are equal. Some have impressive strength and apply their resources effectively across a wide range of human activities. Others have little to no strength and a correspondingly limited scope of action. The ideology a state adopts to manage conflict, such as the social democratic or minimal liberal state models, also has a determining influence on the strength and scope of its government's practices and policies. Weak and failing states are concentrated in the developing world, and there is a growing chorus of scholars and political observers who warn that failed states are likely to be a major source of global instability in the twenty-first century. Whether such states can alter their conditions and avoid disintegration remains to be seen. What is certain is that their governments will play a central role in determining their future, given that a primary role of government is to "steer the ship of state," and they can do so well or badly. But what do governments look like and how do their basic characteristics differ with regime type, specifically with whether the regime is authoritarian or democratic? Governance, or the process of governing, in the two types of regime is the subject matter of the next three chapters.

3 How Governments Work

This chapter shifts our attention away from states and toward how governments work. How do the three main branches of government – the executive, the legislature, and the judiciary – interact in the daily task of governing in democratic and authoritarian regimes? What is the business of governing like across these regime types? We argue that there are important similarities and differences between them when it comes to governing. For example, governments of both types face a similar set of constraints, such as the need to maintain popular legitimacy and to engage in inter-branch negotiation and adjustments when making policy. Equally, executives dominate the governance process no matter the regime type. Thus, even in democracies, executives possess more levers of power than do legislatures. Still, the spread of democracy around the globe has led authoritarian regimes to establish legislatures and courts that, among other things, function to constrain (however mildly) the exercise of arbitrary power. Such similarities notwithstanding, however, there remains considerable variation in both types of regime in regard to how the three branches of government interact.

In this chapter, we explore these issues by addressing the following themes: (1) the rules of governance (such as constitutions, both written and unwritten); (2) the structures of governance (executive, legislative, judicial) in democratic regimes; and (3) the structures of governance in authoritarian regimes. We begin with a discussion of the concept of government.

WHAT IS GOVERNMENT?

The term "government" is used in different ways. Sometimes it is used to refer to the collectivity of institutions and personnel that make and implement political decisions in a state. In this sense, it is an impersonal entity that can exist at various levels of society, including, most commonly, federal, state, and local. At other times, it is used more narrowly to refer to those individuals collectively responsible for ruling and directing the affairs of a state – for example, the leading members of the governing party in a democracy. This book will use the term "government" in this second sense – that is, to refer to the collective political decision-making body. The term "political executive" will refer to the leadership group in this decision-making body, and the term "chief executive" will denote the most prominent member of this group – the president in the United States, the prime minister or chancellor in countries like the United Kingdom and Germany, the leader of a military junta, and so on.

National governments are the public face of the state. They are not the same as the state, however, and can take many forms from one state to the next and within the same state over time. Viewed from an international perspective, some governments are authoritarian, some democratic; some are left-wing in ideological orientation, others right-wing; some enjoy overwhelming public support, others are unpopular; and so on. Individual states are similar in that they too will likely experience different types of government over a period of time as, for example, parties of the right unseat parties of the left in elections or military leaders overthrow civilian governments. This variation does not mean, however, that each government is unique unto itself. Rather, the very act of governing forces certain similarities on governments, just as, for example, the act of playing football makes football teams from different leagues and even countries resemble each other in many critical respects. Amid great diversity, in other words, there is uniformity that stems from being subject to common rules and having shared goals, whether these, in the case of governments, are to provide a coordinated response to social problems or security threats or, in the case of football teams, to win a game or a championship.

The job of government is evident from the origins of the word itself. It comes from the old French *governer*, which is from the Latin *gubernare* (to direct, rule, guide), which in turn comes from the Greek *kybernan* (to steer or pilot a ship, direct). The emphasis here is that governments are responsible for steering the ship of state. In practice, they can do a good job or a bad job of it; their decisions and actions can make the state stronger and more legitimate in the eyes of its population, or they can have the opposite effect, or no effect at all. But whatever the eventual outcome of their stewardship, governments do not come to the job entirely free to act as they please and see fit. Rather, their room for maneuver is always constrained to some degree. Comparability is introduced into their behaviors by two sets of forces: (1) the rules in place about what kinds of laws they can pass and the procedures they must follow in making and passing them; and (2) the structures in place to allow established, new, and returning governments to perform their fundamental task of steering the ship of state by making and enforcing laws. These two sets of forces are labeled the *rules* and *structures* of governance, respectively. *Governance* means simply the act or manner of governing, *rules* are the authoritative regulations governing the conduct of public officials, and *structures* are the offices, roles, and institutions that public officials occupy. Together, they form the governing framework of a state and thereby play an important role in constraining and shaping the decisions and actions of all governments. Let us now turn to each of them separately and draw attention to how they differ in general between authoritarian and democratic regimes.

RULES OF GOVERNANCE

Governments perform their stewardship role by making laws that are intended to be binding on the citizens of the state. These laws encourage public behavior that the government judges to be in the best interests of the state and they range widely from those that are permanent, relatively unchanging, and found in all states to those that are put in place temporarily and may even be unique to a single state in a specific set of circumstances. An example of a permanent law is taxation. Even though the rate of taxation and the objects taxed may vary from state to state or from one time period to the next in a single state, every government levies taxes of one kind or other on its citizens in order to fund the activities that it chooses to undertake. An example of a temporary, or ad hoc, law is a short-lived hose pipe ban to conserve water for essential purposes in a time of severe drought. Importantly, however, to make the observation that governments pass laws that affect the lives of their populations from the cradle to the grave is not to imply that governments can pass whatever laws they want. One imperative all governments would be wise to respect is not to undertake any actions that become so unpopular that they undermine public acceptance of their right to govern and the people's need to comply. For governments to lose sight of the limits of public tolerance could lead to outcomes as diverse as the loss of elections in democratic regimes or some more violent ejection from power – a coup, for example – in authoritarian ones.

All governments, then, have some limits on the laws that they make, limits defined at the extreme by the practical need to maintain popular support, or at least avoid inciting popular rebellion. Importantly, however, these limits are not the same for all governments. A safe generalization is that authoritarian governments, by their very nature, enjoy more unconstrained freedom of action in their dealings with their populations than do democratic governments. This is because the latter are more likely to be subject not only to the need to maintain their right to govern in the people's eyes, but also to practice politics-as-process in abiding by a set of rules, principles, and procedures, usually set out in a constitution, designed to regularize and limit their power over citizens. These principles might include, for example, the right to organize and challenge specific government policies as well as guarantees of freedom of speech, association, and communication to allow such challenges the potential to be effective.

Generally speaking, authoritarian governments do not accept the legitimacy of such challenges because their ideological predisposition is to be guided in their actions less by the will of the people and more by the desire to hold on to political power – despite the will of the people, if necessary. They may on occasion be responsive to popular pressure if such responsiveness helps achieve their higher-order goal of holding on to power. Their more common strategy, however, is, first, to encourage public apathy by denying people the political rights, like elections and freedom of speech, that condone and legitimize challenges to government power, and, second, to practice politics-as-war, resorting, if necessary, to forceful repression if and when public opposition to their rule shows itself. Still, it is worth reiterating that authoritarian governments cannot always be arbitrary and unconstrained in their day-to-day interactions with those they govern. The need to retain some degree of popular support is one type of constraint on their freedom of action; religion might be another. It can trump politics as theocracies "do more than grant exclusive recognition and support to a given state religion: Laws must conform to the principles of religious doctrine and no statute may be enacted that is repugnant to these principles" (Hirschl 2008, 73). Thus, some Islamic scholars argue that Islam contains embryonic democratic values. In particular, they note the stipulation in the Quran that rulers should engage in *shura*, which is basically a consultative decision-making process, in matters of governance (Esposito and Voll 1996).

Nonetheless, it is a truism that, compared to their democratic counterparts, authoritarian governments are relatively free to govern as they see fit and can therefore be relatively arbitrary and whimsical in their relationship with those under their rule. In most circumstances they enjoy the freedom to act in ways necessary to keep themselves protected from political challenges and in control of government, regardless of whether their actions are lawful or acceptable to the public.

Constitutionalism

A fundamental characteristic of democratic government, by contrast, is that the potential for arbitrary rule is limited by the fact of constitutionalism. Otherwise known as the rule of law, constitutionalism is "the constraining of government in order to better effectuate the fundamental principles of the regime" (Whittington 2008, 282). Put differently, constitutionalism holds that governments cannot arbitrarily pass whatever laws they please, but are limited in the things they can do and in the way they can behave by a set of authoritative principles, rules, and procedures set out in the constitution. Thus, governments cannot, for example, whimsically deprive citizens of constitutionally guaranteed rights or bypass the normal process by which laws are made and govern by decree. Constitutional law is higher law, as is evident in the fact that, generally speaking, it can be amended only with the approval of some kind of special majority in the legislature, the population, or both. In most democracies, ordinary laws – for example, the legal speed limit – can be changed with the support of a simple majority in the lower house of the legislature, but changes to the constitution – for example, the legal voting age – are more demanding and commonly require a special (perhaps two-thirds) majority for passage and in others the acquiescence as well of regional legislatures, again often with some kind of special majority.

Possession of a constitution is the sine qua non of constitutional government. Two important caveats have to be made before we go on to examine constitutions, however. First, possession of a constitution is not itself a guarantee of constitutional government. The totalitarian Soviet Union, for example, had a very elaborate constitution that included among other political rights freedom of speech, freedom of assembly, and freedom of religion. In practice, however, citizens were systematically deprived of these rights. The constitution, in other words, was a façade designed to promote the communist regime's legitimacy without at the same time constraining the ability of its rulers to act as and how they saw fit. The second caveat is that some constitutions are *codified* and some are *uncodified*. All democracies are constitutional in the sense of being characterized by the rule of law, yet not all constitutions are the same. Most of them are codified and are usually the product of a dramatic political event, like defeat in war or revolution, that points the country in a new direction – transforming it from a monarchy into a republic as in the case of the United States, for example. The defining characteristic of codified constitutions is that they are written down in a single document, although some, like those of Australia and Canada, also include separate statutes that emerged after the original constitution was enacted. Israel, New Zealand, and the United Kingdom, in contrast, have uncodified constitutions, which are so because their provisions have cumulated incrementally over long periods of evolutionary, as opposed to dramatic, political change. Uncodified constitutions include written sources – the Scotland Act of 1998 in the United Kingdom established an elected assembly with tax-raising powers in Scotland – and unwritten sources. Taking the United Kingdom as an example, the latter include constitutional conventions (e.g., the duty of the monarch to act on the advice of government ministers and not unilaterally), royal prerogatives (e.g., declaring war), customs and tradition (e.g., always holding national parliamentary elections on a Thursday), and the observation of precedent. In addition to being unwritten, a second important characteristic of uncodified constitutions is that they can be amended by a simple legislative majority because, in the absence of a higher constitutional law, a legislature that derives its legitimacy from being directly elected by the people is seen as being incapable of doing legal wrong.

Bearing these two caveats in mind, what can be said about constitutions in general? In essence, they serve three functions. First, they set out the social and political ideals to which the state aspires and that define its character; these are the "fundamental principles" referred to in the earlier definition of constitutionalism. The preamble to the U.S. constitution provides a clear example of this function:

> We the People of the United States, in Order to form a more perfect Union, establish Justice, insure domestic Tranquility, provide for the common defense, promote the general Welfare, and secure the Blessings of Liberty to ourselves and our Posterity, do ordain and establish this Constitution for the United States of America.

Similarly, Article 79 of the Basic Law for the Federal Republic of Germany rejects the country's Nazi past by stipulating that the country has to be a democratic, federal, and social republic where all state powers have to leave the dignity of man inviolable, where rule of law has to prevail, and where sovereignty has to lie with the people.

The second function of constitutions relates to what Sartori (1994, 198) considers to be their defining feature: the provision of a frame of government. Constitutions, in other words, specify the pathways to governmental office, the structure, powers, and duties of the branches of government, and the procedures for their internal cooperation and conflict in the making of laws. Examples of specific items falling under these three subheadings include how individuals attain governmental office (direct election versus indirect election versus appointment), how concentrated at the center is the lawmaking power (centralized versus decentralized government), how territories or regions are represented in national lawmaking (unicameral versus bicameral legislatures), and how the power to pass laws will be distributed among government actors (separation-of-powers systems of government versus fusion-of-powers systems).

The final function of constitutions is to define the nature of the relationship between the state and citizen – that is, their rights and responsibilities relative to each other. Democracies confer on their citizens the right to choose their government in regular, free, and competitive elections, and constitutions specify who has the right to vote in those elections. Passed in 1971, for example, a recent successful change to the U.S. constitution was the Twenty-Sixth Amendment, which extended the franchise, or right to vote, to eighteen-year-olds. Previously citizens had to be twenty-one years or older to enjoy this right. Some constitutions go even further and tell eligible citizens that they must exercise their right to vote or face a monetary fine if they fail to do so. Australia and Belgium are examples of states where voting is compulsory. More strikingly, however, constitutions define and protect the range of rights that citizens enjoy and that the state cannot take away; these rights are "inalienable." In this regard, constitutions enunciate a higher law that limits government discretion. An example of an early incursion into the right of rulers to treat their subjects as they pleased is the Magna Carta, signed under pressure from his barons by King John of England in 1215, and the single most important article of which introduced the notion of habeas corpus. This article stipulated that the king was no longer permitted to imprison, outlaw, exile, or kill anyone at whim; there must be due process of law first. The article in question reads:

> No free man shall be arrested, or imprisoned, or deprived of his property, or outlawed, or exiled, or in any way destroyed, nor shall we go against

him or send against him, unless by legal judgement of his peers, or by the law of the land.

In sum, then, governance, or the act of governing, always occurs within the framework of a set of rules that limit to a greater or lesser degree the freedom of governments to act arbitrarily and whimsically toward those they govern. The precise content of this framework varies from state to state and the frameworks themselves have different roots across states, originating perhaps in religious doctrine in some, in monarchical convention and tradition in others, and in constitutional doctrine in yet others. Most importantly, however, governance frameworks vary in the degree to which they are binding on governments, with authoritarian governments generally speaking being freer to ignore constituent rules, principles, and procedures than democratic counterparts with their deeply rooted traditions and habits of constitutionalism. But even within democracies, these frameworks are differentially binding on governments, not least because they are more easily amended in some than others. As mentioned previously, where democratic constitutions are uncodified (Israel, New Zealand, and the United Kingdom), specific constitutional provisions can be amended by simple majority vote in the lower house – just like ordinary legislation.

The argument made to this point is that the myriad forms of government found in the world today have in common that they are rule-bound, and therefore constrained, to a greater or lesser degree in the ways they can behave toward those they govern. A related limitation on the ability of governments to act as they see fit in steering the ship of state is the structure of governance, or the set of institutional arrangements by which public policy proposals are initiated, debated, passed, and reviewed to become laws binding on the population. It is to the discussion of the structure of governance, again from a comparative perspective, that we now turn.

WAIT A MINUTE. **CONSIDER THIS.** Why are constitutions effective at constraining governments? Does their effectiveness stem from being either codified or uncodified? Is it tradition or habit, or perhaps even the religious roots, of a constitution? Another possibility is that adherence to constitutional norms ensures greater citizen compliance with government initiatives and policies. Still another is the fear of public backlash that can occur against politicians who flagrantly violate constitutional norms. Essentially, why do governments accept the constraints that constitutions impose on them?

▓ STRUCTURES OF GOVERNANCE

Discussion of how governments should be structured, or organized, so as to strengthen the state involves many of the issues found in the rules-of-governance debate. In particular, there is the fundamental question of whether governments should be organized so as to limit or to strengthen the power of the state vis-à-vis its citizens. An early leading theorist in the debate on rational government structure was Baron de Montesquieu (1689–1755), a French nobleman who came down firmly in favor of limited government. Looking across the channel, he championed in his home country what he saw to be the "English" notions of freedom, toleration, moderation, and constitutional government. He was not a reformist who wanted to empower the common people. Rather, he wanted to elevate the French aristocracy to a position comparable to that of its English counterpart by giving it back the rights it had enjoyed prior to the emergence of absolute monarchy in seventeenth-century France. For him, a politically potent aristocracy would serve to preserve liberty against the potential for despotic rule inherent in both an unchecked monarch and the common people.

In his classical work, *On the Spirit of Laws* (1748), Montesquieu essentially argued that the limited government he advocated was best realized when the lawmaking power was shared between three groups of officials, as in England where, he argued, it was divided between a Parliament (which made laws), a King (who enforced them), and the judges of the courts (who interpreted them). This "separation of powers," as he termed it, was at its optimum when the three separate branches of government enjoyed equal but different powers so that no one of them could have too much power and each branch could limit the other two through the exercise of countervailing power. He wrote:

> When the legislative and executive powers are united in the same person, or in the same body of magistrates, there can be no liberty, because apprehensions may arise lest the same monarch or senate should enact tyrannical laws to execute them in a tyrannical manner. (Quoted in Madison, Federalist No. 47)

To the extent that this same separation-of-powers doctrine played a key role in the design of the very first democratic constitution – that of the newly independent United States of America in the late eighteenth-century – and that democracy is everywhere equated with the distribution of political power among a plurality of actors, it is clear that Montesquieu was a revolutionary in his political thinking. Before and after him, however, there have been many expressions of the opposite viewpoint, seeing separated powers as a wasteful and counterproductive way of structuring governance. A recent example is found in many of the leaders of the independent states created in Africa and Asia from European colonial empires after World War II. They rejected democracy on the grounds that it was inefficient and distracted attention from a more pressing goal whose realization would contribute far more to the common good: economic development. Almost immediately upon taking power, therefore, they ended the flirtation with a democratic constitution imposed by departing colonial rulers, outlawed political opposition, and vested all political power in a single political party of which they were usually the unopposed leader (Zolberg 1966).

These contrasting views of the best structure for the governance of states once again highlight the tension between the political dynamics of contemporary world democratic and authoritarian regimes; in the former, lawmaking power tends to be shared among the legislative, executive, and judicial branches of government, and in the latter it is more concentrated in the hands of a ruling individual or minority. But as in the case of the earlier discussion of rules of governance, *this difference should be recognized as being one of degree, not kind*. In other words, many of the governance practices of democratic and authoritarian regimes are actually quite similar. This is evident when we examine patterns of governance in each of them more closely.

Separation of Powers: Democratic Governance

Unlike their authoritarian counterparts, all democratic regimes have legislative, executive, and judicial branches of government. They are also different in that each branch's powers are entrenched by being constitutionally specified, which means that no one branch can always dominate the others. This is because the power to make laws is shared so that no one branch can consistently ignore the others in performing this key function of government. Take a simple example. To pass a legislative proposal to increase the rate of taxation on personal incomes into law is not the prerogative of any one branch. Instead and minimally, the agreement of representatives of both the executive and legislative branches is required. If one of them refuses to sign off on the proposal and the other cannot persuade it to do so, then the proposal remains precisely that – a plan of action that did not make it on to the statute books. To note, however, that the branches of democratic governments share powers in the making of laws is not to imply that they have the same or equal powers. Rather, in theory at least, the basic division of labor is that legislatures make the laws, executives implement and administer them, and judiciaries adjudicate disputes arising from their implementation. The evolution and character of each of the three branches of government will now be explored, starting with political executives.

Executives

Political executives are the moving force of democratic politics and bear the main responsibility for governance; they take the lead in setting national priorities, crafting legislation, shepherding it through the approval process, overseeing its implementation and administration, and coordinating the myriad activities of the state on the domestic and international scenes. To understand their role and its limits, an important distinction that needs to be made early is the one between head of state and head of government. The head of state plays no direct role in governance. Instead, he/she is a ceremonial figure whose job is to reinforce national identity and pride by personifying the country's ideals and values and placing them on display before national and international audiences. Monarchs are often the head of state – the United Kingdom is an obvious example, but countries like Belgium, Denmark, Japan, and Spain also have a monarch in this role. Others, including Austria, Germany, Ireland, and Italy, have an appointed president as head of state. The United States is notable for combining the roles of head of state and head of government in one person, the president.

The head of government is the chief executive and, in cooperation with other members of the political executive, has two principal roles. The first is to set and coordinate the government's goals in both domestic and international affairs and to initiate legislation and undertake other actions necessary to achieve them. Success in this endeavor requires that the political executive fill a second role effectively, and it is to exercise control over a bureaucracy that exists to implement and administer public policies decided on by governments. Let us look at this second role more closely.

The term "bureaucracy" basically means "rule by office" and its origins are found in the clerical servants who administered the affairs of royal households. Even today, bureaucrats, or civil servants, in the United Kingdom are described as servants of the crown. More generally, the term refers to the administrative arm of government, the organizational machinery by which policies are implemented and administered. As the modern state grew in size and complexity, traditional forms of bureaucracy became inappropriate for its needs. Accordingly, the organization of the administrative arm of government expanded and adapted to meet the managerial needs of the evolving state. There were many important stepping stones. Napoleon, for example, introduced a hierarchically structured and centrally controlled bureaucracy to France in the early nineteenth century. The Prussians also pioneered bureaucratic reform, introducing the notion of recruitment and promotion on the basis of merit rather than patronage, personal loyalty, family membership, or other premodern criteria. It is this Prussian model that underpins Max Weber's classic study of rational-legal authority and the onset of the modern bureaucracy. For Weber (who is considered a founding father of modern social science), a rational-efficient bureaucracy possesses the following characteristics:

1. a carefully defined division of tasks;
2. merit-based recruitment and promotion coupled with secure jobs and salaries;
3. methodical adherence to formal rules and procedures;
4. disciplined hierarchy of command in which there is a clear line of authority from senior to junior officials;
5. rationality in the sense of choosing the most efficient means to achieve specified ends.

This model promised efficiency and effectiveness in public administration, but, as Weber himself realized, it also raised serious political problems. In particular, it highlighted the dilemma of political control of the bureaucracy in a democracy. Bureaucrats have expertise through their qualifications and permanence through job security, whereas governments are amateur and fleeting, putting the latter at a distinct disadvantage in their relationship. As Weber himself recognized:

> Under normal conditions, the power position of a fully developed bureaucracy is always overwhelming. The "political master" finds himself in the position of the "dilettante" who stands opposite the "expert", facing the trained official who stands within the management of administration. (Gerth and Mills 1946, 232)

The risks are serious. Without effective political control, bureaucracies could, at the worst, become increasingly self-serving, corrupt, and neglectful of their political masters and the citizens they represent. Less serious perhaps, but more likely is the problem of misplaced loyalties. The norm is for government bureaucracies to be divided into specialized ministries, or departments. Examples found in all democracies are the Ministries of Agriculture, Defense, Finance, and Foreign Affairs. One of the responsibilities of these ministries is to maintain regular contacts and consultation with domestic interest groups in their domain of specialization to canvass their policy views and monitor their compliance with government policies. Thus, for example, the Ministry of Agriculture maintains close relations with farmers, listens to their concerns, and regulates their activities to ensure compliance with the law. The problem is that these relationships are institutionalized and outlast individual governments, with the result that bureaucratic agencies can develop close relations with the industries they are supposed to regulate and actually end up championing those interests rather than regulating them. This phenomenon is known as "agency capture" (Stigler 1971) and its occurrence essentially means that the elected government serves the unelected bureaucracy rather than vice versa. Other problems can include lack of responsiveness and inertia as standard operating procedures become entrenched and even the smallest changes become difficult to implement.

How have governments sought to keep the bureaucracy responsive and accountable for its actions? In addition to routine micromanagement strategies like auditing, performance reviews, and outcome reviews, four major mechanisms of political oversight can be identified. The first of them might be called the British model and involves having career professionals fill even the most senior positions in the civil service and making them answerable to the party politician – the minister – appointed to run their department. The strategy involves hiring and promoting individuals of talent, integrity, and vision and imbuing them with an ethos of professionalism and public service that enables them to adapt their skills, chameleon-like, to the service of elected political masters of different political complexions. The second mechanism is the American model, which is skeptical that such selflessness is possible and so its control strategy is to place presidential appointees not only at the head of each department of the federal bureaucracy – the Secretary of Defense, for example – but also to fill the senior bureaucratic positions immediately below them with presidential sympathizers. Thus, when George W. Bush assumed the presidency in January 2001, he had approximately 1,200 full-time positions to fill. Over time, however, these two models have become less mutually distinct. The same ethos of professionalism and service is imbued in permanent bureaucrats in the United States, and there are signs of European convergence on the American model. Members of the political executive (ministers) in France, for example, have since the early 1970s had their own *cabinets*, made up mostly of seconded civil servants, to assist them, whereas Britain has witnessed the rise of *personal political advisors*. These are individuals appointed by senior politicians to be their political eyes and ears in the corridors of power and, unlike civil servants, they retain their position only as long as the minister employing them remains in office.

The third oversight mechanism is the administrative court. In the discharge of their duties, bureaucrats are subject to administrative law, which is the law created by government regulatory agencies through decisions, orders, regulations, and rules. A number of countries, including France, Germany, Greece, and the Scandinavian countries (Denmark, Norway, Sweden, Finland, and Iceland), have established a separate system of administrative courts whose jurisdiction does not overlap with that of general courts and in which citizens can appeal administrative decisions. The United States is different in that administrative courts are tribunals within government agencies. A similar avenue of appeal in some countries is the ombudsman, a word that comes from the Swedish for "representative." An ombudsman is a person appointed to investigate complaints against maladministration and to protect against the abuse of power by government and the civil service. Ombudsmen are found in a number of countries, including Canada, Denmark, Nigeria, and Peru (Reif 1999).

The final mechanism for improving bureaucratic efficiency and responsiveness has its roots in the neoliberal reforms of the Reagan-Thatcher period and imports private-sector principles into the public sector. It is called the New Public Management and its basic goal is to introduce market efficiency into the provision of public services. Among its key principles are decentralizing management through the creation of autonomous public agencies, increasing the use of markets and competition through, for example, contracting out services, and placing increased emphasis on the measurement of performance, outputs, and attentiveness to customers (Osborne and Gaebler 1992).

Legitimized largely by the "roll back the state" crusade of Ronald Reagan and Margaret Thatcher in the 1980s, this privatization of the state has affected all democracies to some degree. It is perhaps most evident in the United States where both Democratic (Clinton) and Republican (Reagan, Bush Sr., and Bush Jr.) administrations have argued strongly that small government, limited intervention in the economy, and the free operation of markets are superior to state intervention in addressing social problems. Grover Norquist, a top Republican strategist during the 2000–2008 presidency of George W. Bush, captured this "small government" ethos succinctly when he proclaimed his party's goal to be to cut government "down to the size where we can drown it in the bathtub." The private sector has even come to play a prominent role in the conduct of America's foreign affairs. Prosecuting the war in Iraq, the U.S. government employed approximately 25,000 private security agents (who constitute 16 percent of all coalition military forces) and between 50,000 and 70,000 nonmilitary, privately contracted workers (Bergner 2005).

Whereas it is debated whether the privatization of the state actually improves bureaucratic efficiency and responsiveness, it undoubtedly represents a substantial challenge to traditional ideas of (1) government as the embodiment of the public interest; (2) government officials as "civil servants"; and (3) the state as the sole provider of law and domestic order.

*W**AIT A MINUTE. CONSIDER THIS.** What is your stand on the issue of "rolling back" or privatizing traditional functions of the state, like schools, prisons, and the military? Should state institutions be assessed on a market or efficiency basis? What happens to the public interest when private actors are charged with carrying out state policy? What is lost and what is gained by such an approach?*

Legislatures

The term "legislature" comes from the Latin word for law – *lex, legis*. Thus, the legislature might be taken at first glance to be the lawmaking branch of government, but in fact this was never the intent for this kind of body. Its precursors were feudal assemblies of medieval, precapitalistic Europe that arose from monarchs becoming obliged to convene assemblies of feudal lords from whom they required money and manpower to prosecute their endless wars. These assemblies were convened by kings to consult – to *parler* (the French word for "to speak") – and not to govern, hence another name for legislatures is parliaments. Those consulted in turn wanted protection against despotic royal rule by obliging the king to make concessions to their demands in return for the taxes and manpower he extracted. The first notable outcome of this trade-off of political influence for taxation income occurred when the principle of parliamentary consent to taxation gained constitutional recognition in the Magna Carta in 1215.

This victory for the barons, however, represented the beginning, not the end, of a struggle that was to last centuries and to become one into which more and more social groups were drawn as monarchs sought to expand their tax base beyond the nobility.

Legislatures developed from such incursions into monarchical power across Europe, following different trajectories country by country. In England, the story is one of the steady, if uneven, erosion of the king's power as the "Model Parliament" was formally adopted in 1265 and its membership comprised "commoners" (knights and burgesses) as well as the nobility and clergy. In 1341, the Commons met separately from the nobility and clergy for the first time, creating an Upper Chamber and a Lower Chamber that formally became the House of Lords and House of Commons, respectively, in the middle of the sixteenth century. By the middle of the seventeenth century, parliament had replaced the monarchy as the supreme source of power in England, because Oliver Cromwell's Roundheads staged a revolution, defeated the royalists, deposed and executed the king in 1649, only for the monarchy to be reinstated, a politically diminished institution, in 1660. In France, by contrast, the initial legislative assembly was called the Estates General and its membership included the different classes (or estates) of French subjects: First Estate (clergy), Second Estate (nobility), and Third Estate (commoners). First convened in 1302, it initially enjoyed substantial power; the king could not levy many taxes without its consent. In the second half of the fourteenth century, however, its power declined as the result of the king's success in having most taxes made permanent. The assembly was not even convened between 1484 and 1560. It then enjoyed a renaissance until 1614 only to fall again as France entered a long period of divine-right monarchy. It did not meet again before the French Revolution of 1789, after which it became the National Constituent Assembly in the newly founded republic (Mariongu 1968).

The changed balance of power between monarchy and parliament is evidenced by what is, according to the online *Oxford English Dictionary*, the first reference to "legislature"; it is found in Hale's 1713 *History of Common Law*: "Without the concurrent Consent of all Three Parts of the Legislature, no . . . law . . . can be made." With the three parts being the House of Lords, the House of Commons, and the king, repeated extensions of the suffrage in Britain from the middle of the nineteenth century onward promised to rebalance this triangular relationship to the advantage of the ever-more popularly elected lower house. It did not turn out this way, however. Instead, attention has centered on the "decline of legislatures" in the sense that lawmaking power, and particularly the power to initiate legislation, has largely migrated to political executives in the modern world (Loewenberg 1971).

Concern for the increase in executive power is evident, for example, in characterizations of the U.S. presidency as having become an "imperial presidency" or the British prime ministership an "elective dictatorship." A commonly cited example of the allegedly overweening power of both offices is that both President Bush and Prime Minister Blair falsified intelligence evidence about Saddam Hussein's possession of weapons of mass destruction to justify their largely personal decision to commit American and British troops to the invasion of Iraq in 2003. Indeed, some question just how effective is countervailing power in the contemporary United States. Take the example of the "signing statement." This is a prerogative that presidents have increasingly claimed for themselves and that is of questionable constitutionality insofar as it allows them to specify what part of a law they will execute and enforce. Its basis is the president's claim that he has the constitutional discretion to write a paragraph under any legislation he signs explaining how he will interpret it. Although used infrequently by his predecessors, President George W. Bush invoked this discretion to ignore more than 750 laws passed by Congress, compelling the Constitution Project, a bipartisan, nonprofit organization, to state publicly that it is "deeply concerned about the risk of permanent and unchecked presidential power, and the accompanying failure of Congress to exercise its responsibility as a separate and independent branch of government" (Drew 2006).

Lord Bryce (1921, 368) was among the first to note, and regret, this departure from a legislature-centered model of representative government:

> By the representative system, the executive would . . . be duly guided and controlled; by it the best wisdom of the country would be gathered into deliberative bodies whose debates would enlighten the people, and in which men fit for leadership could show their powers. Whoever now looks back to read the speeches and writings of statesmen and students between 1830 and 1870, comparing them with the complaints and criticisms directed against the legislatures of the twentieth century, will be struck by the contrast, noting how many of the defects now visible in representative government were then unforeseen.

How is the contemporary departure from Bryce's ideal legislature-led government to be explained? A number of factors have played a role. Party discipline has been especially important in bringing about legislative decline insofar as it is a convention whereby legislators are obliged to vote in the way determined by the leadership of their party (alternatively, the political executive when the party is in office) or suffer some kind of punishment – for example, being denied promotion. A second important contributor has been massive growth in the volume and complexity of government business. From the fairly minimal responsibilities of the "night watchman state" (principally maintaining domestic order and keeping the state safe from foreign invasion), governments have expanded their responsibilities to cover areas ranging from the economy, to workplace safety, to the regulation of nuclear power. Its business, in other words, is ever more wide-ranging and technically complex, and neither individual legislators nor the legislature collectively have the expertise or resources that would enable them to write or modify laws across the whole range of government business. Indeed, in some cases, the legislature, recognizing its own limitations, has delegated important responsibilities to the executive branch. In 1921, for example, the U.S. Congress passed the Budget and Accounting Act, which required the president to submit to Congress an annual budget for the entire federal government. This was a huge transfer of power because, in deciding how much money is to be allocated to which goals, the budget defines national priorities for the year to come – and whether a budget privileges defense over welfare spending or vice versa has significant political consequences.

The political bureaucracy is another contributing factor. As already seen, it commands the expertise and resources needed by governments to make laws in ever broader and more specialized areas of human activity. But as the scope of government has grown, the expertise and experience it has accumulated have also enabled it to play a supportive role to the executive in the crafting of legislative proposals before they are introduced into the legislature.

The final major culprit helping account for the decline of legislatures is the growth of organized interests. Interest, or pressure, groups (for example, employer associations, trade associations, the Sierra Club, and the British Medical Association) are alternative channels of political representation to political parties in democracies and they serve useful purposes for both supporters and the government (see Chapter 5). Their goal is to influence public policy in areas of interest to their members and supporters and they are valued by governments both because they perform a legitimate representation function and because they provide advice, data, and cooperation in the formulation of the very policy they seek to influence. Two characteristics of these groups have worked to the disadvantage of legislatures. First, their number has increased as the scope of government activity has widened. One 1979 directory of pressure groups in Britain noted that more than 40 percent of the listed groups had come into existence since 1960. Second, these groups focus their lobbying activities mainly on the executive branch of government and therefore strengthen the executive vis-à-vis the legislature. Governments in turn co-opt many of these groups into the process of policy deliberation to take advantage of their expertise and insight and often even develop policy proposals suggested by them into full-blown legislation. The legislature plays little or no role in this consultative process and finds it difficult to challenge the policy proposals that are its outcome, partly because of executive dominance, partly because it does not have the knowledge or resources to assess the logic or material evidence underlying them, and partly because the proposals have the approval of the affected groups and their supporters.

*W*AIT A MINUTE. **CONSIDER THIS.** Do you find it troubling that legislative power has declined in the modern era? After all, in democratic regimes, the legislature is the one branch of government considered to be the "house of the people." Is democracy therefore jeopardized by the migration of lawmaking power away from the legislature and towards the executive? Would you like to return to Lord Bryce's ideal of the legislature–led government? Is this possible in the modern era?

Despite the origins of the term, modern legislatures do not make laws. Indeed, to the extent the making of laws is seen as their responsibility alone, they never have; the political executive, whether it was in the form of a monarch or now of the leaders of a democratic government, has usually been the pre-eminent partner in the execution of this governmental responsibility. But if the legislatures' active involvement in the lawmaking process has diminished as states have become more complex, does this mean that they do not play a useful role in modern democratic governance? The answer to this question is an emphatic no. Legislatures generally may not be the workshop where legislative proposals are mooted, their content debated and the final proposal crafted, but they still perform a number of valuable functions that enhance the quality of democratic governance. These functions can be organized into three categories, the first focusing on the legislature's contribution to the lawmaking process, the second to its oversight of the executive and the third to its role in linking governors and governed.

Legislatures and Lawmaking

It has already been established that legislatures generally play only a limited role in the making of laws and that the role they have in this regard has diminished in the modern era. They do, however, have a reactive role in the process. Even though they may have the constitutional power to do so, it is rare for legislatures to initiate legislation and rarer still for them to block legislation introduced by the government, or political executive. An extreme example is Britain where 97 percent of the bills proposed by the executive between 1945 and 1987 became law (Rose 1989, 173). Nonetheless, legislatures can shape legislation by offering amendments that bring the bill closer to the preferences of their members. The right of amendment is not always unlimited and governments most often can get around amendments they do not like. It is the case, however, that governments do accept many amendments either because they improve the quality of the legislation by, for example, closing loopholes or because the legislature threatens some sanction if the amendment is not accepted – perhaps the invocation of its constitutional right to delay, if not reject, pending legislative proposals.

Legislatures and Executive Oversight

Oversight of the executive branch of government by the people's elected representatives is at the heart of democratic governance because it is an important means by which the goals of governmental responsiveness and accountability to the people are achieved. Debate on the floor of the house is the most highly visible form of oversight, especially in the era of televised legislative proceedings. Generally, however, the more effective routine oversight mechanism is the parliamentary committee with the power to meet at will, to demand evidential material from the executive branch, to summon witnesses to appear before it, and to issue reports. But such committees are not equally powerful in all democratic legislatures because there is considerable variation in their constitutional mandate, the resources at their disposal, and their will to confront the executive, especially when the majority on the committee is from the party in government. Similar oversight mechanisms are questions and emergency debates. Questions refer to direct queries of members of the political executive and can take either written or verbal form. Again, however, there is variation in the importance of this oversight mechanism. In Britain, the House of Commons asks more than 70,000 questions a year and they are usually answered, whereas members of the French executive often fail to answer them at all. Emergency debates are relatively rare because they normally require some minimum number of parliamentarians to support the call for one, but, when held, they are still an effective means of holding the government to account because they generate publicity and require the government to explain itself to the general public more fully than it might normally do.

Legislatures and Linkage

In most democracies, the legislature, specifically its lower house, is the only directly elected part of the national government. For this reason, it is often the preeminent institution linking governors and governed in a two-way relationship of communication and influence. This relationship lies at the heart of democratic governance (See Chapter 5). An important component of this broader linkage function is for individual members of the legislature to represent their constituents in the legislative process and thereby protect their interests. The common dilemma facing elected representatives is whether to be a *delegate* and simply give voice in the legislature to the explicitly stated wishes and preferences of constituents, or a *trustee*, using one's own judgment to pursue policies deemed to be in the best interests of those same constituents. Faced with the need to be reelected periodically, most legislators judiciously combine both approaches to representing their constituents and constituency, hoping thereby to maximize both their effectiveness in the legislature and their popularity at home. A by-product of linkage and representation has already been discussed in the context of authoritarian regimes, and it is legitimation. Democratic legislatures are forums for debate in which opposing views are aired and reconciled through the peaceful processes of negotiation and compromise. By way of their elected representatives, people are brought into the political system, try to manipulate it to their own advantage, and develop an emotional attachment to it that transcends bouts of discontent that might otherwise lead them to seek to get their way by, for example, resorting to violent or nonviolent protest on the streets.

Courts

In contrast to legislatures, courts are gaining in political influence in democracies, so much so that it is now common to talk about the "judicialization of politics," by which is meant

> the reliance on courts and judicial means for addressing core moral predicaments, public policy questions, and political controversies... Armed with newly acquired judicial review procedures, national high courts worldwide have been frequently asked to resolve a range of issues, varying from the scope of expression and religious liberties, equality rights, privacy, and reproductive freedoms, to public policies pertaining to criminal justice, property, trade and commerce, education, immigration, labor, and environmental protection. (Hirschl 2008b, 94)

To the extent that they interpret the law and in the process create winners and losers, courts have, of course, always been political institutions. Historically speaking, however, the most contentious issue surrounding them has been whether the judicial branch should have the right to determine whether legislation passed by any level of government – federal, state, or local – accords with the letter and spirit of the constitution and to strike it down if it deems it does not. This right was first claimed by the U.S. Supreme Court in 1803 in the case of *Marbury vs. Madison* when Chief Justice John Marshall struck down part of the Judiciary Act (1789) as unconstitutional, observing that "it is emphatically the province and duty of the judicial department to say what the law is." In so doing, he established in the United States the doctrine of judicial review, which, although not specifically mentioned in the constitution, gives ordinary courts the power to nullify both legislative and executive acts that they deem to contravene the constitution. The Supreme Court is the ultimate arbiter in disputes about the constitutionality of legislation and its decisions are not subject to further appeal.

Over the centuries, the Supreme Court has varied in the extent to which it has asserted its power of judicial review and in the conservatism or liberalism of its judgments. Early in Franklin Delano Roosevelt's presidency, for example, the Supreme Court resisted New Deal legislation that expanded the federal government's regulation of the economy. Some argue that it eventually capitulated not out of deference to the popularly elected president, but out of fear of his threat to "pack the court" by increasing its membership from nine to sixteen and appointing six new liberal justices. A mere thirty years or so later, the court became much more liberal under Chief Justice Earl Warren and in the 1954 case of *Brown vs. Board of Education*, it outlawed racial segregation in schools, overturning a previous Supreme Court decision (*Plessy vs. Ferguson* in 1896) that held "separate but equal" facilities for blacks to be constitutional. Judicial review, then, has always been controversial in the United States partly because some argue that the Supreme Court has sometimes overstepped its constitutional role in its activism and partly because the decisions taken by individual Supreme Courts have tended systematically to favor some constituencies over others.

For more than 140 years after *Marbury vs. Madison*, the notion of constitutional review was absent from a Europe where the doctrine of legislative supremacy held uniform sway. According to this doctrine, only elected representatives in the legislature have the right to make laws and the statutes that they do create can be adjudged constitutional or otherwise and changed if necessary only by them. Similarly, legislative supremacy constitutions deny the existence of other constraints on the authority of lawmakers, like the notion of inalienable rights. The rights to which people may be entitled are granted by parliament and enshrined in statute. In neither case, in other words, is there a legitimate oversight role for a higher body. In his 1885 book, *Law of the Constitution*, A. V. Dicey (1835–1922) defined parliamentary sovereignty thus: "Parliament has the right to make or unmake any law whatever . . . and . . . no person or body is recognized by the law of England as having the right to override or set aside the legislation of Parliament."

The comparative study of courts languished in political science as long as the right of constitutional review of legislation was restricted to the United States. Since World War II, however, there has been a "rights revolution" in much of the world insofar as the clear trend has been for democracies, old and new, to adopt entrenched constitutions that limit governmental authority by granting citizens political and social rights, establishing an independent judiciary to protect those rights, and specifying amendment procedures. These are called "higher law" constitutions and their legislative supremacy opponents have all but disappeared in face of the global popularity they have acquired. The constitutional scholar Sweet (2008, 233–34), for example, identifies 106 constitutions that were adopted after 1985 and notes that all of them incorporate a catalog of rights and all but five of them – Iraq (1990), Laos, North Korea, Saudi Arabia, and Vietnam – allow for judicial review. Another source concludes that "as of this writing, 158 out of 191 constitutional systems include some formal provision for constitutional review" (Ginsburg 2008: 81).

Why has this judicialization of politics taken place? There is no simple answer to this question because the reasons for it are many and they interact to form complex explanatory patterns. Nonetheless, four main categories of explanation have been identified and are labeled: (1) functionalist; (2) rights-centered; (3) institutionalist; and (4) court-centered (Hirschl 2008b). The functionalist explanation focuses on the increasing complexity of governance combined with states' ever greater involvement in supranational organizations, like the European Union, that themselves make laws, many of which are binding on member states. Especially in face of parliaments lacking appropriate expertise, binding review by an active and independent judiciary is an efficient means of monitoring today's ever-expanding administrative states. Moreover, as regulatory state agencies have expanded their reach into different areas of social life, it has become widely accepted that citizens' rights require the protection against abuse that only constitutionally mandated judicial review can provide.

The rights-centered explanation might also be described as "judicialization from below." As is reflected in the fact that all modern constitutions contain a catalog of political and social rights, people in the world today are simply more aware of their rights, more protective of them, and more trusting of judicial than political institutions to protect them. Seeing the judiciary as more impartial and responsive, historically underrepresented or disenfranchised groups and/or individuals often seek redress through the courts rather than the political system; witness African-American success in achieving racial equality and equal voting rights through mid-1960s Supreme Court decisions after decades of frustration in Congress.

A third explanation is institutionalist in character. To put it simply, the wave of democratization that spread across the globe in the last quarter of the twentieth century has created conditions conducive to commitment to the rule of law and acceptance of a legal system with judicial review power. This power is essential because democracy, with its separation of powers between the legislative, executive, and judicial branches of government as well as between national and subnational governments, creates conflicts between different levels of government and between governments and citizens that have to be authoritatively resolved.

The final, court-centered explanation holds that the courts and judges themselves are the main driving force behind the expansion of judicial power. Judges are condemned for being too "assertive" and becoming overly involved in moral and political decision making that is rightly the preserve of elected public officials. At the same time, however, it has sometimes been in the interests of government officials to delegate power to the judiciary as a means of avoiding legislative gridlock or having to make hard choices that might cost them electorally or politically. Delegation may even be seen as a defense mechanism for governmental actors, especially in transitional regimes like new democracies, whose hold on power is uncertain or under threat and who want to be treated fairly by successors and/or have the opportunity to return to power in the future. Institutionalizing the rule of law and judicial review under a functioning system of constitutional government is an effective means of securing a democratic political future and one's ability to be part of it.

Separation of Powers: Authoritarian Governance

Political Executives

The preeminence of political executives is especially pronounced in authoritarian regimes precisely because those entrenched in power go to great lengths to maintain their control of both state and society by ensuring that there are few competitors to threaten it. Not only is power valued for itself, but also loss of it can carry great personal risk.

There are various routes to governmental office in authoritarian regimes, some of them being more institutionalized (in the sense of being routinized and largely nonviolent) than others. The principal route in many of them, however, involves violence, or the threat of it. Staging a coup, for example, a military clique overthrows a civilian government or another military government in an unpredictable and utterly ad hoc succession. In theocracies, by contrast, executive succession is more predictable because religious and political leadership are fused. The leading cleric becomes the head of government and runs the country according to religious doctrine. Thus, the Supreme Leader is Iran's highest-ranking political and religious authority and plays a leading role in selecting a Guardian Council that can reject legislation and/or election candidates for being insufficiently Islamic. While not as predictable in terms of who precisely will become king, succession in the hereditary monarchies of the Middle East has also been managed largely without violence. The ruler has generally emerged after discussions and machinations within a ruling family concerned, above all, with providing strong and capable leadership, although there are some weak signs of primogeniture (i.e., the firstborn's right of inheritance) emerging as the hereditary principle.

The pattern of succession profoundly affects the character of authoritarian regimes. If it is relatively institutionalized and peaceful, it can be conducive to political stability and better governance. Not fearful of being the victim of an unpredictable, violent, and possibly deadly seizure of power, rulers can seek to consolidate their political position by striving to neutralize political opposition and at the same time creating better living conditions for citizens, thereby keeping them politically compliant. "The creation of welfare states in the Gulf was not only an obligation under tribal and Islamic norms, but it fulfilled the basic requirements of a more modern legitimacy" (Peterson 2001, 183). By contrast, if the pattern of succession is uninstitutionalized, violent, and unpredictable, it can promote a different brand of political authoritarianism: personal rule. This phenomenon is defined thus:

> A system of relations linking rulers not with the "public" or even with the ruled but with patrons, associates, clients, supporters and rivals who constitute the "system." The system is "structured" not by institutions but by politicians themselves. The fact that it is ultimately dependent upon persons rather than institutions is its essential vulnerability. (Jackso nd Rosberg 1982, 19)

Put differently, authoritarian leaders seek less to build lasting institutions that store the wisdom that comes with experience of governing and more to concentrate power in themselves and their supporters. Ruthlessness, selfishness, and survival become central concerns because the costs of political overthrow can be high, ranging from a prison sentence through exile overseas to, most dramatically, execution. Good governance is a secondary concern and administration of the state becomes a source of jobs for ethnic group, family, or tribal members who are rewarded for personal loyalty rather than for professional competence.

Legislatures

A siege mentality is but one common facet of authoritarian rule. Another is the use of the other institutions of governance – legislatures and courts – to consolidate the executive's hold on power. At first blush, it might be thought that the existence of, say, a legislature signals significantly diminished control from the center in authoritarian regimes. But a compelling reason to question this assumption is the large number of such regimes that in fact have a separate legislature. Arraying the world's states along an implicit authoritarian/democratic continuum, Freedom House places each of them into one of three categories: "Not Free," "Partly Free," and "Free." It turns out that in 2006, fully 45 of the 192 members of the United Nations fall in the "Not Free" category and, according to the Inter-Parliamentary Union, all but 2 of them (Brunei and Myanmar – formerly Burma) had some kind of national parliament. This is not to argue that these parliaments are as powerful as those found in "Free" states or even that all those in the "Not Free" category enjoy similar powers. It is simply to draw attention to the ubiquity of some kind of legislature in authoritarian regimes and to raise the question of why they are there if rulers are intent on stifling opposition in order to hold on to the power that comes with control of government.

There are a number of answers to this question. Among the more common of them is that the existence of a legislature, even one with little or no role or influence in the lawmaking process, may be exploited to enhance the public's sense of political participation and representation, thereby enhancing the legitimacy of the authoritarian regime. The legislature may also provide the government with the kinds of linkages that, in the absence of more formal and institutionalized consultation mechanisms (like elections and a free press), allow it to reach into society to get important feedback on controversial plans and policies on the one hand or to exercise more effective social control on the other. In other words, legislatures exist under authoritarianism because they are instrumental in facilitating manipulation of public perceptions, expectations, and behaviors to the ruling group's advantage. This dynamic is especially apparent when such a government chooses to break with the status quo and move the country in a new direction. A sine qua non of success in such an endeavor is to avoid arousing any overt or latent hostility there may be toward the authoritarian regime and instead mobilize the support of a normally quiescent public behind a set of collective goals it has had no role in defining. The experience of communist China in the last quarter of the twentieth century indicates that legislatures can play an important role in legitimating great change without at the same time inciting demands for political change and democratic reform.

The communist revolution took place in China in 1949 and a totalitarian one-party regime in which opposition was not tolerated at all was put into place immediately. The National People's Congress (NPC) was founded in 1954 and, despite the constitution giving it the responsibility, for example, to provide oversight of the state's budget, it was clearly never meant to play an active role in the lawmaking process. Its members are indirectly elected, they number in the thousands, and they meet in congress for only about two weeks a year. The rest of the time, the NPC's Standing Committee of around 150 members meets regularly and serves as the working legislative assembly. Up until the death of Mao Zedong in 1976, the NPC was effectively a "rubber stamp" assembly that routinely did the bidding of China's communist party. By 1978, Deng Xiaoping had emerged as party leader and was intent on moving China in a new direction by freeing economic activity from suffocating state control but without at the same time undermining the communist party's political hegemony by allowing citizens greater freedoms. To this end, Deng's followers advocated reform of the NPC with three goals in mind: (1) to create political conditions conducive to economic development; (2) to improve government efficiency; and (3) to promote political stability by "check[ing] wayward government leaders and dispers[ing] influence" (O'Brien 1988, 347).

Amid opposition from traditionalists in the communist party, constitutional change was introduced in 1982 and the NPC gradually became less supine and more assertive. Its more active governmental role was evident in, for example, a large increase in delegate motions and, more tellingly, dissenting votes. The political status and influence of the NPC's Standing Committee were also enhanced as it assumed a more prominent role in organizing the legislature as well as in lawmaking. On two occasions, the NPC even neglected to pass legislation submitted to it. But while representing genuine change, the larger political significance of these reforms should not be overstated. They may have helped bring about fundamental economic change, but they did little to undermine the authoritarian character of governance in China. "Reform did not recast the NPC into a liberal democratic legislature; those who had hoped for such a development had forgotten the realities of one-party rule" (O'Brien 1988, 368).

Thus, legislatures in authoritarian states are not constitutionally entrenched and the role they play in lawmaking remains overwhelmingly at the whim of the ruling group. Ironically, however, the limited constraints they place on the arbitrary power of this group may actually strengthen authoritarian control by making the regime more legitimate and efficient. A very similar logic explains the existence in many authoritarian states of courts with some degree of judicial independence.

Courts

The role of law and the courts in authoritarian regimes has been described as "rule *by* law" in contrast to the "rule *of* law" that characterizes democratic government. The essence of the difference is that authoritarian governments pass laws that are binding on their population, but they themselves are not subject to a higher, constitutional law and can still act arbitrarily toward citizens as and when they see fit. But why establish courts at all when their simple existence may raise popular expectations of standardized treatment by public officials that then provide a basis for rightful resistance if the regime fails to live up to its own proclaimed standards? Why do authoritarian regimes bother with judicial institutions?

Experts on judicial forms of governance in such regimes have identified five answers to this question (Ginsburg and Moustafa 2008). First, and as in democracies, an obvious role for courts is the exercise of social control. Criminal law is a particularly salient example of this function; courts chastise those who break the law of the land. There is also a peculiarly authoritarian dimension to social control, however, and it is in evidence when the ruling group uses the courts to stave off challenges to its dominance and authority. In "partly free" Turkey in 2008, for example, the long-dominant secular ruling elite used the courts to try to close down the Islamist AKP (Justice and Development Party) that had won control of the Turkish Grand National Assembly in 2007 national elections. The initiative was supported by six of the eleven justices on the Supreme Court – one vote short of the seven needed to disband a political party.

The second reason for judicial forms of governance under authoritarianism is again shared with democracies, and it is legitimation. People are easier to govern if they perceive their government as legitimate, and courts, like legislatures discussed earlier, can give the impression of being an effective check on arbitrary rule. This function may be especially important in helping authoritarian rulers avoid blame when they fail to deliver on material promises of land reform, economic development, income redistribution, and the like.

The third reason for judicial institutions with some degree of independence is, again as in democracies, better monitoring and control of administrative agents. All governments delegate the implementation of laws to a large, often complex bureaucracy and all have the problem of ensuring that bureaucrats do not undermine the intent of their policies by being corrupt, nepotistic, or arbitrary in their dealings with the public. Without such oversight, governments risk becoming more inefficient and wasteful, thereby weakening their hold on power. Especially when authoritarian regimes ban channels of protest like a free press and independent watchdog groups, courts provide an important venue in which individuals and groups in society can challenge and seek redress for abuse on the part of government functionaries.

The fourth function served by semi-independent judiciaries in authoritarian states is economic in that their existence can serve to encourage internal and external investment by protecting property rights and enforcing contracts. This kind of economic protection is taken for granted in democracies, but courts' independence (to some degree) from authoritarian governments enhances the credibility of commitments that private property will not be seized by the government or some other representative of the state – perhaps when the country falls on economic hard times. Especially in a globalizing world where flows of investment capital are huge and interstate competition for them is fierce (see Chapter 6), the advantage of independent and effective courts is that they encourage exchange between contracting parties by reducing uncertainty and risk.

The fifth function of courts is more patently political and is shared to some degree with democracies. Authoritarian rulers who often find themselves forced to make controversial decisions can delegate the making of at least some of those decisions to courts whose veneer of objectivity and neutrality can help make them more palatable to an aggrieved public. The political fallout from reneging on promises of, say, land reform or price subsidies may well be less if these policies are determined in court to be unacceptable under the law than if they are simply announced by a government that had previously promised to enact them.

The general conclusion to follow from this account of authoritarian governance is that it cannot be identified simply by the legislative, executive, and judicial powers being compounded in a single individual or ruling group. Its structure and dynamics are far more complex. With goals like improving legitimacy and efficiency, this type of regime has commonly introduced separate institutions exercising some semblance of legislative or judicial power under tight control from the center. Nonetheless, the introduction of these institutions has produced significant change. Today, authoritarian governments are more constrained by laws and their citizens freer from political arbitrariness than ever before. In this sense, the reforms that these governments have themselves introduced have changed regime political dynamics by expanding the space for political contention and creating greater potential for activist mobilization against the prevailing political order. Still, to appreciate the nature of these dynamics requires a clear understanding of the continuing power inequalities in authoritarian states. To put it simply, the executive power lords it over the legislative and judicial branches of government that may exist. Equally, however, an understanding of the governance of democratic states requires one to acknowledge the top-heavy role played by the executive branch in them. Idealistic notions that authoritarian and democratic regimes are different because lawmaking power in the latter is distinctive for being distributed more or less equally between the three branches of government must not be overstated.

CONCLUSION

Two major conclusions would seem to follow from this chapter's comparison of the governance characteristics of democratic and authoritarian regimes. The first is that Montesquieu's separation of the lawmaking power into its legislative, executive, and judicial components is a useful way of understanding the dynamics of governance in both of them and of comparing how governments work across them. Two important qualifications are in order, however. First, it is misleading to think of governance in either type of regime in terms of the separation of powers. Rather, discussion should be framed in terms of the sharing of powers by different branches of government to emphasize that no one branch can govern on its own. Even in authoritarian states, the branches need each other and have to cooperate if effective government and political stability are to be maintained. Second, to emphasize their interdependence is not to imply that the branches of government enjoy equal powers. In both types of regime, the executive branch is the leading partner in the triumvirate. This is especially so in authoritarian states despite legislatures and courts now hemming in the executive more than they did in the past.

The second major conclusion is that the extent to which governments are authoritarian or democratic in their behaviors can vary over time so that they can look more or less like each other depending on circumstances. The growth of executive power in democracies, for example, has brought about a concentration of power in one branch of government that might on occasion be akin to that found under authoritarianism. Nor is it obvious that the "judicialization of politics" has counteracted this dilution of democracy in many countries. After all, judges are largely unelected figures who do not face periodic elections where they can be held accountable for their actions. Without such accountability, there is no democracy. Thus, to the extent that the unaccountable judicial branch plays a role in lawmaking, it might be argued that democracy is weakened, not strengthened, despite the constitutional check it can bring to bear on the executive branch. An opposing viewpoint is that judges are often appointed by the elected representatives of the people and, in this way, the membership of courts changes and their decisions evolve to represent the prevailing tide of public opinion; witness how the U.S. Supreme Court at one point condoned racial segregation and some decades later declared it unconstitutional. From this viewpoint, it is countervailing power and not popular election that matters for the quality of democracy.

W*AIT A MINUTE.* **CONSIDER THIS.** How can the growth of power in the modern executive branch be limited? There are two mechanisms for limiting the power of political executives in democratic governance. The first is popular accountability through elections and the second is the constitutional provision for countervailing centers of power in government. From the standpoint of enhancing the quality of democracy in a society, which is more important: elections or countervailing governmental powers? Is it better, for example, to elect judges, or to institutionalize their independence from momentary electoral passions? In what other ways can executive power be constrained?

▉4▉ *Frameworks of Governance*

*T*he previous chapter focused on how executives, legislatures, and courts interact in the making of public policy in both democratic and authoritarian regimes. In this chapter, we continue the theme of describing how governments work by expanding our investigation to cover the broader institutional framework within which governance takes place. Governance frameworks comprise the institutional landscape that surrounds and conditions the routine behaviors and interactions of political executives, legislatures, and courts. This framework is made up of the basic structures that all states must choose for themselves. Their first choice is whether these structures will be designed and coordinated to promote authoritarian or democratic governance. This decision made, more particularistic ones follow. Will there be a legislature, and, if yes, will it have two chambers (bicameralism) or just one (unicameralism)? Will the law making power be concentrated at the center (unitarism) or will it be shared with constituent territorial units (federalism)? How will governments be chosen, and, if by direct election, will plurality, proportional, or mixed electoral systems be used to elect candidates and parties to office?

These are some examples of the choices states have to make in establishing the institutional framework within which day-to-day governance takes place. In the pages that follow, these issues are addressed sequentially. The political costs and benefits associated with these choices will be discussed, first for authoritarian regimes and then for democratic ones. This discussion of governance framework begins, however, with an explication of an important foundational term of discourse: political institution.

◼ POLITICAL INSTITUTIONS

The notion of an institution is ambiguous and can be conceptualized in different ways. From one perspective, an institution is an established organization with a physical presence. Thus, the Smithsonian Institution, located in Washington, DC, is the world's largest museum and research complex, with nineteen separate museums and nine research centers. It might be described as the archetypal cultural icon in the United States and its eminence results partly from just being there, and having been there for a long time. In the same way, political institutions are often associated in the popular mind with bricks and mortar. To mention the British Parliament, for example, conjures up for many pictures of a grandiose building on the banks of the River Thames in London. Similarly, many associate the institution that is the French presidency with the Elysée Palace in Paris. Such bricks-and-mortar buildings are noteworthy for housing the political actors routinely engaged in the law-making process.

But a more important sense in which the term "institution" is commonly used in political science focuses not on the inanimate buildings themselves, but on what goes on inside them. From this vantage point, a political institution is conceptualized as a set of relationships between political actors that is predictable, stable over time, evolves to meet changing political circumstances, and comes to be valued for its own sake – in other words, it acquires legitimacy. When this state of affairs is reached, the relationships are said to have become "institutionalized," or, put differently, a political institution has been put in place. This institution may be of interest in its own right or in its interactions with other institutions. For example, a legislature might be examined to understand how it routinely arrives at its own decisions or how it interacts, equally routinely, with other institutions, like the political executive, to arrive at joint decisions. Thus, the study of governance focuses on the institutions, or patterned interactions and predictable behaviors, involved in the making of public policy.

Any one state will have many political institutions within its borders. In addition to executive, legislative, and judicial branches of government, others include political parties, interest groups, the army, and the police. The act of governing requires these institutions to interact with each other on different issues at different points in time. Moreover, single institutions often play multiple roles in this complex and dynamic pattern of interactions. Take the U.S. presidency as an example. Textbooks often try to convey the complexity of the president's role in American government by describing it in terms of the various "hats" he wears. He is simultaneously "chief of state," "chief executive," "commander-in-chief," "chief diplomat," "chief legislator," "chief of party," "voice of the people," "protector of the peace," "manager of prosperity," and "world leader" (Rossiter 1956).

An important caveat about political institutions, however, is that they need not remain durable, effective, or legitimate. Rather, they acquire and retain these characteristics to the extent they form part of a governance framework that works according to established procedures, rules, norms, and values. In democracies, this framework is laid out largely in an entrenched constitution that is binding on institutional behaviors. In contrast, the frameworks found in authoritarian regimes are generally less organizationally complex, less permanent, and less binding on how political institutions behave. In cases of personalistic rule, for example, political competition might not be tolerated so that to talk of institutions interacting in the making of public policy makes limited sense at best. Moreover, even if an authoritarian governance framework were to promote this kind of interaction to some degree, it would likely be fragile. It has been common, for instance, for military leaders to overthrow civilian governments and replace them with a completely different pattern of rule by military junta. Finally, even where an authoritarian governance framework persists over time, the influence enjoyed by a political competitor to, say, a hereditary ruler will most likely be inconsistent and unpredictable for being subject to his whim. The prevalence and persistence of the Middle Eastern hereditary monarchies are examples here.

The important message is that the governance frameworks in authoritarian regimes vary widely in character over space and time and do not readily lend themselves to general, lasting statements about their origins, structure, or impact on policy outcomes. Democracies, in contrast, have much more in common. At the very least, all of them have a legislature that, being directly and popularly elected, is durable and commands the authority to compete with other institutions, like the political executive, for power and influence. The contrast with authoritarian regimes is stark, many of which do not have a legislature of any kind, let alone an elected one. "During the post–World War II period, the proportion of nondemocratic regimes with legislatures varies from 60 to 88 percent" (Gandhi 2008, xvi). Moreover, those legislatures that are allowed to exist function less to share influence and power with the authoritarian ruler and more to advance his objectives.

Authoritarian governance, then, tends to be relatively idiosyncratic and unpatterned because political institutions are often less developed in them, and, when they do exist, their role in governance is determined more by the needs of those in power and less by the dictates of a democratic ethos enshrining a set of constitutional principles and rules of procedure that transcend the individuals who happen to be in office at any one point in time.

Authoritarian Frameworks of Governance

To provide some insight into the wide variation in the dynamics of authoritarian governance, we look in a little more detail at the role of legislatures in a range of nondemocratic regimes: (1) Myanmar; (2) Kuwait; and (3) Paraguay. Freedom House places Myanmar (which it still calls Burma) firmly in the "Not Free" category, with the lowest possible score of 7 on both its political rights and civil liberties scales. Kuwait is in the "Partly Free" category, with scores of 4 on these same democratic freedom measures. Lastly, Paraguay squeaks into the "Partly Free" category, with scores of 3 on the two measures. The "Free" category begins with a score of 2.5 on the 7-point scales.

Myanmar

A contemporary example of governance without a legislature is to be found in Myanmar's military government. Burma became a parliamentary republic after becoming independent from Britain in 1948. A 1962 military coup then brought a repressive socialist government to power that suspended the constitution and banned political opposition as it introduced the "Burmese way to socialism." This doctrine sought to blend elements of Marxism and Buddhism as a means, first, of transforming Burma's political economy through national self-help and, second, of lending legitimacy to the new order. It included such measures as severe isolationism, the nationalization of industry, repression of minorities, and a police state. Its Buddhist element was intended to make people more selfless. The new regime introduced a constitution and a People's Assembly in 1974, but these actions did little to quell popular discontent. Massive demonstrations in 1987 and 1988 were squashed by a military junta called the State Law and Order Restoration Council (SLORC) and it again suspended the constitution. Legislative elections were held in 1990, but these produced a landslide for the opposition National League for Democracy (NLD).

SLORC denied the legislature the right to assemble and proceeded to crack down ruthlessly on all opposition. In 2008, a new draft constitution passed in what was widely regarded as a fraudulent national referendum. It promised elections and these were held in November 2010, but they were boycotted by the NLD for being heavily rigged. The party was consequently dissolved and this decision was upheld by the Special Appellant Court in January 2011.

Despite the elections and the appointment of a new parliament dominated by military personnel at the end of January 2011, Freedom House continued to give the country its lowest score of 7 on both its political rights and civil liberties scales. Only eight other countries in the world received this same rating.

Kuwait

This sovereign Arab emirate is another story; it has a legislature but keeps it under strict control. A constitutional monarchy, it is governed within a separated-powers framework that was established in 1962 after independence. The country's ruler is a hereditary monarch, the emir, who appoints the prime minister and approves his choice of cabinet members. Its parliament, the National Assembly, consists of both elected and appointed members and is the oldest among the Arab states in the Persian Gulf. Being banned, political parties are not found in a legislature that can nonetheless exercise some degree of influence over the executive, partly because some members of the cabinet come from the parliament and partly because it has the constitutional power to dismiss the prime minister or any member of the cabinet. Ultimately, however, the Kuwaiti emir is the reservoir of power, holding what Linz and Stepan call "reserve domains of power" (1996). In addition to appointing the prime minister and a number of legislators, he has the power to legislate by decree and to veto legislation passed in parliament. As a last resort, he can also dissolve parliament and call new elections, as he did in May 2009 in face of a deadlock between the cabinet and legislature. Alternatively, he may also suspend the parliament at his pleasure, which he did from 1976 to 1981, from 1986 to 1992, and from May to July 1999.

Paraguay

A long history of legislative influence was brought to an end in Paraguay when General Alfredo Stroessner seized power in 1954 and then held on to it for the next three decades. A new constitution followed his removal from office in 1989, and it established a separated-powers political framework, with the directly elected president being both the head of state and head of government and the legislative power being shared by the government and parliament, formally called the National Congress. Congress has substantial powers overall even if its strength vis-à-vis the executive is limited. It cannot appoint the president or ministers, its members cannot serve in government, and it cannot eject the government from office with a vote of no confidence. It can, however, impeach the president, call his ministers to account, and investigate the executive. In addition, and among other things, its members have the democratic stamp of popular election, it cannot be dissolved by the president, it can override presidential vetoes by a majority vote, and it can initiate bills in all policy jurisdictions. Finally, its approval is needed for declarations of war, the ratification of treaties, and judicial appointments. This constitutional dispersal of power notwithstanding, however, the conservative and nationalist Colorado Party won all four presidential elections between 1989 and 2008 and has used its power to cement its dominance and stall the consolidation of democracy (Fish and Kroenig 2009).

The major conclusion to be drawn from these three brief examples is that *differences in political framework* help make for very different patterns of authoritarian governance. At times, a single political institution (e.g., the military in Myanmar) all but monopolizes the lawmaking power and exercises it with little or no legal or constitutional constraint. At other times, in contrast, there is a meaningful constitutional order that prescribes both how political institutions take part in the governance process and the limits of their influence. True, a constitution like the Kuwaiti one might be criticized for placing disproportionate power in the hands of a hereditary ruler, the emir, but it also has the advantage of establishing a governance framework that routinizes and, to some degree, makes predictable how and on what principles the country is governed.

Democratic Frameworks of Governance

The political frameworks of democracies are more uniform, not least because they have a number of characteristics in common, including constitutionalism, separated powers, elected governments, and the promotion, not just tolerance, of political opposition. Nonetheless, it would be misleading to imply that there is a single framework of democratic governance. There are structural differences between democratic regimes that have substantial implications for the way political institutions organize themselves, for how they interact, and for the policy output of governments. We identify four such framework differences and explore some of their more important impacts on the patterns of governance found in democracies. The four differences are: (1) unitarism versus federalism; (2) unicameralism versus bicameralism; (3) presidentialism versus parliamentarism; and (4) electoral systems and government formation.

Our argument is not that these are the only framework differences to be found in democratic regimes. They are, however, the most important ones because they encapsulate the fundamental institutional choices that founders of a new democracy would have to make.

Unitarism versus Federalism

The unitary/federal distinction relates to the territorial governance of states. To speak of the separation of powers evokes first the horizontal power relations between branches of government, be it at the national or subnational level. To speak of territorial governance, in contrast, refers to the vertical power relations between levels of government within states. All democratic states have two or more levels of territorial governance; a common typology distinguishes between national, regional, and local governments. Whatever their number, however, their actions have to be coordinated to ensure efficient and effective governance across the territory of the state. The unitary/federal distinction speaks to the manner of this coordination, in particular to the distribution of authority between, and relative powers of, the national (otherwise called federal or central) and subnational (otherwise called state, provincial, or regional) governments. A useful way to understand these contrasting philosophies of territorial governance is to provide a background to the enumeration of their key characteristics by placing their emergence in historical context.

The observation has already been made that the modern state emerged during the period of monarchical rule in Western Europe, and the form that each state takes is the product of a specific pattern of coercion and compromise during the state-building period. Kings basically found themselves anxious to exert their control over increasing swathes of territory, partly to subjugate political rivals and partly to enhance their power and national security vis-à-vis other European expansionist powers. Central to the achievement of these goals were the needs (1) to increase their fiscal resources, mainly tax revenues, and (2) to widen their military recruitment pool so as to be able to prosecute their incessant wars and to maintain internal order. Louis XIV of France, for example, fought four wars between 1667 and 1714 to increase the territory of France at the expense of the German states and Spain. It was also Louis XIV who enlarged and centralized the royal bureaucracy, turning it into a highly efficient tax-collecting machine. Other rulers may have been less successful than the kings of France in building a highly centralized state, but most adopted basically the same approach to state-building. Take Count-Duke Olivares of Spain (1587–1645), who, trying to integrate a collection of principalities into a more centralized state, reformed the tax system and required all territories to contribute to the national defense. In the end, however, he failed to reproduce the absolutist state of France because of military defeat abroad and internal opposition at home. In Britain and the Netherlands, by contrast, centralized states emerged, but power in them did not rest in the hands of an absolutist monarch. Indeed, Charles I of England was put on trial, convicted, and executed in 1649. The House of Commons then eliminated the monarchy and established a republic under the rule of the army's commander-in-chief, Oliver Cromwell. The monarchy was restored after his death in 1658, but as a much-reduced political force (Levack et al. 2007).

One outcome of a pattern of state-building in which a core acquired peripheral territories (usually forcibly but also through purchase, treaties, intermarriage, and the like) was suspicion of the loyalty of newly acquired subjects. They were, therefore, to be governed from the center and kept under strict control and supervision by the army and the monarch's administrative representatives in the localities. To take France as an example again, in the early state-building years, Louis XIII and his chief minister, Cardinal Richelieu, suppressed rebellions led by nobles, limited the independence of regional supreme courts or parliaments, and established a system of professional bureaucrats called intendants both to supervise local administration and to ensure the cooperation of city councils, judges, and parish priests in enforcing the royal will. Today, the unitary state is the predominant form of territorial governance in Western Europe. Thirteen of the region's current seventeen states are unitary in structure, the exceptions being Austria, Belgium, Germany, and Switzerland, with Belgium having ceased to be a unitary state only in the early 1990s. Moreover, the same picture prevails in the many modern states that have been created by different means. Take Africa as an example. Colonial powers generally drew the boundaries of states there to suit their own administrative and political convenience, paying little or no attention to their ethnic and tribal make-up and to the compatibility of their populations. Internecine strife, even civil war, inevitably followed and unitarism emerged as the preferred form of territorial governance in the post-colonial era. Thus, of the fifty-four countries in Africa (excluding Western Sahara) in 2010, only three are federal in state structure: Ethiopia, Nigeria, and South Africa.

This historical sketch indicates that the choice of a unitary territorial governance structure is rooted in the fear that popular disloyalty will threaten the integrity of the new state unless its political expression is quashed and national unity imposed from the center. This impression is only reinforced if we look at political unitarism in action. Its key characteristic is that the national government has the constitutional right to monopolize the lawmaking power. Subnational governments may exist at the regional and local levels, and some of them may even be popularly elected. Nonetheless, they exist less to compete with, and more to act as the administrative agents of, the national government. Indeed, the measure of the ascendancy of unitary governments is that they generally have the constitutional power unilaterally to refashion or even eliminate subnational governments whose policies and/or performance displease them. Nor is this an empty threat. In 1985, the British Conservative prime minister, Margaret Thatcher, eliminated the popularly elected Greater London Council (GLC) simply by passing an Act of Parliament in a House of Commons controlled by her own party. She took this drastic action after losing patience with the allegedly socialist (high taxation, high spending) policies of the Labour-led GLC. It used Conservative government subsidies, for example, to go against national policy and reduce fares on London's public transport system. The Prime Minister also wearied of its constant posturing designed to irritate her Conservative government. For instance, the GLC endorsed the erection of a statue of Nelson Mandela, a man who had not yet become President of South Africa and whom Mrs. Thatcher publicly condemned at the time as a terrorist.

In practice, however, the hierarchical nature of political unitarism should not be overstated. As is amply demonstrated by the GLC and Mrs. Thatcher, subnational governments have the ability to frustrate national governments as they seek to bend national policies to their local or regional needs, especially when the two levels of government are under the control of different political parties. Another consideration is that informal channels of influence may exist to give localities and regions a voice in the decision-making centers of national government, as well as vice versa. In Belgium and France, for example, many members of the national legislative assemblies hold a "dual mandate," which means that they also hold elected office in local and/or regional government – perhaps as mayor of a town, or local councilor. Decentralization is another way subnational governments have been empowered vis-à-vis the center to some degree. This is a process whereby policy execution is delegated to such subnational bodies as local authorities. They may, for example, be allocated a block grant for public libraries but be given the authority to spend it as, in their view, local circumstances dictate. Finally, a number of unitary states, including Belgium, Britain, Italy, Spain, and, perhaps most surprising of all, the archetypal "one and indivisible" France have devolved power to the regions by creating popularly elected regional assemblies with decision-making powers, and sometimes even with the power to make laws in certain areas. Take the case of the Scottish Parliament created in 1999. It passes primary legislation in many domestic areas, including education, justice, agriculture, and health. It also has some power over taxation levels. In Spain, the Catalans of Catalonia were even recognized as a "distinct nationality" in 2006.

Especially in the twenty-first century, then, it would be misleading to equate political unitarism with the total concentration of the lawmaking power at the center. Many unitary states have moved in the direction of a meaningful sharing of this power between levels of government. Their motives vary. In some cases, the changes might have been introduced in the name of efficient governance or enhanced democracy (bringing government closer to the people). In others, for example, India, Spain and the United Kingdom, the rationale included defusing secessionist pressures from territorially concentrated ethnic groups. Ultimately, however, they are no less unitary for having made these concessions given that their central governments have retained, in theory at least, the power to reshape or dissolve subnational governments at will. In the words of Enoch Powell, a Conservative and strong supporter of the union of England, Scotland, Wales, and Northern Ireland: "Power devolved is power retained."

W*AIT A MINUTE.* **CONSIDER THIS.** Do you agree with this sentiment? Does devolution actually enhance the overall unity of the state? If you were a decision-maker, would you support the devolution of power to an ethnic or regionally concentrated group as a means to undermine secessionist sentiments? Or would you see such devolution as the first step on the "slippery slope" to the breakup of multinational states? The multinational and federal states of Yugoslavia, Czechoslovakia, and the USSR broke up when communism collapsed. Does a similar fate await multinational Western states like Belgium, Britain, Canada, and Spain?

Federalism, the major worldwide alternative to unitary territorial governance, entails the notion of a compact, covenant, or treaty and has its political origins in the successful American struggle for independence from Britain in the late eighteenth century. The revolutionaries were spread over thirteen colonies, each of which had enjoyed a large degree of political autonomy and self-government during the colonial period. The difficulty the colonies had in subordinating their deeply ingrained habits of autonomy to the pursuit of common goals became evident immediately after the signing of the Declaration of Independence on July 4, 1776. Defining the relative powers of the thirteen states and the Continental Congress, the "Articles of Confederation" became the first constitutional agreement for the newly independent United States of America. Adopted by Congress in November 1777, they created a nation that was "a league of friendship and a perpetual union," but its governmental system proved to be flawed because state governments retained most of the lawmaking power, granting the central government little jurisdiction over states or individuals. Thus, Congress could not raise money by collecting taxes, had no control over foreign commerce, and could pass laws but could not force the states to comply with them. According to George Washington, governance under confederalism was "little more than the shadow without the substance," and support for a stronger national government grew as his opinion became more widely shared. In 1787, the Articles were replaced when the Federal Constitutional Convention drafted a new constitution – the one that prevails, if occasionally amended, to this day.

If confederalism is the opposite of unitarism in that it implies a system of territorial governance where the preponderance of power lies with the subnational units at the expense of the national government, federalism represents a compromise between these two extremes and is best understood in terms of partnership rather than hierarchy. This is because the formation of federal states is the culmination of a process of more or less voluntary "coming together" rather than the often forcible annexation of peripheries on the part of an expanding core group. In this case, there may not even be a core with the military capacity and/or political desire to impose itself on other groups. Federalism is instead a merger based more in voluntary union.

> A federal bargain is struck . . . when two conditions are met. First, there
> exists a desire on the part of those offering the bargain to expand territory
> by combining constituent governments into a new political entity in order

to secure a public good such as security or a common market. Second, for those accepting the bargain, there must be some willingness to sacrifice political control in exchange for access to the public good provided by the new federal government. (Ziblatt 2004, 74)

Thus, federal states tend to be of two types. One, they are geographically large and naturally diverse so that uniform governance from the center is inappropriate because of its potential disregard for regional differences. Thomas Jefferson said of the United States, for example: "Our country is too large to have all its affairs directed by a single government." Two, they emerge to accommodate potential centrifugal strains that might arise from multiethnic or multinational populations being concentrated in different geographical regions of the state. Belgium, Canada, and Switzerland are instances of federalism as a conflict management mechanism for states with centrifugal political strains. But what is it about federalism that makes it seem appropriate to such political circumstances?

Bednar (2009) has identified three characteristics a state must possess to be called federal; they combine to guarantee the regional autonomy and self-governance that are at the heart of the federal compact. They are:

1. *Geopolitical division:* The territory of the state must be divided into a number of regions each of which has its own government that is constitutionally entrenched and that cannot be unilaterally reshaped or dissolved by the national government.
2. *Independence:* The national and subnational governments must have independent bases of authority. These usually come from their direct election by different constituencies, but may have other sources in authoritarian federations.
3. *Direct governance:* The sharing of the lawmaking power between national and subnational governments is constitutionally mandated, with each governing its citizens directly so that each citizen is governed by two authorities. In addition, each level of government must have the constitutional authority to act independently of the other in at least one policy realm.

Needing to possess all three of these structural characteristics, federal states are relatively rare in the modern world. Some states possess one or two of them; devolution, for example, has meant that Italy, Spain, and the United Kingdom satisfy at least partially the independence and direct governance criteria. They fall down, however, on the geopolitical criterion of constitutional protection against unilateral abolition by the national government. Thus, no more than twenty-four countries existing between 1990 and 2000 could be classified as federal, and three of them, Czechoslovakia, the Union of Soviet Socialist Republics (USSR), and Yugoslavia, no longer exist. With about 90 percent of the world's countries being unitary in state structure, the current federal ones are: Argentina, Australia, Austria, Belgium, Bosnia & Herzegovina, Brazil, Canada, Ethiopia, Germany, Malaysia, Mexico, Micronesia, Nigeria, Pakistan, Russia, South Africa, Switzerland, the United Arab Emirates, the United States of America, and Venezuela (Bednar, 2009, 23–24).

Their common characteristics notwithstanding, not all federations have the same pattern of relations and balance of power between the national and subnational governments. One commonly drawn distinction is between *dual federalism* and *cooperative federalism*. The former is a system where the two levels of government operate largely independently of each other, with each tier enjoying autonomy within its own sphere of authority. Examples are held to be Australia and the United States. Cooperative federations are Germany and Switzerland and in them the tiers of government share powers and so are required to cooperate closely in furthering the interests of the whole community. Another common distinction is between *symmetric* and *asymmetric federalism*. The former refers to a situation in which the territorial units enjoy equal powers relative to the national government. The United States is an example; it grants each of its states equal representation in the Senate regardless of sometimes huge differences in their population sizes. A federation is asymmetric when one or more territorial units enjoy greater powers than others relative to the national government. In Canada, for example, the French-speaking province of Quebec has been granted special powers to fend off English-speaking "pollution" of its French-Canadian culture. The nine English-speaking provinces do not enjoy similar powers. In the end, however, while such differences may throw light on distinctive patterns of territorial governance under federalism, they pale beside the basic observation that federalism, unlike unitarism, is not about hierarchy. Instead, its defining features are cooperation, intergovernmental relations, and interdependence in the exercise of the lawmaking power.

*W**AIT A MINUTE.* **CONSIDER THIS.** Which of the two – federalism or unitarism – makes for better governance? Does one appear to promote freedom more than the other? Should the central government be able to override local interests, or should the latter always trump the former? If given a choice, would you prefer to live in a unitary or federal state?

We next consider another dimension of the governance framework of democratic states: the cameral structure of parliaments.

Unicameralism versus Bicameralism

The unitary/federal distinction points to a real difference in the political autonomy and influence of subnational governments, with those in federal states benefiting from their own constitutionally protected existence and powers. But how is this difference in the pattern of territorial governance reflected in the way that government is organized at the center? The answer to this question is complex, but two major institutional differences stand out. We have already discussed the judicial branch of government. Suffice it at this point to reiterate that an important function of the judiciary in federal states is to adjudicate jurisdictional disputes between levels (national versus subnational) as well as branches (executive versus legislature) of government. Thus, federal states will generally have some kind of judicial body with some power of constitutional review. Unitary states, in contrast, do not usually allocate this power to their judiciaries because for them, the lawmaking power is properly the preserve of the elected national government; it is rightly the judge and jury of its own (in)actions (the doctrine of parliamentary supremacy) and answers ultimately to the electorate for them. The second institutional difference pertaining to the unitary/federal distinction concerns the cameral structure of the national parliament – specifically, how many houses comprise it, one or two? More formally, the distinction at issue is between unicameralism and bicameralism, with the former meaning that the legislature has only one house and the latter that it has two, an upper and a lower one.

Considerable overlap between the pattern of territorial governance and the cameral structure of the national legislature might be expected. Such is indeed the case with federations. Of the twenty currently existing federations (see the list earlier in the chapter), seventeen are bicameral in parliamentary structure, boasting an upper house, or second chamber, that goes by various names, the most common of which, and the one used herein, is the senate. Others include *Bundesrat* in Austria and Germany, *Rayja Sabha* in India, *Soviet Federatsii* in Russia, and *House of Lords* in the United Kingdom. The unicameral exceptions among federations are Micronesia, the United Arab Emirates (UAE), and Venezuela, and their exceptionalism is easily explained. Micronesia is a small country whose directly elected congress has a total of only fourteen members, including one member from each of its four constituent states. The UAE is not an electoral democracy, and the lawmaking power rests entirely with the dynastic rulers of the seven constituent emirates. Together, they form the Federal Supreme Council, which is the highest executive and legislative body in the country, so a second house is not deemed necessary to the governance process. Finally, Venezuela became unicameral in 1999 as part of Hugo Chavez's new constitution designed to strengthen the presidency. With voter approval of this constitution in a referendum, the bicameral Congress and Supreme Court of Justice were dismissed and a single house introduced. In contrast, there is not an equally close correspondence between unitarism and unicameralism. The Inter-Parliamentary Union Web site identifies 162 unitary states, of which 108, or 66.7 percent, are unicameral.

It is easy to understand why federal states generally have a bicameral legislature; it allows for territorially-based political representation. The regions enjoy a political identity and a constitutional legitimacy that mandate that their voice be heard in the national government. Equally, the equation between unitary states and unicameralism seems to follow. Unitary states came into being hoarding political power at the center and denying the periphery the right to voice territorially-based political opposition to the state. Thus, having one house has been justified for increasing the efficiency of government, for integrating the periphery into a national political process, and for maintaining political control over those same peripheral regions. What is less easily intuitively understood, however, is why more than one in three unitary states has opted for a bicameral legislature. To be sure, some unitary states (Costa Rica, Denmark, New Zealand, and Sweden) have put this apparent anomaly to rights by switching from bicameralism to unicameralism, but they are the exception rather than the rule. The attraction of bicameralism for so many unitary states is best explained by looking at bicameralism's origins.

Origins of Bicameralism

The intellectual underpinnings of bicameralism can be traced back to two ideas that have influenced thinking about government and governance since at least Ancient Greece and Rome. These ideas are: (1) the power of government should not be concentrated in a single individual or institution, or even a single class of people; rather, the authority and legitimacy of government is greater to the extent that its decisions are the product of a mixture of sources and interests; and (2) there is a need for wisdom in government so that there should be input from a variety of sources, but especially from the wise, the experienced, the elderly, and the distinguished. The famous Greek philosopher, Aristotle, identified three major forms of government: monarchy, aristocracy, and democracy – the rule of the one, the few, and the many. He argued that good government required all three to be blended together in a mixed or balanced form. In this way, society would be bound together and more stable government would follow. In ancient Greece and Rome, councils of elders that generally represented wealthy and powerful classes would sit alongside more broadly based assemblies designed to represent the citizens. Thus, the logic that would eventually produce the bicameral parliament reflects "the communal spirit of the medieval world" (Marongiu 1968, 54).

This so-called classical theory of mixed government may have been the yardstick against which some measured good government, but it was not directly responsible for the emergence of parliaments across Europe in medieval times. Rather, this process was heavily dependent on the needs of monarchs on the one hand and contingent circumstance on the other. Parliaments arose for the practical reason that the monarch needed a forum for consultation with those whose relative status or power meant that they could not be ignored and whose wealth helped replenish ever-thirsty royal coffers. Their division into two houses crystallized gradually in the thirteenth and fourteenth centuries, and England's historical experience was influential throughout Europe. Over time, the ever-present need for money and soldiers obliged English kings to expand the Great Council beyond the nobles and bishops who constituted its original membership. Representatives of the shires and the land were also gradually incorporated and they too gained influence from advising the king and setting taxation. The House of Lords emerged in the fourteenth century when the nobility and clergy, as opposed to the townspeople and the peasants, composing distinct classes, or "estates," began to meet separately so that there eventually emerged an "upper" chamber comprising the nobility and bishops and a "lower" chamber representing the people, or "commons." A similar evolution took place across a medieval Europe where society was commonly seen as comprising distinctive estates, most commonly the clergy, nobility, and others. The French parliament, for example, initially had three chambers representing each of these estates. Fifteenth-century Sweden actually recognized four estates (nobility, clergy, business, and peasants) and each met in its own chamber.

Given these beginnings, what do modern senates look like? We address this question now and then turn to the theory of bicameralism (Patterson and Mughan 1999).

Parliaments' Upper Houses

The Inter-Parliamentary Union identifies 193 legislatures in the world today; of them, 114, or 59.6 percent, are unicameral and 78, or 40.4 percent, are bicameral. Unicameral parliaments are found largely in small states, whereas their bicameral counterparts tend to be located in larger countries. There are exceptions, of course. China, the world's most populous country, has a very large unicameral body, whereas tiny Belize (with a population of less than 400,000 people) has two legislative houses. Bicameral parliaments are also to be found in all parts of the world – the Americas, Western Europe, Eastern Europe, Asia, the Middle East, South Asia, and the Western Pacific. Their memberships also vary tremendously in size. At one end of the scale used to be the British House of Lords. Prior to the expulsion of most of its hereditary members in 1999, its membership numbered around 1,300 and consisted largely of hereditary peers and peers appointed for life. At the other end of the scale is, once again, the senate of Belize, with eight members. Discounting the House of Lords, the average senate consists of eighty-three members. The tenure of senators is just as variable. In the United Kingdom and Canada, members of the upper chamber can serve for life. Elsewhere, senators serve for a fixed term, which varies from three years in Burkina Faso and Malaysia to nine years in France. In some cases, the terms of members are stratified so that only a third or half of the senate membership is chosen in any one election. Finally, there is the question of how people become senators, and the answer is in many different ways. Indeed, there is often more than one method of selection in the same institution. Direct or indirect election is the most common of them, with all members being directly elected in only nineteen of the sixty-one upper chambers in the world today. In Italy and Spain, most senators are directly elected, but some are indirectly elected or appointed. In yet another seventeen upper chambers, all of the senators are appointed by the government, the head of state, or the king. Members of the German Bundesrat are appointed by the state governments in numbers allocated to them roughly in proportion to the state's population size.

By way of summary, members of senates are appointed on the basis of varying criteria and premises, and they take on different responsibilities and constitutional obligations. Indeed, these bodies are, outwardly at least, unique aggregations, each with its own history, its special traditions and customs, its time-honored norms and practices, its constitutional status, and its impact on the laws of the land. Yet, beneath this variety, they share an underlying justification, purpose, and rationale. This brings us to the question of what senates do, or the theory of bicameralism.

Theory of Bicameralism

The purposes of senates is to allow for differentiation in political representation and to provide the redundancy in policy making that may prevent error, delay action until alternatives have been vetted satisfactorily, or postpone decisions until the disputants achieve consensus. Accordingly, the theory of bicameralism underscores both *representation* and *redundancy*.

A powerful justification for two-chamber parliaments lies in demands for *representation*. According to the theory, one chamber, the lower one, is composed of popularly elected members representing the citizens directly. The other chamber, with a different basis of representation, may give voice to the interests of social classes, economic interests, or territorial diversity. The most common basis on which senates have been constitutionally founded is territorial representation. This explains the close relationship between federal systems and bicameralism in which a senate serves as a federal house whose members are selected to represent subnational territorial entities, like states or provinces. The paradigmatic federal house is the U.S. Senate, whose 100 members are distributed territorially on the basis of 2 senators for each of the 50 states. Territorial considerations can be reflected in the parliamentary structures of unitary states as well. In France with its unitary constitution, for example, senators are chosen so as to represent the country's departments and overseas territories as well as French citizens living outside France. Spain is also unitary and its senate is based on territorial representation, with each province having four senators. There are senators from islands and other territories as well. In the same way, Chilean senators are elected from the country's thirteen regions, six of which return four senators and seven of which return two.

Territory is not the only possible basis for senatorial representation. As noted, upper chambers emerged as class-based institutions and they have often been associated with the protection of the interests of the privileged, although this role has diminished as democracy has progressed. The British House of Lords, for example, was often accused of being an undemocratic institution that served to entrench aristocratic position and privilege in the governance of Britain. Similarly, at the time of the founding of the American republic, many advocated a senate that would especially represent the gentry, the rich. Functional representation can also serve as the basis of senate membership. Most members of the present Senead of Ireland, for example, are chosen in vocational, or functional, clusters – in culture and education, agriculture, labor, industry and commerce, public administration, and social services.

A second line of theorizing about bicameralism concerns the value of *redundancy*, meaning that the upper chamber "provides for a second opinion" (Wheare 1967, 140). Occasionally, this opinion on proposed legislation is equal in importance to that of the lower house. For example, the American and Italian upper houses have the same powers as their lower houses, and laws must be approved by both as they provide a checking and balancing of one another in the two countries. In most parliaments, by contrast, the upper house is subordinate to the lower. Like the British House of Lords, upper houses are commonly empowered only to revise, reconsider, or delay, and individual constitutions specify the circumstances under which the upper house can be overridden by the lower house. The strength of bicameralism thus lies in the capacity of the senate to check the actions of the putatively more popular lower house. In the mid-nineteenth-century words of John Stuart Mill (1861, 249): "(A) majority in a single assembly, when it has assumed a permanent character... easily becomes despotic and overweening, if released from the necessity of considering whether its acts will be concurred in by another constituted authority."

In addition to checking the power of lower houses, senates are also held to contribute to legislative performance and good governance through reviewing and revising proposed legislation. Thus, for Lord Bryce, a British diplomat and member of the House of Lords, "the chief advantage of dividing a legislature into two branches is that the one may check the haste and correct the mistakes of the other" (Bryce 1893, 183). The senate may, for example, ferret out and correct errors in laws proposed by the popular house, permit second thoughts about provisions of law, and check the influence of interest groups. They may also delay or reconsider legislative proposals by the lower house to allow the expression of public sentiments on policy issues of the day or to dampen or mitigate popular passions or hasty judgments. "Great advantages" said Oliver Wentworth to the U.S. Constitutional Convention, "will result in having a second branch endowed with the qualifications ... [of] weight and wisdom [which] may check the inconsiderate and hasty proceedings of the first branch" (quoted in Wood 1969, 556).

For the lawmaking process to reach closure in a system of cameral redundancy, processes have to be invented by means of which legislative differences between the two houses may be resolved. Generally speaking, parliaments have developed two core procedures for intercameral resolution: conference committees and a "shuttle" system. Some senates are primarily involved in one process, some utilize the other, and some senates practice both. For the conference committee procedure, each house chooses some of its members to serve on a joint committee, the conference committee, to iron out differences. When the shuttle system (in some places called the "navette" system) operates in countries like France, bills simply pass from lower to upper house until both have adopted the same version of the bill (Tsebelis and Money 1997).

But despite their performance of these representation and redundancy functions, senates remain "essentially contested" institutions in the sense that their very existence is inherently a matter of dispute. Most countries are unicameral and choose not to have an upper house, others have them but then do away with them, and still others keep them but are engaged in an apparently incessant debate about their reform. None of this is true, of course, of the United States where a governing philosophy of minoritarian democracy legitimizes opposition to the directly elected House of Representatives, even if it comes from political actors who are not themselves directly elected, for example, the president, Supreme Court justices, or senators before they became directly elected in 1913. The overriding democratic ethos in America is to protect the interests of political minorities against potential majority tyranny. By contrast, parliamentary systems of government tend to be based on a more majoritarian philosophy of democracy. Their principal goal is to allow the will of the majority, as expressed in periodic elections, to be put into practice for as long as the government legally holds office and retains majority support in the directly elected assembly. This view is strongly held by advocates of unicameralism, who criticize senates on both democratic and practical grounds. The former include the charge that to the extent they are not directly elected, senates are undemocratic institutions because not only do they breach the fundamental majority rule principle, but also are not popularly accountable for their actions. They are often also held to be unrepresentative and elitist when senators, as with hereditary peers in the British House of Lords, owe their membership to accident of birth, or, as in the Canadian Senate, to patronage appointment. The final subversion of the democratic spirit is said to occur when, as in Australia and the United States, equal representation is provided to territories of sometimes dramatically unequal population sizes.

A second line of attack on bicameralism is on purely operational grounds. Senates are said to obstruct and frustrate the popular will more often than they contribute to constructive, salutary delay, and they may particularly do so when the two houses are in the hands of different political party majorities. They are also accused of introducing inefficiencies and unnecessary duplication in the processing of important legislation, and of sometimes failing to produce an adequately critical review of legislative proposals. Thus, it may come as no surprise that a former Australian prime minister, Paul Keating, described his country's senators as the "unrepresentative swill" of Australian politics or that a Canadian counterpart, Robert Mulroney, dismissed the members of his country's upper house as "has-beens and never-weres."

Presidential versus Parliamentary Government

This distinction refers to the form that relations take between the executive and legislative branches of government and, as such, involves the horizontal dimension of the separation of powers in democratic governments. How, in other words, is the lawmaking power distributed between the political executive and the legislature? The answer to this question is that three broad models of executive-legislative relations can be found in the world's democracies. They are: (1) the presidential model; (2) the parliamentary model; and (3) the semi-presidential model. Another way of conceptualizing these models is to array them on a separated-fused powers continuum, with the presidential model at its separated powers end and the parliamentary model at the other. In tracing the philosophical basis and institutional characteristics of these two models, it is customary to take the United States as the exemplar of the presidential model and the United Kingdom – often called the Mother of Parliaments – as that of the parliamentary model. We will next elucidate the philosophical basis and major institutional characteristics of each of these models and explain how, together, they inspired the semi-presidential model created initially to suit the singular political needs of the French Fifth Republic in the late 1950s and early 1960s.

Before proceeding, however, it is important to emphasize that the relationship between the executive and legislature powers is always dynamic rather than static. The last chapter, for example, considered the "decline of legislatures" thesis, which holds that the increasingly complex demands of democratic governance have redistributed the lawmaking power toward executives at the expense of legislatures. In the shorter term as well, the relationship can fluctuate with personality and circumstance. U.S. presidents, for example, are usually better able to impose themselves on Congress when they enjoy high public standing and/or their party holds a majority in one or both of its houses. With this proviso in mind, we look at presidential government first.

Presidential Government

To reiterate, the philosophical basis of American government is *minoritarian democracy*. Separating the executive and legislative powers, along with federalism and bicameralism, was seen by the Founding Fathers as essential to preventing the potential majority domination and repression of political minorities. The first defining feature of presidential government, therefore, is the *separate popular election of the executive and legislature so as to endow each of them with an independent base of authority and legitimacy*. Initially at least, only the House of Representatives was directly elected; the Senate became so in 1913 with the passage of the Seventeenth Amendment to the constitution. The president remains indirectly elected to this day. He was to be insulated against pressure from the distrusted masses by being chosen by an Electoral College consisting of appointees from each state equal in number to that state's two senators plus its number of lower-house members. The indirect election of the president in this way became very controversial in the 2000 race, when the Democratic Party's Al Gore won the popular vote, while his Republican rival, George W. Bush, won the Electoral College vote. The U.S. Supreme Court allowed Bush's "victory" to stand. This was the fourth time in U.S. history that the college rather than the people was decisive in the choice of president, and the episode resurrected widespread debate over whether the U.S. president can really be said to be democratically elected even when, as is the norm, the Electoral College and popular mandates coincide.

Separate election assures the mutual independence of the two branches of government. Elections take place at fixed times and at fixed intervals. The president cannot dismiss the legislature and call new elections, whereas the legislature can dismiss the president only if it chooses to impeach him "for, and on Conviction of, Treason, Bribery, or other high crimes and Misdemeanors." Andrew Johnson and Bill Clinton are the only presidents to have been impeached, but both were acquitted at trial. Richard Nixon resigned when it looked certain that he would be impeached. Reinforcing this mutual independence is a *separation of personnel*. Individuals cannot hold positions in the executive and legislative branches simultaneously. This is of particular consequence for the president's constitutional responsibility to oversee the federal bureaucracy. Unable to recruit serving members of Congress to help him in this task, he usually looks outside the political process to find the supporters who will lead the various departments of state – Agriculture, Defense, Housing and Urban Development, State, Treasury, and so on – and who will use their leadership position to advance his political agenda. Occasionally, however, members of Congress resign their elected office to assume this role. Hillary Clinton, for example, resigned her Senate seat to become President Barack Obama's Secretary of State in 2009. Collectively, the leaders of the major government departments are called the Cabinet and, being appointed by the president, its members serve at his pleasure and, like the president himself, are normally beyond the reach of Congress.

Paradoxically, the second defining characteristic of presidential government is *mutual dependence*. That is, despite being elected separately and usually being beyond each other's censure, the executive and legislature need each other to govern. Each does not enjoy autonomy within its own constitutionally defined sphere of policy responsibility. Rather, they share powers across policy areas and must coordinate their actions if laws are to be passed. Among the more salient, and consequential, examples of shared power are:

1. Both branches are required to sign legislative proposals before they can pass into law.
2. The president can veto legislative proposals arising in Congress, but Congress can override this veto with a two-thirds majority in both houses.
3. The president may generally have the upper hand in initiating legislative proposals, but it is Congress that controls the purse strings and allocates monies for the execution of legislation.
4. The president is commander-in-chief of the armed forces, but it is Congress that has the power to declare war.

5. The president appoints Supreme Court justices, cabinet secretaries, diplomats, and other government officials, but only with "the advice and consent" of the Senate.

In this sense, "the separation of institutions sharing powers" is a more accurate description of the essence of governance in the United States than the more conventional "separation of powers" (Neustadt 1960).

In and of themselves, however, separate institutions and shared powers need not separately or in combination guarantee minority protection against majority domination. After all, what is to stop a party that occupies the White House and enjoys a majority in both houses of Congress from imposing its will on those out of power? For the Founding Father James Madison, the solution to this problem lay "in giving to those who administer each department the necessary constitutional means and personal motives to resist encroachment of the others . . . Ambition must be made to counteract ambition" (Madison 1893, Federalist 51). Thus, the constitution was designed to place the elected members of the executive and legislative branches perpetually at odds with each other for reasons of serving different constituencies and having different time horizons. The president is the only nationally elected political figure, whereas senators represent states and members of the house the country's 435 electoral districts. Tension necessarily follows from this division of labor, because what is good for the country may not be good for individual states or congressional districts. A reduction in defense spending might, for example, help balance the national budget, but it could cause unemployment in states and districts in whose economies the defense industry looms large. Thus, even if from the same party as the president, representatives from these states and districts will resist budget cuts for fear of voter retribution at the next election. Different time horizons similarly build permanent tension into relations between elected representatives in a separated-powers system. The president is elected for four years and can be reelected for only one additional term, whereas, facing no term limits, senators are elected for six-year and house members for two-year periods. Again, a president might want to write himself into history by eliminating the country's economic deficit before leaving office, but unpopular measures like raising taxes or cutting spending will likely be anathema to legislators whose reelection is imminent, and especially to those among them whose constituents and/or districts will be disproportionately hurt by such measures. Again, regardless of whether or not they belong to the same party as the president, members of Congress may well choose to resist his initiatives in their own self-interest and/or that of those they represent.

The minoritarian democracy ethos, then, makes for consensual government. Laws are the outcome of an incessant process of negotiation, compromise, and concession in a governance system in which multiple actors have the potential to stall legislative proposals, if not derail them altogether. Parliamentary government, at least as practiced in the United Kingdom, is a quite different story.

Parliamentary Government

The philosophical basis of parliamentary government is majoritarian democracy. Political power is rightly the preserve of the only directly elected government body, which is the lower house in virtually all parliamentary democracies. The lawmaking power is fused in two senses. One, it is concentrated in the lower house and not widely shared with government bodies – upper houses, for example – that are unelected or indirectly elected. Two, the concentration of power entails parliamentary lower houses necessarily performing the executive and legislative functions that fall to distinct branches of government in separated-powers systems. This makes for a very different pattern of governance than that found in the U.S.-style presidential system of government.

For a start, there is only one political prize to compete for at election time, which is control of the lower house, and control comes with winning a majority of the seats in it. Partly explained by differences in national population size, there is enormous variation in the size of democratic lower houses across the world, ranging from 200 or fewer seats in some European countries (including Belgium, Denmark, Finland, and Ireland) to around 600 or more in France, Germany, and the United Kingdom. The winning formula in all them, however, is the same: command of a majority of those parliamentary seats. Majority support gives governments the votes they need to pass legislation while at the same time conferring the stamp of democratic legitimacy on that same legislation. But majority victories are not automatic in parliamentary elections. Instead, there are three broad types of parliamentary government: *single-party*, *coalition*, and *minority*. Single-party governments are formed when one party wins a majority of seats in its own right and assumes sole responsibility for governing the country. This is the least common type of parliamentary government and is most notably the norm in the United Kingdom. Coalition governments, in contrast, are formed when no single party wins a majority so that two or more parties formally band together behind a negotiated set of common goals to acquire the majority of seats needed to pass legislation and govern the country. Coalition government is the norm across most of the parliamentary world. On occasion, however, a party or even a coalition of them may control a large number of parliamentary seats but be unable to cross the threshold of majority status. Under these circumstances, a minority government might be formed comprising either a single large party or a coalition of parties. Single-party minority governments have been common in contemporary Norway and coalition minority governments in contemporary Denmark. Minority governments of both types will usually obtain the majority they need to pass legislation by brokering deals with parties outside the governing coalition one piece of legislation at a time. They might, for example, agree to amend the legislation in ways attractive to a non-governing party in exchange for its promise not to oppose it or, better still, to support it when the vote is called.

Generally speaking, then, a bill effectively becomes a law in parliamentary systems when approved by a majority in the lower house. Moreover, unlike U.S.-style presidential government where the executive and legislative powers are independent of each other, the responsibility for executing laws emanating from the legislature is the responsibility of that same lower house. Thus, the government, or executive power, emerges from it and is dependent on its support to remain in office. The leader of the government, commonly known as the prime minister, premier, or chancellor, is not popularly elected, but is chosen from within the legislature and is usually the leader of the governing party or the largest party in the coalition. Among his or her roles is that of chief executive, which entails the selection of a team of senior politicians from within parliament, usually around twenty in number, to run the government. This team is often called a cabinet or council of ministers, just like its similarly named U.S. counterpart. Each member of the cabinet assumes responsibility for overseeing and directing one of the major departments of state – Defense, Foreign Affairs, Treasury, Agriculture, and so on. Unlike in the United States, however, the cabinet must have the confidence of the lower house to assume the executive function. This sometimes manifests itself in passage of a positive majority (or investiture) vote in the lower house, sometimes in not being rejected in such a vote and sometimes in being allowed to take up office without a formal vote. The important point is that the executive and legislature are not independent of each other; the former needs to have the confidence of the latter to take up its responsibilities. It also needs to maintain that confidence if it is to remain in office and continue to execute those responsibilities.

A number of key features of parliamentary government follow. First, governments are directly dependent on the legislature and accountable to it for their (in)actions. If they lose the confidence of a majority of its members, they can be ejected from office in a clear signal that they have forfeited their democratic right to lead in the eyes of their parliamentary colleagues. The usual procedure by which dismissal occurs is *the vote of no confidence*, which is basically a parliamentary decision on the question of whether the government should be allowed to remain in office. If the vote is successful, the government resigns. A no-confidence vote can be called at any point in the life of a parliament and any number of them can be called during this same period. In view of the role of this parliamentary tactic in destabilizing the Weimar Republic and vaulting Hitler to power, Germany in its post-World War II constitution introduced the notion of *the constructive vote of no confidence*. Under this procedure, it is not enough to show dissatisfaction with the incumbent government by ejecting it prematurely from office; a simultaneous requirement is that an alternative government has to be chosen to replace it if the no-confidence vote is to take effect. Thus, Germany's Free Democratic party (FDP) was in coalition with the Social Democrats (SDP) when, in 1982, it switched its support to Helmut Kohl's Christian Democrats (CDU-CSU) and they jointly passed a vote of no confidence in the incumbent SDP/FDP government and at the same time voted into office a replacement CDU-CSU/FDP coalition. Kohl remained chancellor of Germany until 1998, most notably overseeing the reunification of East and West Germany after 1990.

This episode highlights an interesting feature of no-confidence votes. Successful ones are very rare under single-party governments because such parties are almost always able to impose discipline on their parliamentary members. *Party discipline* involves Members of Parliament (MPs) voting as their party leadership instructs them to for reasons including a sense of shared ideology and common fate, a fear of giving political competitors of a different ideological stripe the opportunity to wrest power away from their party, or a reluctance to put their own political career – advancement to cabinet rank, for example – at risk by disobeying their party leadership. The vote of no confidence is more of a threat in coalition governments where member parties, acting as a disciplined whole, may withdraw their support out of electoral strategizing, policy disagreement, personality clash, or whatever.

Should a vote of no confidence be successful, two responses are possible. In the case of coalition governments, an attempt can be made to build a different coalition and have it accepted by the legislature. This response is not possible, however, when, as in Britain, two large parties dominate the struggle for office and eschew political cooperation. The usual response in this case is the second one and it is to dissolve parliament and call new elections so that the voters are given the opportunity to resolve the gridlock between the two competitors by taking the opportunity to redistribute seats in favor of one or the other. This is also the response when a new coalition cannot be built from the constellation of parties already in the legislature. This resort of calling on voters to resolve parliamentary gridlock highlights a final distinctive feature of parliamentary government, which is that elections to the national legislature do not take place at fixed times and intervals. To be sure, the lifetime of parliaments is fixed, ranging typically between three years in countries like Australia and Belgium and five years in Britain and France. But the prime minister can request a dissolution and call new elections at any point in the parliamentary cycle. Moreover, the exercise of this prerogative is not restricted to the need to resolve parliamentary gridlock. Rather, its use is at the chief executive's discretion, hedged in only by calculations of voter tolerance of premature elections, the likelihood of adverse electoral consequences, and fear of losing control of government. It is nonetheless a powerful weapon in any prime minister's armory. He can avoid an electoral backlash, for example, by calling an election before an economic recession hits, or he can improve his party's electoral prospects by calling one after a successful war.

Presidential and parliamentary forms of government, then, are different because they are rooted in contrasting conceptions of democracy, the former minoritarian and separating political powers in the name of protecting minority interests, the latter majoritarian and fusing them with a view to allowing the directly elected majority to govern in accord with the promises it made to voters when running for office. In institutional terms, this basic philosophical difference translates into the legislature not being able to remove the government in presidential systems and its being able to do so in parliamentary ones. Direct election makes for parliamentary sovereignty in the latter, but not the former. Semi-presidential systems are an amalgam of these two sets of institutional arrangements and allow for the dismissal of the government by both the president and the legislature. The archetypal such system, the Fifth French Republic, will now be described.

Semi-Presidential Government

The semi-presidential system of government is relatively uncommon in the democratic world. In Western Europe, it is to be found in France, Finland, and Portugal and in Eastern Europe, in the Czech Republic, Estonia, Lithuania, Poland, and Slovenia. Its origins lie less in the desire to put into practice a particular vision of democracy and more in the desire to strike a workable balance between the executive and legislative powers. Between 1871 and 1958, the guiding principle of French government was parliamentary supremacy, which translated into a weak executive, a rapid turnover of multiparty coalition governments, a long history of unstable and ineffective governance, and, eventually, regime change (see Chapter 2). Among the more notable consequences were occupation by Germany on three separate occasions (1870, 1914, and 1939) and a feeble economic performance that earned the country the title "the weak man of Europe." In 1958, a threatened military coup gave Charles de Gaulle the opportunity to bring to an end the era of parliamentary supremacy and introduce a constitution for the new Fifth Republic that introduced a strong executive, or president, with the power to override the destructive force of the country's deep and long-standing internal political divisions and thereby introduce stable and effective governance to France.

This constitution was the blueprint for the semi-presidential model of democratic government, and its distinctive feature is that it combines elements of the "purer" parliamentary and presidential systems. The goal was to continue to allow for the democratic expression of the various interests in French society in the legislature while at the same time introducing a popularly elected president who could protect and advance a national interest that was held to have been neglected in the previous Third and Fourth Republics. To this end, a dual executive comprising a prime minister and a president was created. The prime minister and the government have the constitutional duty to "determine and direct the policy of the nation," are accountable to the lower house of parliament, and, broadly speaking, are concerned with domestic affairs, with the prime minister's major task being to manage parliament and its business. The parliamentary credentials of the Fifth Republic lie in the lower house's ability to pass a vote of no confidence in the government. Its presidential credentials come from the president being popularly elected (initially by an electoral college and later directly) and from his not being removable by the parliament except for impeachment. His actual governance role, however, is complex. On the one hand, he is largely responsible for the conduct of the country's foreign affairs. Thus, he is chief of the armed forces, chairs the main defense committee, and negotiates treaties. On the other hand, he is responsible for the smooth functioning of parliament and has powers that allow him to intervene in domestic governance if parliament proves to be, as in earlier Republics, too internally divided to govern effectively. At the extreme, he has strong emergency powers that allow him to take sole responsibility for the governance of the country. More routinely, he has the constitutional power to bypass parliament by calling referendums, to appoint (but not dismiss) the prime minister, and, most tellingly, to dissolve parliament, whereas parliament cannot remove him by similar means. The sharing of the dissolution power with parliament is the essence of the distinctiveness of semi-presidential government (Cheibub 2007).

Semi-presidential government has had a checkered history in the Fifth Republic. It has worked well when presidents have enjoyed loyal majority support in the lower house. In this situation – and it has been the norm in the Fifth Republic – presidents have been able to appoint premiers not only of the same ideological stripe as themselves but also ones who have been acceptant of presidential primacy in the governance of the country. More tellingly, these same prime ministers also accepted the president's de facto right to dismiss them. In normal times, therefore, the president has been the unquestioned chief executive. On occasion, however, presidents have not enjoyed a loyal parliamentary majority and have been obliged to appoint a prime minister of an ideological stripe acceptable to the legislative majority rather than themselves. Given the president's inability to dismiss the prime minister, the result has been a struggle for primacy between the two ideologically opposed "heads" of the political executive. The term *cohabitation* is used to describe this situation of potential deadlock, and there have been three such periods in the Fifth Republic. Between 1986 and 1988, a socialist President coexisted with a prime minister belonging to the ideologically rightist party founded by General de Gaulle in the early days of the republic. This situation repeated itself between 1993 and 1995. Then from 1997 to 2002, a Gaullist president found himself compelled to cope with a socialist prime minister. When in operation, the net effect of cohabitation has been to increase prime ministerial influence at the expense of the president. In no case, however, has it resulted in a return to the kind of presidential-prime ministerial stand-off that would risk reintroducing the unstable and ineffective governance characteristic of the Third and Fourth Republics.

If only for this reason, semi-presidentialism in France can be counted a success.

> *W**AIT A MINUTE.** **CONSIDER THIS.** We have just outlined the three basic models of governance: presidential, parliamentary, and semi-presidential systems. Are you more in favor of the minoritarian approach of presidentialism or the majoritarian approach of parliamentarism? Does the semi-presidential model represent the best of both worlds? If you were charged with writing a new constitution, which one would you adopt, and why?*

Majoritarian versus Proportional Electoral Systems

All democratic elections take place within the framework of a body of laws and regulations that stipulate, among other things, who enjoys the legal right to vote, who is eligible to stand for election to specific public offices, when the election will take place, the structure of the ballot, and the hours during which the polling booths will remain open. Particularly important facets of election law are (1) the electoral formula by means of which individual votes are translated into parliamentary seats and (2) the district magnitude that determines the number of representatives per electoral district. The electoral formula and district magnitude are the principal elements of the electoral system and together provide the solution to the basic puzzle of democratic elections, which is how are millions of votes aggregated to produce a much smaller number of representatives holding a seat in parliament. How, for example, were the more than 112 million votes cast in the 2008 election to the U.S. House of Representatives translated into the election of 435 individuals, each representing a single congressional district? The first step in understanding cross-national similarities and differences in this translation process is to note that there are three major types of electoral system in the world of democratic elections: plurality/majoritarian, proportional, and mixed (Norris 2004). These will now be described and their implications for the governance of countries explored.

Plurality/Majority Electoral Systems

Three major variants of this type of electoral system exist. In descending order of use in democratic elections, they are: (1) single-member district plurality (SMDP), (2) two-round (TR), and (3) alternative-vote (AV) systems. All usually have single-member districts (SMDs). In other words, there is one seat per district (otherwise called a constituency in the United Kingdom, a riding in Canada, or an electorate in Australia) up for grabs in elections. The major differences between them lie in the share of the vote needed to win and how that share is accumulated by the winning party.

The SMDP system is used in many countries around the world, including the United States (for elections to the House of Representatives,) and the United Kingdom along with many of its former colonies, Canada, India, and Nigeria being among the largest of them. It is also known as first-past-the post system because it is a winner-take-all system that allows for only one ballot per person and the winner is the candidate who gets a *plurality* of the votes cast (i.e., more votes than anyone else). Thus, in a three-person election, candidate A might get 34 percent of the total constituency vote and candidates B and C 33 percent each. Candidate A wins the seat despite being barely more popular than both her rivals and not commanding anything near a *majority* (50 percent + 1) of support among the district's voters.

The TR and AV systems are somewhat different in that they are designed to enhance the legitimacy of winning candidates by manufacturing an enhanced vote share for them. In the TR system, if no candidate wins a set percentage on the first round, or ballot (usually a majority), then a second round is held at some later date and only the top candidates on the first ballot proceed to this second one. Sometimes only two candidates are allowed to proceed, thereby guaranteeing a majority for one of them in the second round election. If more than two candidates contest the second round, a plurality of votes will usually carry the day for the winner. Some form of the AV system is used in Australia, Fiji, and Papua New Guinea. Again, it usually entails SMDs and, if there are more than two candidates running for election, the voter ranks them in her order of preference on her ballot. If one candidate wins an absolute majority on the basis of first-preference votes, he wins the seat. If no candidate wins such a majority, then the candidate with the smallest first-preference vote share is eliminated and her votes redistributed among the remaining candidates on the basis of stated second preferences. This process of elimination and redistribution continues until one candidate comes to enjoy a majority of the votes cast and is declared the winner.

There are a number of advantages to plurality/majority electoral systems. The first is that they present the voter with a relatively simple choice. Only one seat is at stake and a single person has to be identified and chosen to fill it. A single candidate is chosen directly in SMDP elections, voters choose on two separate occasions in TR elections or, most demandingly, they rank a number of candidates on a single ballot in AV elections. But whatever the method of choice, a single elected official represents voters' interests, which makes it relatively straightforward for them to know who their representative is and to hold her accountable for her and her party's performance in office. The basic democratic mechanism of accountability is thereby strengthened, as it also is by the tendency of this type of electoral system to produce single-party governments. In contests where there can be only one winner, larger parties are more likely than smaller parties to come out on top; this is the reason they are larger in the first place. The responsibility for governing is therefore more likely to fall on a single party that is readily blamed or rewarded for its performance in office when it comes to election time.

Proportional Electoral Systems

The second major body of electoral systems falls under the proportional representation (PR) label. Their common goal is to award legislative seats to parties in proportion to the share of the vote they win. Thus, if a party wins 20 percent of the popular vote, PR systems are designed to award it a similar proportion of the seats in the legislature. PR electoral systems are the more common worldwide, and they fall into two main types: list PR and the single transferable vote (STV), with the former easily outnumbering the latter in the world's democracies.

A defining difference between plurality/majority and PR systems is that the latter use multimember districts (MMDs) as opposed to the former's SMDs. In other words, more than one representative is elected in MMDs. They are used for the simple reason that it is impossible to distribute anything proportionally if there is only one seat to be won. The actual number of seats per MMD can range from as low as 2 or 3 to more than 100 in countries like Israel, the Netherlands, and Slovakia, where the whole country is treated as a single MMD for purposes of electing a legislature. The votes are summed within each district and formulae exist to award seats in proportion to vote share. Perfect proportionality is rarely achieved, but it is approximated far more closely than in plurality/majority systems. District size plays an important role because the larger a district is, the greater the proportionality that can be achieved.

The allocation of seats is different for the two PR models. Under list PR, seats are awarded to parties on the basis of votes cast for party lists of candidates. The lists are usually drawn up by the parties themselves and contain the same number of candidates as there are seats to be won. The parties determine where individual candidates are placed on the list and voters respond according to the list PR system in place. In *closed-list* systems, voters can cast their ballot only for their party's list as a whole; there is no mechanism for them to express a preference for individual candidates on the list. In *open-list* systems, voters do not have to accept the party's ordering of the candidates. Instead, they can alter it by expressing a preference for candidates within the party list. The least restrictive system of all is the *free-list* system, which usually gives voters as many votes are there are seats to be filled and allows them to distribute those votes among multiple candidates within a single party list or among candidates from different party lists.

STV, the second type of PR system, works differently. It does not employ a party list, but requires voters to rank candidates in the district. To win a seat, a candidate must obtain a particular quota of votes, which is roughly the total number of valid votes in the district divided by the number of seats plus one. All candidates who exceed this quota on first-preference votes are elected. If seats then remain unfilled, the elected candidates' "surplus" votes are distributed to other candidates on the basis of the second preferences shown on the individual ballot papers. If no candidate manages to reach the quota on the first count, the bottom candidate is eliminated and her votes redistributed on the basis of second preferences. The redistribution continues until all the seats are filled.

In producing a closer correspondence between parties' vote and seat shares, PR electoral systems have their champions and their critics. One advantage is their greater fairness in rewarding parties in accord with their popularity among voters. This is seen as being preferable to the tendency of winner-take-all plurality/majority electoral systems to over-reward large parties. Let us take a hypothetical example based on an SMDP electoral system. Imagine a country made up of three SMDs, 1, 2, and 3, with three parties, A, B, and C, contesting each of them. Party A gets, respectively a 35, 33, and 33 percent vote share, Party B gets 33, 34, and 35 percent, and Party C gets the remaining 32, 33, and 32 percent shares. Under SMDP aggregation rules, Party A wins District 1, Party B wins Districts 2 and 3, and Party C, despite winning almost an average of one-third of the total vote, receives no seats. Party C's basic problem is that it is popular in all three districts, but not popular enough to win a plurality of the vote in any of them. This predicament is especially acute when a smaller party's support is distributed more or less evenly across districts and becomes less so when its support is geographically concentrated so that achieving plurality status in at least some districts becomes more likely. Thus, in the 2005 British general election, the Liberal Democrats, which put up candidates in all constituencies, needed an average 0.36 percent share of the national vote for each seat that it won. In contrast, the Scottish Nationalists, contesting only Scottish seats, needed only 0.25 percent of it, and the Welsh Nationalists, fighting only in Wales, even less at 0.20 percent.

PR systems are praised for producing roughly proportional seat to vote shares for each party in the election and for not "wasting" the support given to smaller parties that have no chance of winning government office in plurality/majoritarian electoral systems specifically designed to create governing majorities for larger parties. They are not without their critics, however. For a start, their tendency to create the need for coalition governments is claimed to hold out the potential for the kind of rapid governmental turnover that in the past helped undermine democratic stability and pave the way for periods of authoritarian rule in countries like Germany, France, and Italy. In addition, the "tyranny of the majority" so feared by America's Founding Fathers can be replaced by a potential minority tyranny whereby members of the governing coalition, even very small ones, can gain disproportionate influence over policy by threatening to withdraw and bring the coalition down if they do not get their way. A problem with this criticism, of course, is that, as previously noted, many healthy democracies in the world today have a tradition of multiparty coalition, and often even minority, government. What seems to matter is less the letter of the electoral law and more the ability and willingness of political elites to make political institutions operate to achieve the common good rather than their own immediate political goals (Gunther and Mughan 1993).

Coalition government in the French Fourth Republic, for example, did not work because two large groups in the parliament, the Communists and the Gaullists, deliberately sabotaged delicately balanced coalitions in order to make them fail, the former in the hope of replacing capitalism with a socialist economic and political order and the latter of replacing a parliamentary with a presidential form of government. But a more telling criticism of PR electoral systems is that the link between voters and their elected representative is less clear and unambiguous in multimember districts, and democratic accountability is thereby weakened. If a person votes for a party list, for example, who among the several candidates elected from that list is his representative? This is an especially vexing question when none of them comes from the part of the district in which he resides. Another accountability criticism is how is blame to be apportioned, and punishment at the polls meted out, when a coalition government does not live up to its campaign promises and its members blame each other for their collective failure?

> *WAIT A MINUTE.* **CONSIDER THIS.** The issues in this debate are multiple and complex, but you might start by asking whether the political benefits of plurality/majority electoral systems, like that for the U.S. House of Representatives, outweigh their democratic costs. PR does a better job of representing the variety of political interests and viewpoints in an electorate, but SMDP promises greater accountability of governors to the governed. Between representation and accountability, in other words, lies a fundamental democratic conundrum. Which of these two democratic principles – representation and accountability – is more important to you, and is this choice linked to the electoral system you support?

Mixed Electoral Systems

Representing an effort to combine party and geographical representation, mixed electoral systems are a hybrid in which there are two groups of elected members, one of which is elected under a plurality/majority system and the other under a PR system. The two sets of elections can be linked to produce a relatively proportional result (mixed-member proportional, or MMP), or they can be conducted independently of each other to produce a non-proportional mixed-member majority (MMM) outcome.

The MMP system was first introduced in Germany after World War II and was designed to avoid the twin pitfalls of the Weimar Republic between the wars. The first was fragmented coalition government in the democratically elected legislature, and the second excessive concentration of power at the center under Hitler. Thus, German voters have two votes, one for candidates elected by plurality voting in SMDs, which was intended to simplify the party system by encouraging fewer and larger parties. The second vote is for a regional party list, which was intended to empower the German states at the expense of the center. Each electoral system accounts for half the seats in the national legislature. The party list vote determines the overall number of seats to be awarded to each party in each region and candidates from the party lists are added to the directly elected candidates until proportionality between vote share and seat share is achieved. In addition to Germany, this system is used in, among other countries, Hungary, Italy, Mexico, Venezuela, and New Zealand. The MMM system is also called the parallel system and is used in twenty-one countries across the globe, including Japan and the Russian Federation. It involves the use of majoritarian and proportional electoral formulae in what are essentially two separate elections conducted independently of each other. Countries vary in the balance that they try to strike between the numbers of each type of seat in the national legislature. Russia, for example, allocates 225 of them using an SMDP system and another 225 of them using list PR with the whole country as a single electoral district.

Consensual and Majoritarian Democracies

In sum, like the previous institutional arrangements we have discussed – unitarism/federalism, unicameralism/bicameralism, and parliamentarism/ presidentialism – electoral systems help influence the distribution of political power in democracies, with plurality/majority variants concentrating it in relatively few hands and PR ones dispersing it more evenly among those political parties able to command popular support. Looking at these institutional arrangements one by one, it is not easy to order individual democracies according to how much they concentrate or disperse lawmaking power. The problem is that if an individual democracy concentrates power in one dimension, say parliamentarism, it need not in another, say federalism. Australia, Canada, and Germany, for example, are parliamentary regimes, but they are also federations that select upper-house members with methods ranging from direct election to prime ministerial appointment. One way of getting around this difficulty is to look at a regime's institutional arrangements as a package and then to place democracies on a continuum running from their being more or less majoritarian or consensual in character (Lijphart 1999).

Basically, majoritarian democracies are those in which the preponderance of power lies with the winning party or coalition of parties in the lower house; checks and balances on the exercise of the executive power are effectively few and far between, and there are clear and consistent winners and losers in the competition for power and influence. These two groups may change roles with different election outcomes, but a structural characteristic of the political system is that until such time as they become winners, losers are basically outsiders in the governance process. Great Britain, with its fusion of the executive and legislative powers, its unitary state, weak upper house, and SMDP electoral system, would typify democracies falling toward the majoritarian end of this continuum. Consensual democracies, by contrast, are characterized by the sharing rather than concentration of power, the existence of checks and balances on the exercise of the executive power, and respect for, and often inclusion of, minorities in the governance process. Examples toward the consensual end of the scale are the U.S. presidential system and Belgium and Switzerland among parliamentary democracies.

As Table 4.1 indicates, the differences between the two types of democracy are not only institutional. With their relative concentration of power, majoritarian democracies are associated with efficient and coordinated decision making, clearer lines of accountability to voters, and the uniform treatment and expectations of groups across the territory of the state. On the other side of the coin, however, they can be associated with the neglect of minorities, which can lead to political instability. The strengths of consensual democracies, by contrast, are constraints on the majority's abuse of power in its own interests, government being closer to the people, including an influence for a wider range of preferences in the formulation of public policy and accommodating more readily and easily the special interests of ethnic and regional minorities. Thus, consensual democracies come to score higher on democratic quality as well as on state generosity in the areas of social welfare, environmental policy, criminal justice, and foreign aid (Lijphart 1999, chapter 16). The weaknesses of this type of democracy, however, include minority groups exerting political influence and power out of proportion to their size, governments having to negotiate and compromise to such a degree that they can have difficulty passing laws adequate for the purposes they are intended to achieve, and minority groups using political institutions as weapons to advance goals harmful to the state. Federalism, for example, may give regional minorities influence in the federal government that helps protect them against majority domination. But at the same time, the political power that federalism affords them can be used as leverage to extract yet more concessions from the center and perhaps even to advance a secessionist agenda (Roeder 1999). While political science can provide a detailed description of the merits and demerits of

TABLE 4.1 Strengths and weaknesses of majoritarian and consensual forms of democracy

Advantages	Disadvantages
Majoritarian democracies	
More centralized government means greater accountability to voters.	More centralized government power can lead to its abuse.
More centralized government promotes efficient and coordinated decision making.	More centralized government can lead to the neglect of opposing and minority viewpoints. Can neglect or exploit regional minorities by denying their special concerns/circumstances.
More centralized government means policies more uniform across the whole state.	More centralized government can become rigid and deaf to opposing viewpoints.
Citizens' rights and responsibilities more uniform across the whole state.	Neglect of regional diversity can encourage regional sentiment and secessionist tendencies.
Consensual Democracies	
Checks and balances that come with decentralization help discourage "tyranny of the majority."	Dispersion of power weakens accountability and can encourage "tyranny of the minority" as small groups are granted special rights.
Decentralization of power brings government closer to citizens and makes it more responsive to them.	Decentralization of power weakens public confidence in government because of perception of needless bureaucratic duplication.
Broader satisfaction with public policy because more preferences are taken into account.	Public policy a compromise between competing interests and inadequate for the purposes it is designed to achieve.
Asymmetric federalism can accommodate special interests of regional minorities and strengthen national unity.	Asymmetric federalism often exacerbates regional inequalities and provides institutional weapons that can encourage secession.

consensual and majoritarian approaches, evaluation and choice between them necessarily falls to you, the reader.

CONCLUSION

This chapter has examined the basic frameworks of governance found in the authoritarian and democratic regimes of the contemporary world. Whether a state is unitary or federal, its legislature unicameral or bicameral, its form of government presidential, parliamentary, or semi-presidential, and its electoral system majoritarian or proportional has enormous bearing on the quality of democracy and the effectiveness of governance. So critical are these institutional choices that they can make a difference to how countries are governed even in authoritarian regimes. Governance itself, however, is more than the study of the institutions of government. It is a relationship, a two-way process of communication and influence between those holding political power and those subject to its exercise. It is to the nature of the linkage between governors and governed in the two different types of regime that we turn in the next chapter.

5 Linkage and Representation

The last chapter outlined the major political institutions whose interactions shape the contrasting patterns of governance found in democratic and authoritarian regimes. Taken together, these institutions comprise the governance framework within which political deliberation and discussion take place and public policy outcomes are decided. These outcomes involve in large part the passage of laws that are binding on the people to whom they apply, which is more often than not the population of the state as a whole. New laws are introduced, existing ones are amended, and some are repealed as governments respond to changes in their domestic and international social, economic, and political circumstances. Income tax levels may be raised, for example, to compensate for increased government spending as the result of involvement in war. Alternatively, the voting age may be reduced to allow for changing definitions of adulthood in society as a whole. Seen from an institutional perspective, governance could easily be seen as a one-way process of imposition from above – those in government decide what is best for their charges and shape and reshape their legal environment to promote newly appropriate behaviors and outcomes.

It is misleading to see the governance process in this light, however. Previous chapters have reiterated that governments, even authoritarian ones, cannot ignore the wishes of their people without risking a popular reaction that might lead ultimately to their ejection from power. Such ejection will probably be peaceful and uncomplicated in democracies as governments forfeit the next election for having failed to satisfy their citizens. By contrast, it might take longer and be less than peaceful in authoritarian regimes where there is not the same shared expectation of responsiveness and accountability to the people and governmental power is forfeited only begrudgingly. Nonetheless, the bottom line in both types of regime is that governance is a two-way process; governors cannot function in the absence of the governed, and vice versa.

The dynamics of this relationship is commonly discussed in terms of linkage politics, and this is the subject matter of this chapter. The notion of linkage is used to signal that governors and governed are connected, or tied together in a relationship of mutual dependence and influence. Each provides goods that the other values and needs. Governments, for example, provide security against foreign invasion or domestic crime, while the governed provide the support, or at least passive acceptance, that keeps governments in power. The essence of this relationship is that it is dynamic in character. Most obviously, it varies across regime type. Authoritarian governments by definition make only the concessions that are necessary to guarantee the continued passivity and quiescence of their populations. Democratic governments, in contrast, have to represent their citizens or pay the price at the next election. Representation means essentially that governments have to remain attentive and responsive to the interests and demands of their citizens, or at least those of them who put them in office. But even though democratic citizenries have the power to hire and fire, the balance of power in their relationship to government should not be understood as always being skewed in their favor. Generally speaking, governments will enjoy greater decision-making autonomy in times of crisis or in areas about which their citizens are not knowledgeable or in which they have little interest or involvement. Those in power will enjoy a much freer hand, for example, in regulating nuclear power stations than they will in setting taxation levels. Linkage exists, then, in all political regimes, but what does it look like in practice? Put differently, who or what mediates the relationship between governors and governed, and how?

Distinguishing again between democratic and authoritarian regimes, this chapter will address this question by examining two distinct dimensions of linkage politics. The first of them concerns mechanisms of intermediation, focusing in particular on elections because they are a large, inclusive, and politically important exercise in linkage politics. The second focuses on the political institutions that act as intermediaries between governments and their people. Two such institutions are identified and explored: (1) political parties and (2) interest groups.

MECHANISMS OF INTERMEDIATION

The term "mechanism" is used here to denote a structured pattern of behavior by means of which governors and governed routinely interact with each other. In the diverse world of politics, mechanisms of inter-mediation can take many forms, with some operating primarily from the bottom up and others primarily from the top down. In democracies, for example, bottom-up efforts by citizens to influence governments and hold them accountable for their actions in office take the form of popular participation in politics, but this participation is itself a multifaceted phe-nomenon. To vote in elections so as to take part in the basic democratic act of choosing one's government is its minimal and most widespread form. Democratic citizens are usually allowed to choose whether or not they will bother to vote, but in countries like Argentina, Australia, Belgium, Cyprus, and the Netherlands (until 1970), the act is compulsory and citizens risk a small fine if they fail to exercise their right to cast a ballot.

There are many other ways of getting involved in politics beyond the vote, however, and these are usually categorized into *conventional* and *unconventional* forms of political participation (Barnes and Kaase 1979). The former involves taking advantage of freedoms and opportunities that are officially sanctioned and put in place to encourage citizen engagement in the political process so as to encourage its responsiveness to their wishes and interests. Its forms include: (1) discussing politics with friends; (2) trying to convince friends to vote for a particular party; (3) working to solve community problems; (4) attending political meetings; (5) contact-ing officials or politicians; and (6) working on election campaigns. Uncon-ventional participation takes places outside normal democratic channels and practices and is usually a reaction to the perception that the political process, even in democracies, is closed and unresponsive. Its forms include: (1) signing petitions; (2) taking part in lawful demonstrations; (3) organizing and taking part in boycotts; (4) occupying buildings; (5) blocking traffic; (6) damaging property; and (7) personal violence.

Political participation in authoritarian regimes resembles unconven-tional more than conventional participation. This is because the political goal of authoritarianism is not to involve the people in political discus-sion and represent them in the political process. Rather, it is to encour-age a passive and quiescent mass public that has little or no expectation of being served by the government. Thus, without the means to regis-ter its disapproval peacefully, the public's frustration with an inattentive and unresponsive government sometimes erupts spontaneously into street demonstrations, property damage, clashes with the police, and the like. A good example is the popular unrest, known as the Arab Spring, that shook authoritarian North Africa and the Middle East in 2011. Tunisia, Egypt, Bahrain, Libya, Syria, and Yemen were all rocked by a contagion of mass uprisings, while minor street protests occurred in many other states in the region (Nematt 2011). Sometimes the regime is able to withstand such assaults on its right to govern the way it does and sometimes it crumbles before them, as Ben Ali's government did after twenty-eight days of protest in Tunisia, followed by Hosni Mubarak's government after eighteen days of protest in Egypt.

But just as there are various mechanisms by which the people can reach out to seek to influence governments, there are a variety of mechanisms by which governments can seek to influence the behavior of the governed. For a start, there is the law. All governments make laws that are binding on their peoples and that they break only at the risk of being punished in some way or other. Some laws are common across regime types; others are not. Both authoritarian and democratic regimes, for example, have a clear interest in maintaining social order and both outlaw the likes of treason, murder, and robbery because of the threat they pose to that order. In other areas, however, the two types of regime can be very different. Democracies use the law to guarantee basic freedoms, or rights – like freedom of speech, freedom of association, and freedom of movement. Authoritarian regimes, in stark contrast, are more likely to use the law to limit such rights as part of a larger strategy of repression.

Another top-down mechanism of intermediation is a regime's propagandistic use of the mass media in its efforts to shape popular attitudes and perceptions and build support for the government and regime. Democracies enjoy freedom of the press, which means that government interacts with the media in one of two ways. It can purchase broadcast time or newspaper space, as with, for example, paid political advertising during election campaigns. More commonly, though, governments strategize to gain sympathetic coverage from an independent media. A minister might, for example, announce a change in health care policy in a hospital setting surrounded by enthusiastic doctors and nurses. Authoritarian governments usually stand in a much more direct relationship to the media – they control it and often blatantly manipulate it to further their own political ends. Finally, governments can penetrate society itself by setting up organizational units to facilitate their interaction with, and control over, the governed. The smallest organizational unit in communist societies, for example, is the party cell (composed of at least three members). The Soviet communist party inserted one within all institutions in society, including the military, the media, schools, hospitals, factories, and farms. The cell was intended to initiate the upward flow of information through the party hierarchy so as to facilitate highly centralized party control from above. In democracies, political parties create organizations that generally correspond with electoral districts and are called local party organizations. Their purpose is to educate and inform the people in the constituency about party ideology and goals and to mobilize their support behind it at election time in particular.

In short, many mechanisms of intermediation can be identified in the two-way relationship between governors and governed. They may take similar forms in authoritarian and democratic regimes, but they often serve different purposes. This is nowhere more evident than in the case of elections, which are a particularly large-scale, inclusive, and politically important intermediation mechanism found in both types of regime, although not always in authoritarian ones. We will now look more closely at the role of elections in each of them.

Elections

A general dictionary definition of an election is that of a formal decision-making process by which a population chooses an individual to hold an office. Elections take place in all walks of life; many organizations choose their leaders by popular consultation of the membership. For many, they are the defining characteristic of democratic politics. Samuel Huntington, for example, declares a twentieth century political system to be democratic "to the extent that its most powerful collective decision-makers are selected through fair, honest and periodic elections in which candidates clearly compete for votes and in which virtually all the adult population is eligible to vote" (Huntington 1991, 7). An unfortunate by-product of the tendency to equate democracy with the holding of elections, however, is neglect of their role in authoritarian regimes, and this despite the fact that elections are far more common in them than many of us might think. Indeed, about half of the legislative and presidential elections held around the world between 1946 and 2000 took place in nondemocracies (Golder 2005, 106).

How do elections in the two types of regime differ? In particular, how do they differ in their performance of the role as intermediation mechanism linking governors and governed? Let us start with elections in authoritarian regimes.

Authoritarian Elections

The first thing that must be said is that elections in authoritarian regimes, like those in democracies, take place at various levels; some are for heads of government, some for national legislatures, and some for local councils. Whatever the level, however, authoritarian elections generally share the distinction of being limited forms of public consultation. They are limited in that the suffrage in them is not always universal and in that they are not intended to give participants in them meaningful choice as to who governs them. The bottom-up channel of influence from the governed to governors is underdeveloped by design in this type of electoral regime. This is evident in the limited competition that is built into their structure. Entry into electoral competition is not open to all political forces in society, but is strictly regulated by the ruling group acting as gatekeepers. At one extreme is the exclusion from the election of all candidates except for those endorsed by, and representing, the regime itself. The classic example here is elections in the totalitarian Soviet Union. For most of its history, there was only one candidate per district, hand-picked to run for office by the ruling communist party. Reported turnout was always high at more than 99 percent and, inevitably, all the votes were cast for the communist party candidate. The outcome was then hailed as a resounding vote of confidence in the ruling communist party and its goals. This fiction proved hard to maintain over time so that, especially in Soviet-controlled Eastern Europe, the minimalist concession was made that entry rules were relaxed and some limited choice allowed by having more than one communist party candidate per district.

At the other extreme is the semi-competitive authoritarian election, characterized by a tolerance of limited political opposition in the electoral process. The regime may allow universal suffrage, but at the same time it devalues the vote by keeping the range of political options for which it can be cast within strictly acceptable limits. Opposition groups may be tolerated, but they are strictly controlled. In Egypt prior to the Arab Spring of 2011, for example, the parties allowed to run in national legislative elections were selected by a committee controlled by the long-serving and authoritarian President Mubarak's National Democratic Party (*Economist*, July 15, 2010). Such practices ensure that elections do not offer voters real alternatives to the current regime itself or to the institutional rules by which the political game is played. Rather, their purpose is more to preempt public discontent by presenting a façade of choice and representation. The tolerance of limited opposition is usually intended to help strengthen this façade, although this is not to say that it never backfires and promotes the emergence of an opposition that comes to threaten the hegemony of the entrenched ruling group. The fact that an opposition comes into being, for example, has been argued to reflect deep divisions within the hegemonic group's ranks that may even undermine the authoritarian regime itself eventually (Brownlee 2007).

But why bother with elections at all given that they are expensive and commonly have few immediate political consequences in that governments do not turn over and policies do not change as a result of their outcome? The answer to this question is simple. Authoritarian governments hold elections because they are virtually certain of victory in them and the elections themselves serve a number of useful purposes for the regime.

Two conditions make for the almost certain victory of incumbent governments in authoritarian regimes. "Generally, when incumbents hold elections, they have overwhelming advantages through their monopolies of state resources and the means of coercion" (Gandhi and Lust-Okar 2009, 407). Their monopoly of resources means that incumbent governments are in a position to bestow patronage on supporters and to distribute the spoils of office to a wider public in order to win broader support. Patronage is important for retaining the loyalty of existing supporters and for dividing the opposition by co-opting at least some of its members with a promise of a share of the spoils, and maybe even some limited influence on decisions important to them. This control of the spoils of office also helps account for a pervasive linkage between governors and governed in the authoritarian world, known as patron-client relations. These relations involve the exchange of goods and services between unequal actors. Patrons can provide clients with basic necessities, like physical protection, food, medicine, and jobs. In return, clients offer patrons votes in particular, but also political acquiescence, and/or a loyal labor force (Hutchcroft 1997). The client's material dependence on the patron often means that the former vote against their personal preferences and consolidates the hold on office of the latter's preferred party.

Authoritarian governments' monopoly of the means of coercion gives them the power to rig elections to ensure a favorable outcome, and to do so more or less with impunity. Rigging involves numerous practices in addition to banning meaningful competition outright. To take the example of pre-Arab Spring Egypt again, against a background of numerous other restrictive practices including the selective registration of voters, supervision of the polls, and fraudulent vote counting, one of President Mubarak's potential opponents in the aborted 2011 presidential election complained: "I am suffocated. We can't have a headquarters, can't raise funds, can't hold public meetings. All I can do is go and visit a few places, and then after I leave they arrest a few" (*Economist*, July 15, 2010).

The inevitable question is why authoritarian governments go to all this trouble when their concern is not to consult or represent public opinion, and the result of the election is all but a foregone conclusion. The answer is that elections serve a number of purposes, or functions, that help such governments consolidate both their own hold on power and the integrity of the authoritarian regime itself. Four such purposes can be identified: (1) communication; (2) information; (3) legitimation; and (4) safety valve (Gandhi and Lust-Okar 2009, 405–07).

Communication involves authoritarian regimes implementing their strong preference for political passivity and inactivity by reaching out unilaterally to the people to issue orders, explanations, and cues as to appropriate expectations and behaviors at present and in the future. The information provided even by noncompetitive or semi-competitive elections can be of great value to the regime. Unusually high levels of support for opposition candidates or of voter abstention and ballot nullification, for example, will alert the ruling group to popular dissatisfaction to which they might choose to be attentive. Alternatively, election dynamics might show those in control where their own support is weak and that of the opposition strong so that they can respond before this imbalance gets out of hand. Similarly, elections can provide them with information about the loyalty and competence of their own party cadres. A third function of elections is to help authoritarian rulers appear legitimate in the eyes of pro-democracy advocates at home and abroad. To put it simply, elections can, on the surface at least, be taken as signs of good behavior and political movement in the right direction by both these audiences. Finally, elections can function to reduce pressure for change on authoritarian regimes and, in this sense, act as a safety valve. They can, for example, give the impression of listening to the people, they can become an opportunity to isolate, divide, and perhaps even co-opt oppositional elites, or they can help the incumbent rulers adapt, rejuvenate, and become even more firmly in political control. In light of the advantages and information that elections provide, it is perhaps no surprise that authoritarian rulers who hold them remain in power longer on average than those who do not (Gandhi 2008).

WAIT A MINUTE. **CONSIDER THIS.** Imagine you are an advisor to a dictator in the fictional country of Ruritania. Would you allow the holding of elections? As we note earlier, this may promote a longer time in power for the authoritarian ruler. At the same time, as indicated in Chapter 2, electoral authoritarian regimes with a limited multiparty system are the most fragile of all authoritarian regime types, having a short life span of only nine years on average. So if the dictator summons you to his office and asks if he should hold elections, what would you say?

In short, if linkage is seen as a process of mutual dependence and influence, elections are poor linkage mechanisms in authoritarian regimes because the bottom-up flow of information and influence is weak in them. As a direct result, so too is political representation of the people and government accountability. Paradoxically, an important reason for holding authoritarian elections is to help ensure that the ruling group does not depend on the governed to retain political office and power. In sharp contrast, elections are the major source of office and power in democracies.

Democratic Elections

Democracy enshrines the notion of popular sovereignty – the primacy of the people over the state. As in authoritarian regimes, elections are the major intermediation mechanism in liberal democracies, but a number of features of democratic elections make them a more effective channel of upward influence, thereby ensuring that the governed are better able to make their voice heard in government. For a start, there is the cultural expectation shared by both parties to the interaction that elections should matter – in other words, that citizens should take part in them and that politicians should listen and be responsive to what the people want and what is good for them. Democratic elections can truly be said to be the sovereign voice of the people because virtually all adults (usually defined as eighteen-year-olds and older) have the right to vote in them. By definition, the suffrage is all but universal today, with it usually being denied only to four categories of people, which we can think of as the four "i's" of exclusion: the incarcerated, the insane, infants, and immigrants without citizenship status. Moreover, not only is it the case that most adults have the right to vote, but also elections are open in the sense that virtually everybody has the right to stand for public office in them as long as they satisfy minimal criteria relating to age, country of birth, citizenship, and the like. U.S. presidential candidates, for example, must be natural-born citizens of the United States, at least thirty-five years of age, and permanently resident in the United States for at least fourteen years. Senatorial candidates, in contrast, only need to be at least thirty years old, a U.S. citizen for no less than nine years at the time of election to the Senate, and a resident of the state they are seeking to represent in the upper house. A little reminiscent of authoritarianism, however, is the fact that political criteria are sometimes used to restrict eligibility to compete electorally. Take Europe as an example. Germany, Italy, and France all have laws allowing the government to ban extremist groups, especially far-right and/or neo-nazi organizations. Whether such moves protect or tarnish democracy is a matter of political interpretation and argumentation.

*W**AIT A MINUTE.* **CONSIDER THIS.** Should elections be open to all political forces in democratic societies, even those that reject civil liberties and free elections, such as fascists and communists? Or should participation in them be restricted to those groups that support the principles and practices of democracy itself? Can democracies restrict participation and still be democratic?

The strongest guarantee of citizen influence in government is the right of democratic electorates to hire and fire those who govern them. Popular election is the primary path to political office in democracies, and aspiring power-holders campaign for the votes necessary to win this prize by making a package of promises and commitments, commonly called a manifesto or platform, that they think will be more attractive to voters than that of their competitors in the election. Moreover, the fact that elections must by law be held at regular intervals means that a government is acutely aware that voters can withdraw their support and throw it behind a competitor if they conclude retrospectively that, in office, it has not lived up to the promises and commitments it made when campaigning for office. This is very different from authoritarian elections in which governments are not threatened by meaningful competition for office and, as such, are not held to account for their behaviors and overall performance in office.

Undoubtedly, then, democratic elections are an effective intermediation mechanism linking governors and governed, promoting a dependence of the former on the latter and thereby a meaningful flow of influence from the bottom up. At the same time, however, there is a strong top-down character to their pattern of interaction, even in democracies. Governors are not mere puppets in the hands of voters. Indeed, some radicals see little difference between authoritarian and democratic regimes in this regard, holding that both make for elite domination of the masses. For them, direct coercion may play little role in the democratic context, but elections remain no more than a mechanism that deludes the "sovereign" people into voluntarily handing power over to the rich, clever, and powerful while getting little in return. Antonio Gramsci, for example, dismisses elections in liberal democracies as *"electoral putsches"* (or coups) of the bourgeoisie. But even if claims of the inevitable political dominance of the bourgeoisie are rejected, it is still obvious that, even in democracies, the governors enjoy resources and opportunities that allow them to place their own top-down imprint on their interaction with the governed.

Ironically, perhaps the greatest weapon that governors have in their efforts to shape the expectations and behaviors of the governed is the legitimacy that elections themselves confer on the regime and the office-holders acting in its name. Popular election is tantamount to the consent of the governed and it is the principal source from which democratic governments derive their authority. The consequent voluntary compliance makes it easier for those in government to perform their duties effectively and efficiently. The collection of taxes, for example, is far easier when citizens accept, albeit perhaps reluctantly, that they have a moral and legal obligation to pay the taxes levied on them by elected officials. At the same time, however, legitimacy goes hand in hand with trust and confidence in the government's honesty and good intentions, which in turn reduces the public's political attentiveness and vigilance. With legitimacy, in other words, the accountability linkage is weakened and governments enjoy greater freedom from public scrutiny and become better able to shape popular expectations and behaviors rather than just respond to them. People will be readier, for example, to accept an erosion of their civil liberties if a legitimate government claims that a terrorist attack is imminent than if an illegitimate one does. Similarly, voters will be more willing to accept that a government is acting in a national interest that demands painful sacrifices from them if they think that the government is legitimate.

It is not only legitimacy that plays a top-down role in governments shaping popular expectations and behaviors. They have a variety of other weapons at their disposal as well. Parliamentary governments have the ability to call an election at any point during the legal lifetime commonly of a parliament. Thus, they may call one before the onset of an economic recession and in the process avoid electoral blame for bringing it about. Or they can call one in the aftermath of a successful and popular military expedition, as Margaret Thatcher did after Britain's victory in its Falklands War with Argentina in 1982. This legal maneuver grants the ruling party considerable advantage over its opponents. Similarly, all governments go to great lengths to slant in their own favor the political information reaching the people through the print and broadcast media in particular. In authoritarian regimes, this is achieved through direct government control of the media and strict oversight of its content.

This situation is untenable in democracies where freedom of speech and the press are usually constitutionally guaranteed. Instead, governments there try to convey the images and messages they want by paid commercial advertising or by strategies designed to have the independent press voluntarily present and frame information, and especially in news broadcasts that reach a large audience, in the way that they want. A triumphant George W. Bush, for example, celebrated U.S. "victory" in the Iraq war by announcing it from the deck of an aircraft carrier and with a banner announcing "Mission Completed" in the background. While such political theater helped raise Bush's popularity to new levels, the subsequent civil war between the Shia and Sunni communities in Iraq proved this claim of victory to be premature. Finally, it is governments and their competitors for office that set the political agenda, and in doing so, they are commonly tempted to place less emphasis on what the people might want and more on what serves their own electoral advantage. Thus, parties construct election campaigns to persuade the voter of the overriding importance of issues that they "own" in the sense of being perceived by voters as handling better than their competitors. Thus, left-wing parties might want voters to believe that the election revolves around matters of redistribution and social and economic justice, whereas their right-wing counterparts might prefer to focus the public's attention on issues like tax cuts and law and order (Budge and Farlie 1983).

Democratically elected leaders, then, are as likely to try to shape popular perceptions and demands as they are to feel obliged to be responsive to them. Indeed, it is not unknown for them to lie to their citizens in order to get them to accept policy decisions that run counter to popular preferences. A recent example of this scenario occurred when Prime Minister Blair of Britain and President Bush of the United States made the claim, without conclusive evidence, that Iraq possessed weapons of mass destruction, in order to justify invading that country in 2003. As the secret memo written by MI6, the British spy agency, later revealed, "intelligence and facts were being fixed around the policy" of military invasion, which Bush had already committed to by 2002 and perhaps even earlier (Danner 2005). The continuous refrain of "mushroom clouds over America" by members of his administration were repeated by the mass media and effectively shaped public opinion in favor of war.

Perhaps even worse than lying is the practice of competing in elections in order to bring down the very democratic political system that makes those elections possible. This was the intention of the French and Italian communist parties for three to four decades after World War II when their strategy was to win seats and refuse to join any coalition in the hope that majority government formation would become impossible and governance unworkable. The eventual result, it was hoped, would be the collapse of liberal democracy and its replacement with a socialist state more to their liking (Sartori 1966).

Elections then are at the core of democracy; they are the mechanism through which the consent of the governed is translated into responsive and accountable government. It is important to note, however, that the presence of elections is no guarantee of the stability and success of democracy itself. To put it simply, "the necessary condition . . . of democratic stability is that political elites must want to make prevailing political arrangements work" (Gunther and Mughan 1993, 301). In other words, elections are central to a healthy democracy, but their existence in and of itself is no guarantee of democracy's success. This is immediately obvious in the case of contemporary electoral authoritarian regimes. With the post-1974 "third wave" of democratization (see Chapter 2), democratic governance norms became necessary for domestic and international legitimacy across the globe. The common response was the introduction of competitive elections to choose a new generation of leaders. Initially, many of these elections could be considered democratic in the sense of being free and fair. Their integrity was quickly subverted, however, by authoritarian leaders reluctant to sacrifice their long-standing prerogatives to the demands of popular sovereignty. The outcome was *electoral authoritarianism*, which describes regimes in which elections are held regularly, which allow for some multiparty competition and produce leaders who then claim to derive their authority to govern from their election victory. In reality, however, this victory is based not on free and fair competition, but on practices like oppressing serious opposition, media censorship, and restricting freedom of assembly and speech (Schedler 2006).

WAIT A MINUTE. **CONSIDER THIS.** Do you accept the argument that democratic elections are not too dissimilar from authoritarian ones in that they offer not a meaningful choice, but a limited choice defined by a governing class that is concerned more with maintaining the political status quo and less with upholding the popular will? Are

Marxists, like Gramsci, correct to argue that elections are essentially games controlled in their own self-interest by oligarchs (the powerful few) and plutocrats (the wealthy), or are democrats like Abraham Lincoln right that elections create government "of the people, by the people, and for the people"?

Having examined the major mechanism of intermediation, or linkage between governors and governed, we now turn to the two principal institutions that drive this mechanism: the political party and the interest group. Both can be found in authoritarian as well as democratic regimes, although, again, they do not function in the same way in each of them. Let us start with the definition of a political party and then proceed to an examination of their political role in the two types of regime.

Political Parties

Political parties are organizations that serve to allow their leaders to win and/or retain political office and power according to the rules and procedures of the society in which they operate. In democracies, for example, power comes with contesting and winning elections, and parties tailor their political strategy above all to this end. As one eminent scholar has put it: "[Political] parties formulate policies in order to win elections, rather than win elections in order to formulate policies" (Downs 1957, 28).

Political parties are pervasive political institutions and, like elections, can be found in different types of regime throughout the world. Moreover, their global presence means that they vary in a large number of important and politically consequential ways. Some, for example, are organized to contest competitive elections, others might not have to fight elections, and still others take part in contests whose outcome is known in advance. Some are built around complex ideologies that transcend their leaders, whereas others are the creatures of the ruling individual or group in a society. Another difference is that some are highly articulated, permanent organizations that reach out to society to educate, inform, and mobilize actual and would-be supporters, whereas others have little life or organizational reach beyond the group or individual at their head. The list could go on, but the important point is that it is this core characteristic of being power-seeking organizations that accounts for their role as the critical linkage institution in the modern world. Parties seek both to control government and to shape public acceptance of this control and, in so doing, they fundamentally shape the nature of the relationship between governors and governed. Let us turn to a closer examination of this relationship, starting once again with authoritarian regimes.

Authoritarian Political Parties and Party Systems

Like elections, political parties are commonly associated in the popular mind with democracy, but are surprisingly common in the nondemocratic world (Gandhi 2008, 39). Indeed, if we think of parties as operating within a system of dynamic interaction with other political actors who also pursue political influence and control, three types of "party system" can be identified in the world of authoritarian political regimes: (1) the no-party system; (2) the one-party system; and (3) the semi-competitive party system. Considerable ideological and institutional variation can be found within each of these categories, but all share the basic characteristic of a ruling group or individual using censorship, manipulation, and repression to promote political passivity and quiescence in the population, thereby consolidating its hold on power.

Usually found in ruling monarchies and military regimes, no-party systems forbid the existence of political parties altogether. Current examples are a number of ruling monarchies in the Middle East, including Saudi Arabia, Jordan, the United Arab Emirates, and the Sultanate of Oman. The banning of political parties in such regimes sends two clear signals. The first is that organized political opposition is unwelcome, albeit for different reasons in monarchies as opposed to military regimes. Monarchies are deeply conservative regimes that base their legitimacy more in custom, tradition, and religion and less in any kind of popular mandate. Military regimes, in contrast, ban opposition because they have often come to power by deposing a civilian (or other military) regime they claim has lost its legitimacy for being corrupt, inefficient and self-serving. The period of military rule is promised to be used to root out corruption, to implement sound government, and eventually to restore civilian rule, perhaps even democracy. Because they promote themselves as "saviors" acting in the national interest, military governments commonly deny the need for organized opposition during this period of national rehabilitation. The second clear signal that the banning of political parties sends is that the ruling group or individual is content with the economic, social, and political status quo and has no desire or plans to reshape society or to engage in any other kind of national reform project. Thus, precisely because the regime has no plans to reach out and mobilize the population behind some reform project that involves change and uncertainty, it has no need of an organization that can help mobilize the people at the same time that it monitors its continuing loyalty. The political party, in other words, holds no value for traditionalist authoritarian regimes with an entrenched status quo. Indeed, if allowed to function, an organized political grouping like a party represents a potential threat in that it risks serving as a pole of attraction around which opposition to, say, economic mismanagement or self-interested monarchical rule and/or abuse of power can potentially crystallize.

The party system most readily associated in the popular mind with political authoritarianism is the one-party system. This is partly because, historically speaking, it has been more common than its no-party counterpart and partly because it has fallen into two highly salient variants: the totalitarian model and the later postcolonial model found largely in Africa. The totalitarian one-party state is rooted in a Marxist-Leninist theory that proclaims the transition from capitalism to socialism to be historically determined, socially just, and therefore inevitable. Further, this transition meets resistance from those who had been the dominant class under capitalism so that members of this class, the bourgeoisie, and members of the newly dominant class, the proletariat, have to be socialized to the values, norms, and practices of their new life under socialism. The communist party plays a key role in managing this transition. Consisting of an elite group of committed and specially selected individuals, it brooks no opposition because its Marxist ideology lays out the path to follow to reach the communist utopia and its job is simply to move society along that path. Labeled by Lenin (1932) as "the vanguard of the proletariat," the communist party functions not to represent the wishes of the newly promoted proletariat, but to impose the will and wisdom of a party leadership that has to be obeyed because to question it is to question the underlying ideology and goals of the communist revolution itself.

As an example of this type of party, the Communist Party of the Soviet Union's (CPSU) role was almost entirely top-down and consisted essentially of "spreading the leadership-dictated gospel" through an orchestrated strategy combining education, indoctrination, mobilization, and – when faced with resistance-coercion. Of the latter, a case in point is the kulaks. These were farmers who, prior to the 1917 revolution, owned their own land and whom Lenin, the first leader of the CPSU, described as "bloodsuckers, vampires, plunderers of the people and profiteers who batten on famine." Doggedly opposed to a collectivization policy that involved the forced expropriation of their land to allow for large-scale agricultural production, they incurred the wrath of the CPSU leadership; hundreds of thousands of them were killed or sent to prison or labor camps as a result (Conquest 1986).

Eventually, and especially under Lenin's successor, Josef Stalin, the CPSU became less an independent, goal-oriented ruling institution and more an instrument of rule at the disposal of the party leader. A similar trend is characteristic of the second common type of one-party system emerging from British and French decolonization, mostly in Africa, in the 1950s and 1960s. The departing colonial powers sought to leave behind functioning democracies, and the nationalist movements that had spearheaded the drive for independence usually came out as winners in the elections that took place. They had little time for democracy and party competition, however, and soon banned all political opposition, arguing, among other things, that competition and democracy (1) were an unacceptable luxury that only exacerbated ethnic and regional divisions that already threatened the new state's integrity, and (2) also detracted from the larger, more pressing and important goal of promoting economic development. In practice, however, this type of single party never sought to penetrate society in the same way that totalitarian parties did. Nor did they have the same ambition to create a new kind of world based on a utopian ideology and redefined set of social relations. Rather, the party rapidly degenerated into becoming the leader's personal vehicle and its primary purpose became to keep him in power. Thus began the African tradition of long-serving dictators. The longest-serving of them all is Omar Bongo, who was president of Gabon for forty-two years until his death in office in 2009. His Gabonese Democratic Party tolerated no opposition until 1990, and even the introduction of multiparty politics in that year did not loosen Bongo's hold on the presidency (Wallechinsky 2006).

The Gabonese example highlights the earlier observation that the presence of elections and multiple parties is not a reliable indicator of successful democratization. Nor does it mean that political parties play a very different a role in semi-competitive systems of authoritarian government to the one they play in single-party regimes. The primary function of the party remains the same: to consolidate the power of the ruling group or individual by promoting political passivity and quiescence in the population at large. What moves states in the direction of a semi-competitive party system is that the authoritarian ruler, as with Omar Bongo in 1990, comes to see that holding elections and allowing other parties to compete in them actually serves his interests. As touched on in the earlier discussion of elections under authoritarianism, there may be any number of reasons for such a decision. It may be, for example, that powerful forces have arisen in society that can no longer be denied a political voice, and attempts must be made to co-opt them and turn them into political allies. Alternatively, it may be that the authoritarian ruler is seeking greater international respectability and acceptance in an effort to win more foreign aid or foreign direct investment from richer countries. Whatever the reason(s), however, the introduction of limited political pluralism is basically an effort to enhance authoritarian legitimacy while sacrificing little or no power. The hope is that the appearance of choice will be as effective in consolidating the legitimacy of authoritarian rule as the reality of it is in democracies.

A good example of this dynamic is modern Egypt. The country's modern political history can be said to have begun with the 1952 military coup that overthrew King Farouk and paved the way for the rise to political power of the charismatic Gamel Abdel Nasser. An Arab socialist, Nasser did not allow political opposition and sought to mobilize the Egyptian public behind his socialist reform drive initially through an organization called the Liberation Rally (1953–1956) and then the National Union (1956–1962). In 1962, he announced the formation of a political party called the Arab Socialist Union (ASU) that was supposed to serve as the supreme authority of the state, but in actuality lacked real authority and served as Nasser's instrument for indoctrinating the people. Egypt remained a one-party state until Nasser's death in 1971 and the ascendance to the presidency of his deputy, Anwar el-Sadat. Following Egypt's defeat in the 1967 and 1973 Arab-Israeli wars, Sadat acknowledged public unrest and reformed the structure of the ASU, at the same time introducing some pluralism into Egypt's political life. Importantly, however, pluralism did not mean new and independent political parties. Rather, it involved no more than establishing three forums within the ASU to represent the right (Liberal Socialist Organization), the center (Egypt Arab Socialist Organization), and the left (National Progressive Unionist Organization).

These forums became political parties in 1976 and were allowed to contest elections. They never won more than a handful of seats and never functioned as meaningful alternatives to the National Democratic Party (NDP) established by Sadat in 1978. The 1976 reforms were not without political consequence, however, for they allowed Islamists, including the Muslim Brotherhood, to start organizing politically, particularly on university campuses. This organization rapidly became Egypt's most important opposition, with the Society of the Muslim Brothers running as independents or through alliances with other political parties and, for example, capturing some 20 percent of the seats in the People's Assembly in 2005. Still, Hosni Mubarak, Sadat's successor in 1981, remained firmly in control of the political process until he was deposed by the mass protests of 2011. There are two main reasons for his longevity. One, the Muslim Brotherhood was a banned organization and was not allowed to form a political party with prerogatives that would help it function as a real alternative to the NDP. Two, his NDP continued to control state resources, to maintain close ties with the state's security forces, and to benefit from an electoral law designed to protect its privileged position. For instance, the registration of political parties was the responsibility of a body controlled by the ruling NDP. In short, authoritarian rule remained intact in Egypt for thirty-five years after the ostensible onset of political pluralism.

Democratic Political Parties and Party Systems

Political parties may exist in many authoritarian regimes today, but their origins as linkage institutions date back well more than 100 years to the advent of political democracy, or the gradual expansion of the franchise beyond the privileged few to virtually all adult men and women beginning around the mid-nineteenth century and culminating more or less by the mid-twentieth century. A key change associated with the spread of the franchise involved the means by which individuals gained membership in national parliaments. Traditionally, it was achieved largely through ascriptive criteria like noble birth, ecclesiastical rank, or wealth and position in a community. Democracy changed all this as the key to holding political power became popular election; the people had won the right to determine who governed them and to pass judgment periodically on their performance in office.

Not everybody got the vote at once. Rather, the franchise was extended gradually to encompass a wider and wider range of people. Its extension got underway in Britain, for example, with the 1832 Reform Act, which increased the size of the electorate by more than 50 percent, but it remained the case that only one in six adult males had the right to vote. Under the prevailing electoral law, possession of this right was determined by property ownership and effectively excluded the working class. This restriction was eased in the second wave of franchise expansion, the 1867 Reform Act. Its major impacts were to increase the size of the electorate close to threefold and to extend the franchise for the first time to male householders in the urban working class. Subsequently, universal male suffrage was granted after World War I and universal female suffrage in 1928.

The calculus of gaining political office had changed dramatically. It was now necessary for aspiring officeholders to appeal beyond a small, select few notables in the constituency to a more diverse, mass audience. In addition, effective election contestation entailed not only educating, informing, and appealing to the interests of the new waves of voters, but also to organizing them for political action, and especially contesting elections. The political party evolved to perform these basic, essentially organizational tasks. Indeed, broadly speaking, two kinds of party emerged with the spread of the franchise: (1) those committed to defending the economic, political, and social status quo against forces of change; and (2) those seeking to redefine this status quo to the advantage of their own supporters. In organizational terms, these parties are commonly classified respectively as "cadre" and "mass" parties and they can be differentiated along two dimensions: organization and ideology (Duverger 1954).

Cadre parties are sometimes referred to alternatively as internally created parties. This is because they were established and nurtured by established parliamentary elites responding to the political assault on their power and privilege by an expanding, urban working class in particular that demanded egalitarian reform in virtually all spheres of public life. "An internally created political party is one that emerges gradually from the activities of the legislators themselves. As the need for creating legislative blocs and of assuring the re-election of members of these blocs is increasingly felt, political organization at the local level or in the electoral constituency occur" (LaPalombara and Weiner 1966, 9). Examples of this party type are the Democratic and Republican parties in the United States and the Conservative and Liberal parties in Australia, Britain, and Canada. All share the important characteristic that the party organization outside the parliament, and especially in the constituencies, has always willingly subordinated itself to the parliamentary party and been acceptant of the ultimate authority of its leader.

The contrasting party type is the mass, or externally created, party and it is labeled as such because it originated outside parliament with the specific purpose of challenging and extracting political reforms, especially the right to vote, from the established ruling class. Created to assault the "citadels of power," mass parties differed organizationally as well as ideologically from their cadre counterparts. In Duverger's words, "they tend to be more centralized . . . more ideologically coherent and disciplined, less subject to influence from the legislative contingents of the parties, and generally less willing to ascribe major importance or to be deferential toward parliament" (cited in LaPalombara and Weiner 1966, 10). Perhaps the best examples of externally created parties are the Labour, Social Democratic, and Socialist parties that emerged in Western Europe around the turn of the twentieth century.

As it turned out, however, the differences between the two types of party started to erode after the struggle for universal suffrage heated up. The main force for change was the externally created party that saw organization and discipline as being essential to success in their battle for economic and political rights. Their emergence and rapid growth quickly led internally created parties to adopt these same two characteristics (i.e., organization and discipline) in their efforts to fend off the sustained and aggressive challenge to their hegemony. Thus, for example, they set up an equally extensive, if more subordinate, extra-parliamentary party organization at the local level and, later, equally embraced the need for party discipline in the parliament, voting as a single, coherent unit in the parliamentary division lobbies. At the same time, however, the legislative wings of externally created parties soon started to mimic their internally created counterparts, seeking to establish their preeminence in the party hierarchy once parliamentary representation had been achieved and reelection become as an overriding party goal. The parliamentary representatives of externally created parties were those who had been elected to office and they reasoned that democratic accountability required them to be seen as being in control of party policy if they were to retain the confidence of the voters who had put them there (Epstein 1967).

Thus, competing in the same electorate under the same rules, the imperative to win elections encouraged organizational convergence between mass and cadre parties. The same logic encouraged ideological convergence as well, but let us look first at parties' ideological origins.

Cleavages and Parties

But where do parties come from and what accounts for the scope of their electoral reach – that is, whether they are national or regional in structure and organization? With regard to electoral reach, the crucial variable would seem to be the location of economic and political power in society. National parties arise when this power rests with the central government, whereas regional parties flourish when it gravitates downward to subnational levels of government (Chhibber and Kollman 2004). More attention has been paid, however, to the origins of political parties, and the dominant view is that these are to be found in the pattern of social conflict, or social cleavages, that divided societies during their democratic awakening and that, as a result, helped shape lasting party divisions and voting behavior. In their seminal essay, Lipset and Rokkan (1967) argue that twentieth-century democratic party systems are the political product of the earlier National and Industrial Revolutions. The National Revolution began in France with the 1789 revolution and encompassed the struggles involved in state building, and two social cleavages proved to be of particular long-term political relevance: center-periphery conflict and church-state tensions. The former refers to the conflict between the core nation builders at the center (southeast England, for example) and ethnic, linguistic, or religious groups often located in the peripheries and threatened with absorption into the nation-building group's language and culture (Scotland and Wales in Britain, for example). The church-state cleavage in turn pitted states intent on establishing sovereignty within their territories against a Catholic Church that sought to retain historic corporate rights transcending state boundaries. Over time, however, this confessional divide (Catholic versus Protestant) subsided in salience and church-state, or clerical-anticlerical, tensions became the main source of religious division as issues like the role of the church in the education of the young became a source of contention. In the Netherlands, for example, Catholic and Protestant religious groups worked together from the end of the nineteenth century to promote their shared interest in the state funding of religious schools. They even presented a common list at the 1977 general election under the name Christian Democratic Appeal. Across Western Europe, resistance to such clerical groups came from anti-clericals who wanted to remove the church's political influence and whose demands ranged from no state funding for religious schools to the complete separation of church and state.

The Industrial Revolution got underway in the late eighteenth century and continued through the nineteenth century. It too generated two principal cleavages. These pitted rural interests (primarily industry, including agriculture) against urban industry on the one hand and owners and employers against workers on the other.

These two revolutions had two profound and related consequences for the pattern of democratic politics in Western Europe. First, they put in place the principal ideological divides along which national populations would cleave and parties form. Second, they played a prominent role in shaping the contours of national party systems. We will now examine each of these developments in turn.

A cleavage is a division pitting competing social groups against each other and providing each of them with a collective identity and a permanent organizational presence in society. The National and Industrial Revolutions produced four main types of party in Western Europe. From the center-periphery conflict in the former came various regional parties with a distinct ethnic or linguistic basis (e.g., the Scottish National party in Britain and various Flemish nationalist parties in Belgium). The National Revolution's church-state conflict produced mainly Catholic and Christian Democratic religious parties (e.g., the Austrian People's Party and the Swiss Catholic Party). The Industrial Revolution came later and encompassed two cleavages: urban-rural and employer-worker. The former gave rise to such agrarian and peasant parties as the Finnish Centre Party and the Australian Country (now National) Party. The products of the class conflict between workers and employers are perhaps the best-known political parties, and prominent among these are the British Labour Party, the French Socialist Party, and German Social Democratic Party. Of these four cleavages, social class and religion have proved to be the most encompassing and resilient, not least because they have taken organizational forms other than political parties, including churches, trade unions, and employer associations, all of which seek to influence the actions, ideology, and policy pursuits of parties to their own advantage.

Many parties that emerged in the early days of the franchise expansion in Western Europe persist to this day, and an important reason for their resilience is their continuous adaptation to changing circumstances, and particularly their efforts to extend their appeal beyond the cleavage groupings that originally spawned them. Catholic parties are a good example. With the weakening of confessional tensions over the course of the twentieth century, they sought power and influence by diluting their identity as parties of religious defense in favor of becoming reformist parties of the center-right whose appeal extended to non-Catholic members of the working class. Their strategy was essentially to become Christian Democratic in name and social democratic in policy advocacy. A good case in point is the post-World War II transformation of Germany's prewar Catholic party, which became known as the Christian Democratic Union (CDU) after the war and began to champion generous welfare provision – a stance they described as "capitalism with a human face." The CDU has regularly been in and out of government ever since (Gehler and Kaiser 2004).

Class parties followed a similar evolutionary pattern as Western European societies developed economically and the notion of class warfare became less meaningful to their increasingly affluent working-class supporters. The essence of this change was that left-wing parties moderated, or even abandoned, their Marxist rhetoric and committed themselves unequivocally to achieving what remained of their traditionally left-wing political ideology and goals through parliamentary means. The German Social Democratic Party is a good example of this evolution, as it dropped Marxism and the class struggle from its program in 1959 and then formed a "grand coalition" with the CDU to take part in governing postwar Germany for the first time in 1966.

The path was thus cleared for the emergence of the catch-all party type, which represents the negation of politics based on cleavage groups insofar as the aim of such parties is to win elections by appealing to a wide variety of interests rather than to the demands and interests of well-defined social groups. It "exchange(s) effectiveness in depth for a wider audience and more immediate electoral success" (Kircheimer 1966, 184). Emphasizing their search for a broader appeal, these parties became less dependent on traditional party mechanisms, like local party members and interest organization ties with the likes of unions to achieve their electoral goals. Instead, they turned to a greater reliance on the mass media and political professionals, like pollsters and media consultants. As the importance of party members and local party organizations declined, that of party leaders went up as they became more and more the public face of the party in an age when political communications increasingly took place through the medium of television (Mughan 2000).

WAIT A MINUTE. **CONSIDER THIS.** Otto Kircheimer, the scholar associated with the idea of catch-all parties, was actually troubled by their emergence. He felt, among other things, that democratic representation would be damaged if a party spoke for "everyone" rather than specific cleavages and interests. By the same token, he reasoned that the role of political opposition in a democracy – namely to advance alternative solutions – would deteriorate if all parties began to look and speak alike. What do you think? Consider the political party you support. Does it represent specific cleavages and interests, or does it represent "everyone"? Is this good or bad for democracy?

Cleavages have proved important not only for the patterns of social conflict that they embody, but also for the number of such conflicts that have received political expression in, and thereby shaped, national party systems. Two types of "cleavage constellations" can be identified: homogeneous and heterogeneous (Caramani 2004). The first is characterized by the presence of one predominant political cleavage, usually class, and political life is dominated by competition between a working-class party and a middle-class party. A well-known example is Britain where, until the late 1960s, the conventional wisdom was that "(c)lass is the basis of British party politics; all else is embellishment and detail" (Pulzer 1967, 98). Heterogeneous constellations, in contrast, have multiple cleavages that are expressed in the political party system. Examples of such plural democracies are Belgium, Canada, South Africa, and Switzerland, where parties based on class, religious, and language (ethnic) group loyalties compete for the popular vote (Lijphart 1979). The cleavage structures of individual societies, in other words, play an important role in shaping their party systems, particularly the number of parties in them.

The striking feature of this relationship between cleavage structures and party systems is that it has remained remarkably stable over time. The names of individual parties may have changed and smaller parties may have come and gone, but by and large, the party systems of Western Europe today continue to mirror the political conflict patterns that gave rise to them early in the twentieth century. This stability was first noted in Lipset and Rokkan's famous "freezing hypothesis": "(T)he party systems of the 1960s reflect, with few but significant exceptions, the cleavage structures of the 1920s" (Lipset and Rokkan 1967, 50). It has been confirmed more recently in a study of change in the inter-party distribution of the vote from one election to the next – otherwise called electoral volatility – over the period between 1885 and 1985 (Bartolini and Mair 1990). Their analysis of volatility patterns found them stable over time and concluded that there was little reason to believe that the continent's party systems had been redefined by new cleavages.

Its success in explaining the shape of Western European party systems notwithstanding, the cleavage model has not performed as well in explaining party system formation and development in the new democracies of Eastern Europe that emerged with the collapse of the communist bloc and the Soviet Union. An important reason is that cleavage structures in Eastern Europe were not as clearly crystallized because the communist political authorities there had long repressed the expression of differences in societies that they held to be well on their way to achieving an egalitarian, harmonious social order. With cleavages in these societies being less clearly articulated and well developed, they were not as able to shape the organizational structure and ideology of the political parties that emerged during the transition to democracy. Indeed, partly because of the availability of advanced electronic communications technologies that could substitute for extra-parliamentary organization, the parties that were formed generally resembled the loosely organized catch-all party type far more than the mass or cadre types whose interaction had done so much to shape Western European party system development. Eastern European parties, in other words, tended to "jump" a developmental stage and, as a result, to be less ideological, more leader-centered, and more pragmatic in adopting strategies that consolidated their own existence and promoted party system stability (Sitter 2002).

The Continuing Centrality of Parties

Following this kind of pattern of adaptation to a social, economic, and technological environment that has changed greatly over the course of the twentieth and twenty-first centuries, parties in established democracies have evolved in the way they perform their linkage function. They no longer need to educate newly enfranchised citizens to the norms and procedures of democracy, for example. Nor do they play the same overwhelmingly important role in disseminating information to voters and mobilizing their support at election time. In an age of highly sophisticated communications technologies, they now share this role with television, the Internet, and other forms of mass communication. Nonetheless, they continue to perform functions that make them central to the operation of modern democracies. In the often quoted words of the scholar E. E. Schattschneider (1942, 1): "Political parties created democracy, and . . . modern democracy is unthinkable save in terms of parties."

This continuing centrality is evident in the two basic functions they perform, which are (1) to organize voters and (2) to organize governments. Let us start with voters. Parties are important to voters in a number of ways. One, they serve as a reference point that makes a complex political world manageable by allowing voters to align themselves with a party and interpret the political world through the ideological lens and political cues that this identification provides. Two, they mobilize voters at election time partly by aggregating diverse interests into manifestos, or platforms, among which voters can choose, and partly by working to get out the vote through knocking on doors and organizing advertising and publicity campaigns. Finally, parties make the voice of voters heard in the governance process by harnessing the power of government to deliver on the promises they made to win election to office. As for their role in government, parties give structure to the governance process. They recruit the candidates who run for office and socialize them into the ways of the party and the political world in which it operates. Some of these candidates eventually become elected officials and even members of governments formed by successful parties. When party leaders become government officials (or ministers), they oversee the permanent bureaucracy with a view to ensuring that policies are implemented in a manner consistent with the intentions of a government responding to electoral incentives and pressures. Finally, parties organize the work of parliaments. Virtually all parliamentarians across the democratic world are elected under a party label, caucus with others of the same, or similar, label, and coordinate their actions in support of, or opposition to, the political executive that enjoys primary responsibility for lawmaking. In short, by simultaneously organizing and linking governors and governed in the cut-and-thrust of democratic politics, parties allow for the latter's institutionalized representation in the lawmaking process.

Interest Groups

Interest groups are the second major linkage institution to be found in both authoritarian and democratic regimes. Individuals form groups to achieve a huge variety of shared goals, including, for example, sports clubs, professional associations, labor unions, and environmental advocacy groups. Such groups become interest groups when, individually or in cooperation with like-minded groups, they take action to influence the content of public policy in their own favor. An interest group, in other words, can be defined as any formally organized association of individuals or groups that attempts to influence government decisions so as to benefit themselves or their larger causes. Based on their practice of bringing pressure on government to enact policy with certain content, these groups are sometimes called pressure groups. Another name for them is lobby groups, which derives from the tradition of group representatives meeting with politicians in the lobby of the British Parliament; visitors are not allowed to enter deeper into the building without being escorted.

Interest groups are like political parties in that they represent their members and supporters in the lawmaking process by promoting and protecting their interests. They are unlike political parties, however, in three important respects. First, not seeking to win elections, they generally do not strive to appeal broadly. Instead, they limit their attention to well-defined segments of the population. An employer's association, for example, is unconcerned about winning support from employees in the workforce, whereas an environmental advocacy group may even welcome a hostile reaction from the coal industry for the heightened sense of unity and determination it elicits among its members. Second, unlike parties, interest groups do not seek to influence the whole range of government policy by themselves becoming the government. Rather, their more limited goal is to wield influence in the relatively small number of policy areas that impinge directly on the concerns of their members and supporters. Third, because both serve as mechanisms linking governors and governed, political parties and interest groups are usually found in authoritarian as well as democratic regimes. This is not always the case, however. We have seen that a number of authoritarian regimes ban political parties for fear of their serving as poles around which political opposition might organize, but such a ban does not always apply to interest groups as well. Saudi Arabia, for instance, bans political parties but encourages professional associations for the country's journalists, lawyers, and teachers. A Human Rights Association can even be found there. The explanation of this difference is that interest groups stand in a different relationship to the governance process than do political parties. Let us examine this relationship in the context of authoritarian regimes first.

Interest Groups: Authoritarian Regimes

The term "interest group" is found most commonly in the study of the governance of democratic states where they are seen as organized, autonomous entities that enjoy the right to define their own self-interest and to pursue it vis-à-vis governments. It is a term that is also commonly found in the study of authoritarian regimes where a very different picture of them prevails. One study of communist interest groups concludes, for example, that "political groups in the Soviet Union are seldom organized, and *if* (emphasis in original) organized, are dominated by functionaries who are usually not elected and not responsive to the wishes of their constituents" (Skilling 1971, 382). Given this authoritarian aversion to organized groups independent of the state, the question has been raised of whether it is a misnomer to speak of interest groups when studying associational activity in this type of regime. Responding affirmatively to this question, one suggestion is that their political role is more accurately characterized by the label "administered mass organizations" (AMOs), which can be defined as "mass civilian organization[s] created and managed by a political regime to implement public policy" (Kasza 1995, 7).

This definition is valuable for highlighting once again the predominantly top-down nature of the pattern of governor-governed interactions under authoritarianism. AMOs are not part of the ruling group, but are created by it for its own purposes. Important among these purposes are to co-opt and stifle the emergence of autonomous interest groups and political parties, to control the population in the regime's interest, and to mobilize resources for the achievement of the goals that it sets. Regime-created political parties perform similar functions, but they are notable for also participating in national policy making and serving as a channel of recruitment to political office, no matter how limited their influence on outcomes in these areas. AMOs, in contrast, are separate from the formal governing structure and their role is to help the ruling group control society at the same time as contributing to the realization of whatever political agenda it might have. The relationship is one of control and bears no hint of equality.

The degree of control to which AMOs are subject varies with the ideological clarity of the regime and its degree of organization and penetration of society. An entity with the organizational articulation of the Communist Party of the Soviet Union, for example, was able to control AMOs like its industrial unions or youth groups far more tightly than African single-party or dictatorial regimes could. But even highly effective control does not mean a complete lack of AMO influence and impact on political and social outcomes. Rather, it means simply that any influence or impact that they might have falls within parameters set and maintained by their authoritarian political masters. The key to understanding this hierarchy is that these rulers may place their primary emphasis on keeping themselves in power, but they might also pursue other, secondary goals that further this end and also serve the country more generally. "Asian Tigers" like South Korea and Taiwan, for example, pursued an aggressive economic development program in their pre-democratic days. Similarly, China's communist government has encouraged the formation of a large number of organizations that can perform useful socioeconomic functions. This host of associations includes, among others, trade and business associations, community and social welfare organizations, and scholarly societies.

There is little evidence, however, that these creations of the ruling group enjoy "associational autonomy or associational contestation vis-à-vis the state" (Foster 2001, 98). Nor is it clear that all of them are designed explicitly to strengthen the authoritarian state by cementing the political position of its rulers. Rather, their role is more commonly to help the ruling communist party carry out its plans and projects for society, and to the extent they are successful, the state becomes legitimate in the eyes of the population and is strengthened indirectly, making it more stable and deeply entrenched.

The ironic conclusion follows that associational activity is not inimical to successful authoritarian rule. Indeed, the opposite can be the case. A common belief is that interest groups strengthen democracy by bringing governors and governed together more regularly and in a greater number of policy arenas, thereby improving the representation of the latter in the making of laws. While perhaps inadvertently, AMOs appear able to do the same to some degree for authoritarianism.

Interest Groups: Democratic Regimes

Interest groups operating in democracies differ in that they are independent of the state, not creatures of it. Democratic regimes can surely regulate some of the activities of organized interests; they may, for example, curb the right of labor unions to strike or the lending activities of financial institutions. But as long as groups act within the law, they place few limits on their specifically political – that is, lobbying – activities. A rare exception to this rule is limits on monetary contributions donated to election campaigns in the United States, although indirect spending by interest groups and individuals on parties, issue advocacy, and candidate advertising independent of party organizations is less heavily regulated.

Four stages can be identified in the evolution of the modern interest group system in the democratic world, and these largely reflect patterns of industrialization, their effects on society, and the associational response to these effects (Thomas 1993, 12). In a preindustrial phase lasting from about the 1830s to 1870s, associational life consisted mainly of middle-class charitable organizations, including church groups, ministering to the poor, organizations seeking expansion of the franchise, and the like. Class came into the picture during the period of intense industrialization that stretched from the 1860s to the early 1900s, and producer groups, working-class labor unions and middle-class employers' associations emerged on the political scene. Agricultural groups were also active at this time, advocating for rural interests. The third stage lasted from about 1920 until the 1950s and witnessed the emergence of groups representing the professions – for example, teachers and doctors – as well as advocacy groups promoting various causes and whose membership was less defined than in the past by economic self-interest. These included arts and veterans groups. The final stage continues to this day and reflects the concerns of a postindustrial era. Groups have emerged that are not rooted in economic interests, but rather advocate for quality-of-life issues like the environment, civil and minority rights, and sexual freedoms. The upshot of this pattern of development is that there has been a steady increase in the number of interest groups and the diversity of the causes and audiences they protect and promote. The interest group universe, in other words, has expanded and become more plural.

However, it is their interaction with government in the making of policy, not their number or character, that makes interest groups politically important. But why should governments allow groups that often represent minority interests to influence their policy deliberations, and what form does this involvement take? Let us address the "why" question first.

Governments have a number of reasons for accommodating interest groups. Most importantly, governments accept that they are entitled to be involved in the political process. They speak for citizens, and in democracies, citizens have a right – indeed, are encouraged – to engage in political life beyond mere participation in elections. When they do, the basic democratic principles of representation, responsiveness, and accountability are strengthened. Moreover, as long as all citizens enjoy this right, governments cannot legitimately ignore those citizens or their representatives who choose to exercise it between elections simply because other members of society may choose not to do so. Another reason for including interest groups in policy making is that their participation can improve the quality of both deliberations and outcomes. Specialist groups bring experience, evidence, expertise, and insight to discussions of, say, agricultural, nuclear regulation, or drug use policy, and the decisions that governments make can be the better for this input. As an example, it is the pharmaceutical companies themselves that conduct the experiments on which the U.S. Food and Drug Administration makes its decisions about the safety and availability to the general public of potentially dangerous drugs designed to treat ailments like heartburn, arthritis, and depression.

But how precisely do governments and interest groups interact in the democratic political process? Two models predominate in the political science literature, usually labeled *pluralism* and *corporatism*. The pluralist model enjoys special currency in the United States with its dispersion of lawmaking power over several branches and levels of government, whereas the corporatist model has been more popular in Europe where this power tends to be more heavily concentrated in a small number of political institutions and actors. Let us turn to the pluralism model first.

Pluralism is a doctrine that holds interest groups to lie at the heart of democracy. Its basic principles are:

- Individuals have the right to form groups and all groups (except those forbidden by law) have the right to involve themselves in the lawmaking process in pursuit of political goals.
- All significant interests in society will eventually form groups and become politically active in defense and promotion of their interests.
- The lawmaking arena thus becomes a marketplace to which all groups enjoy equal access and in which competition for influence over public policy is more or less perfect.
- No one group or small number of groups is able consistently to impose its views on other groups over the range of public policy partly because each group limits itself to its own area(s) of interest (banking, education, the environment, for example) and partly because the government acts as arbiter and "honest broker" in mediating the interplay of interests.

Thus, pluralism claims that interest group activity enhances democracy because everybody is free to organize into groups to advance and protect their interests, and all groups are equal in a political marketplace operating under the watchful eye of a neutral government that ensures fair play. The reality is less utopian, however, because four major departures from the assumption of group equality are evident when pluralism is examined in practice. First, not all citizens are equally likely to form groups intended to compete in the political marketplace. Early on, the American political scientist E. E. Schattschneider (1960, 35) noted wryly that "the flaw in the pluralist heaven is that the heavenly chorus sings with a strong upper-class accent." Second, different groups have different resources at their disposal; business groups, for example, are usually better organized and better financed than advocacy groups for the poor or the environment, and such disparities can easily translate into unequal policy influence. Third, governments are not always neutral in arbitrating group differences and conflicts. Some groups enjoy easier access to, and a more sympathetic ear from, government for a number of reasons. Perhaps they are ideologically similar so that, for example, labor unions tend to be favored by parties of the left and kept at a distance by parties of the right. Alternatively, a government may favor some groups over others because it is more dependent on them for the realization of its political agenda or the smooth functioning of society. In a dispute over public spending cuts, for example, governments will usually favor employer interests over those of welfare recipients or the artistic community. Fourth, groups advocating radical change are among those kept at a distance, or even blacklisted, by governments so that pluralist conflict ends up representing no more than a limited selection of the full range of political options open to a society, thereby strengthening the economic, social, and political status quo.

The reality of unequal access to government is explicitly recognized and built into the second major model of interest group influence on public policy: corporatism. This model shares with pluralism the view that interest groups are legitimate players in the democratic political process and, as such, warrant direct access to public policy makers. It differs, however, in how this access is granted and in taking the form of only a few powerful interest groups being invited into a direct partnership with the government in the making of policy. The roots of this arrangement lie in the state corporatism of authoritarian regimes of the late nineteenth century and later found in Franco's Spain, Mussolini's Italy, and Hitler's Germany. State corporatism saw society as a unified and hierarchical body in which the government's role is to orchestrate the activities of special interests like business and labor so as to promote a public interest that it itself defines. Democratic corporatism retains these essential features with the exception that the relationship between the government and the interest groups is voluntary and contains no element of coercion. The major interest groups are represented in their interactions with government by their peak associations, which are single organizations formed by like-minded interest groups so as to be able to promote their shared interests vis-à-vis government more effectively. The peak associations for industry and labor in Britain, for example, are the Confederation of British Industry and the Trades Union Congress, respectively. Such associations derive their policy influence (1) from being members of deliberative institutions like ministerial committees and advisory boards and (2) from being able to assure governments that their membership will accept the policy decision to which they have been party. In some cases, corporatism is taken a step further by institutionalizing the representation of functional interest groups in the national legislature. Thus, the Austrian parliament has chambers of representation for business, labor, and agriculture, whereas the Senate in Ireland is composed of representatives from five distinct social interests: agriculture and fishing, labor, industry and commerce, public administration, and language, culture, and literature.

Pluralist and corporatist interest group systems have elements in common; for example, both institutionalize the consultation of interest groups and allow for their formal representation on policy deliberation committees within the bureaucracy. The essential difference between them lies in the intensity and intimacy of the group-government relationship, and it is best to think of individual countries as lying on a pluralist-corporatist continuum. The highly pluralist United States would lie at one end of the continuum, whereas countries combining elements of both, like Belgium, Britain, and France, would be found toward the middle of the continuum, and the Scandinavian countries, Austria, Germany, and Switzerland toward its corporatist end.

Expertise, access, and acceptability, then, are three important sources of interest group policy influence in democratic regimes. What other factors might help account for variation in the amount of influence that individual groups enjoy? This question is difficult to answer conclusively because it is very difficult to measure influence directly, but a number of such factors suggest themselves. The *size* of a group will likely have some bearing on its influence if only because sheer numbers are a source of legitimacy in the democratic political calculus. Moreover, size will be particularly important when it is coupled with *density* of membership, or the proportion of the eligible membership who are actually members of the group in question. The higher this proportion, the greater will be the group's legitimacy because its claim to be speaking for the whole group is more credible. In addition, its blackmail potential will be greater if it threatens to resort to direct action out of frustration with the government's perceived failure to listen to its demands. If a prison warders union threatens a strike, for example, its threat will ring hollow if it counts only a minority of all wardens in its membership. *Financial resources* are a similarly quantifiable indicator of influence. These are needed to sustain the kind of permanent organization that is essential to successful lobbying. Money buys expertise, publicity, sustained pressure, and, in the case of campaign contributions, the goodwill of politicians – all of which are important ingredients of successful policy influence. It also allows groups to undertake punitive action when adversaries fail to accede to their demands. Labor unions, for example, can compensate workers who go on strike for lost wages, just as employers can dig deep into their reserve funds and forsake short-term profits in the hope that breaking this same strike will ensure higher profits in the future. A less tangible and quantifiable source of interest group policy influence is *quality of leadership*. Good leaders set realistic goals and devise sound strategies for achieving them, maintain good relations with their counterparts in government and other organizations, and ensure that their members have realistic expectations of what can be delivered in policy terms. To fall short in any of these areas risks a diminished stature that could translate into less influence for the group as a whole.

The disturbing conclusion to be drawn from this survey of interest group systems in democratic regimes is that groups and the influence they wield are characterized above all by inequality. This conclusion runs counter to the fundamental tenet, encapsulated in the aphorism "one person, one vote, one value," that political equality is the hallmark of democratic government. The million-dollar question, therefore, is whether interest groups add to, or detract from, the democratic political process.

There is a number of ways in which interest groups can be argued to enhance democracy. First, for voters, they supplement electoral democracy by giving individuals the chance to participate in political life between elections that are held only once every several years. In so doing, they enable governments to maintain regular contact with at least some elements of public opinion. A related consideration is that, especially in majoritarian systems of government, associational activity can give political voice to permanent minority groups and to groups that happened to support the losing side in the last election. They are, in other words, alternative channels of representation to the political party. As such, they stimulate the kind of political discussion and debate that makes for a better-educated and informed electorate, which in turn helps keep governments more informed, responsible, and accountable for their actions. Interest groups can also be argued to improve the quality of government outputs by widening the range of opinions heard during the design phase of the policy-making process and providing technical expertise and practical advice. In exchange for their input into the making of policy, they often play a key role in the smooth, efficient, and effective implementation of public policy. The fact, for example, that their peak association, the British Medical Association, was among the chief architects of the at-the-time controversial postwar National Health Care system meant that British doctors found it more difficult to refuse cooperation with it once introduced (Eckstein 1960).

But just as it is often argued that interest groups enhance democracy, the counterargument that they detract from is also common. For a start, they exacerbate political inequality and concentrate power by strengthening the voice of the well organized and well resourced in society, usually the already wealthy and privileged. In addition, because they are not popularly elected, interest groups are not accountable to the broader public for their actions and influence; they exercise power without responsibility. Moreover, to the extent that group leaders are rarely elected, they are not even accountable to their own members whose views, therefore, they may or may not represent in to government. A third criticism is that they undermine democracy because (1) they bypass the representation mechanisms built into the legislative process, and (2) their actions promote a closed and secretive policy-making process that is removed from public scrutiny. Finally, interest groups are so numerous and diverse in their goals that the promotion and protection of vested interests can stalemate governments, making it difficult for them to formulate and implement policy initiatives that are adequate to meet the nation's needs. Olson (1982), for example, argues that the accumulation of interest groups in a democratic society may lead to its economic stagnation as groups representing small numbers of firms in oligopolistic industries promote monopolistic or protectionist legislation that damages the broader economy and the country. He terms this state of affairs *"institutional sclerosis."*

*W**AIT A MINUTE.* **CONSIDER THIS.** Do interest groups facilitate or debilitate democracy? Which argument do you find convincing? Would democracy be better off without them? Can this possibility even be imagined?

CONCLUSION

This chapter has explored how governors and the governed in both authoritarian and democratic regimes are linked by way of elections, parties, and interest groups. It is worth reiterating at this point, however, that governments are handmaidens of the state; their role is, above all, to "steer the ship of state" by governing wisely and making decisions that consolidate and enhance its legitimacy in the eyes of its people. But whether they operate in authoritarian or democratic governance frameworks, not all governments succeed in this task. We have seen that states have commonly experienced internal insurrection, succumbed to foreign invasion, and, in some cases, have even gone out of existence, like the USSR, Yugoslavia, and Czechoslovakia in modern times. Failures of these kinds occur because governments have not proved equal to the problems they have been called on to confront, and the integrity of the state has been the casualty in the sense that its sovereignty has been brought into question. Symptoms of a state's weakened sovereignty include inability to protect and control borders, loss of legitimacy in the eyes of (usually ethnically defined) sections of its population, inability to exercise control over portions of its own territory, and, at the extreme, failure to guarantee its continued existence.

Thus, a basic truism of political life is that the simple existence of a state does not guarantee its sovereignty. The attributes of statehood are not set in stone, but are continuously under threat from political forces arising within states' own borders or within the international system in which they operate. The job of government is to counter these forces, but what form do they take? We now turn to answer this question by examining some of the major challenges that confront states in the contemporary world. These are: (1) globalization; (2) ethnic nationalism; (3) terrorism; and (4) organized crime. The next chapter examines how globalization is changing the character of the modern state, some would even say hastening its demise.

6 Globalization

Wherever you are in the world at this moment, look at the products that populate your immediate surroundings. From where did they all come? As I survey my home office, I notice that the table I sit at was manufactured in China, as was the lamp that lights my workstation. The tablecloth on my table was woven in India, and so was the rug that covers my floor. While my coffee mug was made in Greenbush, New York, my shirt comes from Bangladesh, my pants from Mexico, some of my novels from Argentina and some of my music from Trinidad. Thousands of different workers living in numerous countries have produced and shipped the products that fill my immediate space. Even though I live in a small, quiet, relatively insular community, global forces have shaped what I wear, what I consume, how I work, and how I entertain myself. What is more, they are doing so increasingly and this incursion of the global on the local is what we refer to as globalization.

The starting point for understanding globalization is the everyday observation that people, goods, money, and ideas have moved across geographical distances since humankind began to trade. The entrepreneurial search for new markets, the development of trade routes, and the gradual expansion of the number and variety of goods bought and sold across distances all contributed to a process whereby different peoples and cultures were brought into closer and closer economic, cultural, and political contact. Although the term "globalization" has only entered the English language in recent decades, the integration and mutual dependency of peoples that constitute its essence are (1) as old as human civilization and (2) the product of interactions that include commerce, warfare and invasion, intermarriage, and migration from place of birth. Seen in this light, a useful definition of this phenomenon is the "proliferation of worldwide economic, social, and cultural networks, and people's dependence on these global networks for prosperity and security" (Mansbach 2000). People's lives and daily experiences, in other words, are broadened as they find themselves increasingly subject to people, ideas, food, information, and entertainment from territories more or less distant from their own. Life experiences and social relations become "*deterritorialized*" (Scholte 2005). This process has been neither smooth nor linear, however. Rather, it has been shaped at different times by different combinations of economic expansionism, technological advance, and political ambition (Bordo et al. 2003; Chanda 2007).

Globalization then entails an erosion of the importance of state boundaries in the international system; where there were once barriers, there are now bridges to the free flow of goods, services, people, ideas, culture, and so on. It has not been a politically neutral process of change, however. By eroding barriers, globalization presents a challenge to state sovereignty. Part of this challenge is the result of states' own actions and decisions. For example, in choosing to join avowedly free trade organizations like the European Union (EU) or the North American Free Trade Association (NAFTA), states sacrifice their ability to impose import quotas and tariffs on competitors to protect domestic industry. Moreover, accompanying the free flow of consumer goods is the free flow of investment capital. Every day, trillions of dollars race around the globe in search of investment opportunities in stock, bonds, and currency markets. When state control over the movement of goods and capital in and out of their national economies begins to erode, a substantial dimension of traditional state power is the casualty. According to one observer, "there is no doubt that these measures represent an expansion of the rights of private enterprise vis-à-vis government. The question is: Is this a good thing?" (DePalma 2001).

This chapter introduces students to some of the more important facets of the relationship between globalization and state sovereignty. To highlight that globalization is a matter of choice and not economic inevitability, it starts by tracing its up-and-down trajectory over the last several centuries. It then identifies and defines the three main dimensions of globalization: economic, political, and cultural. We finish by examining not only major challenges that snowballing globalization poses to state sovereignty, but also how states have responded to them.

■ BACKGROUND TO GLOBALIZATION

Globalization has its roots in international trade and, as such, goes back deep into human history. At first, the trade involved was overland and small in scale, but it slowly expanded territorially to involve larger and larger numbers of people. The classic example is the Silk Road that began with an internal silk trade in China around 200 BCE and ended up passing through India and progressing as far the Roman Empire in Europe, a distance of approximately 7,000 miles. It was a trade route that grew slowly because the major means of transportation was the pack animal, and traders were frequently subject to predatory attacks along the way. Nonetheless, trading partners were inevitably introduced to alien goods, religions, and cultures. Silk, for example, was traded for medicines, perfumes, precious stones and metals, and even slaves. Foreign merchants in turn established a presence in China, and Buddhism spread to there from India.

Then, starting in the seventeenth century, international trade assumed a different scale with the expansion of Western European power, influence, and dominion into Asia, Africa, Latin America, and the Caribbean. European expansionism and the associated spread of the capitalist economic system was facilitated by faster and better ships and encouraged by the more powerful of the continent's newly formed states, most prominently Britain and France. Its goals included conquest and empire, economic profit, opening up new trade routes, providing slaves for the labor-intensive plantations that were opening up in the sparsely populated New World, and converting "heathen" peoples to Christianity. Over time, the outcome was the unprecedented incorporation of the New World into an international economy dominated by Europe, and organized for its benefit. An important mechanism of incorporation was colonialism, which was a successful enterprise because of Europe's superior weapons technology, sea power, and commercial prowess and was attractive because it held out the promise of new lands, raw materials, cheap labor, and export markets for surplus goods produced in the factories of the colonial masters. The nature of this relationship is strikingly conveyed by the African slave trade, which was but one leg of a highly efficient trading triangle. Ships containing goods such as guns, cloth, and household implements would sail from Europe to West Africa. There, Africans would be either forcibly abducted or bought in exchange for these goods. The ships would then sail to the Caribbean or coasts of North or South America and the Africans sold as slaves for cash. This cash would then be used to purchase the products of the plantations and mines in the New World, which would be brought back for sale in Europe. But in shaping the New World, Europe was simultaneously influenced by it economically and culturally. Along with profits from overseas ventures and investments, it experienced an influx of new

TABLE 6.1 The four waves of globalization

Time period	Triggers	Some manifestations
1870–1914	Reduction in transport costs and falling trade barriers; primary commodities boom; improved communications technology	Mass emigration from Europe to Australasia and Americas; European economic ascendancy
1914–1945	Outbreak of World War I; Great Depression; outbreak of World War II	Economic globalization retreats; resurgence of protectionism; mass migration plummets
1945–1980	End of World War II; reassertion of free trade in the West; less developed countries remain essentially commodity suppliers	European postwar recovery; trade between Western countries rebounds; capital and migration flows lag behind
1980–current day	Spread of free-trade ethos; less developed world becomes integrated into liberalized international economy	Unprecedented volumes of global trade and investment flows; trade barriers fall and the gap between more and less developed worlds narrows; huge increase in migration from the latter to the former

foodstuffs – tea, tobacco, sugar, potatoes, and a range of exotic spices, for example.

The two fundamental legacies of this period of history were (1) the spread of European power and influence over the rest of the globe and (2) the rise to prominence of New World countries like Argentina, Australia, Canada, and the United States that were to be prime movers in a process of globalization that got underway around 1870 and whose first wave, or phase, lasted until the outbreak of World War I in 1914.

The Four Waves of Globalization

It is common to date the globalization process from the end of the nineteenth century and to identify four waves, or phases, in its evolution to the modern day. The timing and major characteristics of these waves are summarized in Table 6.1. Its contents are highly selective, and, reading it, it needs to be borne in mind that there is a number of contributors to globalization that are constant over the whole period. The steady spread of the free-trade ethos is one of them. Others are the constant improvements in production, communications, and transportation technologies that facilitated the massive, if uneven, growth in the flows of trade, capital, and people.

As mentioned, the *first wave* lasted from 1870 to 1914. It retained the earlier period's basic dynamic of movement in the direction of an ever more integrated international economy founded on capitalist principles, but it also differed from it qualitatively in a number of very important respects. First, integration picked up pace as many countries reduced their protectionist tariffs, ships and railroads got faster and penetrated further, transportation costs fell sharply, and communication became more efficient with the invention of the telegraph and, later, telephone. Second, mechanization brought tremendous increases in agricultural and industrial productivity and, as a result, in the volume and reach of international trade. An example is the large-scale farming that took root in the north-central United States in the last quarter of the nineteenth century. The territory was made accessible by the coming of the railroad and secured by state intervention in the form of (1) gifts of land in return for settlement and cultivation and (2) protection against both criminals and displaced indigenous peoples. Investment capital and people from home and abroad poured in, landholdings were consolidated rather than dispersed among many tenant farmers and the large-scale, for-profit "bonanza" farm was born. The railroad was indispensable because it made for a reliable flow of supplies and provided a cheap and speedy way of getting produce to market, and the telegraph and telephone allowed for the day-to-day planning and coordination of a complex set of activities over long distances. North Dakota became the breadbasket to the world (Lechner 2009, 22–24).

North Dakota is but one small example of a worldwide process of rapid social change facilitated by technological advance and information diffusion. It was not evenly spread, but its scale in total was unprecedented. A few examples will suffice to illustrate globalization's acceleration during this period. From 1500 to 1800, the rate of growth of international trade (as measured by exports) averaged a little more than 1 percent per year. This figure then jumped to 3.5 percent between 1815 and 1914. This increase meant that exports nearly doubled relative to world gross domestic product (GDP), accounting for about 8 percent of it. At the same time, foreign investment nearly tripled relative to the GDP of developing countries. The final distinguishing characteristic of the 1870–1914 period was the surge in the flow of people across borders, or international migration. Three stages can be identified in migration from the Old to the New World. Between 1600 and 1790, migrants were mainly slaves and contract labor as Europe sought to consolidate its hold over its newly acquired territories. Attention then turned to settling these territories, and from 1790 to 1850, it was mainly free settlers who migrated. The period from 1850 to 1920 was the era of mass migration. During this period, about 10 percent of the world's population moved from Europe to the New World and from China and India to less populated neighboring countries. For example, in the case of mass migration to primarily the United States, Canada, Australia, and Argentina, 300,000 per annum moved between 1850 and 1880, 600,000 between 1880 and 1900, and more than a million between 1900 and 1910. This surge in international migration was the product of a number of factors. Governments encouraged it to help relieve some of their own social and economic problems at home, transportation costs fell and became affordable for many, and the New World was attractive for holding out the promise of greater opportunity and higher wages.

In its *second phase*, lasting from 1914 to 1945, globalization lurched sharply into retreat under the combined impact of the two world wars and the Great Depression. Trade and migration plummeted, strict controls on the flow of capital were introduced, and countries erected high tariff barriers against foreign goods. Take migration to the United States as an example. Between 1900 and 1930, an average 621,000 people entered the country annually. This figure then dropped to 53,000 in the 1930s and 1940s. As for international trade as a share of GDP, by the end of the 1940s, it had fallen back in the U.S. to about the same level that it had been in 1870.

The *third wave* dates from 1945 to about 1980, when globalization's trajectory picked up again as the growth of trade and investment flows resumed, transportation costs continued to fall, and barriers to the trade of manufactured goods were dismantled. However, this upswing was mostly limited to the countries of Europe, North America, Australasia, and Japan, countries that were all members of the General Agreement on Tariffs and Trade (GATT, the forerunner of the current World Trade Organization (WTO)), which, along with other multilateral organizations like the International Monetary Fund (IMF) and the World Bank, were postwar creations designed to promote free trade over the protectionism of the interwar years. Most countries in the developing world maintained trade barriers and were consigned to the role of primary goods exporter and benefitted little from international capital flows.

Getting underway around 1980 with the election of aggressively free-market governments in the United Kingdom and United States in particular, globalization's *fourth wave* has been contagious, and unprecedentedly so. The integration of markets, transportation systems, and

TABLE 6.2 Worldwide global flows of foreign direct investment (FDI) and trade

Time period	Mean global FDI outflows	Mean global FDI inflows	Trade as % of global GDP
1960–1969	n.a.	n.a.	12.1%
1970–1979	$28.3bn	$24.0bn	15.9
1980–1989	$93.5bn	$92.9bn	18.5
1990–1999	$416.6bn	$402.0bn	20.7
2000–2007(05)[a]	$1,161.0bn	$1,158.3bn	25.1

Note: [a] The FDI figures cover the period 2000–2007 and the trade figures 2000–2005.
Sources: FDI: <http://unctadstat.unctad.org/TableViewer/tableView.aspx>;
Trade: <http://earthtrends.wri.org>. Accessed December 8, 2010.

communication systems has progressed "farther, faster, deeper, and cheaper" than ever before (Friedman 1999). Two factors account for this acceleration. The first is technological advance, which has so lowered the costs and increased the speed of international communication and transportation that it often makes good economic sense to locate different phases of production in a number of geographically distant countries. Goods, in other words, may be manufactured in one or several countries and transported to, and assembled in, another, as is the case, for example, with automobiles. The second is the increasing liberalization of trade and capital markets among less developed countries, most notably Brazil, China, and India, that had previously protected their economies from foreign competition through the imposition of measures like import quotas and tariffs. Table 6.2 provides illustrative evidence of these developments in the form of global trends since the 1960s in (1) the global dollar value of outflows and inflows of foreign direct investment and (2) international trade (measured as the export of goods and services) as a percentage of global GDP.

Table 6.2 strikingly conveys just how rapid the escalation in international economic interactions has been over recent decades. What it does not show, however, is the unprecedented degree to which the developing world has become integrated into the globalized international economy. Take trade. In the 1970s, developing world exports accounted for only an average of 19.7 percent per annum of the world's GDP. This figure rose steeply to 22.6 percent in the 1980s, to 27.4 percent in the 1990s, and to 38.3 percent between 2000 and 2006. The same rapid change is evident in foreign direct investment in the developing world. It averaged $5.9 billion per annum in the 1970s, $42.2 billion in the 1980s, $118.1 billion in the 1990s, and $356.1 billion between 2000 and 2009. In other words, foreign direct investment in the developing world increased more than sixtyfold between 1970 and 2009. The matching figure for the developed world is lower at a little under fiftyfold.

The West's unprecedented penetration of a hitherto relatively isolated developing world brought increased interdependence in its wake and intensified more than just its purely economic influence. The spread of capitalism entailed the global expansion not only of the capitalist economic philosophy, but also of cultural and political influences associated with the strongest carriers of that philosophy, particularly the United States. Think, for example, of the global diffusion of the McDonalds restaurant chain on the one hand and English language on the other. George Ritzer has written of the "McDonaldization" of the planet, and the 1990s were a high watermark for this phenomenon as 900–1,200 new restaurants opened around the world each year (Ritzer 2007). The growing dominance of the English language is even more incredible. Rated the world's most influential language, English is understood in some form by one-quarter of the world's population and it represents 80 percent of the electronically stored information on the Internet. It is essentially the lingua franca of the globe (Mydans 2007). A full appreciation of the notion of globalization, in other words, means that we must look beyond its economic dimension to evaluate its other dimensions as well. We now turn to a discussion of the dimensions of globalization.

> **W**AIT A MINUTE. **CONSIDER THIS.** Given the nonlinear, zigzag development of globalization over time, can you imagine conditions that would lead to its retreat once again? Do you foresee this happening during your lifetime?

DIMENSIONS OF GLOBALIZATION

Globalization is rooted in changes in the pattern of international economic interactions, but it is a special pattern of change. There is always, of course, a relationship of dependence when one country imports the goods and services that another one exports. But this dependence intensifies when the exporting country's economic well-being comes to rely more heavily on the goods and services that it exports. When, by contrast, GDP grows at the same rate as exports, a country's international interactions may have increased, but exports are no larger a proportion of its GDP so that its national wealth has become no more dependent on them. Importantly, the essence of globalization is not an increased volume of international interactions, but states' growing dependence on such interactions, whether or not their volume increases, for their economic well-being. The interdependence of states, in turn, intensifies when they become more reliant on each other for the goods, services, labor, and capital needed to fuel their economies' growth. Its economic roots notwithstanding, however, globalization should not be seen as a hermetically sealed process affecting only domestic and international economic relations. Rather, it has implications for social relations more generally. Recognition of its complex character is behind its common disaggregation into three distinct dimensions: economic, political, and cultural. All share the notion of growing interdependence, but they improve our understanding of globalization and its myriad effects by looking at this interdependence from different angles rather than as an undifferentiated whole. Let us examine each of them in turn.

Economic Globalization

A definition of economic globalization is "the increasingly close international integration of markets for goods, services and factors of production, labor and capital" (Bordo et al. 2003). Put more prosaically, national market economies are coming together more and more to form a single, deeply integrated international economy whose working is governed by neoliberal principles. These preach the economic superiority and efficiency of free markets and of governments playing a minimal role in regulating them. The profit motive and entrepreneurial initiative – in other words, capitalism – should be the driving forces behind economic activity. Today, economic globalization is accelerating at a faster pace than ever before largely because, on the one hand, governments of virtually all political stripes have accepted free trade and enacted policies of deregulation and liberalization and, on the other hand, transportation costs have fallen and communications technology has made – and continues to make – rapid advances that have spread throughout the world. The Internet, for example, belongs to no single country, has a global reach, and is in principle available to anybody with the technology and software to access it.

An important driver of economic globalization has been the consolidation of global production and distribution in the hands of a few hundred multinational corporations that, in an age of cheap transportation and instant communication, locate themselves in a number of states and coordinate their operations across them. Another driver, however, has been the retreat from regulation by governments of both the left and the right as they have come equally to embrace free market economics.

The consequent consolidation of economic power in a relatively small number of multinational corporations (MNCs) stands out in the contemporary world. If we compare the GDP of states to the total revenues of corporations, we find that of the top 100 economic entities in the world, 44 are MNCs. If we expand our list to cover the top 175 economic entities, then we discover that MNCs make up 109 (or 62.3 percent) of the total. The largest corporation in the world is Wal-Mart, which ranks twenty-third on the aforementioned list, meaning it has more assets at its command than such states as Sweden, Austria, Norway, Saudi Arabia, Iran, Argentina, and South Africa, to name just a few. Table 6.3 lists the top 100 economic entities in the world.

The importance of the economic might and power of MNCs lies in the bargaining power that it affords them vis-à-vis states. Those states eager for private capital investment can be played off against one another as each scrambles to create ever more favorable conditions to attract economic investment. This typically means states reducing, if not eliminating, corporate taxes, creating lax environmental impact rules, subsidizing the construction of factories and facilities, and guaranteeing a low-wage, union-free workforce. Of course, not all states stand in the same relationship to the political power of mobile capital. Particularly vulnerable are those with small, fragile economies in which foreign capital and investment plays a particularly important role. A case in point involves Diageo, a rum distillery conglomerate based in the United Kingdom and the maker of the popular brand "Captain Morgan." It recently set off a furious "race to the bottom" between Puerto Rico and the Virgin Islands, as each of them competed to offer a more lucrative business environment in the hope of having the company locate its production facilities on its territory. The Virgin Islands eventually won this race by offering, among other things, the construction of a brand-new plant at taxpayer expense, exemption from property taxes and gross receipt taxes, a 90 percent reduction in corporate taxes, and marketing and production support worth tens of millions of dollars (Kocieniewski 2010).

The great advantage that MNCs enjoy when negotiating with states is their global mobility. When one state fails to offer the right incentives, MNCs can look elsewhere for better investment opportunities. States, in contrast, are both desperate for investment and "glued more or less to one piece of territory" (Isaak 1995, 264). Statesmen and politicians are thus driven, hat in hand, to ask business leaders: "What do you need?" One must wonder what is to become of state sovereignty and the integrity of democracies when MNCs can use their vast resources to

TABLE 6.3 The world's top 100 economic entities, 2009

Rank	State or MNC	Assets ($m)	Rank	State or MNC	Assets($m)
1	United States	$14,256,300	51	**State Grid**	$184,496
2	Eurozone	$12,455,979	52	Singapore	$182,232
3	Japan	$5,067,526	53	**AXA**	$175,257
4	China	$4,909,280	54	Nigeria	$168,994
5	Germany	$3,346,702	55	Pakistan	$166,545
6	France	$2,649,390	56	**China National Petro.**	$165,496
7	United Kingdom	$2,174,530	57	Chile	$163,670
8	Italy	$2,112,780	58	**Chevron**	$163,527
9	Brazil	$1,571,979	59	**ING Group**	$163,204
10	Spain	$1,460,250	60	Romania	$161,110
11	Canada	$1,336,067	61	Philippines	$160,476
12	India	$1,296,085	62	**General Electric**	$156,779
13	Russia	$1,230,726	63	**Total**	$155,877
14	Australia	$924,843	64	**Bank of America**	$150,450
15	Mexico	$874,902	65	Kuwait	$148,024
16	South Korea	$832,512	66	**Volkswagen**	$146,205
17	Netherlands	$792,128	67	Algeria	$140,577
18	Turkey	$617,099	68	**ConocoPhillips**	$139,515
19	Indonesia	$540,277	69	**BNP Paribas**	$130,708
20	Switzerland	$500,260	70	Hungary	$128,964
21	Belgium	$468,522	71	Peru	$126,734
22	Poland	$430,079	72	**Assicurazioni Gen.**	$126,012
23	**Wal-Mart**	$408,214	73	**Allianz**	$125,160
24	Sweden	$406,072	74	New Zealand	$125,160
25	Austria	$384,908	75	**AT&T**	$123,018
26	Norway	$381,766	76	**Carrefour**	$121,452
27	Saudi Arabia	$369,179	77	**Ford Motor**	$118,308
28	Iran	$331,015	78	**ENI**	$117,235
29	Greece	$329,924	79	**J.P. Morgan Chase**	$115,632
30	Venezuela	$326,498	80	**Hewlett-Packard**	$114,552
31	Denmark	$309,596	81	**E.ON**	$113,849
32	Argentina	$308,741	82	Ukraine	$113,545
33	South Africa	$285,983	83	**Berkshire Hathaway**	$112,493
34	**Royal Dutch Shell**	$285,129	84	**GDF Suez**	$111,069
35	**Exxon Mobil**	$284,650	85	**Daimler**	$109,700
36	Thailand	$263,856	86	**Nippon T & T**	$109,656
37	United Arab Emirates	$261,348	87	Kazakhstan	$109,115
38	**British Petroleum**	$246,138	88	**Samsung Electronics**	$108,927
39	Finland	$237,512	89	**Citigroup**	$108,785
40	Colombia	$230,844	90	**McKeeson**	$108,702
41	Portugal	$227,676	91	**Verizon**	$107,808
42	Ireland	$227,193	92	**Crédit Agricole**	$106,538
43	Hong Kong	$215,355	93	**Banco Santander**	$106,538
44	**Toyota Motor**	$204,106	94	**General Motors**	$104,589
45	**Japan Post Holdings**	$202,196	95	**HSBC Holdings**	$103,736
46	Israel	$194,790	96	**Siemens**	$103,605
47	Malaysia	$191,601	97	**American Int. Group**	$103,189
48	Czech Republic	$190,274	98	**Lloyds Banking Group**	$102,967
49	Egypt	$188,334	99	**Cardinal Health**	$99,613
50	**Sinopec**	$187,518	100	**Nestlé**	$99,114

Note: MNCs in bold script.

Sources: World Bank (July 1, 2010); *Fortune Magazine* (July 26, 2010). Compilation and Web reproduction:
<http://dstevenwhite.com/2010/09/13/the-top-175-global-economic-entities-2009-2/>.

weaken regulation, shape public opinion, influence legislation, and, more generally, ensure the triumph of their private interests in the public arena.

Left-oriented political parties at one time represented an ideological and political barrier to the triumph of the interests of capital, but this is no longer the case. When Social Democratic and Socialist parties come to power, they face the same set of constraints as any other party. If they hope to reward their supporters, expand the national economy, and increase employment, it is imperative that they not scare away the own-ers of capital. Thus, when the Socialist Party of Spain ran its successful election campaigns in the 1980s, they openly courted business interests, declared their commitment to the free market, and prioritized economic growth over redistributive policies. After a brief and flirtatious "break with the international capitalist order," the Socialist Party of France under the leadership of François Mitterrand adopted the same pro-market orienta-tion in the 1980s. More than any other traditional left party in Europe, Tony Blair's Labour Party codified this new business-friendly approach, christening it the "Third Way" (Giddens 1998). One wonders in fact if "left-wing" as a political label continues to make sense in this age of globalization.

Political Globalization

Political globalization can be defined as "an increasing trend toward mul-tilateralism (in which the United Nations plays a key role), toward an emerging 'transnational state apparatus,' and toward the emergence of national and international nongovernmental organizations that act as watchdogs over governments" with ever-increasing intensity and influ-ence (Moghadam 2005, 35). A commonly used measure of political glob-alization is the growth in the number of multilateral organizations in the international system. These fall into two types: intergovernmental orga-nizations (IGOs) and nongovernmental organizations (NGOs). IGOs are organizations whose membership is made up of states pursuing common objectives. Prominent examples include the United Nations, the Euro-pean Union, and the Organization of African States. NGOs are different in that they are non-state actors, although they sometimes cooperate with governments to achieve shared goals. Depending on these goals, NGOs fall into several categories: (1) economic organizations (e.g., transnational corporations and the World Economic Forum); (2) advocacy organiza-tions (e.g., Amnesty International and Greenpeace); (3) service organiza-tions (Doctors without Borders and the International Rescue Committee);

(4) transnational terrorist organizations (e.g., Al Qaeda); and (5) transnational criminal organizations. In 1909, there were 37 IGOs and 176 NGOs. Matching numbers for the early 2000s were approximately 300 and 40,000 respectively.

The importance of these organizations is that they are the partners of states in international governance. "Today's world is . . . one of 'transnational' relations and governance, where governmental actors at various levels interact with their counterparts abroad but also with IGOs and private actors to manage international issues" (Thompson and Snidal, 2012). IGOs are state organs that are created to achieve goals that states cannot aspire to individually. Seeking to ensure that states abide by their free-market commitments, for example, is the responsibility of the World Trade Organization (WTO). Any member country can challenge the laws and regulations of another country before the WTO on the grounds that they violate the organization's rules. Disputes are heard behind closed doors and tough sanctions can be imposed on countries that are found in breach of global trade rules. Its reach is substantial as well. Environmental laws, labor standards, human rights legislation, cultural protection, or other policies deemed to be in the national interest are subject to its review and the only way to overturn a decisions is for every WTO member to oppose it. For example, one WTO tribunal ordered Mexico to pay an American company $16.7 million after concluding that environmental laws in Mexico regulating toxic waste violated the company's free trade rights. In another case, the U.S.-based United Parcel Services (UPS) filed suit against Canada alleging that the state's postal system represented unfair competition against private industry (DePalma 2001). NGOs, in contrast, are not state organs and are perhaps best thought of as acting as interest groups in the international political system. Like interest groups, they represent a wide variety of specific concerns, including education, the economy, the environment, consumer rights, nuclear disarmament, and human rights. And again like interest groups, they can exercise considerable influence on policy. They have been particularly active and influential in the areas of the environment, human rights, and the banning of landmines (Keck and Sikkink 1998). More recently, the fight against corruption has been elevated to the top of the global agenda thanks to the tireless work of the NGO Transparency International, which has national chapters around the globe. And a wide array of NGOs are essentially "on call" when environmental and humanitarian crises strike states. This was seen most recently in the aftermath of the 2010 earthquake in Haiti, which prompted approximately 120 NGOs from around the world to respond by sending rescue teams, medical personnel, food, water, medicine, soap, blankets, tents, building materials, and just about every conceivable type of lifesaving supplies and goods.

Cultural Globalization

Cultural globalization is distinctive for not being a state-sponsored project. Economic and political globalization is in large part the product of agreements into which states have voluntarily entered. Cultural globalization, in contrast, is more accurately seen as a by-product of those agreements. It involves the growing and accelerating exchange of ideas, products, sports, values, technology, business practices, foods, music, dance, and fashion across more or less distant national boundaries. The outcome has been a growing standardization of cultural expression around the world. The usual example of this cultural homogenization trend is the global diffusion of American fast food, sometimes referred to as the aforementioned "McDonaldization" of the world (Ritzer 2007). Other prominent examples of contemporary cultural globalization might include sushi, Hollywood (and Bollywood) movies, Harry Potter, soccer, and the growing use of the English language for academic and business purposes in particular.

To note that cultural globalization is not primarily a state-sponsored project is not to claim that states have not made efforts to export their cultural and political institutions and values beyond their borders. Missionaries are as old as the exploration of new lands and were encouraged, among other things, as forces for "civilizing" native peoples who might resent exploration and occupation by foreigners. In a similar vein, making the world safe for democracy, has been a central plank of U.S. foreign policy since President Woodrow Wilson used it to justify his request to a joint session of Congress in April 1917 for a declaration of war against Germany. Pursuit of this goal has involved the U.S. in numerous wars since then and has also led it to conduct propaganda wars against its enemies, and particularly the communist Soviet Union. For example, Radio Free Europe was founded in 1950. An instrument of the CIA, its goal was to "promote democratic values and institutions by disseminating factual information and ideas" in societies where the free flow of information was restricted by their governments. The principal target was the Soviet-dominated states of Eastern Europe. Earlier in 1934, private individuals and the British government came together to establish the less directly political and propagandist British Council. It describes itself on its Web site as "the United Kingdom's international non-profit organization for cultural relations and education opportunities. We build engagement and trust for the UK through the exchange of knowledge and ideas between people worldwide."

The current wave of cultural globalization is different from these earlier government propaganda efforts in two important respects, however. First, it is largely self-generating and mass media and ever more advanced communication technologies are its primary vehicles. News services like BBC and CNN have a global reach and they disseminate many of the same stories and programs exposing people even in remote parts of the world to foreign ideas, lifestyles, and cultural practices. The World Wide Web, along with the development of computer technology, has only accelerated this process of global diffusion as it has permitted people everywhere unprecedented access to an unprecedented amount of information through social networking sites, blogs, Web pages, and the like. The second distinctive characteristic of cultural globalization is its two-way flow. It is not just a story of rich and powerful states imposing their ideas and institutions on smaller, more vulnerable ones. To be sure, economic and military power certainly enhances cultural influence either by force or by attraction. It remains the case, however, that cultural influence can flow in the other direction. Take food. In Britain, the Indian curry dish, chicken tikka masala, overtook fish and chips in the 1990s as the country's national dish and its rise captures perfectly the dynamics of states' cultural interdependence. In the words of Robin Cook, Britain's Foreign Secretary at the time: "Chicken Tikka Massala is now a true British national dish, not only because it is the most popular, but because it is a perfect illustration of the way Britain absorbs and adapts external influences. Chicken Tikka is an Indian dish. The Massala sauce was added to satisfy the desire of British people to have their meat served in gravy" (Cook 2001).

GLOBALIZATION AND THE STATE

In its totality, then, globalization combines accumulating interdependence across a number of dimensions, all of which share the characteristic of meaning a lesser role for the state in shaping its own economic, social, political, and cultural destiny. Their sovereignty has been, and is being, compromised in that what goes on within their borders is increasingly influenced by actions and decisions taken by actors outside those borders. The efforts of a rich country's government to bring down domestic unemployment, for example, are vitiated by newly industrializing states offering corporations such inducements as tax abatements, lower wage costs, and a pliable labor movement to relocate there. States, of course, have never been hermetically sealed in the sense of being unaffected by influences from outside their borders. Nonetheless, their heightened susceptibility to such influences in the contemporary globalization phase has occasioned some to argue that the state is less and less able to perform its key function of providing for the security of its citizens and, as a result, will "wither away" in the same way that earlier structures of governance, such as empire, did.

According to this argument, a basic problem facing states is that they are too small to deal with the pressing global problems currently facing humankind, a few of which are highly mobile investment capital, global warming, the depletion of the ozone layer, wider possession of nuclear, biological, and chemical weapons of mass destruction, the power of multinational corporations, and the global spread of AIDS and other diseases. Susan Strange (1999) has identified three areas of state failure: (1) financial regulation; (2) the environment; and (3) social inequality. More fully, she argues that states are unequal to the tasks of supervising, regulating, and controlling the banks and other institutions that create and trade in credit instruments, of correcting and reversing the processes of environmental damage that threaten the survival of not only our own but other species, and of maintaining a balance between the constantly growing power of what neo-Gramscians call the hegemony of the transnational capitalist class (TCC) and the masses who feel left behind by globalization and abandoned by the established political class that promotes it (Strange 1999).

The counterargument, however, is that the challenges confronting states as a result of globalization are different in degree, but not kind. States have never come anywhere near fully controlling the international forces impinging on them. To take a few examples, war and occupation have always threatened their ability to provide for the security of their people. Indeed, states themselves have historically been among the biggest threats to this security as they have repressed dissent, incited war, and developed ever more lethal instruments of violence. Similarly, plagues and pestilence have long wiped out people by the thousands, if not hundreds of thousands, and states were powerless to stop this. The pursuit of national economic advancement has commonly placed a low value on human life and happiness at the same time as ignoring environmental degradation. Finally, the struggle to establish international rules that impinge on state sovereignty by forcing political leaders to treat their subjects in a certain way is not new either. Initially, efforts in this area concentrated on promoting religious tolerance. The Vienna Settlement that followed the Napoleonic Wars in early-nineteenth-century Europe, for example, guaranteed religious toleration for Catholics in the Netherlands. Over time, the emphasis on achieving universal human rights has shifted from religious freedom to protecting minority rights, but the fact remains that the attempted imposition of universal values that constrain how states can act toward their subjects is not unique to the current period (Krasner 2001).

Thus, while the challenges to states' ability to decide for themselves and act in their own interests may be more numerous and intense in today's global age than they were in the past, they are not qualitatively different. For states, sovereignty has always involved near, but not complete, authority and control over their own destinies. They have learned to cooperate with other states to minimize the effects of changes and challenges to their own sovereignty; they have learned, in other words, how to lose battles in order to win the bigger war for survival. Thus, a common and long-standing behavior for them has been to compromise their autonomy by forming alliances or joining organizations to achieve goals that they could not reach on their own. Balance-of-power theory in international relations, for example, holds that states' primary interest is to protect themselves from aggression so that they will, even if reluctantly, form an alliance with other states to balance the threat posed by a superior, potentially hostile power. The loss of sovereignty involved in such a cooperative venture is preferred to potential defeat in war and occupation. An example is Western European states willingly joining the U.S.-led North Atlantic Treaty Organization (NATO) after World War II. The threat faced in this instance was the potential expansion of the Soviet Union beyond Eastern Europe. In the same vein, free-trade agreements become attractive when governments convince themselves that the diminution of sovereignty is worth the gain in national economic prosperity compared to regulated trade.

It is also the case that agreements that diminish the sovereignty of individual states in pursuit of collective goals are commonly written to allow signatory states to behave unilaterally if they perceive a threat to their national interest. Thus, for example, in 1972, Britain finally opted to join the European Economic Community (established in 1958) for the proven economic benefits that membership of this large and successful free-trade association would bring to it and its people. But when European integration subsequently deepened and a single currency, the euro, was proposed for all member states, Britain, among others, negotiated an exemption from joining it on the ground that membership was not in its national interest at the time. It had still not adopted the euro, a decade after the currency entered circulation in January 2002. Moreover, even if states choose not to abide by agreements they have signed, there are usually limited sanctions at best that can be imposed on them. In rare cases, war might result or economic sanctions might be levied against them. Normally, however, little can be done.

The bottom line is that states are not static entities. They have always had to strive both to shape their international environment to their own advantage and at the same time to adjust their priorities and adapt their behaviors to changes in that environment. Caught up in this dynamic, they may be obliged to dilute their sovereignty to attain a higher good, but they will not offer up any more of their sovereign authority than is necessary. Thus, striking the right balance under conditions of lesser or greater mutual dependency is a never-ending challenge for states. Moreover, it is a challenge that they have continued to confront even as globalization has gathered pace in recent decades. The struggle to maximize both sovereign authority and short-term economic, political, or cultural advantage has always been the hallmark of state behavior, and is no less so today. It is evident in a number of policy areas, and we shall now examine two of them in some detail: (1) international migration; and (2) welfare state policy.

*W**AIT A MINUTE.* **CONSIDER THIS.** Has state sovereignty all but disappeared in this fourth phase of globalization, or is the current dance between sovereign authority and external actors (like MNCs) and structural forces (like the global market) different only in degree from the past? Is it true, as the former Secretary General of the UN, Boutros Boutros-Ghali declared, that "the time of absolute and exclusive sovereignty has passed"? Or do states still possess considerable resources and the will to fight against the unremitting forces of globalization?

The State Pushes Back

States even today remain the only entities on the planet that claim the highest level of authority over a given territory, and this claim is buttressed by both the state's legitimacy in the eyes of its people and its effective monopoly of the legal means of violence within that territory. In the present international order, this means that states alone have the right to determine the laws and the internal organization of their societies. There are many social forces that compete to challenge and shape the legislation and regulations that govern a society, but states have the final say on these matters. Even more, no other state has the legal right to interfere in the domestic affairs of another. How then have states used their resources and power to push back against some of the consequences of globalization that they do not welcome?

Both authoritarian and democratic states have welcomed the economic benefits and rewards that the spread of economic globalization in the form of free-market capitalism has generally brought them. Both embrace the retreat from governmental regulation associated with it, but they differ substantially in their political reaction to globalization. Democratic regimes have long taken for granted that the right to compete in the political marketplace goes hand in hand with the right to compete in the economic marketplace. The latter is defined by the free movement of capital and labor, and its political counterpart by a combination of electoral competition and constitutional protection of rights that all possess. As has always been their wont, however, authoritarian regimes have generally proved reluctant to extend similar electoral and constitutional rights to their peoples. Rather, their reaction to globalization has generally been to use markets to create wealth that can then be directed as political officials, rather than "the market," see fit.

This marriage of economic markets and authoritarian control has been labeled "state capitalism" (Bremmer 2010). There is no hard-and-fast line that divides it from free-market capitalism because all governments regulate, and have always regulated, economic activity to some degree. It may be to promote more rapid economic growth, to advance the interests of their supporters, to protect citizens from unsafe drugs being sold on the market, and so on. The key characteristic of state capitalism, however, is that, despite the deregulation of economic activity, governments continue to dominate and manipulate markets for political gain, with their primary political objective often being to maintain their hold on power by creating political acquiescence and passivity in a population enjoying the fruits of state-led economic growth. Whereas there are numerous examples of state capitalism in the world today, perhaps its exemplar is China, whose ruling communist party has to this point succeeded in retaining its monopoly control of domestic political power while promoting aggressive free-market capitalism and harnessing it to a set of development goals determined by the state (Bremmer 2010, 128–38).

Democratic regimes have been readier to accept the domestic political consequences of economic globalization, such as the deregulation of economic activity, a smaller welfare state that provides less generous benefits to its citizens, and the transfer of some degree of economic sovereignty to supranational institutions like the World Trade Organization, the European Union and the North American Free Trade Association. Even these, however, have resisted the logic of globalization when it has been in the clear political self-interest of their governments to do so. We now examine this resistance in the policy areas of immigration and the welfare state.

Immigration Policy

The salient and controversial topic of international migration highlights the tension between economic efficiency and national interest; it also throws into sharp relief how states strive to retain as much sovereign authority as they can in the resolution of this tension.

The notion of international migration, or living in a country other than the one in which one is born, is predicated on the international system being made up of sovereign states that have the right to determine who can enter and reside within their borders. By contrast, the economic efficiency promised by globalization is predicated on the notion that national borders should not be an impediment to, in the words of our earlier definition, the free flow of "goods, services and factors of production, *labor* (our emphasis) and capital." In point of fact, however, the rich countries of the world in particular go out of their way to have the best of both worlds. Discussion earlier in this chapter has shown that their free-trade doctrine has taken root in developing countries that were previously hostile to it and, partly in consequence, the free flow of goods, services, and capital across national borders has increased substantially during the current globalization phase. At the same time, however, these same rich countries have striven to avoid some of the inevitable and predictable consequences of their free-market doctrine. That is, their trade and investment patterns have promoted modern economies in the developing world and this has meant, among other things, that fewer people are needed on the land. Poverty and an exodus to cities where jobs are scarce have ensued, and a growing number of people have turned their attention to migration to the rich world as a means of making a better life for themselves and their families. Developed countries, however, have generally been less than enthusiastic about unfettered population flows and have reacted by taking numerous, ever more stringent measures to control the number of immigrants entering their territory. They have, in other words, accepted the elements of free-market doctrine that suit their national interest and have invoked their sovereign authority to reject those that do not. A number of reasons explain this contradictory stance.

The first is that the supply of would-be migrants to the rich countries of the Western world far exceeds the demand for them in those same countries. In 1960, the United Nations estimated that about 76 million (about 2.5 percent of the world's population) lived outside their country of birth. By 2005, that figure had jumped to 190 million and it is expected to reach 405 million by 2050. The proportion of international migrants moving from the developing to the developed world, however, is increasing at an even faster rate. This figure was 42 percent in 1975 and it jumped to 60 percent in 2005. Clearly, the rich countries of the world have rapidly become a more attractive destination for the growing number of international migrants over the last part of the twentieth and early part of the twenty-first centuries. At the same time and despite ongoing economic globalization, the developed world has welcomed this influx of newcomers less and less.

There are three types of international migrant and all of them have become subject to a harsher immigration control regime (Cornelius et al. 2004). The three types are: (1) legal migrants who enter through working visa or family reunification programs; (2) refugees or asylum seekers fleeing persecution in their home country; and (3) illegal migrants who seek to enter a country without its permission or blessing. Various mechanisms have been used to make entry more difficult for all three types. For legal immigrants, a general pattern is that their numbers have been strictly limited and entry qualifications tightened. Belgium is a case in point. In 2009, its government determined that henceforth admitted immigrants would, among other things, have to demonstrate their knowledge of Dutch or French, the two official languages of state. Marriages of convenience would be subject to stricter controls and entry under the family reunification program would become more difficult.

Refugees and asylum seekers, in contrast, are individuals who request residency status on the basis of the claim that they are fleeing from political persecution at home. Refugees are different from asylum seekers in that the former have their case heard and a decision made when they are outside the country in which they are seeking residency, whereas the latter make their residency application after having landed in that country.

The difficulty with asylum seekers lies in distinguishing between those genuinely escaping persecution and "economic migrants" who falsely allege persecution in an effort to acquire a materially better life for themselves and their families. This difficulty partly explains why governments in the developed world have become less sympathetic to appeals for asylum. France, for example, has long been a popular destination for asylum seekers, rejecting only 57 percent of applications in 1985. This figure rose to 84 percent in 1995 and 90.2 percent in 2007. Illegal, or undocumented, immigrants are a thornier problem because they avoid all contact with governments so that their comings and goings are less easily regulated. Among the many measures adopted to stem the flow of illegal immigrants include the building of physical barriers, as with the border wall between the United States and Mexico, interdiction on the high seas, and prosecution of employers who hire workers without proper papers.

A second reason for harsher controls is deep-seated popular opposition to further immigration, even in countries that themselves have been settled largely by immigrants. A 2005 Gallup poll, for example, found that 60 percent of Britons thought that the level of immigration to their country should be decreased; the matching figure for Americans was little different at 58 percent. A wider poll of thirteen developed countries in Australasia, North America, and Western Europe reached similar conclusions. Fifty-six percent of the total number of respondents thought that the number of immigrants coming to their country should be decreased and this was the majority viewpoint in nine of the thirteen countries covered (ISSP 2004). There are two basic reasons for this negative view of immigration and immigrants. The first is that they are perceived to present a material threat to the native population. In other words, the popular perception is that they threaten living standards by taking jobs away from the native-born population, working for lower wages relative to unskilled sections of the population in particular, and are a fiscal drain on the country for the government services they consume in areas like welfare, public schooling, and health care. The second, and more potent, reason for anti-immigrant prejudice is that they are perceived to represent a cultural threat. The essence of this claim is not just that immigrants are somehow different. Rather, it is that their desire to retain their traditional culture in their new country of residence threatens the national identity and cultural integrity of the country they have voluntarily adopted. In the words of Pauline Hanson, the leader of Australia's now-defunct right-wing populist One Nation party: "Australians, like other peoples of the world, have the right to maintain their unique identity and culture. It is never immoral to want to retain one's own independence and identity. Those who say that it is, simply will not realise the existence and importance of Australian culture to our people. However, when it comes to the Third World, peoples' culture is suddenly of the greatest importance" (Quoted in Mughan and Paxton 2006).

A final reason for governments' increasing efforts to control immigration is security, which takes two forms: personal and national. One reason for governments responding sympathetically to popular opposition to immigration is the common feeling that immigrants bring crime in their wake. Looking at the same thirteen-country poll as previously, an average 50.5 percent of respondents across all countries agreed that immigrants increase crime rates, with this being the majority viewpoint in six of the thirteen countries. But national security in an age of terrorism is perceived to be a more serious problem. The twenty-first century has seen a series of deadly terrorist attacks in cities on continents as diverse as Africa (Nairobi and Dar es Salaam), North America (New York), and Western Europe (London and Madrid), and numerous other planned attacks have been foiled. This spate of terrorist activity has virtually always involved immigrants in the country legally or the native-born children of immigrant parents. As a result, immigration and terrorism have become overlapping problems, and governments are faced not only with the problem of identifying and denying residency to potential terrorists from overseas, but also with identifying actual and potential terrorists born within their borders. The major casualty of their consequent efforts to "defend the homeland" has been the civil liberties, privacy, and democratic rights of citizens and noncitizens alike. An example is the USA PATRIOT Act, which President George W. Bush signed into law shortly after the terrorist attack on the World Trade Center on September 11, 2001. This piece of legislation significantly expanded the search and surveillance powers of domestic law enforcement and foreign intelligence agencies and broadened the discretion of law enforcement and immigration authorities in detaining and deporting immigrants suspected of terrorism-related acts. President Obama signed a four-year extension of several key provisions of the Act in May 2011.

The basic challenge facing the rich states of the developed world, then, is how to reconcile the conflicting economic and security priorities associated with an economic globalization strategy they themselves have chosen to pursue. International migration is economically efficient, and these states, faced with declining and aging populations, need immigrant labor to fill shortages across the range of occupations. Their dilemma, however, is that their own populations are often hostile to further immigration both in and of itself and because of the threat it is perceived to pose to their material well-being, cultural identity, and national security. Caught between contradictory pressures to open their borders wider if only for reasons of population decline and aging on the one hand and to control the flow of "foreigners" across them more rigorously on the other, immigration reform is one of the more intractable problems facing the rich states of the world today.

Welfare State Policy

Under the umbrella of what Strange (1999) calls the "social failure" – that is, the inadequacy of the state to meet the challenges of a globalizing world – is the question of the future of the welfare state. Designed to ensure that the basic human needs (education, employment, health, housing, old-age pensions, and so on) of all citizens were provided for, generous welfare provision occupied pride of place in the social democracies that flourished in rich countries for the thirty years after the end of World War II. In the early 1950s, social security expenditure was less than 10 percent of GDP in most European countries. By the early 1970s, it had risen to more than 20 percent in many of them (e.g., Belgium, Denmark, France, Germany, Italy, the Netherlands, and Sweden) and was greater than 15 percent in the remainder. This expansion of social protection was paid for by a combination of national economic growth and a system of progressive taxation that served to redistribute advantage from the rich to the poor. But then came two oil shocks in the 1970s when the Organization of Petroleum Exporting Countries (OPEC) announced substantial increases in the price of crude oil. Stagflation (mass unemployment combined with high inflation) and high public sector deficits followed, the terms of international trade were rewritten, economic growth in the rich world slowed, and the neoliberal principles of a market economy came to enjoy greater currency and influence among politicians of both left and right. The social democratic principles underwriting the generous welfare state that had been the norm, at least in Western Europe, for the previous thirty years or so were under siege.

There are many reasons why governments have cut back on their welfare generosity. Prominent among them are rapidly aging populations, rising costs of health care, and an increased demand for the public provision of services that used to be provided by nonworking women, particularly child care and elder care. But much has also been made of the role that economic globalization has played in this process as a result, in particular, of the international integration of capital markets. Two forms of capital have flowed with increasing freedom from state regulation during the current globalizing era. The first is foreign direct investment (FDI), which amounted to a worldwide average total (inflows + outflows) of $52 billion in the 1970s and $2,319 billion in the first seven years of the twenty-first century – a 446 percent increase (see Table 6.1). The second is cross-border portfolio investments, which include equity securities and long-term and short-term debt securities. Many governments have tried to attract FDI inflows by lowering corporate tax rates, relaxing restrictions on the repatriation of profits, weakening labor and environmental standards as well as unions, and so on. To attract portfolio investment, in contrast, they have undertaken such actions as removing legal restrictions on the ownership and trading of stocks and bonds by overseas entities, on non-residents holding bank accounts in their territory, and on foreign banks, brokers, and investors not being allowed to participate in their financial markets. The net results of these changes are twofold. One, capital has become highly mobile and very large amounts of it can be transferred from one location to another with a stroke of a computer key. Two, just as with goods and services, states have become more dependent on incoming global capital flows for their economic prosperity and security.

These developments, the argument continues, have increased the dependency of governments on capital markets and thereby made them increasingly sensitive and responsive to the interests of the owners of capital. Specifically, it has reduced the legitimacy of governmental intervention in the economy to protect less fortunate citizens against market outcomes – the very *raison d'être* of the welfare state. Moreover, governments cannot ignore the limits that highly mobile capital effectively places on their welfare spending patterns, otherwise their countries will lose both investors and the support of the international financial institutions that encourage neoliberalism (the ideology of global free markets) in the international economy. Their room for choice, in short, has become severely constrained. "In this view, it hardly matters whether the left or the right wins elections; the constraints of the internationalized economy will oblige either party to follow the same monetary and fiscal policies or else face a loss of national competitiveness and investment" (Berger 2000, 51). Making governments seem even more helpless, David Held observes that "in this 'borderless' economy, national governments are relegated to little more than transmission belts for global capital" (Held et al. 1999, 3). Thus, the argument goes, as with all forms of state regulation of market activity, economic globalization means the eventual demise of the welfare state.

This prediction, of course, could well prove true over some unspecified period of time, but it has proved far from accurate to date. To be sure, there are unmistakable signs of less generous welfare state provision, and one shorthand way of describing this transition is to note that the social democratic welfare state has passed from a pre-OPEC "golden age" to a more modest "silver age of permanent austerity" (Ferrera 2008). This is a far cry, however, from conceding that the welfare state is withering away. Indeed, what is striking is its resilience despite its poor fit to the demands of an ever more integrated international market economy. As with immigration, the state has not simply succumbed to the logic of the market, but has adapted its institutions and practices to reconcile the competing demands of this logic and its own national interest. One good reason for this adaptive behavior is political self-interest. Welfare benefits provide some relief for the losers from globalization – the long-term unemployed, for example – those whose jobs are outsourced overseas where labor is cheaper and government regulation laxer, or those whose wages are stagnant because of labor market competition from immigrants. Absent welfare benefits, there is always the potential for an anti-market backlash among these groups. Other good reasons for continued welfare provision include the enhanced economic competitiveness that occurs when workers are retrained and the economic stimulus that results from unemployment benefits. Regarding the latter, a variety of economic studies in the United States have demonstrated that for every dollar of federal government money spent on income for the unemployed, nearly two dollars of economic activity is generated (Wiseman 2010).

The resilience of the welfare state in a globalized age is attributable to other factors as well (Pierson 1996). The first is that "the welfare state now represents the status quo with all the political advantages this status confers." Changing the status quo is always an uphill battle for politicians, particularly when the passage of legislation requires the consent of a wide variety of significant political actors. The second reason is that welfare programs are popular with voters and to cut them back, especially radically, risks electoral reprisals. Finally, welfare programs have their supporters as well as their opponents, and the former have mobilized successfully to protect them against radical cutbacks. Supporters include the many consumers of welfare benefits as well as the large number of public employees in any modern state.

This last point emphasizes that states retain some degree of autonomy even though confronted by globalizing forces that reduce their room for maneuver. If supporters of the welfare state are strong and well organized, they can defend it with some degree of success. This is nowhere more apparent than in the fate of the welfare state in less developed countries (LDCs) where its beneficiaries have not been as well organized as in more developed ones (MDCs). The evidence suggests that, unlike in MDCs, globalization has undermined the ability of labor in LDCs to prevent the dismantling of the welfare state. The basic explanation for this difference is that the high numbers of low-skilled as compared to skilled workers, together with large volumes of surplus labor, make it harder for labor to organize in LDCs (Rudra 2008). But even in MDCs, the relationship between globalization and welfare state decline is neither simple nor direct because it is mediated by states' existing political institutions, structures of industrial relations, left-wing governments, the programmatic structure of social welfare systems, and contingent acts of political leadership. This complexity is well captured by the conclusion of a study of change in welfare state spending before and after globalization took off around 1980. What the authors of this study found was that between 1980 and 1993, public health spending (as a percentage of total health spending) fell in ten of the seventeen OECD countries, it remained unchanged in another three, and actually increased in the remaining four. But noticeable in this last group of four countries is that the annual rate of increase in spending was much lower than it had been in the previous two decades (Clayton and Pontusson 1998, 80).

In short, economics does not trump politics. States have proved adaptable and have had some success in resisting and molding the pressures emanating from an increasingly interdependent global economy to fit their own traditions, cultures, and domestic political pressures. A number of globalization's outcomes are unpopular, and not to act to moderate their adverse impact on the lives and well-being of many citizens risks a loss of support for the globalization project and perhaps even a loss of legitimacy for the state itself in the longer run.

The People Push Back

It is difficult for people to push back against globalization. Organizing a popular and effective social movement that advances an anti-globalization program has to deal in the first instance with the fact that nearly all of the states in the world, democratic or authoritarian, support the globalization agenda by and large. In democracies, there are few, if any, parties of government that oppose it, and many authoritarian governments have embraced it equally enthusiastically. Even communist China chose in late 2001 to join a World Trade Organization that it knew to be built on unabashedly free-market principles that are enforced with zeal and enthusiasm. In a word, globalization has attained a hegemonic status in the world today. Under these circumstances, opponents of growing international economic interdependence have tended to pursue their anti-globalization agenda outside the political mainstream, ignoring governing elites and established channels of political communication.

Given an unresponsive center, or mainstream, it is not surprising that the main opposition to the globalization project has been found at the extremes of the political spectrum, from political forces of both the left and right. Operating independently of each other, these two poles of opposition have adopted contrasting philosophies, organization, and strategies to achieve their shared goals. Let us take the left-wing opposition first.

The Left-Wing Push

Left-wing opposition is rooted in the belief that capitalism is evil because it breeds unacceptable social and economic inequality, promotes social injustice, and degrades the environment. Its reform agenda ranges from historically familiar social democratic and labor union attempts to reform domestic capitalism to radical Green and anarchist attempts to eliminate it altogether. The basic message among all anti-globalization Left forces is that global corporate capitalism must be resisted because it promotes egregious inequalities between states as well as within them. What needs to be emphasized is that opposition is to the goals and power of free-flowing international capital, not to globalization per se. The kind of increased international interdependence that today's anti-globalization movements seek is one that promotes the rights of people, not those of privileged elites who manipulate the system for their own selfish ends.

The organizational form that this left-wing opposition has chosen is one of many and varied autonomous grassroots movements that operate outside established political channels and come together periodically to strategize about achieving shared goals. Leading examples include ATTAC (Association for the Taxation of Financial Transactions for the Aid of Citizens), Peoples' Global Action (PGA), and Our World Is Not For Sale (OWINFS). Often themselves loose groupings of organizations, activists, and social movements, these groups both operate independently and come together annually at conferences like the World Social Forum (WSF). On its Web site, this forum describes itself as:

> an open meeting place for reflective thinking, democratic debate of ideas, formulation of proposals, free exchange of experiences and inter-linking for effective action, by groups and movements of civil society that are opposed to neo-liberalism and to domination of the world by capital and any form of imperialism, and are committed to building a society centred on the human person.

The WSF adopted its name to highlight its distinctiveness from the well-known, pro-globalization World Economic Forum (WEF), which meets in Davos, Switzerland, every year and "is an independent international organization committed to improving the state of the world by engaging business, political, academic and other leaders of society to shape global, regional and industry agendas." The annual meetings at Davos attract the world's top business and political elites as well as celebrities and the very wealthy who socialize and exchange ideas on economic and political issues. As an exclusive playground for the global power elite, Davos has come to represent, to the left wing, everything that is wrong with globalization.

Anti-globalization groups operate outside conventional political channels, functioning as neither a political party nor an interest group. Rather, their hallmark strategy is to mount mass decentralized campaigns of direct action and civil disobedience. Although violence is anathema to many in the movement, these campaigns have sometimes involved rioting, fighting with the authorities in the streets, and destruction of property. Some anti-globalization groups are prepared to go to great lengths to stop the meetings of organizations like the WTO and the G8 (an organization comprising representatives of the eight largest economies in the world). There have been numerous instances of violent confrontation between anti-globalization protesters and the forces of law and order, and perhaps the most famous one occurred in Seattle in 1999. There, protesters blocked the entrance of delegates to the November WTO meeting and forced the cancellation of the opening ceremonies. Protests were sustained for all four days of the meeting, and police and National Guard responded with nightsticks, pepper spray, tear gas, and rubber bullets. More than 600 protesters were arrested and dozens more, including four policemen, were injured. The storefronts of global corporations like McDonalds, Starbucks, and Nike were destroyed. The mayor eventually declared the municipal equivalent of martial law and put the city under curfew. There have been numerous other violent confrontations before and since, and one of them, at a G8 meeting in Genoa, Italy, in 2001, even resulted in the death of a protester.

Where anti-globalization movements and activists disagree, however, is in regard to the question of how international capitalism is best rolled back and kept in check. Broadly speaking, two camps can be identified in this debate. The first sees the globalization "problem" as lying in the reluctance of states to limit and regulate the forces of capitalist accumulation. For them, a neoliberal economic doctrine that advocates state weakness lies at the heart of the globalization challenge and the way to meet it is to rebuild and reinforce state sovereignty. Their solution to the ills of a globalized world, therefore, is to strengthen national sovereignty, to restore the status quo ante. The alternative viewpoint within the anti-globalization movement sees the problem as lying in capital itself and the solution not in the restoration of state sovereignty but in transcending state boundaries and building a global world order founded on democratic principles in preference to the current one dominated by supranational, pro-globalization organizations like the G8, the WTO, the World Bank, and the IMF. In the absence of mechanisms for representation in this type of organization (such as accountability, elections, public debate over goals and strategies, and so on), protest at their rule often spills over into the streets. The goal is not to return to a world of states, but to rewrite the public agenda with a view to building a democratic, globalized polity that will provide for greater equality between the rich and the poor, the powerful and the powerless, and that will advance social justice and self-determination for all (Hardt 2002).

The Right-Wing Push

The principal right-wing opposition to globalization is very different in that it takes a highly structured form – the radical right populist party – and operates in the same mainstream political arena as the established political elites that it despises. Part of the political scene in many of the world's established democracies, right-wing populist parties contest elections, court public opinion, and sometimes even take part in government as coalition partners. In cases like Pauline Hanson's One Nation Party in Australia and Ross Perot's Reform Party in the United States, they have flourished and then faded. Others, by contrast, have proved unexpectedly resilient. Prominent among these are Jean-Marie LePen's National Front in France, Jörg Haider's Austrian Freedom Party, Umberto Bossi's Lega

Nord in Italy, Christoph Blocher's Swiss People's Party, and Pia Kjærs-gaard's Danish People's Party. Differences in longevity notwithstanding, all have been among the strongest opponents of neoliberalism, immigration, and (where applicable) European integration in their respective countries.

These parties' hostility to globalization is embedded in a broader populist philosophy that divides the world into "good and bad" and "us and them." In addition, it identifies "us," the in-group, mainly through the demonization and vilification of "them," the out-group. Their strongest criticism is reserved for established political elites and institutions within their own countries. These are condemned for having served the interests of those with power and influence at the expense of the "ordinary people," or the "little Aussie battler," as Pauline Hanson phrased it. Populist parties depict globalization as, on the one hand, a self-serving project launched and maintained by established financial, political, and cultural elites and, on the other, a threat to national identity, national sovereignty, and domestic civil society. For them, it is to be condemned because it has a deleterious impact on all aspects of national life – economic, political, and cultural (Mudde 2007).

Radical right populist parties resent economic globalization for a number of reasons. For a start, their ideology combines economic nationalism and welfare chauvinism. In other words, it is their strong belief that the economy should serve the nation and should be controlled by it; they also support a welfare state, but only for their "own people." Globalization weakens national control of the domestic economy, leading, for example, to the outsourcing of jobs overseas and bringing ruin and unemployment to national industries and communities. This concern is especially central to populist radical right politics outside of Europe. In the 1992 U.S. presidential race, for example, Ross Perot made much of that "giant sucking sound to the south" by which he was referring to the loss of "good paying" (sic) jobs to Mexico that would come with the imminent signing the North American Free Trade Association treaty. Pauline Hanson similarly argued that Australia should strive for "industrial self-sufficiency." In Europe, by contrast, this type of economic concern has not been as central for this party type. This is because, not themselves being societies built on immigration, the perception that newcomers represent a threat to national identity and cultural integrity trumps economics in their hierarchy of concerns.

Nativism refers to "an intense opposition to an internal minority on the ground of its foreign (i.e., 'un-American') connections . . . While drawing on much broader cultural antipathies and ethnocentric judgments, nativism translates them into a zeal to destroy the enemies of a distinctly American way of life" (Higham 1955, 4). Seen from this perspective, economic globalization is resented less because it diminishes state control of the national economy and more because it promotes the mass immigration that is seen to threaten the distinctive way of life of receiving states. A similar logic governs the negative reaction of these parties to the European Union and the ever-closer economic and political integration that it brings in its wake. Right-wing activists need only point to the more than 100,000 pages of legislation passed by the EU since 1957 and compiled in its *Acquis Communautaire* (the official register of all legislation, legal acts, and court decisions) as tangible evidence of the threat it poses to the sovereignty of their respective states.

Similar concerns about loss of national identity and sovereignty lie at the heart of other groups' deep fear of political globalization. Centered around somewhat bizarre conspiracy theories about a "New World Order (NWO)," these groups balk at the ever-growing international political cooperation between states, and in particular the involvement of the UN. Claims of left-wing globalist conspiracies orchestrated by the UN to achieve world domination are found particularly in the United States among militias, the Christian Right, and even the right wing of the Republican Party. Relying on obscure biblical passages, they fear that the UN represents the beginnings of a world government that will inevitability foster the return of the devil to rule the planet. In Europe, the orchestrating role in constructing this NWO falls more to the EU. For example, Jean-Marie LePen, the former, long-time leader of France's Front National, has described the EU as a "link to one-worldness."

The fear of cultural globalization is attributable to technological innovation as well. It is getting cheaper and easier to reach into all corners of the globe via broadcast media, satellite, the Internet, and the like. Indeed, movies, television programs, sound recordings, even fashion designs are increasingly made with exactly this objective in mind. The problem is that not all states are equal in this competition for global market share. Rather, American culture is dominant and diffuses all the more easily for the global reach of the English language. Europe's populist parties are among the many groups in the world to resent what they think of as American cultural imperialism. Similar sentiments can be found in the Islamic world where, for example, a French-Tunisian businessman produced the soft drink "Mecca Cola" in 2002 and marketed it as a politically correct alternative to Coca-Cola. The common fear is not just the homogenization of cultures around the world, but also a belief that the American culture is the wrong one to be emulated. Reminiscent of the philosophy of Herbert Marcuse (Chapter 2 of this book), for example, the CP '86, a Dutch populist radical party, described the Netherlands' increasingly Americanized culture as material and hedonist, full of "consumer slaves who are devoid of culture." Fighting the same battle, there is also an Organisation Internationale de la Francophonie that was created in 1970 with the primary mission of promoting both French as an international language and worldwide cultural and linguistic diversity in an era of economic globalization. Even Canada has joined this battle. On the ground that broadcast programming provides a public service essential to national identity and cultural integrity, it has introduced "Canadian content" legislation stipulating that the national broadcasting system should provide a wide range of programming that reflects Canadian attitudes, values, artistic creativity, and talent. Numerous other countries have introduced similar quota systems that limit foreign broadcasting content.

WAIT A MINUTE. **CONSIDER THIS.** Globalization has brought economic gains that states would often not otherwise have experienced, although it has at the same time aggravated social, economic, and political inequalities within states as well as between them. Have the social, political, and cultural costs been worth the economic gains? Do you advocate that globalization proceed deeper and farther, or do you support its rollback? If you are pushing for a rollback, which hand do you think should do the pushing, the Right or the Left?

CONCLUSION

While not new in essence, globalization accelerated rapidly in the last quarter of the twentieth and first decade of the twenty-first centuries. Manifesting economic, political, and cultural dimensions, it is one of the most comprehensive, far-reaching, and consequential processes of change in the modern world. It carries immense implications for the relations between states as the search for freer and freer markets and weaker and weaker government regulation strengthens supranational economic and political institutions and weakens the decision-making autonomy of states. Global capitalism has no respect for national boundaries as its economic logic, and associated social, political, and cultural consequences increasingly hold sway in the international arena. States have willingly traded off sovereignty against economic gain because their ruling classes perceive it to be in their national interest to do so. It is also the case, however, that this trade-off has met with some public resistance and its limits have become apparent. While mass publics appear largely to have accepted the enhanced national and economic inequalities fostered by globalization, they have resisted other of its consequences and obliged states to assert their sovereign decision-making power for fear of risking a public backlash against the whole globalization project. We have examined two such areas of resistance to the globalization imperative: immigration and the welfare state. In both of them, states have asserted their sovereign right to act as domestic constituencies dictate, despite it being at some free-market economic cost. On the one hand, they have resisted the free flow of people across state borders at the same time that they have made the free flow of goods, services, and capital ever easier. On the other hand, many have maintained often generous welfare states despite the actual and threatened flight of capital to high-return, low-tax, low-wage, and relatively unregulated investment destinations.

In short, states have embraced the globalization project because they deem its benefits to outweigh its costs. At the same time, however, they have shown themselves able and willing to resist its logic in instances where there is risk of this calculus being reversed and the political costs outweighing the benefits. While certainly buffeted, diminished, and altered in an era of unprecedented globalization, the state has not withered away. Instead, it continues to stand tall in the international arena.

7 Ethnic Nationalism

Multiethnic states are the norm in the world today. Currently, there are only six states on the planet that are, to all intents and purposes, ethnically homogeneous. South Korea, North Korea, Lesotho, Algeria, Morocco, and Egypt all have a single ethnic group that accounts for 99 percent or more of their total populations. (Japan at 98.5 percent and Tunisia at 98 percent are close to the mark.) This means that the remainder of the world's states are, to one degree or another, multiethnic. A great variety of political consequences arise from this basic fact, with some states being peaceful and cooperative across ethnic cleavage lines and others being an intolerable, violent hell as warring groups collide. In between are states where ethnic politics is institutionally contained and expressed in struggles for, among other things, language rights, constitutional recognition of ethnic symbols and status, economic equality, educational opportunities, immigrant rights, and pathways to citizenship.

Although most multiethnic societies are stable and peaceful (Fearon and Laitin 1996), many experience some kind of turbulence along their ethnic fault lines. The typical pattern of ethnic politics can be described variously as competitive coexistence, interethnic rivalry, multiculturalism, and/or identity politics. In these situations, groups compete peacefully over perceived political, economic, and cultural injustices (past and present). Because such points of contention are normally fraught with emotional content and extremely difficult to solve definitively, even long-established and peaceful forms of ethnic competition can put the governing capacity of states to the test. This is especially the case when political parties organize around ethnic cleavages. Ethnic parties often gain electoral advantage by raising the temperature of ethnic relations and saturating the national discourse with a rhetoric based on interethnic suspicion, stereotype, and chauvinism. Under these circumstances, a polity can expect little relief from ethnic tensions.

At its most extreme, ethnic nationalism promotes secession, which is a political act designed to divide the territory of the state so as to allow the aggrieved group to acquire its own independent state. The desire of ethnic groups to signal their political independence by possessing their own state is a powerful political goal encapsulated neatly in the slogan of the nineteenth-century Italian nationalist Giuseppe Mazzini, "for every nation a state." This goal still resonates around the globe today.

It is also true that states challenge ethnic groups just as much as the other way around. Dominant groups who rule the state are frequently loath to concede equal recognition to minorities for fear that it will jeopardize their constitutional monopoly of sovereignty and undermine their status as the preeminent national grouping within the state. Consequently, such groups are commonly the main promoters of ethnic tension and perpetrators of violence. Programs of genocide and expulsion are typically the work of states, or of actors and groups who enjoy state support. States can also act as third-party instigators and interveners who stir the ethnic cauldron of neighboring states in the hope of benefiting coethnics who reside in them. In sum, the state is a both a prized object and repressive agent over and against which ethnic groups struggle in their demand for rights, recognition, and self-rule.

This chapter explores the multiple and complex frictions between ethnic nationalism and states in the modern world. Patterns of post–Cold War ethnic conflict are identified and explanations for its surge are offered in the first section. In the second section, distinct forms of nationalism and competing definitions of ethnicity are presented. In the third section, the processes by which politicized ethnic groups challenge the state and threaten democratic instability are explored. And in the fourth section, the range of state responses to such challenges is mapped. Let us first begin by explaining why ethnic and nationalist conflict escalated in the 1990s after communism in Eastern Europe and the Soviet Union collapsed.

THE POST–COLD WAR ACCELERATION OF ETHNIC CONFLICT

When communism disintegrated in Eastern Europe and the Soviet Union in the late 1980s and early 1990s, ethnic conflicts and identity politics spread like a contagion throughout the region. There were horrific wars, including three in Yugoslavia (Croatia [1991–1995], Bosnia-Herzegovina

[1992–1995], and Kosovo [1999]), two secessionist wars in Georgia (South Ossetia [1990–1992] and Abkhazia [1992–1993]), a war involving the secession of Transnistria from Moldova (1992), a civil war in Tajikistan (1992–1997), the Nagorno-Karabakh war between Armenia and Azerbaijan (1988–1994), and two rounds of war between Russia and Chechnya (1994–1996 and 1999–2009). In more global terms, *The New York Times* counted forty-eight ethnic conflicts and tension spots in 1993, the majority of which were concentrated in sub-Saharan Africa (fifteen) and Asia (thirteen) (Binder and Crossette 1993). In another study of the time, Ted Robert Gurr's *Minorities at Risk* project identified twenty-five wars being fought in 1994, eighteen of which involved rival ethnic groups as the principle adversaries (Gurr 1994).

Why was there such an upsurge in nationalist and ethnic conflict in the 1990s? In the broadest sense, ethnic turmoil tends to increase during moments of transition in the international order. The wave of nationalism that emerged as the Cold War ended is actually the third large-scale outbreak of nationalism in the twentieth century. The previous two waves occurred at the end of each of the two world wars, when colonial empires gave way to national liberation movements and periods of new state creation, first in Eastern Europe with the collapse of the Ottoman and Austro-Hungarian empires at the close of World War I, and then in Asia, Africa, and the Caribbean as Europe relinquished its colonial territories in the decades following World War II. Powerful national liberation movements fueled Europe's retreat from its colonial possessions and, having achieved independence, such movements turned to the even more difficult task of constructing viable states from multi-ethnic societies. The underlying logic would seem to be that great power transitions in the international sphere signal an alteration in the status and influence of states, render alliance commitments uncertain and, in general, increase anarchy; they thus create opportunities for aggrieved groups to undertake remedial action to improve their lot.

Just as in the international order, transitions of power within states increase uncertainty for all. Gurr's global study of minorities at risk, for example, found that compared to other potential causes of intergroup conflict, like material inequalities and civilizational or religious cleavages, political transitions are correlated with a greater frequency of interethnic violence. Moreover, such violence is more intense and deadly (meaning more deaths and more refugees) than conflicts that do not follow transitions (Gurr 1994). This is so because ethnic groups with a history of victimization and unfair treatment face *security dilemmas* (that is, real uncertainty about their future safety) during regime transitions and this is especially so when the institutions of the state that manage conflict begin to atrophy (Posen 1993).

Will my rights be protected in the new regime, or will my ethnic neighbors repress me? In many places, this is a rational question to ask because it is grounded in the living memory of past persecutions. Security dilemmas occur within states when the apparatus of law and order weakens and is unable to provide public safety and prosecute perpetrators of violence. In such conditions, real fears and anxieties can grip a community, leading to a dangerous escalation of brinkmanship moves and countermoves by ethnic entrepreneurs and nationalist parties. This danger is greatest when a politically dominant group is about to be transformed into a national minority, which was the fate facing, for example, the Serb population scattered throughout Yugoslavia and, later, the Sunni population in Iraq after the U.S.-led invasion toppled Saddam Hussein in 2003. As long as Yugoslavia remained intact, Serbs could rest comfortably wherever they resided for they were the largest ethnic group overall. The break-up of Yugoslavia promised to alter the demographic status quo profoundly and turn Serbs everywhere, except in Serbia itself, into an unprotected minority overnight.

Irredentist ambitions (or the desire to reclaim land and peoples perceived to have been captured by other states) are likewise kindled during transitions. When state integrity and legitimacy are weakened, territorial boundaries and the treaties that sanction them can all be thrown into question. "Why should we be a minority in your state when you can be one in ours?" neatly sums up the perilous security dilemma involved in territorial revision (Hitchens 1994).

In Eastern Europe and the former Soviet Union, many observers emphasize that the collapse of communism reopened grievances that had been papered over and/or repressed by the all-powerful communist party. As part of the classic Leninist ethnic strategy, ethnic groups were formally recognized throughout the Soviet bloc (or alliance system), subsidized with monies for language development, schools, media, and other institutions of cultural maintenance, and granted the status of either titular nations charged with administering republics or minority "nationalities" with autonomous territories in the federal states of Yugoslavia, Czechoslovakia, and the USSR. But while giving ethnic groups the political institutions and jurisdictional territory of formal self-rule with one hand, the Leninist state took away the de facto right of secession with the other and repressed any form of nationalism that threatened communist party hegemony.

Furthermore, the state's granting recognition and support to some groups was often perceived as coming at the expense of others, such that Serbs in Yugoslavia were convinced that Tito deliberately tried to weaken their status by carving out two autonomous provinces (Vojvodina and Kosovo) from their republic and essentially pursuing a "weak Serbia, strong Yugoslavia" policy. Communist redistribution policies in which subsidies from productive regions were sent to underdeveloped areas was another source of frustration, irritating in particular Czechs and Slovenes, who perceived that their hard-earned wealth was being squandered in, respectively, Slovakia and Kosovo (Bookman 1994; Burg 1983). In these ways and in many others, ethnic resentments festered under communism and exploded once the heavy hand of the Leninist state was lifted.

Sub-Saharan Africa has experienced the largest number of interethnic conflicts in the post–Cold War period. In 1993, full-scale civil wars were being fought in Somalia, Rwanda, Burundi, Zaire (later renamed the Democratic Republic of Congo), Angola, Liberia, and Sierra Leone, while less intense violent conflicts were taking place in Mauritania, Mali, Senegal, Djibouti, Togo, Chad, Nigeria, Uganda, Kenya, and South Africa. As the decade rolled on, so did the violence, intensifying in some of the countries already mentioned (namely the Democratic Republic of Congo, Chad, Liberia, Rwanda, and Burundi) at the same time as spreading to Republic of the Congo (Brazzaville) (1997–1999), Guinea-Bissau (1998–1999), and Côte d'Ivoire (2002–2007).

What accounts for this alarming amount of interethnic violence in Africa? First of all, the legacy of colonialism is directly culpable. When Europe began conquering Africa in the late nineteenth and early twentieth centuries, it drew borders to suit its own administrative convenience and largely ignored the geographical distribution of prevailing ethnic identities, languages, cultures, and historical experience. The formation of independent states therefore had to proceed with populations that either had no particular desire to live together or were outright rivals with one another. Furthermore, in classic divide-and-rule fashion, the colonial powers invented and cultivated some ethnic identities while others were promoted or demoted according to political expediency. For instance, in Rwanda, the Belgians favored the minority Tutsi and denigrated the majority Hutu on the premise that the former had more "European" physical features and were therefore more suitable for training as junior partners in administering the colonial state. For similar reasons, the Germans preferred the Ewe in Togo, the French praised the Moors of Mauritania and the Kabyle Berbers of Algeria, the Belgians lauded the Kasai Baluba of Congo, and the British promoted the Baganda in Uganda and the Yoruba of Nigeria. The problem for the postcolonial setting was that these pernicious external distinctions between "advanced" and "backward" groups took hold via cultural socialization and institutional reinforcement and consequently became the basis for postcolonial conflicts (Horowitz 1985). Lest one doubt the causal effectiveness of colonialism in shaping the present on the grounds that it occurred a "long time ago," it is instructive and sobering to note that virtually all of the countries of Africa became independent states only as recently as the 1960s!

The legacy of colonialism feeds into another cause of Africa's frightening ethnic wars, and that is the weakness of its states. Comparative statistics have much to reveal about this, as African states are regularly found among the poorest in terms of performance. For example, in the 2011 failed states index composed by the journal *Foreign Policy*, African states comprise more than half (thirteen) of the twenty worst cases (The Failed States Index 2011). According to Transparency International's 2011 corruption perceptions index, nine of the twenty most corrupt states on the planet are African (Transparency International 2011). And in the 2011 UN-sponsored Human Development Index, a ranking that measures quality-of-life indicators like life expectancy, education, and per capita GDP, African states constitute thirty-six of the forty-six countries within the "Low Human Development" category (United Nations Development Program 2011). In everyday life, these statistics are manifested in the inability of African states to deliver basic services like law and order, paved roads, functional hospitals and schools, and adequate power, water, and sewage systems. Indeed, in many places, the African state has only a nominal presence outside its capital cities.

The scholar Robert Jackson uses the label "quasi-state" to describe Africa's "limited empirical statehood." According to Jackson, quasi-states are a "parody of statehood," which is "indicated by pervasive incompetence, deflated credibility, and systematized corruption," as well as deficiencies in "the political will, institutional authority, and organized power to protect human rights or provide socioeconomic welfare" (Jackson 1990, 21). During the Cold War, Africa's fictional sovereignty was masked as the United States and the Soviet Union militarily, diplomatically, and financially supported their clients in the global chess game that was superpower rivalry. But with the end of this rivalry, Africa's barely legitimate and malfunctioning states were left exposed and powerless to manage the competing and conflicting interests of ethnic and tribal groups within them.

Moreover, Africa's states have been weak because the capitalist class in them is weak. For much of sub-Saharan Africa, the national bourgeoisie has failed to unite as a class and impose on the state apparatus its generalized interest in the impartial application of the rule of law. Instead, only factions of the bourgeoisie control the state at any given time. Once captured, they turn it into a machine for patron-client relations and exploit it for exclusive personal and tribal gains. This helps explain the prevalence of so much resource predation, corruption, and internal violence across the continent. In short, African states lack *hegemony* (see Chapter 1). Until the capitalist class unifies and imposes the rule of law on all strata of society (including itself), the African state will remain the target of, rather than the setting for, politics (Fatton 1988).

The sheer volume of ethnic wars began to decline at the dawn of the twenty-first century. Of the fifty-nine armed ethnic conflicts ongoing in 1999, Ted Robert Gurr found that twenty-three were de-escalating, twenty-nine were holding constant, and only seven were escalating. Among the reasons for this were the onset of war fatigue in many former hotspots, the replacement of chauvinist elites with more accommodating leaders, and the stepped-up presence of NGOs and human rights organizations (Gurr 2000). But even though ethnic warfare appears to be declining across the world, the march of globalization has continued to serve as a steady source of ethnic friction.

Globalization promotes tension along ethnic fault lines for a number of reasons. First and foremost, technological advances in communications makes it easier for diaspora groups (i.e., ethnic communities living outside their homeland) to keep in contact with their home countries, inform the world of ethnic injustices, raise money for nationalist causes, and forge transnational alliances. The scholar Benedict Anderson calls this phenomenon "email and web nationalism" (Rao 2010). Secondly, globalization has prompted an unprecedented movement of peoples around the world as laborers from poor countries flock to the wealthier societies of the West in search of economic opportunities. The growing presence of Turks in Germany (Berlin, incidentally, is the second largest "Turkish" city in the world), Africans in France and Italy, Mexicans in the United States, and Muslims throughout Europe has fostered a sharp rise in identity politics as dominant groups react with xenophobia and chauvinism against what they perceive as encroachments on their economic rights and cultural traditions (see Chapter 6). Additionally, growing economic insecurity in Western countries brought on by globalization has prompted many to search for scapegoats who can be blamed for unemployment and declining wages as well as the general disorientation caused by a rapidly changing world.

Ethnic and national identities are seductively simple tools that ethnic entrepreneurs can deploy to mobilize aggrieved peoples, because nationalist sentiments provide easy answers to complicated problems. Class mobilization has always been a more difficult task, for it requires individuals to climb a ladder of abstraction and overcome prejudice to find solidarity with members of different ethnic groups who share the same economic standing but possess possibly distinct languages, religions, phenotypes (the observable characteristics of people, like skin color, hair, and facial features), clothing styles, food consumption habits, and mores. The mobilization of ethnicity involves the relatively simpler task of "sliding down" the psychological gradient from complex cognitive levels to unsophisticated and crude notions of prejudice and stereotype based on selectively invidious contrasts between the in-group and the out-group (Rothschild 1981). If nothing else, the comparative ease of ethnic mobilization ensures its staying power in the modern world.

Let us now examine the various and contested meanings of ethnicity and nationalism.

THE POWER OF ETHNIC IDENTITIES AND THE FORMS OF NATIONALISM

An ethnic group is a social collectivity that shares cultural traits (such as language, religion, and common historical experiences) and/or ascriptive markers of common biological heritage or phenotypic distinction. In other words, ethnicity is a general concept within which one may locate linguistic, religious, cultural, and racial identities. Because the bases of ethnic group identity vary tremendously across societies, any definition of it must be broad and inclusive.

The classic definition of an ethnic group comes from the anthropologist Clifford Geertz (1963, 109), who wrote the bonds of "blood, speech, custom, and so on, are seen to have an ineffable, and at times overpowering, coerciveness in and of themselves." What specifically makes ethnicity so "ineffable, overpowering, and coercive" is that ethnic categories are immediately imposed on individuals at birth lending them a "sense of natural – some would even say spiritual – affinity." And so they remain throughout the course of an individual's life even if she consciously rejects them. For example, let us imagine a college student from a Catholic family living in Belfast who studies philosophy and decides to jettison Catholicism and adopt atheism. While this conversion is of utmost importance to the student and reflects her personal independence and autonomy from the sectarian strife of Northern Ireland, in the eyes of Protestant loyalists she is, and will forever remain, a Catholic. Because of this "inherited and inescapable fate" (Horowitz 1985, 90), questions of identity in ethnically divided societies are never framed in terms of "which side are you on?" but rather in the form of "who are you?" As Samuel Huntington (1993a, 27) usefully warns us, in some societies, "the wrong answer to that question can mean a bullet in the head."

The definition of ethnicity we have been discussing is usually labeled "primordialism." According to this view, ethnicity is a fundamental and natural form of human identity. Because of its deep psychological and even biological roots, individuals are conditioned to practice in-group amity and out-group enmity. In other words, for primordialists, favoritism toward one's "own kind" and prejudice toward outsiders are part of the natural human condition. Many scholars in anthropology, sociology, and political science criticize this perspective and argue instead for the virtues of "constructivism." This theory holds that society or the state (and sometimes both) manufacture ethnicity. Rejected is the premise that ethnic identities are fixed, innate, or genetically coded. Instead, constructivists contend that individual identities are always multiple and that ethnicity need not be preeminent among them. When it is useful, profitable, or politically expedient, powerful vested interests in society encourage some types of ethnic identities and discourage others. Furthermore, ethnic identities and enmities themselves are constantly changing and adapting in response to new social circumstances. In nineteenth-century American history, for instance, Irish immigrants were not considered "white" – they were in fact often called "white negroes." Accordingly, they were denied equal rights and employment opportunities. In business storefronts, signs reading "Help Wanted – No Irish Need Apply" were commonplace. Over time, the Irish "became white," which indicates the mutable quality of ethnicity. In short, the constructivist holds that ethnic groups are not born, but made.

WAIT A MINUTE. **CONSIDER THIS.** In the attempt to debunk primordialism, constructivist scholars deny the role of ethnicity in conflict and sometimes even the very existence of ethnic groups. For them, ethnic conflict is not a struggle between two distinguishable *ethnie* (or ethnic communities) who have mutual animosity and irreconcilable interests, but rather is a product of deliberate elite and media manipulation. Thus, John Bowen (1996) writes of the "myth of global ethnic conflict" referring to places like Rwanda and Yugoslavia. Similarly, V. P. Gagnon (2004) advances arguments about "the myth of ethnic war" in the Balkans. These and other authors question the usefulness of ethnicity as an explanation of political outcomes.

Are ethnic groups natural or constructed? Is race a function of biology or an invention of racists? Do you consider yourself a member of an ethnic or racial group, or does society impose these categories on you? Medical science has determined that ethnic and racial groups are susceptible to different types of diseases and even have different levels of tolerance for lactose digestion. For example, in the United States, African Americans die from hypertension in greater numbers than European Americans, and European Americans die from heart attacks more than African Americans. Similarly, Jews tend to carry the genetic mutation for Tay-Sachs disease, and Africans for sickle cell anemia. Are these biological facts relevant for political questions? The renowned African-American novelist James Baldwin (1924–1987) once said, "Color is not a human or personal reality; it is a political reality." What do you think?

Forms of Nationalism: Civic and Ethnic

Just as definitions of ethnicity split into primordial and constructivist versions, so too is nationalism divided into civic and ethnic forms. Civic nationalism is congruent with the political philosophy of classical liberalism, and is the doctrine that influenced the American, French, and Latin American revolutions of the eighteenth century. In this model, nations are constructed on the basis of individual consent and composed of those willing to submit to, and participate in, the laws of the land. Two quotes from French thinkers neatly convey the spirit of civic nationalism. The first comes from Ernest Renan (1823–1892) who pithily described the nation as a "daily plebiscite." In other words, the foundation of nations rests on nothing more than individual decisions to belong and to stay. Abbé Sieyès (1748–1836), an important theorist of the 1789 French Revolution, provides the second quote with his declaration that a nation is a "body of associates living under one common law and represented by the same legislature" (Alter 1989). Both statements underscore the close connection with the social contract theories of Locke and Rousseau.

If a nation is a "body of *associates*" that hangs together by individual consent, then essentially what is created is a *political nation* that is open to all for membership. As the motto on America's Statue of Liberty (a gift from the French) reads: "Give us your tired, your poor, your huddled masses yearning to breathe free, the wretched refuse of your teeming shore. Send these, the homeless, tempest-tost to me." The French revolutionaries also acted in accordance with such premises, repudiating a language criterion for citizenship and electing the American radical and non-French-speaker Thomas Paine (1737–1809) to their National Convention in 1792. Both America and France defined citizenship on the principle of *jus soli* (or the right of soil), meaning that citizenship is immediately conferred on any child born on the territory of the state or who enters the state as an adult and willingly embraces its values and culture.

Despite the ostensibly open-door policy to membership in the "body of associates," eighteenth- and nineteenth-century American liberals partook in a long list of hideous practices against those deemed unfit for citizenship, including genocide against Native Americans, enslavement of Africans, and the later denial of political rights and full citizenship to both groups as well as to the immigrant Asian community. The incalculable human destruction produced in the New World is an inconvenient fact for proponents of civic nationalism. It also brings into sharp relief the question just how different this conception is from the other main form of nationalist ideology: ethnic nationalism.

Ethnic nationalism is the grounding of nationhood in the ascriptive traits of language, common biological descent, and religion. Politically, ethnic nationalism makes the demand that nation and state should correspond, meaning all members of the nation should reside within the same state and political leaders should be of the same ethnic composition as the citizenry. According to this formula, membership in the nation is restricted to those who share the designated ascriptive markers. The concept of citizenship that follows is based on the principle of *jus sanguinis* (or the right of blood), which grants citizenship only to individuals whose ancestors were citizens. What is produced then are not the political nations of civic nationalism, but rather *cultural nations*.

Ethnic nationalism has its origins in the nineteenth-century state-building experiences of Italy and Germany. In these cases, a limited but real sense of nationhood was intact among cultural elites long before states were founded. Gifted philosophers, literary writers, artists, and musical composers had been making great contributions to Western civilization since the sixteenth century in Germany and since the fourteenth century in Italy. Machiavelli captures a rudimentary and proto-sense of ethnic nationalism percolating among some sections of the Italian educated classes when he famously concludes *The Prince*, written in 1513, with a chapter entitled "An Exhortation to Liberate Italy from the Barbarians." Once France and later Britain forged the path to modern statehood in the late eighteenth and early nineteenth centuries, the state ideal became the highest aspiration for Italian and German national awakeners. In contradistinction to the liberty and equality of all citizens championed by French and American nationalists, however, their German and Italian counterparts promoted claims of political priority for those inhabitants of the state embodying their preferred and unique ascriptive attributes (Greenfeld 1992; Hobsbawm 1990). This internal authoritarianism was matched by external aggression. Thus, Italians decried the fate of "*Italia irredenta*" (unredeemed Italy) and made claims on lands of the Austrian empire where Italian communities lived. Germans, for their part, demanded a "*lebensraum*" (living space) that included all of their coethnics who resided in neighboring states and were presumably "trapped" or "lost."

As nationalism continued to spread eastward to the lands of Eastern Europe over the course of the nineteenth century and southward to Asia, Africa, and the Middle East in the twentieth century, it was mostly ethnic nationalism, not the civic version, that made the journey. This is most unfortunate because virtually everywhere, nascent states confronted multiethnic societies making for a poor fit between ideology and reality. Is it any wonder, then, that the building of states and nations around the globe in modern times has been associated with unusual brutality?

*W**AIT A MINUTE.* **CONSIDER THIS.** The differences between civic and ethnic nationalism are routinely presented in the scholarly literature and in political science textbooks, with the former being praised and the latter condemned. Is this differential moral evaluation supported by the historical facts? We have already alluded to the practices of genocide and slavery in American history. How can these catastrophic events be squared with the liberal precepts of civic nationalism? According to critics like Benjamin Schwarz, even the normally vaunted idea of the American "melting pot" flies in the face of the "coercive conformity" and cultural hegemony imposed on all minorities and immigrants by the dominant Anglo-Saxon population (Schwarz 1995). Still, liberalism and civic nationalism celebrate a set of values – a rhetoric of rights, if you will – which aggrieved groups have continually employed to rectify abuses and reform institutions. Martin Luther King, Jr.'s skillful use of liberal rhetoric to convince whites to honor the Constitution is the best-known, but in no way the only, example.

Are there, in fact, significant philosophical and practical differences between civic and ethnic nationalism? What do you think?

POLITICIZED ETHNICITY AND THE CHALLENGES FOR DEMOCRACY AND THE STATE

Thus far, we have presented data on the prevalence of ethnic conflict after the Cold War, provided competing definitions of ethnicity, and argued about the lethal forms nationalism can take. In this section, our goal is to demonstrate specific processes by which politicized ethnicity can damage democracies and undermine states.

Fears, Memories, and Resentments

Verbal expressions of stereotype and prejudice are common in multi-ethnic societies. Think for a moment of the catalog of nasty epithets that white Anglo-Saxons in America have historically directed at the Irish, Italians, Catholics, Japanese, Germans, Chinese, Vietnamese, African Americans, Hispanics, Jews, Arabs, and, most recently, Muslims. From where does this urge to demonize the "other" come, and what are its political consequences?

Scholars who investigate this question often start with insights from the field of social psychology. Henri Tajfel's (1919–1982) work in this area is considered groundbreaking and well supported by subsequent research. Tajfel's scientific experiments involved the random assignment of individuals to groups where they were given opportunities to distribute goods in numerous ways, including those that rewarded all members of all groups. And yet the subjects consistently displayed attachment to their own artificial laboratory group by favoring distributions that maximized differences among the groups in their own group's favor, even in circumstances when more equitable distributions would have brought greater benefits to both the in-group and the out-groups (Horowitz 1985).

On the basis of Tajfel's findings, we can begin to appreciate why in multiethnic societies, where ethnic affiliations are critical components of individual identities, there is such a pronounced tendency to bigotry and a lack of empathy for the "other." The relationship between welfare and racial diversity provides a powerful example. Several studies have demonstrated that welfare distribution is less generous in the United States than in Western Europe in part because European Americans are opposed to spending tax dollars on African Americans who are disproportionately concentrated at low-income levels. European countries are traditionally less heterogeneous, and therefore the middle class does not face the same psychological hurdle when imagining the beneficiaries of public spending. Instead, most can comfortably assume that their tax monies are going to "people like us" (Alesina, Glaecer, and Sacerdote 2001).

The differential group evaluation seen in the United States is discernible around the globe. In the southern Balkan country of Macedonia, relations have always been frayed between majority ethnic Macedonians (64 percent) and minority Albanians (25 percent). Neither side trusts or holds a positive estimation of the other. In one poll, it was revealed that 77 percent of Macedonians held an unfavorable view of Albanians, whereas 43 percent of Albanians felt the same way toward Macedonians. Political perspectives clash so consistently that one can predict with near-absolute certainty that if Macedonians support a policy option, Albanians will oppose it, and vice versa. Not surprisingly, the acceptance of interethnic marriage is very low for both sides. In a 2001 poll, 66 percent of respondents agreed with the statement "most citizens of Macedonia are not ready to marry outside their ethnic group" (Hislope 2007).

In Rwanda, anti-Tutsi prejudice comprised a core element of Hutu postcolonial discourse. The minority Tutsi population was regularly portrayed by Hutus as alien invaders belonging to a different race of people that secretly aimed at keeping the majority Hutus in a state of virtual slavery; "to be forever subaltern workers" is how Rwanda's first president, Grégoire Kayibanda (1962–1973), described it (Uvin 1997). Prejudice is also no stranger in the far more tranquil lands of Western Europe. One study of attitudes toward immigrants found that 45 percent of those interviewed felt there were "too many" foreigners residing in their state. The country breakdown for this attitude is as follows: Greece – 71 percent, Belgium – 60 percent, Italy – 53 percent, Germany – 52 percent, Austria – 50 percent, France – 46 percent, Denmark – 46 percent, United Kingdom – 42 percent, the Netherlands – 40 percent, Sweden – 38 percent, Luxembourg – 33 percent, Portugal – 28 percent, Spain – 20 percent, Ireland – 19 percent, and Finland – 10 percent (Zick et al. 2008).

Hostile feelings toward out-groups are exacerbated when there is a shared history of interethnic strife. Some writers on ethnic conflict speak of "ancient animosities" between groups, but the historical reality is that relatively few, if any, current interethnic problems date back to antiquity. A more realistic conceptualization of the interethnic strife dynamic is "perennialism," or the recurrence of conflict among groups in modern times (Smith 2000). In Yugoslavia, Rwanda, and Burundi, the bloodbaths of the 1990s were preceded by several recent episodes of brutal violence. The postcolonial history of Rwanda and Burundi moves in tandem not only because they are neighboring states, but also because their ethnic composition is essentially identical, namely majority Hutu (85 percent) and minority Tutsi (14 percent). The bloodletting that took place in each country in the first half of the 1990s (Burundi in 1993 and Rwanda in 1994) followed on the heels of one destructive rampage after another. Thus, in 1959, 10,000 Tutsis fled Rwanda following Hutu-led violence; in 1963, 20,000 Tutsi were murdered in Rwanda; in 1972, 150,000 Hutus were killed in Burundi; and in 1988, 15,000 Hutus were massacred in Burundi and 50,000 fled to Rwanda (Mann 2005).

In Yugoslavia, the inferno of World War II produced untold sufferings, with the Serb community being particularly hard-hit by a Croatian-led campaign of genocide. The role of historical memory is potent because living representatives use their pain and anguish to keep the fear of domination and extinction alive and to remind fellow group members of the need for eternal vigilance, if not preemptive strikes, against the descendants of the "other" community. Quite telling in this regard are the many Serb political and military leaders involved in the wars of the 1990s whose family members had perished in the murderous ethnic campaigns of World War II (Glenny 1996).

Overall, the emotions of fear, resentment, hatred, and rage permeate the landscape of many multiethnic societies (Petersen 2002). Even in the relatively pacific and successful democracies of Western Europe and the United States, prejudice, chauvinism, and xenophobia are ordinary features of social life. When popular discourse reduces the *demos* (the citizenry) to the *ethnos* (the ethnic group), dangerous conditions begin to develop within a polity.

Political Competition in Ethnically Divided Societies

The disparaging attitudes, frustrations, and mutual animus that exist within many multiethnic societies are insufficient, in and of themselves, to cause ethnic mobilization, damage democracies, and fragment states. They are best conceived as the raw material of ethnic politics. What transforms this raw matter into the finished product of mobilized ethnicity is the work of political agents and agencies (i.e., parties, media, and elites) that mobilize, encourage, and channel latent hostilities in the direction of confrontation and violence.

Ethnic Party Systems and Intra-Ethnic Competition

Political parties play a major role in the political organization of ethnicity. Ethnic parties are different from nonethnic ones in that their base of support comes exclusively from the targeted ethnic group and their ideology and platform are formulated specifically not to appeal beyond that group. Ascription, exclusion, and centrality are the key dimensions of an ethnic party. "The categories that such a party mobilizes are defined according to ascriptive characteristics; the mobilization of the 'insider' ethnic categories is always accompanied by the exclusion of ethnic 'outsiders'; and, while the party may also highlight other issues, the championing of the cause of an ethnic category or categories is central to its mobilizing efforts" (Chandra 2004, 3).

Nonethnic parties, in contrast, seek an inclusive membership and cast a wide net with their political program so as to catch as many voters as possible. The exceptional electoral success of the Republican Party in America in the 1980s is a case in point. A major achievement of Ronald Reagan in the 1980 presidential election was to convince working-class voters to break their allegiance to the "New Deal" coalition of interests united behind the Democratic Party and forged by President Franklin Roosevelt in the 1930s. This was how the term "Reagan Democrats" was born. In nonethnic party systems, competition for votes typically occurs in the ideological middle, as parties tend to take their core support for granted and compete for the uncommitted, independent, floating voters. Because of this gravitation of parties toward the center, such party systems generate incentives for moderate politics.

In party systems in which all the major political parties are ethnic-based, party competition takes place not across ethnic groups but within them. The central question at election time is not "for whom are you voting?" but rather "are you going to vote?" That is, because ethnic parties cannot expect support outside their group, they must maximize the turnout of their community to gain whatever power their numbers allow. To accomplish this, they have an incentive to employ incendiary rhetoric designed to heighten group anxiety and encourage group unity at the same time. Rather than bridge cleavages, ethnic parties reinforce them

(Horowitz 1985). A good example of an ethnic party system is Northern Ireland, where the main ethnic parties draw their support overwhelmingly from "their own" confessional communities. On the Protestant side, the Democratic Unionist Party's support base is 85 percent Protestant, and the Ulster Unionist Party has a following that is 89 percent Protestant. On the Catholic side, 96 percent of the rank-and-file supporters of the Social Democratic and Labor Party are Catholic, and Catholics account for 93 percent of Sinn Féin's supporters (Mitchell 1995).

When there is more than one party per ethnic group, the competition for votes can produce a ratchet effect of belligerent posturing. Insurgent parties in particular attempt to win popularity by outbidding other parties in order to prove their stronger nationalist credentials. Such "flanking parties" make compromise across the ethnic divide very difficult, because any interethnic deal by an accommodative party will be met by accusations of betrayal. In some instances, intra-ethnic party relations can become so tense that violence erupts. As Donald Horowitz (1985, 348) notes, there is "nothing in the competitive equation [that] requires moderation." This dynamic can be seen at work in many ethnically plural societies, such as Northern Ireland and the former Yugoslavia.

In Northern Ireland in the 1980s and 1990s, the more nationalist (Protestant) Democratic Unionist Party and (Catholic) Sinn Féin gained electoral ground on their more moderate rivals, the Ulster Unionist and Social Democratic and Labor parties, respectively. This brought not only "fierce competition" between the parties but also "intense rivalry within [each] nationalist segment" (Mitchell 1995). Over the course of the entire "Troubles" (as the sectarian conflict in Northern Ireland is known), intra-communal violence was common. Paramilitaries on both sides meted out punishment against their coreligionists. Between 1969 and 2001, Republican paramilitaries actually killed 450 Catholics (nearly 30 percent of all Catholic deaths), while Protestant Loyalist groups killed 231 Protestants (amounting to 18 percent of all Protestant deaths) (see Sutton Index of Deaths at <http://cain.ulst.ac.uk/sutton/crosstabs.html>).

Flanking parties were also evident in Serbia and Croatia in the early 1990s. At this time, insurgent, ultranationalist parties, like the Croatian Party of [State] Right (HSP) and the Serbian Radical Party (SRS), emerged to challenge the dominant parties in power in each republic – President Franjo Tuđman's Croatian Democratic Community (HDZ) and President Slobodan Milošević's Socialist Party of Serbia (SPS). Tuđman's government responded to pressure on its right flank by harassing the HSP party organization and arresting its leader, Dobroslav Paraga. In Serbia,

TABLE 7.1	Bosnia-herzegovina's census election, November 1990			
% of the population		**Ethnic parties**	**% of the vote**	**Total seats**
Muslims	43.7	Party of Democratic Action	37.8	87
		Muslim Bosniak Organization	0.8	2
Serbs	31.4	Serbian Democratic Party	26.5	61
		Serbian Renewal Movement	0.4	1
Croats	17.3	Croatian Democratic Community	14.7	34
Totals	92.4		80.2	185

Source: Hislope (1995).

Milošević at first co-opted the SRS by forging a governing coalition with them in 1992, but soon thereafter relations soured and the SRS was subjected to a campaign of repression (Hislope 1996).

Census Elections

Another ominous political pattern that can occur in ethnically divided societies is the census election. Census elections take place when electoral outcomes mirror the ethnic composition of a population. When citizens decide to "think with their blood" (as the Prussian leader Otto von Bismarck [1815–1898] advised) and vote accordingly, minority groups face the prospect of permanent political exclusion. This is what happened in Bosnia-Herzegovina's first democratic election in November 1990. Table 7.1 provides a summary of the election outcome.

All in all, ethnic parties won 80 percent of the vote and 185 of the 240 seats in the National Assembly. The remaining 20 percent of the vote went to nonethnic parties, like the former communist party and an all-Yugoslav liberal, reformist alliance, which translated into 55 seats for nonethnic voices in the parliament. The election results created a serious problem for Bosnia's new democracy, because once the electoral strength of ethnic communities had become apparent in the census election, the endgame of all foreseeable contests became known in advance. Future election outcomes, in other words, become predictable and unalterable by normal democratic procedures. An ethnic party representing a minority may propose reforming the electoral law in a proportional direction or devolving power to local levels where the minority is the majority, but unless the party of the majority group agrees to these plans, they have zero chance of success. This is why, as Horowitz observes, a census election "provides good reason for the excluded minority party to depart from the electoral road to power – since that road in fact does not lead to power" (Horowitz 1985, 360).

Despite a postelectoral agreement mandating legislative consensus among all three of Bosnia's main parties, Muslim and Croat parties immediately began to align, leaving the Serbs out in the cold. With only 61 seats, the Serbs were powerless to block proposals and accordingly began to complain about being "outvoted." The most important issue facing the assembly concerned the sovereignty of Bosnia within the context of a crumbling Yugoslavia. The Muslim and Croat parties agreed that if the neighboring republics of Slovenia and Croatia declared secession from Yugoslavia, then Bosnia would do likewise. Bosnia's Serbs, however, wanted just the opposite – to maintain close ties with the republic of Serbia and therefore remain in Yugoslavia, even a truncated version of it (i.e., without the northern republics). Between these two visions of the future of Bosnia, no compromise was possible and neither vision could be implemented given the ethnic composition of the National Assembly. After a year of political paralysis, grandstanding rhetoric, and threatening moves by all sides, the Serb deputies walked out of the assembly in January 1992 and never returned. War came to Bosnia the following March.

The Caribbean island state of Trinidad and Tobago also has had experience with census elections, yet it has been able both to avoid bloodshed and to keep its democracy and state intact. Trinidad gained independence from Britain in 1962, and relations between its Black (traditionally referred to as Creole or Negro) and East Indian communities have been fractious but not openly violent since. Blacks are the traditionally hegemonic group in political terms. Their party, the People's National Movement (PNM), held power for thirty uninterrupted years, from 1956 to 1986. Of the fifty-two available cabinet positions during this time frame, Black politicians held thirty-nine posts and Indians only six (Parris 1990). By the 1980s, demographic changes gave Indians (40.3 percent) a slight demographic edge over the Afro-Trinidadian community (39.5 percent). Consequently, the PNM lost power in 1986 to a multiethnic coalition involving the National Alliance for Reconstruction (NAR) and the Indian United Labor Front. This was Trinidad's first ever multiethnic ruling coalition, and it presaged the victory of a new Indian party, the United National Congress (UNC), which won the 2000 elections and became Trinidad's first ever Indian-led government.

Over the course of Trinidad's postcolonial history, ethnic voting has been a central tendency. Ethnic parties in fact often receive nearly 100 percent of the popular vote. This is especially so when elections are close, and they have been increasingly so since the 1990s. It is very rare for PNM candidates to win in predominantly Indian districts, even when fielding Indian candidates. The same is true for Indian parties. In the 1995 elections, for example, only five electoral districts in the country were competitive; the PNM won the fifteen Black majority districts, and the UNC won in the fourteen majority Indian districts (Owolabi 2007). There is a sizeable mixed population (18 percent), called *dougla* in the local vernacular. In electoral terms, this group has been most responsive to the multiethnic NAR party.

On two occasions, census elections have produced a tie in the distribution of parliamentary seats. The first time was in 1995, when the PNM (48.8 percent of the vote) and the UNC (45.7 percent) received exactly seventeen seats apiece. This was a totally unexpected outcome and was unprecedented in Trinidad's electoral history. It was resolved when the multiethnic NAR, which had won the remaining two assembly seats in Tobago, swung its support behind the UNC and created a coalition government (Premdas and Ragoonth 1998). The second time, no such remedy was available. In the December 2000 elections, all the seats to the parliament (thirty-six in total) were evenly divided between the PNM (46.5 percent of the vote) and the UNC (49.9 percent), resulting in an eighteen-to-eighteen deadlock. With the PNM unwilling to form a grand coalition and share power with the UNC, Trinidad limped along for a year without a government until October 2001 when new elections were held and the PNM emerged with 51 percent of the vote and twenty of the thirty-six seats in the assembly. Despite the arousal of intense passions among politicians with each hung parliament, Trinidad never spiraled into violence as Bosnia did in the aftermath of its census election.

*W**AIT A MINUTE.* **CONSIDER THIS.** Why do similar political processes produce different results in different multiethnic societies? If you were to investigate why Trinidad's ethnic politics were ultimately governable and Bosnia's were not, what type of explanations would you pursue? What are some plausible causal factors that can account for the different outcomes?

Ethnic Elites and Nationalist Media

Observers of ethnic conflict often note how calm and tolerant interethnic relations were until nationalist elites showed up and poisoned the atmosphere with fear, hatred, and resentment. The reliance on elites to account for ethnic conflict is a crucial, but sometimes overstated, explanation. There is never a shortage of opportunists among politicians. If political advantage can be gained from playing the ethnic card, then many are willing to step forward and play that game. However, treating elites as the sole causal factor for ethnic problems and ignoring the content and distribution of group attitudes, the modern history of interethnic relations, and the context in which politics unfold (such as regime transitions, economic downturns, intense party competition, etc.) does a disservice to the complexity of underlying political problems, forces, and processes. This is not to suggest that elites do not matter, but only to warn that because political leaders (or those who affect national outcomes regularly and substantially) are so easy to locate and observe, they can tempt one into committing explanatory overstatement.

With this caveat in mind, we can cite a wide range of political elites who made, or are currently making, a career out of stoking interethnic anxieties (they would invariably prefer the description "defending their ethnic community"), including, but not limited to, Slobodan Milošević (president of postcommunist Serbia), Radovan Karadžić (postcommunist Bosnian Serb leader), Vladimir Mečiar (postcommunist prime minister of Slovakia), Robert Mugabe (president of Zimbabwe), P. W. Botha (leader of apartheid South Africa), George Wallace (1960s segregationist southern leader, United States), Ian Paisley (former leader of the Protestant Democratic Unionist Party in Northern Ireland), Gerry Adams (leader of the Catholic-oriented Sinn Féin in Northern Ireland), Jean-Marie Le Pen (former French right-wing party leader), Jörg Haider (former Austrian right-wing party leader), Geert Wilders (current Dutch right-wing party leader), and Alex Salmond (current leader of the Scottish National Party and First Minister of Scotland). The inclusion of this diverse set of political elites in the same sentence is not meant to suggest they all have committed the same crimes (or, for some, any crimes at all), or that all share the same degree of responsibility for inflaming interethnic relations. Rather, its purpose is only to indicate the variety of political elites who are frequently charged with making political capital out of exacerbating interethnic tensions.

Ethnic elites need an institutional base to build a national constituency, and one of the most important of institutions in modern politics is the mass media. Opportunities to sell chauvinism and xenophobia are greatly augmented when important media outlets are placed at the service of ethnic nationalism. The most propitious situation is one in which the media is segmented into ethnic audiences such that ethnic groups hear only information tailored to their group and not others. In this way, a population's national consciousness is splintered and the sense of "we the people" either never takes shape or starts to erode. This happened during Hitler's march to power in Germany. As Jack Snyder (2000, 65) explains, "Weimar's liberal, Jewish-owned, mass circulation papers were objective and even erudite, but their ideas failed to penetrate beyond Berlin or Hamburg." The same segmentation of the media happened in Yugoslavia during its transition from communism. Most of the major newspapers and television channels were overtaken by nationalist-oriented messages in the run-up to the democratic elections and various wars. The upshot was a marginalization of voices in favor of multicultural peace and an amplification of the voices of intolerance.

Today, a similarly dangerous game of audience segmentation and the manipulation of information is occurring in the United States. Since the historic election in November 2008 of America's first African-American president, Barack Obama, the Fox News channel has sought systematically to discredit not only Obama's policies, but also the legitimacy of his presidency. By constantly questioning where Obama was born and his religious affiliation over the course of the twenty-four-hour news cycle, Fox News, along with the hugely successful conservative media personalities like Glenn Beck and Rush Limbaugh, have helped convince an astonishing 46 percent of the Republican base that Obama is a Muslim (he is actually a Christian). Another 27 percent believe that the president was born outside the United States and is therefore not a legal citizen (he was actually born in the state of Hawaii) (Egan 2010). The deliberate obfuscation of Obama's religion and birthplace by Fox News commentators functions to reinforce white suspicions (only 1.38 percent of Fox viewers are black) that America's first African-American president is "not one of us" – a point echoed in the popular Republican slogan "Give us our country back." Although the motto of Fox News is "fair and balanced," it is closely tied to the Republican political establishment, donating $1 million to the party in 2010.

Republican Party rhetoric and strategy is geared toward capitalizing on white fears, for this traditionally dominant segment of American society is shrinking and aging as immigration continues to darken the complexion of the country. The most recent estimates are that by the year 2050, non-Hispanic whites will fall to 46 percent of the population (from their current level of 66 percent). According to one demographer, "no other country has experienced such rapid racial and ethnic change"

(Roberts 2008). In comparative terms, the trajectory of events in other ethnically frayed societies where demographics rapidly change, the economy declines, and opportunistic ethnic elites and a chauvinist media find common ground do not bode well for the future of race and ethnic relations in America.

> *W*AIT A MINUTE. **CONSIDER THIS.** Will American political institutions prove capable of managing the changing ethnic and racial landscape of the near future? Samuel Huntington (1993b, 190) expresses his doubts when he asks, "If the United States becomes truly multicultural and pervaded with an internal clash of civilizations, will it survive as a liberal democracy?" What do you think?

STATES AND ETHNIC GROUPS: CHALLENGES AND SOLUTIONS

A broad range of policy options and strategies are available to states and ethnic groups as they struggle to further their interests. Historically, states have chosen to conquer and dominate minorities, expel them from contested territory, subject them to genocide, institutionalize their subordinate status, coercively assimilate them, and accommodate them through a great variety of ways and means. Minority ethnic groups, for their part, have followed various goals and strategies such as the ballot box, economic redistribution, cultural recognition, institutional reforms that devolve or share power, violent rebellion, and secession from the state. What follows in this section is a brief overview of the various strategies and goals that states and ethnic groups around the globe have chosen in their relations with each other.

Secession, Partition, and Violence

Ethnic groups that pursue secession (or the unilateral exit of an ethnic group and the territory it controls) from the state normally choose a military strategy, because no state anywhere in the world happily cedes territory. To do so would signal its loss of an essential attribute of statehood: maintaining territorial integrity. The peaceful partition of states (i.e., territorial divisions that have state consent and/or are brought about by the intervention and support of the international community) is a rare historical event and can be counted, in the twentieth century, on one hand: (1) Senegal and Mali split in 1960; (2) Singapore left Malaysia also in 1960; (3) Sweden and Norway separated in 1905; (4) Czechoslovakia had its famous "velvet divorce" (i.e., a peacefully negotiated separation) in 1992; and (5) in 1991, the dissolution of the USSR occurred peacefully and paved the way for the birth of fifteen new independent states. The partition of British India into the sovereign states of India and Pakistan was planned to proceed peacefully in 1947, but the massive population exchanges that occurred overwhelmed the governing capacity of the new states, and at least 500,000 people were killed.

Elsewhere, militarized ethnic violence accompanies the decision of ethnic groups to seek exit from the state. This is the lesson of Bangladesh's 1971 successful war of liberation against Pakistan, Eritrea's victorious thirty-year war (1961–1991) to secure independence from Ethiopia, the Yugoslav wars of succession in the 1990s, the 1969–1997 armed campaign of the Provisional Irish Republican Army to free Northern Ireland from union with Britain, the failed thirty-three-year effort (1976–2009) of the Tamil Tigers to separate ethnic Tamil areas from Sri Lanka, and the numerous wars fought by regional ethnic groups against the newly independent states that emerged from the Soviet Union (Transnistria from Moldova, Chechnya from Russia, South Ossetia and Abkhazia from Georgia, and Nagorno-Karabakh from Azerbaijan).

One thing that secessions tend to create is a "new" minority in the seceding region that is unhappy with its newfound situation. Because most states in the world are heterogeneous, a seceding region is bound to carry with it groups who do not wish to depart from the former state. The Serb minority in independent Kosovo continues to feel this way, as do the South Ossetians and Abkhazians who rebelled once the former Soviet republic of Georgia declared statehood. Essentially, secession frequently creates a *matrioshka* effect. Named after the Russian doll that has a series of dolls of decreasing sizes inside, this term refers to the nesting of nationalisms within a single region. Once opened, *matrioshka* nationalism creates a spiraling effect of secessionist moves by consecutively smaller ethnic groupings, or what Horowitz labels "reciprocal separatism" (Horowitz 1985, 278–79). In the process of grappling with Bosnia's secession from Yugoslavia, the international community attempted to preempt this *matrioshka* effect by declaring the principle of *uti possidetis*, which means "as you possess," or "keep what you have." In other words, republics and provinces were allowed to leave federal states and have their administrative boundaries transformed into state borders, but regions and areas within those units that tried to secede could expect neither international support nor recognition (Woodward 1995).

Not all cases are structurally conducive to exit from the state. The geographic concentration of ethnic groups in uncontested territorial units, although rare, offers optimal conditions for secession or partition. One reason that Czechs and Slovaks could so amicably split in 1992 was that only 1 percent of the population in Slovakia was Czech, and only 3 percent of the inhabitants of the Czech Republic were Slovak. Once it was concluded by national elites that a postcommunist *modus vivendi* (condition of living together) was impossible, both sides agreed to quit and split. In many other cases of the world, ethnic groups are stuck with one another for reasons of both demography and geography. More specifically, in many states, populations are thickly interspersed, or minority territorial concentrations are spread haphazardly, or such concentrations are located "inland" and not near more easily movable borders. In all of these cases, the creation of a coherent territorial unit for either the departing region or the rump state is not possible. If politically organized ethnic groups have sufficient resolve for ruthlessness and murder, ethnic cleansing can alter the demographic context and pave the way for a more homogeneous state. Short of this hideously immoral option, however, most groups have to figure out some way to coexist, and this means crafting institutions that can reasonably satisfy the interests of all.

Institutional Remedies

A judicious way for states to avoid a protracted secessionist war is to grant some degree of self-rule to alienated ethnic groups. Devolution, federalism, and autonomy are modes of transferring power to local units within the state. They serve as conflict-regulating devices in many ethnically plural societies. India, for example, has made a habit of creating new administrative state units to accommodate its vastly complex multiethnic mosaic. The number of Indian states has steadily increased from eleven in 1962 to twenty-eight today (including seven Union Territories, or subnational administrative units) (Manor 1998). Similarly, ever since its democratic transition in the late 1970s, Spain has granted autonomy to its various regions, first to the culturally and historically distinct regions of Catalonia, the Basque Country, and Galicia, and later to fourteen additional regions (Shabad 1986). In Britain, both Scotland and Wales have slowly accumulated more and more authority, albeit at different paces and competencies, ever since devolution referenda were publicly approved in 1997. Generally speaking, federalism, autonomy, and devolution have the virtue of redirecting nationalist passions away from the center, where they could prove explosive and dangerous to the entire state, to the local level where intra-ethnic competition for local office is fostered. The downside is that by establishing local sites of authority, ethnic groups gain "institutional weapons" that can be used to contest and subvert the decisions of the center (Roeder 1999).

Another approach to interethnic accommodation is the consociational system. Described by the scholar Arend Lijphart, consociationalism contains four institutional recommendations: (1) a grand coalition government that includes the important parties representing all significant ethnic groups; (2) the mutual veto, or unanimity principle, which provides ironclad guarantees to each ethnic segment that it will be able to protect its interests; (3) proportionality, or a quota system, that mandates specific ethnic representation in the staffing of state institutions; and (4) some system of devolution, autonomy, or federalism. Lijphart argues that this model was adopted in the divided European societies of the Netherlands (in 1917), Austria (in 1945), Belgium (in 1960), and Switzerland (in 1959). So successful was consociationalism in mollifying conflict in these otherwise culturally fragmented democracies, argues Lijphart, that it became unnecessary and was phased out in Austria and the Netherlands in the 1960s (Lijphart 1977).

Many scholars are not so convinced of the virtues of this model. Among its many problems, critics point out that the grand coalition, by guaranteeing representation to all significant parties, effectively erodes democratic accountability and establishes an entrenched elite cartel. Essentially, it is not the most democratic of regime types. Furthermore, whereas the unanimity principle is perhaps necessary in some circumstances to convince fractious and mutually suspicious groups to forego politics-as-war, it is at the same time a recipe for political paralysis and ineffective government. If every important decision requires the consent of all significant groups, then it is likely that important decisions will not be made. The quota system that Lijphart recommends also can be a source of problems, particularly if the relative population sizes of each community change and render the quota out of date. Horowitz labels this problem the "frozen quota pitfall" (Horowitz 1985). Finally, many critics point out that Lijphart's argument is circular. The regime type is supposed to pacify ethnic relations, and yet a degree of pacificity is required for consociationalism to be implemented in the first place. As Ian Lustick

(1997, 100) writes: "Accommodation is simultaneously the successful settling of disputes between cultural fragments and the explanation for stable relations among cultural fragments." In short, consociationalism cannot be both cause and effect of the pattern of ethnic group relations.

Power sharing denotes the predetermined division of political offices among all politically significant ethnic groups. The goal is to ensure inclusion, and in this way it approaches the consociational ideas of the grand coalition and proportionality, but without necessarily committing a regime to the requirements of unanimity rules and devolution. Both Lebanon and Northern Ireland are examples of power sharing. In Lebanon, a national pact was instituted in 1943 that determined which government positions would go to its various confessional groups. Thus, the presidency was assigned to Maronite Christians, the prime ministership to Sunni Muslims, the speaker of the parliament to Shiite Muslims, and cabinet positions were evenly split between Christians and Muslims. The 1998 Good Friday Agreement that contributed importantly to the peace process in Northern Ireland is another example. It distributed seats in the following manner: a Protestant was designated prime minister (David Trimble of the Ulster Unionist Party), a Catholic was made deputy prime minister (Seamus Mallon of the Social Democratic and Labor Party), and three cabinet seats were allocated to the Ulster Unionists, three to the Social Democratic and Labor Party, two to Sinn Féin (Catholic), and two to the Democratic Unionists (Protestant). While power sharing includes all significant groups and thereby can pacify interethnic tensions, it can also fall prey to the frozen quota pitfall and to the stalemated decision making noted earlier.

A final innovative approach to interethnic relations is cross-ethnic voting. Advocated by Horowitz, this accommodative device is aimed at engineering the electoral system so as to ensure maximum interethnic support for officeholders. The idea is to create electoral incentives for moderate policy programs by requiring winning candidates to gain a certain degree of support from ethnic communities other than their own. If winning public office depends on support from several different ethnic groups, then candidates wanting to win office are unlikely to run on programs of exclusive ethnic nationalism. Horowitz calls this "making moderation pay" (Horowitz 1990). Both Lebanon's National Pact government and Nigeria's second republic (1979–1983) instituted this procedure. In Nigeria, a presidential candidate was required to receive not only the largest number of votes, but also at least 25 percent of the vote in no less than two-thirds of the nineteen states. While this was certainly a novel idea, very few cases have adopted this electoral mechanism, and the two that did were abruptly halted by a military coup (Nigeria) and civil war (Lebanon).

Ultimately, institutional solutions to interethnic problems are context-dependent. There is no silver bullet that fells the monsters of extreme ethnic nationalism or a foolproof plan for multicultural harmony. What fosters interethnic peace in one setting and at one time will not necessarily do so in the same or another setting at another time. It is therefore up to you, the reader, to use your critical imagination when thinking through the range of potential remedies for a given ethnic problem. The burden is not a light one.

*W**AIT A MINUTE.* **CONSIDER THIS.** Think of any conflict zone in the world. Can you devise a system that simultaneously marginalizes extremists, creates incentives for elite moderation, promotes inclusiveness, ensures the effectiveness of institutions, and protects the integrity of the state?

Coping with Multiculturalism

In April 1992, six days of race riots erupted in Los Angeles when a jury acquitted four white police officers in the brutal beating of an unarmed black man, Rodney King. On the third day of the rioting, King appeared on television and pleaded for calm, poignantly asking, "Can we all get along?" His question is just as relevant today as it was then. Globalization has made for increasingly diverse populations in states around the world, and this trend will undoubtedly persist into the foreseeable future. It is thus imperative that states develop systems of governance that can manage the tensions that invariably accompany the changing demographics of multiethnic societies. Unfortunately, many states are under pressure from traditionally dominant groups to resist accommodation and even to push back against rising multiculturalism.

The demographic context of the Western world is undergoing rapid and profound transformation. As in the United States, the Caucasian population of Western Europe is shrinking and aging and the immigrant population is young and growing. In 2005, immigrant communities stood at over 9 percent of the total population in eight West European countries. Immigrants in Luxembourg are now one-third of the population and

TABLE 7.2 Right-wing parties and parliamentary strength in Europe

Country	Party	Popular vote in last election year	Relative party strength
Austria	Freedom Party	17.5% / 2008	Third-largest party in national parliament
Belgium	Vlaams Belang	15.3% / 2009	Tied for second place in Flemish regional parliament
Denmark	Danish People's Party	13.9% / 2007	Third-largest party in national parliament
Finland	The True Finns	19% / 2011	Third-largest party in national parliament
Netherlands	Party for Freedom	15.4% / 2010	Third-largest party in national parliament
Norway	The Progress Party	22.9% / 2009	Second-largest party in national parliament
Sweden	Sweden Democrats	5.7% / 2010	Sixth-largest party in national parliament
Switzerland	Swiss Peoples Party	29% / 2007	Biggest party in the national parliament

Source: CIA World Factbook, <www.cia.gov/library/publications/the-world-factbook/>.

in Switzerland nearly one-quarter. France has the largest population of Muslims (4.5 million, or 7.5 percent of the French population) in Europe. Germany has 3 million Muslims, Britain 2.5 million, and Italy and the Netherlands a million apiece. In the Dutch city of Rotterdam, Muslims are almost the majority population (Berend 2010; Fukuyama 2006).

Across Europe, right-wing parties have capitalized on the growing anxieties and resentments of native populations. Right-wing populist parties have experienced growing popularity in the Netherlands, Finland, Sweden, Belgium, Austria, Switzerland, and Denmark (Norris 2005; see Table 7.2). Geert Wilders, the leader of the Party for Freedom in the Netherlands, is currently one of the most vocal European opponents of immigration in general and Muslim immigration in particular. His rhetoric is inflammatory: He has equated the Koran to Hitler's *Mein Kampf*, declared that "I'll be the first to go and cement shut the mosques with bricks," and proposed that a penalty be imposed on Muslim women who wear headscarves, calling it the "head rag tax" (Steen 2010). Less radical politicians have also gotten in their verbal shots. The former president of France, Jacques Chirac, said he perceives "something aggressive" in the wearing of veils, and the former prime minister of Britain, Tony Blair, criticized the veil as a "mark of separation." In 2004, the French government evoked its strict tradition of the separation of church and state to ban the wearing of veils and headscarves (along with non-Muslim religious symbols like large crosses and yarmulkes) in public schools. Then, in 2010, the French parliament banned the public wearing of the burqa (or full body veil), fining violators 150 euros. Belgium banned it as well in the same year.

In general, Europe's growing immigrant population is forcing its old states to confront new and challenging problems. The new cultural cleavage lines are intensifying problems in education, welfare, law enforcement, security, and civil liberties. None of these differences can be easily solved. When a Danish newspaper, for example, published cartoon drawings of Mohammed (Islam bars any visual depiction of the prophet) in 2005, it set off a firestorm of protests around the world, including the burning of the Danish embassy in Beirut, Lebanon. The Danish editors proclaimed their decision to publish the cartoons an "act of defiance" against terrorism and religious zealotry. German Chancellor Angela Merkel agreed, awarding the cartoonist a freedom-of-speech prize in 2010. She even declared that Germany had failed to develop a genuine multicultural society. As she told a gathering of young Christian Democrats: "This multicultural approach, saying that we simply live side by side and live happily with each other has failed. Utterly failed" (Eddy 2010). No better indicator of Europe's general failure to cope with multiculturalism was the mass murder (seventy-six casualties) that took place in Norway in July 2011 by a right-wing gunman who was hoping to launch a war against Islam.

It is readily apparent that Europe's new multicultural mosaic contains a host of thorny governance difficulties. Can we all get along? The answer to that question ultimately depends on the dynamic interplay between states and ethnic groups.

CONCLUSION

States are both major instigators of ethnic conflict and providers of indispensable resources for its resolution. The end of the Cold War unleashed a wave of ethnic conflict that swept the globe and then retreated by century's end. Most multiethnic societies are peaceful and, at most, experience competitive coexistence along ethnic fault lines. Bringing different ethnic groups into closer and more sustained contact, the advance of globalization only stokes the potential for more or less acrimonious ethnic conflict and makes more pressing the need to find formulae for moderating this potential. Ethnic diversity is now an existential fact everywhere, and this has turned the old dream of ethnic nationalists – epitomized by Mazzini's phrase "every nation a state" – into an impossible dream. Whether states can ultimately manage the new challenges posed by unprecedented worldwide immigration is anyone's guess.

◑ 8 Terrorism

errorism is, at root, the indiscriminate use of violence against civilians for political ends. Even before the deadly attacks on the World Trade Center in New York City on September 11, 2001, it was a significant problem in the United States and wider world. Readers of this book are probably aware of several ghastly and high-profile terrorist incidents that took place in the United States prior to its current "war on terror." For example, the anti-technology-inspired "Unabomber" (Theodore Kaczynski) sent sixteen letter-bombs to various targets between 1978 and 1995. Timothy McVeigh, a supporter of right-wing, anti–federal government ideology, blew up a federal building in Oklahoma City in 1995 in what was, at the time, the single deadliest act of terrorism in American history. Right-to-life advocates have subjected abortion clinics and their staffs across America to scores of murders, bombings, and arson attacks over the last couple of decades. Assassins' bullets have taken the lives of four American presidents (Lincoln, Garfield, McKinley, and Kennedy), and a total of fourteen presidents have been the targets of failed assassination attempts. During the first eight months of Barack Obama's presidency, he received an average of thirty death threats a day (*Democracy Now*, August 4, 2009).

America, however, is not exceptional when it comes to terrorist violence. In fact, no part of the world has been free of this scourge in the modern age. In the United Kingdom, for instance, the Provisional Irish Republican Army (IRA) and its offshoots killed more than 1,800 people in terrorist attacks from 1969 to 2001. In Spain, the Basque separatist group ETA (or Basque Homeland and Freedom) has murdered more than 800 people since launching its bid for independence in 1968. In Sri Lanka, the separatist Tamil Tigers conducted 171 suicide attacks, often involving female bombers, between 1983 and 2000. It is worth noting too that those who practice politics-as-violence often deliberately target advocates of peaceful political protest and politicians who either promote or sign peace treaties. Such was the fate of the peacemakers Mohandas K. Gandhi, Martin Luther King Jr., Egyptian president Anwar Sadat (who signed the Sinai Treaty recognizing Israel in 1979 and was killed in 1981 by a radical Islamic group opposed to peace with Israel), and Israeli prime minister Yitzhak Rabin (who signed the Oslo Accords with the Palestinian Liberation Organization [PLO] in 1993 and was murdered in 1995 by a right-wing Orthodox Jew opposed to peace with the Palestinians). The inescapable conclusion from all this murder and mayhem is that terrorism is an integral part of modernity.

As such, it is one of the preeminent challenges to the contemporary state. If the chief function of the state is to provide its citizens with peace and security, then terrorism challenges its very *raison d'être*. Certainly in the Western liberal tradition, peace and security constitute the original intent behind state formation. According to John Locke, the pre-state condition is one in which the "lives, liberties, and estates" of all are in jeopardy because of a general manifestation of "enmity, malice, violence, and mutual destruction" (Locke 1980, 15). The state contract represents a way out of this mess by convening a legislature to make common laws, selecting impartial judges to adjudicate disputes, and establishing an executive power to enforce the laws. By creating civil order in this way, a state achieves nothing less than to make freedom possible for all. Terrorism, in contrast, aims precisely at overturning the predictability, trust, civility, and psychic comforts of a law-based society. Indeed, a major objective behind the launching of surprising and spectacular attacks against unarmed civilians is to demonstrate vividly that the state cannot protect its citizens. By sowing collective disorder and disorientation, terrorism represents a strike at the very heart of the state.

Terrorism poses additional threats to democratic regimes, the most obvious of them being the attempt by its practitioners to affect policy outcomes outside normal channels of political input and influence. Less obvious is the fact that terrorist groups often hope to seduce government decision makers into overreacting. If democratic governments respond to too heavy-handedly to terrorism, they may alienate their own populations and potentially undermine respect for the constitutional order. The risk is that they will compromise their basic values if they overreach with too many infringements on the rights of citizens, such as domestic spying, the suspension of habeas corpus, racial profiling, and the extension of secrecy over government decisions – all of which erode transparency and accountability. In short, democracies are especially vulnerable to terrorism not because the indiscriminate killing of civilians will suddenly cause the regime to collapse, but rather because the reaction of governments may involve them violating the most basic rights of citizens, and it is this that is the real threat to democracy.

This chapter distinguishes terrorism from other acts of political violence. What makes terrorism different from the likes of assault, or riots, or civil wars? For that matter, is the terrorist functionally equivalent to other violent actors, such as political rebels or guerrillas, or are the latter somehow qualitatively different? What counts as a terrorist act? If, for example, an insurgent group sabotages state-owned infrastructure or private property but avoids civilian deaths, is the term "terrorism" appropriate? Another key issue concerns whether the state itself is capable of acts that can be described as terrorist. Should terrorism be a concept reserved for non-state actors, or can the term also apply to states? These are necessary questions to ask if one hopes to scale the conceptual barriers that terrorism presents for political analysis.

The final issues this chapter addresses concern the fundamental dilemmas facing democracy and the state in the face of terrorist threats. States generally react to terrorism in one of two ways: (1) they weaken and fragment because of an inability to control the operations of organized terrorist groups on their territory; or (2) they strengthen by expanding executive authority and the institutions of coercive power, such as law enforcement, intelligence, security, prisons, and defense.

A basic irony, as we shall see, is that as terrorists seek to change government policy by weakening the capacity of the state to rule, the response of most states around the globe has in fact been to strengthen their instruments of coercion, surveillance, and punishment. This is true of both authoritarian and democratic regimes. In both, government leaders typically face considerable pressure to do something about terrorism in the aftermath of indiscriminate attacks against civilians. In this way, the very success of terrorism sets in motion adaptations and innovations that often lead to its ultimate defeat. At the same time, what is effective in the fight against terrorism is not always consonant with democratic values. Thus, the irony deepens when one considers how the state, reinvigorated and retooled in the national security arena, has trouble respecting the constitutional rights of its own citizens. State responses to terrorism, therefore, can sometimes pose as great a threat to democracy as terrorists themselves do. Before observing the full impact of such ironies and dilemmas, let us first turn our attention to basic issues of definition.

■ HOW DO YOU KNOW A TERRORIST WHEN YOU SEE ONE?

It is necessary to note at the outset that terrorism is not an ideology or a political movement. Its various practitioners around the globe and throughout history do not have a common political agenda. On the contrary, a group is considered terrorist on the basis of what it does rather than what it thinks and stands for. Terrorism is a method, a technique, a tactic. The Russian anarchist Peter Kropotkin (1842–1921) said it best when he pithily described terrorism as "propaganda by the deed." Not only have diverse groups adopted terrorism as a means to achieve their goals, but also terrorism is but one form of political violence among many.

There are many types of violence in the world – robbery, rape, bar-room brawls, spousal abuse, cruelty to animals, and so on. These are all personal and private types of violence involving direct citizen-to-citizen (or human-to-animal) contact and do not entail a larger desire to challenge the social order. Violence becomes political when its perpetrators seek to promote or impose a set of values and ideas on the rest of society. Consider the act of bank robbing. Most of the time a bank is robbed because, in the famous words of the American bank robber Willie Sutton, "that is where the money is." But when the small, cult-like, ultra-left Symbionese Liberation Army (SLA) robbed a few banks in California in the mid-1970s, their actions had less to do with money and more to do with striking a blow at capitalism. The SLA's acts were distinctive for being political as well as criminal.

Terrorism exists, if you will, on a continuum of political violence that stretches from war on one end to the actions of a lone assailant on the other. The latter category is exemplified by individuals who are unaffiliated with a political group and who act on their own initiative to redress a perceived personal injury. Typically, such people are mentally unstable, which is quite unlike the rational, educated, and middle- to upper-class profile of the average terrorist. An example of such individual level political violence is Dan White who murdered San Francisco's openly gay politician, Harvey Milk, in 1978. White was motivated not by political ideology but by the simple desire to secure reappointment as city supervisor, a move Milk opposed. At the other end of the spectrum is war, which is the expression of political violence on an international scale, involving states in sustained, armed conflict with each other.

Terrorists versus Guerrillas

Civil or guerrilla wars also occupy a position on the continuum of political violence. Unlike war per se, civil wars take place within a state and typically involve the state fighting an organized group of citizens to whom we refer as non-state or substate actors. The term "guerrilla war" is of Spanish origin and means "little war." It was originally used to describe the Spanish and Portuguese irregulars (or *guerrilleros*) who fought in the early nineteenth century to drive the French from the Iberian Peninsula. Terrorism too involves insurgent groups fighting the state, but what distinguishes it is the use of indiscriminate violence against civilian populations for political ends. To be sure, it is a universal fact that innocent civilians get killed or injured in war. However, states have developed, particularly since the end of World War II, norms, treaties, and conventions to guide military planners and professional soldiers in the protection of civilians caught up in warfare. Thus, civilians will certainly die in interstate wars, but killing them is not an explicit military objective, and if it becomes one, then prosecutable war crimes have been committed. In civil wars, too, guerrilla groups, in ideal terms, target agents of the state (particularly the military, the police, politicians, and judges) rather than civilians. Too weak to confront them directly and in sustained combat, the guerrilla group opts for quick, limited, hit-and-run engagements with a state's forces of order. Of course, in the real world, guerrilla groups have meted out horrific abuses against civilians, and when they do so, one may conclude they have committed terrorist acts.

Additional traits separating the guerrilla from the terrorist are that the former seeks to build armies and liberate territory where an alternative government can be established. Guerrillas typically wear uniforms and insignia identifying themselves, brandish their weapons openly, and tend to establish their base of operations in rural settings from where they can launch attacks against government forces. Terrorism, in contrast, operates in an urban environment where populations are dense, providing both easy targets and multiple opportunities to evade capture by blending into the crowd. Rather than mobilizing a mass movement and attempting to seize and hold territory, terrorists organize into small, secretive cells whose members outwardly appear indistinguishable from average citizens. Finally, unlike guerrilla groups, the targets of terrorist action have little

TABLE 8.1 Guerrilla/terrorist groups and types of terrorist tactics			
Group	**Country**	**Period of activity**	**Tactics**
National Liberation Front (FLN)	Algeria	1954–1962	selective and indiscriminate terror
Armed Islamic Group (GIA)	Algeria	1992–present	indiscriminate terror
Liberation Tigers of Tamil Eelam (Tamil Tigers)	Sri Lanka	1983–2009	selective and indiscriminate terror
Kosovo Liberation Army (UCK)	Serbia/Kosovo	1996–1999	selective and indiscriminate terror
Arkan's Tigers	Bosnia – Herzegovina	1992–1995	indiscriminate terror
Kurdistan Workers' Party (PKK)	Turkey	1978–present	selective terror
Hamas	Palestine	1994–present	indiscriminate terror
Revolutionary Armed Forces of Colombia (FARC)	Colombia	1964–present	selective terror
Shining Path	Peru	1980–present	selective and indiscriminate terror
Basque Homeland and Freedom (ETA)	Spain	1968–present	mostly selective terror; some indiscriminate terror
Provisional Irish Republican Army (IRA)	United Kingdom	1969–2001	mostly selective terror; some indiscriminate terror

Note: For a different listing of groups on these same indicators, see Goodwin (2006).

military value and instead are chosen for their promotional and public-relations value. It has been said of the IRA that it measured success not in terms of casualties but in terms of column inches it generated in newspapers. Given this incentive structure, it makes sense that British Prime Minister Margaret Thatcher once decried the media for providing the IRA with the "oxygen of publicity" (Ripley 2001).

Often, a guerrilla group will combine traditional insurgency tactics and terrorist acts, or the group's strategy will evolve from one to the other. Table 8.1 lists several paramilitary groups, all of whom have practiced, at one time or another, some type of terrorism. Indiscriminate terrorism occurs when a terrorist or guerrilla group attacks civilian populations. Selective terrorism occurs when a terrorist or guerrilla group focuses its attacks on selected politicians, state officials, and prominent public figures deemed responsible for policies the group opposes.

Many armed insurgent groups stand at the intersection of guerilla warfare and terrorism. Some start their struggle using conventional insurgency tactics and later switch to terrorist activities. The IRA normally targeted British police and military forces, but during the height of "the

Troubles" (a period of intense sectarian conflict in Northern Ireland) in the mid-1970s, they expanded to target ordinary civilians as well, both at home and on the British mainland. Later, they established the practice of contacting the media and alerting them to public locations where bombs had been planted. Hamas is a political organization with considerable popularity and strength in the Gaza Strip of Palestine. It is a political party, a provider of social welfare, health, and educational services, and a paramilitary group all rolled into one. Beginning in 1994, it began a suicide bombing campaign against Israeli citizens, killing nearly 300 in the process. But then, in 2006, it renounced such tactics, declaring them inappropriate for the political climate (Urquhart 2006). By November 2008, tensions had once again flared up between Hamas and Israel, leading the former to launch hundreds upon hundreds of indiscriminate rocket attacks on Jewish settlements.

Despite the changing tactics that insurgents adopt in different conflict zones, there are many groups that fall clearly into either the guerrilla or terrorist category. On the one hand, we have the Sandinistas of Nicaragua, who successfully overthrew the Somoza dictatorship in 1979 without ever attacking civilians. The closest they came to an act of terrorism was the kidnapping of the entire Nicaraguan congress in 1978. But even then, no one died (Merrill 1993). On the other hand, Al Qaeda is a terrorist group, pure and simple. Osama bin Laden often declared that because the United States is a democracy, all of its citizens are responsible, and therefore accountable, for its actions. In his worldview, "the American people are not innocent"; all are legitimate targets of terror (FBIS Report 2004, 216).

The Thresholds of Terrorism

Thus far, we have seen that it is possible to differentiate guerrillas from terrorists, but this line often becomes blurry. The scholarly literature is equally blurry, as there is no consensus on the precise definition of terrorism. According to one study, there are more than 100 definitions of a terrorist in circulation; different branches of the U.S. government even advance different definitions (Laqueur 1986; Schmid 1984). Government-compiled lists of terrorists are often unreliable because they reveal more about the allies and enemies of a specific state and commonly do not represent an objective assessment of who and who is not a terrorist. An additional complicating factor is that the concept of a terrorist has such a negative connotation that its practitioners and their supporters prefer to refer to themselves as "freedom fighters" or a "national liberation army."

In short, terrorism is an essentially contested concept. As with so many other basic terms of discourse in political science, elaboration and interpretation are required. It thus falls upon you, the reader, to determine and decide what thresholds have to be reached before one "sees" a terrorist. It is likely that all readers will agree with the premise that an indiscriminate attack on a civilian population is, ipso facto, terrorism. But what about selective terrorism? What if only agents of the state (politicians, police, and the military) are the targets? Terrorists and guerrillas alike justify these choices on the basis that it is precisely these groups who produce and coercively enforce repressive policies. But this leads to another question: How much repression justifies a violent response against the state and its representatives? Let us ponder these questions as we examine a few real-world cases.

The National Liberation Army (Republic of Macedonia)

In 2001, the National Liberation Army of Macedonia (NLA), an Albanian paramilitary force that was originally an offshoot of the Kosovo Liberation Army, launched an offensive against the state of Macedonia because of its alleged disregard for, and abuse of, minority Albanian rights. (Albanians comprise 25 percent of the Macedonian population; Macedonians account for 64 percent.) The NLA bombed police stations, ambushed military units, planted explosive devices, and forcibly removed the inhabitants of a few villages. In all, this was a short, six-month conflict (with approximately 200 casualties and 170,000 refugees) that ultimately led to internationally mediated constitutional revisions that improved Albanian rights in this postcommunist republic. The one hitch, however, is that Albanians were hardly repressed politically – they had their own media, they organized their own political parties and competed for all government offices, several Albanian parties held seats in the national parliament, and every Cabinet since independence in 1991 had been a multiparty coalition, with Albanians serving as key partners in that coalition (Hislope 2003).

Still, there was a lingering legacy of institutional inequality against Albanians dating from the communist period. Albanian grievances covered issues like education and language rights, the demand for decentralization of power to Albanian localities, and the desire to upgrade the constitutional status of Albanians from that of a national minority to a co-equal community with Macedonians. The leader of the NLA, Ali Ahmeti, consistently claimed that the Albanian insurgency was all about "equal rights," and not secession from the state.

So did the Albanians have a case that warranted selective terrorism against agents of the state? Does a context of unequal social rights but equal democratic rights to assemble, petition government, and compete for public office justify the bombing of police stations and killing of civilians, as the NLA did in 2000? This is the question that the writer Timothy Garton Ash put to himself when he met and interviewed Ahmeti in November 2001. In his words, "was I drinking whiskey with a terrorist?" (Ash 2001).

The international community, for one, was quite unsure of how to answer this question. U.S. President George W. Bush placed Ahmeti on the terrorist list in the summer of 2001, but then removed him. NATO chief Lord George Robertson decried the NLA as a bunch of "murderous thugs," but later this rhetoric was softened as NATO, the EU, and the United States pressed the Macedonian side to compromise. Timothy Garton Ash as well seemed unsure in his final analysis: "Perhaps the moderation of his [Ahmeti's] goals, the fact that he tried not to target civilians, pulls him just the right side of the line. Just. Perhaps" (Ash 2001: 33).

*W**AIT A MINUTE.* **CONSIDER THIS.** Is Ali Ahmeti a terrorist? What do you think? Can you avoid the wishy-washy and flip-flop evaluations of Ash and others? How weighty in your calculation is the fact that democratic alternatives to violence were available? Is violence ever legitimate if opportunities and institutions are freely available for the peaceful, albeit slow, redress of grievances? It is true that the six-month NLA insurgency brought more rights to the Albanian community than ten years of postcommunist democratic practice had. But do the ends justify the means?

The African National Congress (South Africa)

The African National Congress (ANC) of South Africa operated under a notoriously brutal system of racial segregation called apartheid. Under it, black Africans were denied all political and civil rights, they were limited in their right to move about their country by an internal passport system that restricted their access to white areas, and they were subjected to a segregated state sector that delivered at best inferior education, health care, and other public services. The National Party, an Afrikaner (Dutch) political party, was the main architect of apartheid, and this party ruled South Africa from 1948 to 1994. One illustration of the brutal nature of apartheid rule was the Sharpeville Massacre of March 1960, in which South African police opened fire on peaceful protestors, killing 69 people, including 8 women and 10 children, and injuring 180 more. In short, peaceful modes of promoting black political interests were simply not available.

In 1961, the ANC created a paramilitary wing they named the *Umkhonto we Sizwe* (Spear of the Nation), or MK, for short. Nelson Mandela became its leader, gave it its name, and co-wrote its manifesto. Under his leadership, the organization focused on a policy of sabotage against economic targets. In Mandela's autobiography, *Long Walk to Freedom*, he explains why the ANC chose such methods:

> Because it did not involve the loss of life it [sabotage] offered the best hope for reconciliation among the races afterward. We did not want to start a blood feud between white and black. . . . Sabotage had the added virtue of requiring the least manpower. Our strategy was to make selective forays against military installations, power plants, telephone lines, and transportation links; targets that would not only hamper the military effectiveness of the state, but frighten National Party supporters, scare away foreign capital, and weaken the economy. This we hoped would bring the government to the bargaining table. Strict instructions were given to members of MK that we would countenance no loss of life. But if sabotage did not produce the results we wanted, we were prepared to move on to the next stage: guerrilla warfare and terrorism. (Mandela 1994, 246–47)

Over the course of the anti-apartheid struggle, MK bombs did occasionally and inadvertently injure and kill some whites, but its principal target remained economic infrastructure. ANC president, Oliver Tambo, even went so far as to sign, in 1980, a declaration committing the ANC to the principles of the Geneva Convention (1949), which prescribe rules for the proper treatment of prisoners, civilian populations, and other conduct in time of war. This marked the first time in history that a paramilitary group formally committed itself to the norms of an international human rights document (Goodwin 2006). Nevertheless, U.S. President Ronald Reagan and British Prime Minister Margaret Thatcher regarded the ANC as a terrorist organization and Nelson Mandela himself as a terrorist. During the 1980s, both leaders firmly resisted the growing international anti-apartheid movement that called for the divestment of Western firms from the country and for economic sanctions against the apartheid regime (Ungar and Vale 1985). Whether to label an actor or a group as "terrorist" is thus no mere academic exercise; on the contrary, it is a decision that can have real economic and political consequences.

W*AIT A MINUTE.* **CONSIDER THIS.** Which side are you on? Were Reagan and Thatcher correct in labeling Mandela a terrorist? Does sabotage cross your threshold of terror? In the words of the scholar Elleke Boehmer (2005, 47), "could the 1950s Mandela, advocate of sedition and sabotage, still be called a terrorist today?"

Ecoterrorism

Ecoterrorism is a relatively new construct that has gained traction since the 9/11 attacks. The concept means the use of sabotage to destroy property for the purpose of promoting or defending environmental, ecological, and/or animal rights causes. Recently in the United States, this stigma has attached to both the Animal Liberation Front (ALF) and the Earth Liberation Front (ELF), with the FBI regarding both as "serious terrorist threats." The FBI describes ecoterrorism as the "use or threatened use of violence of a criminal nature against innocent victims or property by an environmentally-oriented, subnational group for environmental-political reasons, or aimed at an audience beyond the target, often of a symbolic nature" (Amster 2006). What is significant about this concept is the extension of the term "terrorism" to acts that target only property and not people. This redefinition has occurred since the passage of the USA PATRIOT Act in 2001, and has been further codified in the United States by the Animal Enterprise Terrorism Act of 2006, which extends the meaning of terrorism to include sabotage against commercial enterprises and academic institutions that use or sell animals or animal products.

Both ALF and ELF groups have suffered arrests on the grounds of "domestic terrorism." Some of the crimes they stand accused of include destroying a sports-utility vehicle (SUV) dealership and a sky lift expansion in Vail, Colorado, burning down five luxury homes in Seattle, and setting fire to the animal diagnostic laboratory at the University of California, Davis (Kaas 1998; Yardley 2008). Both groups insist they are not terrorists. Convinced that modern capitalism is destroying the environment, they practice a form of environmental direct action, known as "monkeywrenching." According to Dave Foreman, who wrote *Ecodefense*, "monkeywrenching is nonviolent resistance to the destruction of natural diversity and wilderness. It is never directed against human beings or other forms of life. It is aimed at inanimate machines and tools that are destroying life" (quoted in Amster 2006, 289).

One obvious risk that this tactic entails is that accidents can happen that involve the loss of human life. When New Left groups in America, like the Weather Underground, turned to violence in the early 1970s, several such accidents occurred. In March 1970, three founding members of Weather died during an explosion at their "bomb factory" in a Greenwich Village townhouse. In August of the same year, another Left terrorist group, the "New Year's Gang," attempted to demolish an Army Mathematics Research Center on the campus of the University of Wisconsin at Madison. Using a car bomb, they mistakenly blew up the Physics department, killing a young postdoctoral fellow who had a wife and three children (O'Neill 2001, 42–43).

*W**AIT A MINUTE.* **CONSIDER THIS.** The concept of ecoterrorism is a clear expansion of the definition of terrorism, but is it a valid one? To say it differently, does property damage for environmental causes warrant a criminal charge equal to the taking of human life? What do you think?

Reflections

Let us reflect again on the fundamentals: a definition of terrorism. In all, there are many types of tactics that have been held to fall within the general rubric of terrorism, including, but not limited to, bank robbing, kidnapping, airline hijacking, indiscriminate attacks against civilians, selective terrorism against agents of the state (including assassination), and attacks against economic infrastructure (or sabotage). Despite this variability, however, the bottom line of terrorism involves attacks against civilians for political goals. Whatever else terrorism might be, this is its defining feature. When an organized group indiscriminately attacks the general population, it directly threatens the authority of the state by disrupting social order. The terrorist hopes to strike fear and panic into the public and thereby undermine the individual and collective security that states uniquely provide. By weakening the state in turn, terrorists hope to achieve some kind of political end, such as a change in government policy, the release of political prisoners, or even no more than publicity for their cause. But what if states themselves are the principle disturbers of the peace? Is it ever reasonable to label states as "terrorist," or do words like repression and domination suffice?

STATES AND TERRORISM

The term "terrorism" actually originated in the behavior of a state. More precisely, its roots lie in the period of Jacobin rule during the French Revolution that was known as the Reign of Terror (September 1793–July 1794). With the country facing both internal rebellion and foreign war with Britain, Austria, Spain, and Holland, power in Paris was delegated to a twelve-member war cabinet called the Committee of Public Safety. Led by Maximilien Robespierre, the tasks of the Committee were nothing less than to rid France of its internal and external enemies and to lay the foundations for a "republic of virtue." To these ends, the Committee unleashed massive state repression. In all, 20,000 "enemies" lost their heads at the guillotine. For the likes of Robespierre, such violence from above was a moral necessity during revolutionary upheavals. In his words, "if the basis of popular government in peacetime is virtue, the basis of popular government during a revolution is both virtue and terror; virtue, without which terror is baneful; terror, without which virtue is powerless. Terror is nothing more than speedy, severe and inflexible justice" (Linton 2006).

It was during France's Reign of Terror that our modern notion of terrorism was born; the first dictionary to include the term is the 1798 edition of the *Dictionnaire de l'Académie Française*, which describes terrorism as a "system, a regime of terror." Conservative critics of the French Revolution instigated the tradition of using terrorism in a pejorative sense, joining the English statesman Edmund Burke's (1729–1797) denunciation of the Committee of Public Safety as "those Hell Hounds called Terrorists" (Dallas 1989).

Like the Jacobins, the Bolsheviks did not shrink from using the full power of the state to induce conditions of terror in the general population when, after the October Revolution of 1917, they were confronted by the twin threats of domestic counterrevolution from the White Army (militarized forces loyal to the monarchy) and foreign war. As organizer and commander of the Soviet Red Army, Leon Trotsky vigorously defended the use of violence by the fledgling proletarian state. In 1920, as Russia faced both civil war and war with Poland, Trotsky wrote *In Defense of Terrorism*. In this essay, he exuberantly advocates violence and justifies it on a class basis. According to Trotsky, it was morally permissible for the Bolsheviks to shoot hostages, suppress competing political parties (like the Socialist-Revolutionaries, anarchists, and the Mensheviks), "militarize" workers by implementing compulsory labor service, and murder the Czar's entire family. The justification for such tactics was the need to suppress class enemies of the proletariat. For Trotsky, the morality of political violence rests on the class on whose behalf it is exercised. In other words, if terror advances the interests of the toiling masses, then its use is justified. In his chilling words, "terror can be very efficient against a reactionary class which does not want to leave the scene of operations. Intimidation is a powerful weapon of policy, both internationally and internally" (Trotsky 1920; Kolakowski 2005).

Trotsky's words are cold and brutal, but it is actually difficult to find a modern state that has not, at one time or another, committed acts of heinous repression that can reasonably be described as terroristic. This was especially the case at the founding of many Western states. Think, for example, of the bloody beginnings of the United States. The founding and expansion of the United States occurred in a context of ethnic cleansing and extermination of the indigenous North American peoples. After examining the complicity of five American presidents (Washington, Jefferson, Jackson, Lincoln, and Teddy Roosevelt) in the systematic mistreatment of Native Americans, the scholar Michael Mann raises the unsettling question, "how many of these presidents would be prosecuted today for genocide by an international war crimes tribunal?" (Mann 2005, 94–95). Andrew Jackson (1767–1845) is one compelling candidate. As a military officer, Jackson commanded his men to kill Native American women and children and boasted that "I have on all occasions preserved the scalps of my killed" (Mann 2005, 93). As president, he broke Indian treaties and supported forcible resettlements, including the Trail of Tears relocations, during which 18,000 Creek, Cherokee, and Choctaw died.

Nazi Germany and Stalinist Russia, the very models of totalitarianism, employed terrorism against civilians on a mass scale. Arbitrary arrest, show trials, extrajudicial killings, targeted violence against subsets of the population, torture, and incessant propaganda warnings of internal and external enemies were cumulatively meant to leave a lasting imprint of insecurity on the psyche of the citizen so as to render each and all helpless before the state. These same tactics were used by many authoritarian regimes in the developing world during the post–World War II era. Chomsky and Herman (1979) meticulously document the multifaceted uses of terror by right-wing governments in the 1970s, particularly in Latin America, the Middle East, and Asia. Dictators like Augusto Pinochet in Chile, Alfredo Stroessner in Paraguay, Jean-Claude ("Baby Doc") Duvalier in Haiti, Shah Reza Pahlavi in Iran, and Ferdinand Marcos in the Philippines used selective terrorism against labor leaders, opposition parties, peasants, journalists, professors, and students. In the words of Naomi Klein (2008, 115), "to be a leftist in those years was to be hunted."

In sum, it is not difficult to find examples from the historical record of state behaviors that can only be described as terroristic. In addition, states, it should be noted, are far more effective terrorists than substate actors. According to the noted expert on terrorism, Walter Laqueur, "the number of victims and the amount of suffering caused by oppressive, tyrannical governments has been infinitely greater than that caused by small groups of rebels. A Hitler or a Stalin killed more people in one year than all terrorists throughout recorded history" (Laqueur 1986, 89). States also sponsor terrorism by providing insurgent groups with a host of critical assets, including training camps, weapons, communications, finances, travel documents, diplomatic support, intelligence, safe houses, and so on. States accused by Western powers in the recent past of being major sponsors of terrorist activities include Iran, Afghanistan, Syria, Libya, and the Sudan.

Another relationship between states and terrorism is causal. Does state terror cause the same behaviors among substate actors, or does causation flow in the opposite direction? In the literature, this is often referred to as the relationship between "wholesale" (i.e., state) and "retail" (oppositional) terrorism. What is the nature of this relationship? How do states respond to terrorist acts, and what are the consequences of those responses for both the quality of civil and human rights and for the state itself?

The next two sections seek to answer these questions by providing a brief survey of state responses to two very different types of terrorist challenges: (1) the threat presented variously by left-wing, nationalist, and/or ethnic-based terrorist groups from the 1960s to the 1980s in both the Third and First Worlds; and (2) the challenge posed by current Islamist terrorist groups, which have become globally significant since 1979, the year of the Islamic Revolution in Iran. Both of these historical periods involve a high level of terrorist activity and consequently prompt vigorous responses from states (Rapoport 2004). Let us consider each period in turn and then reflect on the lessons that each teaches.

The State versus Terrorism, Round One

The 1970s witnessed the full range of violent tactics employed by a diverse set of terrorist groups, including the Provisional IRA, Basque Homeland and Freedom (ETA), the Popular Front for the Liberation of Palestine (PFLP), the Italian Red Brigades, the Japanese Red Army, the German Baader-Meinhof Gang, and the U.S.-based Weather Underground and Symbionese Liberation Army, to name just a few. Bombings, armed attacks, skyjacking, kidnapping, assassination, and bank robbing all occurred with astonishing frequency. The hijacking of airplanes was the main innovation of the period. More than 100 skyjackings occurred every year! In one particularly spectacular instance, the PFLP hijacked, on September 6, 1970, four planes in Zurich, Amsterdam, and Frankfurt and landed them at Dawson's Field in Jordan. This event has since been dubbed "skyjack Sunday."

Both kidnapping and bank robbing became lucrative activities for terrorists. The Palestine Liberation Organization (PLO) and the Christian Phalange of Lebanon, bitter enemies in politics, nevertheless cooperated in 1976 to carry out one of the biggest bank heists in recorded history, grabbing upward of $100 million from the British Bank of the Middle East in Beirut and earning a place in the Guinness Book of World Records in the process. Between 1968 and 1982, 409 international kidnappings took place in 73 countries. Corporations began to take out insurance policies on their executives and pay-offs occurred with regularity, earning terrorists an estimated $350 million. The Rand Corporation conducted a study for the period from 1968 to 1975 and found that there was an 80 percent chance of kidnappers escaping, a 50 percent chance of having some demands met, and a 100 percent chance of media publicity. In another Guinness World Record, the Montoneros of Argentina kidnapped members of two wealthy families and received in return a ransom of $60 million and another $1.2 million to purchase food and clothing for the poor (Midlarsky et al 1980).

Assassinations and executions also occurred with great frequency. To mention just a few instances, the Red Brigades murdered Italian prime minister Aldo Moro in 1978; the Palestinian Black September killed the Jordanian prime minister (1971) and tried to do the same to King

Hussein (1974); the IRA killed the British ambassador to Ireland (1976) and attempted to assassinate both Margaret Thatcher (1984) and her successor John Major (1991); the Rebel Armed Forces (FAR) of Guatemala killed an American ambassador in 1969 and a German ambassador in 1970; and in Canada in 1970, the Quebec Liberation Front (FLQ) abducted and strangled to death Pierre LaPorte, a Quebec labor minister and vice-premier (Rapoport 2004).

So how did states respond to this orgy of violence? Some, like the Federal Republic of Germany, were unprepared. The Munich hostage crisis during the 1972 Olympic Games, at which the Palestinian Black September group kidnapped members of the Israeli team, ended in disaster because the German police were not trained to deal with such contingencies. Other cases were a debacle in the sense that some governments applied heavy-handed violence that resulted in the deaths of terrorists and hostages alike. This is what happened in Colombia in 1985, when the rebel group M-19 tried to replicate the successful Sandinista tactic of kidnapping the entire national congress. M-19 set its sights on the Colombian Supreme Court, but the government refused to negotiate for the release of the 300-plus judges, lawyers, and magistrates and instead sent soldiers to storm the Palace of Justice building where they were being held. In the end, 100 people died, including 11 of the country's 21 Supreme Court justices. Across Latin America, authoritarian governments responded to terrorism with death squads, torture, execution, secret trials, and selective disappearances (in a word, state terrorism), effectively crushing many groups, such as the Tupamaros of Uruguay (in 1972) and the Montoneros of Argentina (in 1977). The infamous Brazilian communist and propagandist of terrorism Carlos Marighella, who wrote the *Minimanual of the Urban Guerrilla* (1969) and thereby influenced revolutionaries and radicals around the world, was gunned down in a police ambush in Sao Paulo, Brazil, in 1969.

In America and Europe, counterterrorist police forces were created and security at airports and embassies was tightened. The introduction of metal detectors, X-ray machines, checkpoints, and other screening devices had become universal by the mid-1980s, substantially reducing the skyjacking phenomenon (Johnson 2001). The UN also swung into action, passing a series of conventions to combat terrorism between the 1970s and 1990s. The European Community (as the European Union was then called) established the TREVI agreement in 1975 and Europol in 1994, both measures enhancing cross-border policing and the development of common counterterrorist strategies.

State responses to terrorism were not consistent, however. What the United States did in 1986 is a perfect example. On the one hand, the Reagan administration punished Libya for terrorist activities; on the other, they traded arms for hostages with terrorist Iran. The bombing of Libya occurred in April after Muammar Gaddafi's government sponsored a string of terrorist events in Europe that targeted Americans (Prunckun and Mohr 1997). Then, in November, it was revealed that Oliver North, an official appointed to Reagan's National Security Council, had arranged for the sale of weapons to Iran in exchange for the release of American hostages held by Hezbollah in Lebanon. President Reagan and other administration officials in the meantime insisted that the United States had not and never would negotiate with terrorists. The event became known as the Iran-Contra Scandal, because money gained from the sale of weapons to Iran was channeled, illegally, to the "contras" of Nicaragua, a right-wing militia the United States was supporting in its attempt to overthrow the leftist Sandinista government.

Other Western countries employed a deliberate policy mixture of repression and reform to contain terrorism, with varying degrees of success. In Canada, the War Measures Act was invoked following the kidnapping and killing of LaPorte. Largely regarded as an overreaction, this Act imposed martial law in Montreal, temporarily suspended civil liberties, and allowed the government to arrest anyone associated with the FLQ (in all, 300 people were taken into custody, including leading French intellectuals and public figures). In the longer term, the government expanded the cultural and linguistic rights of the French minority. Bill 101, for example, made French the official language of Quebec. The respect and cultural protection the French-speaking community received from Ottawa helps explain why the Quebecois voted down a referendum for independence in 1980, and why the violence of 1970 was unique in the history of modern Canada (Miller 2007).

If Canada epitomizes a reformist approach to the problem of terrorism, Spain alternated between conciliation and coercion. ETA was founded in 1959 to fight for Basque cultural and linguistic rights under the dictatorship of General Francisco Franco. It launched its insurrection in 1968, but it only really took off after Franco had died in 1975 and the transition to democracy had begun. In a sign of reconciliation, a new constitution was passed in 1978 granting political autonomy (i.e., self-rule) to the Basque region (called Euskadi). Unfortunately, Basque radicals were not placated and their attacks on politicians and policemen doubled between 1975 and 1983.

The Madrid government, in response, adopted a more repressive approach. In the mid-1980s, the Spanish government secretly supported the organization of a right-wing death squad, the Antiterrorist Groups of Liberation (GAL), which was charged with taking the fight to ETA. Decried as Spain's "dirty war," the GAL kidnapped and murdered suspected ETA members in both Spain and France between 1983 and 1987. When the details of this clandestine program (which included kidnapping the wrong people and killing innocent civilians) was made public, widespread condemnation followed, forcing Spain's first socialist government since the 1930s from office and landing several government officials in jail. This was followed, in the 1990s and early 2000s, by the decision to cultivate closer ties with moderate Basque parties and to isolate the terrorists by banning the party Herri Batasuna (HB), the political wing of ETA. To this end, Madrid signed numerous "pacts against violence" with centrist Basque parties, closed down the offices and Web sites of HB for giving "voice to ETA," arrested suspected ETA operatives, and even shut down seventy "nationalist taverns" in Euskadi thought to be sites for ETA recruiting and fundraising (Chalk 1998). These actions reflected the classic policy of divide-and-rule. In the 2000s, Madrid's fight against ETA received a boost from Nicolas Sarkozy, French interior minister at the time, who mounted a harsh crackdown on Basque separatists in France and worked closely with the Spanish government. Experts agree that the rank and file of ETA has been decimated by arrests and this has led the leadership to declare a cessation of its "military activity" in October 2011 (Burns 2011).

WAIT A MINUTE. **CONSIDER THIS.** What is the best approach to tackling terrorism? If you were an elected official, would you choose coercion, conciliation, or some combination of the two? These are not easy questions to answer for it appears that different policies work in different settings. Surveying three decades of literature on the subject, one scholar concludes "contentious politics sometimes breeds terrorism, and sometimes forestalls it. Appeasement, as does repression, sometimes works, and sometimes fails. Some states seem constitutionally vulnerable to terrorism, and others configuratively immune" (Lichbach 2005, 165). Do you consider the state you reside in "vulnerable to terrorism" or "configuratively immune"? In either case, what makes it so?

Despite differences in the literature on terrorism, there is a basic consensus among experts that the way in which political actors react to terrorism has consequences for the quality of democracy and the integrity of the state. Both could be jeopardized by either too little or too much coercion. In other words, if a state is not proactive in the fields of intelligence and security, unthinkable mayhem and destruction could result. By the same token, too much spying and too much coercion threaten the democratic institutions of a free society, as the Spanish case illustrates. The problem of terrorism thus throws into sharp relief the fundamental tension between liberty and security, which lies at the heart of the democratic state.

The State versus Terrorism, Round Two

Two events occurred in 1979 that fundamentally altered the dynamics of international politics. The first of them – a fundamentalist Islamic revolution in Iran – substantially altered the consciousness and political imagination of Muslims around the world. For the first time in the modern age, a secular leader installed and supported by America, Shah Reza Pahlavi, was overthrown by the street demonstrations of a religious movement. The new Iranian regime, led by the Ayatollah Khomeini, immediately sought to capitalize on this and spread its religious and political influence by supporting and funding Shia terrorist movements in Iraq, Saudi Arabia, Lebanon, and Kuwait. (The two main denominations of Islam are Sunni and Shia. Sunnis constitute the vast majority of Muslims; Shiites are numerically dominant only in Iran, Iraq, Azerbaijan, Bahrain, and Lebanon.)

Also in 1979, but at the end of the year, the Soviets invaded a very unstable Afghanistan to prevent the unrest there spilling over into its Central Asian republics. In reaction, the Reagan administration ordered the CIA to assist local anticommunist insurgents in Afghanistan so as to raise the costs of occupation for the Soviets. This turned out to be the last front of the Cold War. Ten years later, the Soviets were forced into a humiliating withdrawal. Although many in the Western world celebrated the Soviet defeat, it was essentially a hollow victory for the United States, because the very forces it trained and funded included the likes of the Taliban (whose rank-and-file fighters, then as now, were called "mujahedeen") and Osama bin Laden, and these forces soon were engineering terrorist attacks against U.S. targets. The CIA word for this is "blowback," or the unanticipated transformation of clients into enemies (Kinzer 2006, 260–75).

The path of destruction sparked by these two events is a matter of historical record: in 1983, the Iranian-sponsored Hezbollah ran two truck bombs into the U.S. Marines' barracks in Lebanon, killing 241 American soldiers; in 1988, Libyan agents blew up Pan Am flight 103 over Lockerbie, Scotland, causing 270 deaths; in 1993, Afghan-trained terrorists launched the first attack on the World Trade Center, resulting in 6 deaths and more than 1,000 injuries; in 1996, Saudi militants and Afghan war veterans bombed a U.S. housing complex in Saudi Arabia, killing 19 Americans; in 1998, Al Qaeda hit the U.S. embassies in Tanzania and Kenya, causing the deaths of 224 people and injuring 5,000; in 2000, Al Qaeda attacked the USS *Cole* at a Yemeni port, causing the death of 17 sailors; and in 2001, 19 hijackers (15 Saudi Arabians, 2 United Arab Emirates citizens, 1 Lebanese, and 1 Egyptian) hijacked 4 U.S. passenger jets and flew them into the World Trade Center and the Pentagon, resulting in more than 3,000 dead and more than 6,000 injured. In all, between 1980 and 2000, Islamic-based groups were responsible for eleven of sixteen acts of international terrorism. Suicide bombing became the main innovative terrorist technique, in many cases sanctioned and encouraged by extremist Islamic clergy who framed it as a direct path to paradise for perpetrators. The noted political scientist Samuel Huntington labeled this pattern of post–Cold War conflict the "clash of civilizations," holding the tension between the West and Islam to be the main dynamic of the new international order (Huntington 1996).

But what makes Al Qaeda *the* terrorist group of the moment is not its religious affiliation; rather its significance stems from its greater global reach and wider range of targets compared to other groups. The Colombian FARC, the Tamil Tigers, the Kurdish PKK, the IRA, ETA, and Hamas and Hezbollah all focus on local or, at most, regional targets. Al Qaeda is the only one to have acted on a global stage. It is also the only one that targets such a wide variety of states, including both Western countries and governments in the Muslim world it regards as corrupt or run by "infidels." Al Qaeda developed this capacity largely through state sponsorship by the Taliban of Afghanistan. Once the Soviets had been defeated and the Taliban took control of the country, a partnership was developed with Osama bin Laden, allowing him and Al Qaeda (known in Afghanistan as the "Afghan Arabs") to use Afghanistan as a base to train, strategize, communicate, and mobilize for attacks against the West. The invasion and occupation of Afghanistan in 2002 by Western coalition forces broke the back of this relationship, turned the Taliban against Al Qaeda, and severely degraded the capabilities of Osama bin Laden's forces. The weakening of Al Qaeda proper, however, has led to a shadowy proliferation of "Al Qaedaisms," or the rise of multiple, largely independent, and unaffiliated groups inspired by bin Laden but who had no direct connection to him. As Eric Etheridge (2009) explains:

> Whereas eight years ago there was only one address for Al Qaeda, the caves of Tora-Bora in Afghanistan, today there are a number of different addresses for different branches of the organization, which are perhaps stronger and more dangerous than the "main" branch. There is now Al Qaeda in the Arabian peninsula and in the Islamic Maghreb [i.e., North Africa], in addition to branches in Iraq and along the Pakistan-Afghanistan border. There is also a Somali branch, which has revived and rebuilt and is now stronger than it was in a previous iteration.

How have contemporary states reacted to the challenges posed by Islamist-based terrorism? The answer is in two diametrically opposite ways. In the first one, the state strengthens by expanding the discretionary authority of the executive branch and investing in, and mobilizing, the institutions of security, intelligence, and law enforcement. Both democracies and authoritarian regimes have responded to terrorism by taking on the characteristics of a hard security state. The paradox of this approach, for democracies, is that strengthening these institutions of the state invariably places pressure on civil liberties in society. The second reaction is for the state to weaken by losing territory, authority, or the monopoly of violence to organized terrorist groups who then exploit the state's territory as a base of operations.

Hard Security State

Western states have taken the lead in strengthening the institutions of hard, physical power to counter the Islamic-based terrorist threat. They have been prompted to do so by a string of direct terrorist attacks on their soil, most notably the September 2001 attack on the United States, the March 2004 Madrid train bombings (191 killed, 1,800 wounded), and the July 2005 London bombings (56 killed, 700 injured). France, the United States, and Britain, in particular, have pioneered the moves toward a hard security state and thus serve as a model on which other states are converging. A hard security state is characterized by an active and less constrained executive, the expansion of the instruments of coercion and surveillance, and curtailing of civil liberties in the name of national security imperatives.

The French developed this model after a string of terrorist attacks, largely in Paris, by Middle Eastern–based groups in 1986. These attacks increased public anxiety and compelled the authorities to respond with new, tough legislation. Prior to this time, successive French governments had followed a policy of accommodation, known as the sanctuary doctrine, which granted residence to suspected terrorists and prominent opposition figures from other states on the condition that they did not plot terrorist acts against France itself. It was under this policy that the then-dissident and exiled Ayatollah Khomeini was allowed into the country in 1978 and permitted a base of operations (in the suburbs of Paris) to coordinate the overthrow of the Shah of Iran.

A major reason the French state originally developed the sanctuary doctrine was its political class's acute awareness that the country's military apparatus was incapable of projecting sufficient coercive power into the international arena to contain terrorism at that level. Consequently, the idea took hold to create a sanctuary in which terrorists, as well as dissidents, radicals, and human rights refugees from around the world, could find safe haven. In return for its neutrality toward extremist groups, the French state enjoyed a built-in guarantee against future domestic terrorist acts as well as greater diplomatic latitude to pursue relations with states that sponsor terrorism. The sanctuary doctrine produced, in the 1970s and early 1980s, the temporary silence of several radical groups in France, including the PLO, but its dangers soon became evident. The 1986 attacks involved twelve total incidents spread over a period of three frightening months (February, March, and September) by a hitherto obscure group, the Committee for Solidarity with Near Eastern Political Prisoners. The French state was caught completely off guard. The vulnerability of the country having been made blindingly obvious, a powerful public outcry effectively put an end to French accommodationist policies (Shapiro and Suzan 2003).

In response to these events and a subsequent wave of terrorist attacks in 1995 by the Algerian Armed Islamic Group (GIA), the French political class made a series of moves that put in place the foundations of a hard security state. These included:

1. The reform of the judiciary and the expansion of its purview so that normal judges could try terrorism cases. In this way, France regularized the prosecution of terrorism within its existing legal structure

and avoided the creation of separate court system crafted just for terrorists and therefore of dubious constitutionality.

2. Investigating magistrates (*juge d'instruction*), who specialized in terrorism, were granted substantial powers to interrogate, investigate, and indict. Effectively enjoying the powers of prosecutor and judge, investigating magistrates had the power to open court inquiries, authorize wiretaps and search warrants, and issue subpoenas.

3. The DST (*Direction du Surveillance Territorie*), France's domestic intelligence agency, began close surveillance of mosques and extensive wiretapping of immigrant Arab and North African communities.

4. Police powers were liberally augmented and utilized in the form of sweeps, detentions, and deportations, and police were granted the right to hold terrorism suspects without charge for up to three years.

5. Finally, special mention must be made of the French state's unique promotion of secularism and the concerted effort to assimilate immigrants into the French culture, including the monitoring of speech in mosques and regulation of the education of imams. This package of reforms brought condemnation from human rights groups and paved the way for some successful preemptive strikes that foiled terrorist plans to attack the World Cup in 1998, the Strasbourg Cathedral in 2000, and the American embassy in Paris in 2001.

It was this record of achievement that made the French hard security state a model for much of the rest of Europe (Haddad and Balz 2008).

The security measures enacted in the United States after the 9/11 attacks have also been promoted as models for other states to adopt. Whereas the limited international hard power of the French state compelled successive governments to concentrate on domestic threats, the unmatched ability of the United States to project military power around the globe allowed President George W. Bush to fight the terrorists, in his words, "over there" (i.e., Afghanistan and Iraq) so as not to fight them "here" (on U.S. soil). The Bush administration argued that Islamist terrorism was a wholly new phenomenon requiring unprecedented measures. Vice President Dick Cheney was particularly pointed about what the new terrorist threats required, which was for the United States to start operating from the "dark side." This term implied the sidestepping of constitutional constraints and international obligations that interfered with the new counterterrorism strategy.

First to go was the Geneva Convention. Given that Al Qaeda is a nonstate actor, Bush officials argued it could not expect, nor was it entitled to, the rights and protections afforded to prisoners of war. Instead, captive Al Qaeda members were deemed "illegal enemy combatants" and treated as dangerous criminals rather than political actors. White House lawyers wrote secret memoranda to justify the use of harsh torture methods like water boarding (or the simulated drowning of a prisoner), stress positions, holding detainees in small coffin-like boxes, hypothermia, prolonged isolation, threatening prisoners with dogs and guns, forced nudity and sexual humiliation, and the use of psychologists and psychiatrists to exploit the captives' fears. These are just a sampling of the hundreds of "enhanced interrogation techniques" approved for use against detainees (Cole 2009; Danner 2009). Resort was also made to other constitutionally and legally dubious practices, including extraordinary rendition (or the CIA kidnapping of terror suspects around the world), the use of secret "black site" prisons in unidentified states to hold suspects indefinitely without public knowledge, and the deliberate decision to utilize Guantanamo Bay in Cuba as a prison facility because it lies outside the jurisdiction of American constitutional law.

Domestically, the USA PATRIOT Act was passed into law in the stress-filled month following 9/11. In this 342-page document (which, astonishingly, many congresspersons later admitted they did not even read), the government was granted, among other things, the right to intercept the overseas phone calls and e-mails of Americans, as well as the authority to deny terrorist suspects the writ of habeas corpus. The suspension of habeas corpus is deeply troublesome because it is a basic constitutional right of citizens, when arrested, to have their case reviewed by a court to determine the legality of their detention. This provision has long served to differentiate free societies from authoritarian regimes where incarceration occurs without accountability. Furthermore, law enforcement agencies were granted an enormous boost of power with this legislation, including enhanced search-and-seizure powers as well as greater access to individual medical, financial, educational, business, and mental health records. In all, counterterrorism measures in the United States have facilitated the expansion of presidential power and, with that, the power of security and intelligence agencies (like the CIA, the National Security Agency [NSA], and the FBI). (Feldman 2006).

Great Britain has followed a similar path, albeit one shaped by its long struggle with IRA terrorism. Such practices as long-term internment, detention without trial, limiting the rights of the accused in the name of judicial effectiveness, the use of physical maltreatment to obtain confessions, and shoot-to-kill police policies were initially applied only to Northern Ireland but have since been extended to cover the entire United Kingdom in order to meet the new Islamic-based terrorist threat (McEldowney 2005). The London bombings of 2005 were Britain's "7/7," as they were perpetrated by British-born Muslims on the seventh day of July. Echoing the chilly words of American Vice President Cheney, Tony Blair declared that "the rules of the game have changed." Actually, by then, the rules had already changed in Britain, where the 2000 Terrorism Act and the 2001 Anti-Terrorism, Crime and Security Act allowed for the internment of terrorist suspects, the suspension of habeas corpus, and the expansion of police powers. What was different was not that Britain introduced these harsh measures for the first time; they were previously put into practice in the Northern Ireland conflict. Rather, what was different was that they were now extended to the remainder of the United Kingdom.

The 2006 Terrorism Act did amount to a new encroachment on civil liberties, as it contains an "offense of glorification" clause, which deems any celebration of terrorist acts by social groups a punishable offense. The government of Gordon Brown applied this law to a radical Islamist group in January 2010 for its plans to protest the war in Afghanistan along the funeral route taken by Britain's returning war dead. Britain has also exercised, quite regularly, the power of proscription; by 2007, fifty-four groups had been banned, forty of which were linked to international terrorism and fourteen to the conflict in Northern Ireland (Croft 2007; Haubrich 2006). Finally, special mention must be made of Britain's extensive video surveillance system that, by some estimates, can film the movements of a single person an average of 300 times a day (Gray 2003).

WAIT A MINUTE. **CONSIDER THIS.** Between 2001 and 2007, at the behest of the UN Counter-Terrorism Committee and the United States, which are the two main promoters of global antiterrorism legislation, a total of thirty-three countries adopted antiterrorism measures, to a large extent patterned after the USA PATRIOT Act (Whitaker 2007). In other words, many countries are moving toward the hard security state model we have identified in France, the United States, and the United Kingdom. Do you think this is a good omen for the future of democracy? In other words, can the practice of hard security and democracy be reconciled? At what point does the expansion of state power threaten, rather than protect, the democratic order?

Weak and Failing States

The challenge to the state is of an altogether different type in Yemen, Pakistan, and Somalia, countries in which Al Qaeda has found a safe base from which to launch its operations. Yemen and Pakistan are weak, divided states where the central government is unable to enforce its authority over the entire territory; Somalia is a failed state that has had no real central government since 1991. Terrorist groups thrive in these environments where training, recruiting, communications, network building, travel, and so on can proceed under cover of state (or quasi-state) protection. In both Pakistan and Yemen, government actors assign a higher priority to problems other than fighting Al Qaeda, adding to its operational freedom. India is that higher priority for Pakistan. Since the partition of 1947 (the year British colonial rule ended), India and Pakistan have fought three wars and continue to be bitterly divided by their conflicting sovereignty claims to Kashmir. In Yemen, a secessionist movement in the north and an emerging one in the south have created the political space for Al Qaeda to flourish. In both countries, Al Qaeda has forged relationships with elements of the political class, the religious authorities, and the security/intelligence/military apparatuses (Erlanger 2010; Perlez 2009; Shane 2009). These insider connections have allowed the terrorist group to carve out territorial strongholds outside government control and neutralize the efforts of those political forces allied to the war on terror. Al Qaeda has, in short, infiltrated the state. In the clash between states and terrorists, this is one of the worse-case scenarios – a state vertically and horizontally compromised by non-state actors and thereby unable to act coherently and effectively.

CONCLUSION

Based on the conceptual and historical overviews presented in this chapter, we can conclude:

1. Although terrorism is a slippery term to define, its bottom-line meaning is the indiscriminate killing of innocent civilians for political goals. Historically, terrorist groups practice a wide variety of tactics. Bank robbery, economic sabotage, assassination, and kidnapping all form part of the general repertoire of terrorist group acts. For these reasons, terrorism is a capacious and contested concept requiring

you, the reader, to determine its thresholds beyond its minimal core, that being violence against civilians.

2. Terrorism is not a monolithic ideology or organizational entity. Rather, it is a method adopted and practiced in a variety of ways for a variety of reasons by different groups, including states. This means that solutions to terrorism are also plural and contextual. What works in one setting and for one group will not necessarily work elsewhere. In some cases, like Canada's problem with Quebecois terrorism, a large dose of conciliation will dampen the passion for violence. In other cases, like Spain's conflict with the Basques, combinations of conciliation and coercion appear to have produced the same effect. As James Miller writes, "there is no best policy for dealing with all terrorisms" (Miller 2007, 345).

3. It has proved very difficult to reconcile democracy and counterterrorism. Politicians everywhere face strong pressure to act after a terrorist attack, and their failure to do so will most certainly have adverse electoral consequences for them. At the same time, the temptation to adopt harsh repressive measures poses just as serious a threat to the constitutional order as terrorism does. This paradox is difficult to avoid, and many states have traveled down this path. In the words of the expert David Rapoport, "[t]errorist tactics, inter alia, aim at producing rage and frustration, often driving governments to respond in unanticipated, extraordinary illegal, socially destructive, and shameful ways" (Rapoport 2004, 68). If the defeat of terrorism brings in its wake the defeat of democracy, then no one wins.

4. Terrorist attacks provide states with unprecedented opportunity to augment and extend their control into more dimensions and layers of social life. In Western democracies like France, the United States, and the United Kingdom, a hard security state has emerged. More citizens than ever before in human history are under the constant gaze of the intelligence and security apparatuses. For many advocates of individual rights and civil liberties, these are worrying developments. As Mitchell Gray (2003, 319) writes, "dramatic and fearful events like the terrorist attacks of September 11 (and other recent attacks) aggravate . . . society, making more vivid and manipulable the perceptions of risk already present and strengthening the support for surveillance-based methods of risk management."

5. Some states face challenges of a different order, particularly when terrorist groups operate more or less freely on their territory. In such

cases, sovereignty is severely diminished, leaving either a weak or failed state. If the emergence of a hard security state in the West and elsewhere typifies one outcome in the contest between states and terrorists, the divided and fragile states of Pakistan, Somalia, and Yemen throw another into sharp relief.

9 *Organized Crime*

Organized crime is a problem of tremendous economic, social, and political significance in the world today. Criminal organizations operate around the globe, affecting countries both rich and poor, regimes both democratic and authoritarian, and cultures both Western and non-Western. Its practitioners are secretive and elusive, for their behavior necessarily takes place in the shadows, hidden from the gaze of the public eye. Despite this opaqueness, global criminal organizations have an impact on contemporary states that is real, often dramatic, and definitely substantial. Scholars of comparative politics have traditionally not identified organized crime as a core, defining issue of the field in the same way that they have with problems like development, democratization, institutions, or culture. The time has come to correct this oversight.

This chapter is divided into four sections. The first demonstrates the significance of organized crime in the contemporary world. The second provides definitions of key terms, explores how organized crime is structured, and considers how globalization impacts the criminal industry. The third section focuses on patterned interactions between criminals and politicians. Organized crime cannot prosper without the assistance of corrupt politicians. In many places in the world, a political-criminal nexus prevails, in which criminals and state agents derive mutual rewards and benefits from covert networks of cooperation. Finally, the fourth section contains a series of case studies that cast light on the political-criminal nexus in a variety of settings. We start by examining Italy, which is the classic case of a mafia-penetrated state. Next, Russia's postcommunist transition illustrates the emergence of criminal organizations as the state weakened and declined during the country's "roaring '90s." The final case explores the connection between crime and politics in Mexico and, in particular, the rise since the late 1990s of powerful, competing, and extremely violent drug syndicates whose activities spill over into, and threaten, the United States. The chapter ends with a brief reflection on the ever-evolving relationship between crime and the state.

THE CONTEMPORARY SIGNIFICANCE OF ORGANIZED CRIME

Today, organized crime generates more than a trillion dollars annually. It encompasses an amazingly diverse set of activities, including drug trafficking, people trafficking, prostitution, money laundering, illegal weapons sales, the contraband cigarette trade, illegal transactions in energy products and toxic waste, gambling, ponzi and pyramid schemes, copyright fraud and counterfeiting, cybercrime, and the sordid diamond trade in the conflict zones of Africa. The amount of money made from such activities is as staggering and jaw-dropping as the activities themselves. In 2003, a UN study put the annual value of the drug trade alone at $321 billion, which means that global drug revenues are higher than the GDP of 88 percent of the countries in the world. The music piracy industry is worth $12.5 billion; arms trafficking is a $245-million business; toxic waste and illegal trash dumping accounts for another $11 billion; the illegal sale of prescription drugs is valued at $64 billion, and counterfeit pharmaceutical drugs at $200 billion; software piracy creates $51 billion; wildlife and animal smuggling $20 billion; organ trafficking $75 million, and body parts and human tissue $6 million; prostitution $187 billion; illegal logging $15 billion; and approximately $1.5 trillion is laundered worldwide. In the Canadian province of British Columbia alone, a lucrative marijuana industry geared toward U.S. demand (and accounting for only 2 percent of overall U.S. consumption at that), generates $4 billion a year, employs 100,000 workers, and represents 6 percent of the province's GDP. Globally, 2.5 million people are trafficked annually, some for labor and others for sex. The Council of Europe estimates that this trade in human beings produces $42.5 billion in revenue. All in all, illegal transactions and trafficking are estimated, at the high end, to account for 15–20 percent of global trade (Glenny 2009, xix; see also the online database of black market activities at <www.havocscope.com>).

Needless to say, global crime represents a significant challenge for modern states. A state cannot claim to have effective sovereignty when it cannot control its borders, or enforce its laws, or protect its citizens, or, most disconcertingly for state agencies, collect taxes. The tremendous profits made in the shadow economy are, of course, tax-free, and therefore count as lost revenue for the public treasury. This is particularly true with commodities that are legal but are discouraged by governments and subjected to high taxation; an example is cigarettes in the Western world. In reaction to high taxes, a flourishing trade in contraband cigarettes has developed, depriving governments of critical revenue streams. Based on its 2010 report, the EU estimates that the illegal tobacco market annually inhales up to 10 billion euros away from its coffers (see <http://ec.europa.eu/unitedkingdom/press/press_releases/2010/pr1077_en.htm>).

Even more troubling are cases of widespread corruption. Organized crime operates best when under political protection, and it secures this protection by bribing politicians and civil servants to "look the other way." Corruption corrodes democratic equality and transparency by providing an inside advantage to those willing and able to purchase government favors. Corruption also adds significant costs and economic inefficiencies to social programs and state economic projects. In the late 1980s in Italy, for instance, corrupt actors surreptitiously steered the government to spend twice as much as the United States and three times as much as Germany and Britain on cement for public works. According to one study, "at least 80% of these works [in Italy] are unnecessary; some of them are undoubtedly a disaster" (Porta and Vannucci 1997).

Protection rackets are central to the repertoire of organized crime. Local thugs lean on small businesses and demand a regularized form of payment. In return, the business community insures itself against such unfortunate and "unexplained" events as mysterious fires, vandalism, and the nondelivery of supplies. As Charles Tilly puts it, "someone who produces both the danger and, at a price, the shield against it is a racketeer" (Tilly 1985, 173). Racketeers engage in predatory economic behavior (Frye 2002). They diminish the state because a successful racketeer muscles in on the monopoly roles assigned to state agents, be it the local policeman, fire marshal, tax assessor, or health and building code inspectors. If racketeers can ply their trade more or less unimpeded by state agents, the clear conclusion is that the state itself is weak or failing.

Another way that global crime impacts the state is by providing resources to terrorists and rebel groups who hope to damage or overthrow it. The FARC (Revolutionary Armed Forces) of Colombia, the Shining Path of Peru, the Shan of Myanmar, and the Taliban in Afghanistan have all relied on the drug trade to sustain their rebellions. The transformation of "fighters into felons" has been most notable since the end of the Cold War. During the worldwide standoff between the

United States and the Soviet Union, militarized client states and insurrection movements on each side could count on a continuous flow of money and matériel from the two superpowers to prosecute their proxy wars. This happened in places such as Afghanistan (1979–1988), Lebanon (1975–1990), Angola (1975–2002), Mozambique (1975–1992), El Salvador (1980–1992), Nicaragua (1961–1990), Grenada (1979–1983), and Colombia (1964–1990s), to name just a few. Amid a shifting geopolitical landscape and the loss of superpower interest in the old alliance system, many client states and rebel groups alike in Latin America, Africa, and Asia fashioned new criminal alliances that exploit and traffic in precious and natural resources (e.g., diamonds, gold, oil, timber, wildlife, minerals) to sustain their movements and advance their interests (Kaldor 2001).

The "blood diamond" phenomenon in Africa offers a poignant illustration of this problem. Various African states and insurgent groups have used diamond mining to purchase or sell weapons that fuel horrendous civil wars and inflict hideous costs on civilian populations. Angola, Liberia, Sierra Leone, Côte d'Ivoire, Zimbabwe, and the Democratic Republic of Congo have all engineered or suffered from conflicts financed by the illegal diamond market. In a recent celebrated case, the International Court of Justice at The Hague subpoenaed Naomi Campbell, the international supermodel, for reportedly receiving a handful of rough diamonds from deposed Liberian leader and accused war criminal, Charles Taylor. According to the prosecution, Taylor is guilty of using diamonds to support a rebellion in neighboring Sierra Leone, where up to 500,000 people were mutilated, raped, and/or murdered, often by child soldiers (Simons 2010).

Sometimes, pure criminal groups (i.e., those groups without a political ideology or program) become so powerful that they directly confront, intimidate, and, occasionally, take over the state. This happens in a multitude of settings and contexts. In Brazil in May 2006, the powerful syndicate First Capital Command (*Primeiro Comando de Capital*, or PCC) mobilized its 1,000-plus-strong membership to wage a deadly attack on the policemen of Sao Paolo; they killed nearly 100 people in the process. According to Brazil's chief of police, "this is a challenge to the police – they want to show us how powerful they are and that we must negotiate with them at all times" (Glenny 2009, 276). In Turkey in November 1996, a car crash revealed intimate links between the state and organized crime, for the car's passengers included a Turkish mafia boss (who was also a drug-trafficking terrorist), a member of parliament, and a high-ranking police official. Prime Minister Mesut Yilmaz later admitted the state "has been overtaken by organized crime" (Jamieson 2001, 382). Similar stories of criminal takeover can be told about states around the globe, from postcommunist countries like Ukraine, Transnistria, Serbia, Kosovo, and Bulgaria to African countries like Nigeria and Guinea-Bissau, Central Asian countries like Afghanistan and Tajikistan, and Latin American countries like Colombia and Mexico.

Often criminals do not come from outside the state, but rather originate within it. The West African country of Guinea-Bissau is a case in point. Possessing a weak state apparatus and an impoverished economy, Guinea-Bissau has become a major transit point for cocaine destined for Europe. The country's military actually runs this operation; the heads of the army, navy, and air force are all involved and were deemed "drug kingpins" by U.S. officials in April 2010. The situation is virtually identical in the neighboring countries of Guinea and Gambia. Presidents and their extended families, government ministers, policemen, and customs officials are either intimidated into inaction, intimately involved, paid handsomely to avert their eyes, or murdered for getting in the way (United Nations Office on Drugs and Crime 2010). The U.S. State Department's 2010 report on international narcotics control contains similar findings on state collusion in the drug trade. A total of twenty states – Afghanistan, the Bahamas, Bolivia, Brazil, Colombia, Dominican Republic, Ecuador, Guatemala, Haiti, India, Jamaica, Laos, Mexico, Myanmar, Nigeria, Pakistan, Panama, Paraguay, Peru, and Venezuela – are claimed to be either major production sites or strategic transit points for illegal drugs. Of those twenty, three are said to have "failed demonstrably" to abide by international counternarcotics covenants that require them to use state power to combat aggressively the drug trade. Those three are Bolivia, Myanmar, and Venezuela (United States Department of State 2010).

In sum, organized crime is a deadly serious and politically significant phenomenon in the modern world. States are directly threatened by the activities of organized crime groups, perhaps even more so than by those of terrorist groups. Weak states in particular are under heavy duress. When politicians, the police, and the judiciary are easily corrupted, the rule of law becomes nonexistent, and criminal groups can flourish. As one study concludes, "organized crime is more prevalent in countries where the rule of law is less well assured and vice versa. There are very few exceptions to this rule" (Van Dijk 2007, 46). When state actors themselves become criminals, problems of crime and corruption metastasize and eat away at the foundations of the state.

*W**AIT A MINUTE. CONSIDER THIS.** The following are quotes from three experts that describe global organized crime: "At present there is not one region in the world without an indigenous transnational organized crime group or that is not plagued by the activities of an international organized crime group" (Shelley 1995, 472). "The world has never seen a planetwide criminal consortium like the one that came into being with the end of the communist era" (Sterling 1994, 14). "The McMafia is alive and well across the globe" (Glenny 2009, xii). What resources and instruments do contemporary states have available to combat the power of transnational organized crime? If one state is overtaken by criminal elements, what can other states do given the principle of noninterference in the domestic affairs of other states?*

THE ORGANIZATION OF ORGANIZED CRIME: FROM MAN OF HONOR TO CRIMINAL ENTREPRENEUR

Organized crime can be defined as collusion between agents involved in durable, disciplined, and hierarchical social relationships for the purpose of planning and executing criminal activities. Organized criminals are distinguished from petty thieves, burglars, bank robbers, and so on by (1) their membership in a structure of hierarchical authority; (2) their use of corruption and violence to secure their objectives; and (3) the much larger scale of their operations. Although teams of burglars, bank robbers, and even white-collar criminals no doubt have to cooperate and collude to practice their trade, they do not constitute an organized crime group. In other words, crime can be organized without the existence of *organized crime*.

Among scholars and across governments and law enforcement agencies, one finds very little consensus on the definition and characteristics of organized crime (Finckenauer 2005; Hagan 2006; see also <www.organized-crime.de/OCDEF1.htm> for more than 150 definitions of organized crime). This cacophony notwithstanding, a good place to start a definitional quest is to consider the classic cases of mafia organization found in Sicily and its Italian-American offshoots, namely the five historic crime families of New York City: Bonnano, Colombo, Gambino, Genovese, and Lucchese. In these cases, criminal syndicates function like mini-states in the following ways: (1) they are organized in a top-down, pyramidal authority structure; (2) they are marked by internal structural differentiation with functionally specific roles (in the Italian-American mafia, for example, the roles of boss, underboss, capo [captain], consigliere [counselor], and soldier); (3) they have restricted membership and are governed by internal rules of recruitment, promotion, punishment, leadership succession, and dispute resolution; (4) they claim territory or "turf" and seek to monopolize illegal markets within its boundaries; (5) they use violence or the threat of violence to obtain their ends; and (6) they often provide a measure of social order and even public goods and social services to local citizens. Many intellectuals have long recognized the similarity between the state and organized crime, but this comparison was not lost on the ancient world either, as St. Augustine testifies: "[F]or what are states but large bandit bands, and what are bandit bands but small states?" (Augustine 1998).

All criminal syndicates are based on a distinct ethos, or core normative principle, like honor, kinship, or profit. The Sicilian mafia (*Cosa Nostra*, or "Our Thing") was originally an honor-based organization. It took shape in the first half of the nineteenth century in a setting of profound state weakness, severe economic underdevelopment, and rapid social transformation spurred by the founding of the Italian state (in 1861) and the onset of market capitalism. Market forces generated desperate competition for land at the same time that they intensified inequality, but the weakness of the state in the south meant the absence of a centralized organization that could regulate conflict through its monopoly control of the means of violence. In this vacuum, men who successfully exercise violence and display "valor, cunning, brutality, thievery, and trickery" gain the respect of their peers. The Italian expert, Pino Arlacchi, writes: "[T]he word 'honorable' implies one thing only: the assertion of superior force. Honorable means 'exceptional'; 'worthy' means prevailing in power. . . . Mafioso behavior belongs to a system of cultural *mores* focused around the theme of honor and pursued by means of individual violence" (Arlacchi 1979, 54). In America, mafioso men of honor are dubbed "made men," indicating that no one can harm them without facing retribution from the entire criminal organization to which they belong. In return, they are expected to subordinate their personal lives and their immediate family to that organization. Another key element of honor is the absolute duty of *omertà* (the code of silence), the dedicated practice of which brings the organization competitive advantages vis-à-vis the state and rival criminal enterprises (Paoli and Wolfgang 2001).

The Yakuza of Japan are also steeped in an honor culture dating back to the Tokugawa shogunate of the 1600s. They are a highly ritualized underworld society whose members adorn themselves with brilliant and vivid full-body tattoos that symbolize their membership of, and loyalty to, the organization, while also functioning to alert and intimidate outsiders. Russia's famed *vory v zakone* (thieves in law), the underground mafia forged in the Soviet Gulag (prison system), also make extensive use of tattoos as a form of recognition, rank, and criminal achievement. Their members submit to a code that requires them to forsake all personal ties outside the society of thieves. The *vor* must renounce marriage, love for parents, legal employment, and cooperation with the authorities. The only path to membership is by serving time in prison, the center of *vory* power (Volkov 2002).

Other criminal groups may lack similar theatrical rituals and elaborate vows of submission, but they nonetheless maintain high levels of trust and solidarity by exploiting basic sources of identity, such as ethnicity, confession, kinship, and tribe. The Igbo of Nigeria, the Balkan peoples, the Caucasian peoples, the Muslims of India, the Lebanese, Jews, Sicilians, the Vietnamese, the Cantonese, and Fujian Chinese communities are long-standing trading nations who developed their market skills on the frontiers of capitalism where the distinctions between legal and illegal commerce are unclear and poorly policed (Glenny 2009). Many fit the description of "middlemen minorities," or ethnic groups suffering from discrimination in the larger political arena but still able to carve out and specialize in a valuable niche of economic activity. In economic terms, shared cultural heritage and ethnic solidarity work to mitigate the uncertainties involved in market-based criminal activity (Bovenkerk 1998).

These uncertainties are called transaction costs and they amount to the price of participating (i.e., trading, or buying and selling) in a free market. How certain can one trader be that the other will not renege on payment or delivery of goods? Are there risks of robbery during the transaction? Are enforcement mechanisms available to deter and punish cheaters and swindlers in the marketplace? If the exchange is illegal, how can one be sure the other trader is not the police, incognito? Transaction costs are high when information is imperfect in the market, and there is no mechanism to bind the parties to the agreement and prevent predators and opportunists. This is especially true with illegal exchanges, which carry higher risks and costs than do legal ones. Deception, arrest, and murder are some of the normal hazards involved in the shadow economy. Common identities reduce (but do not eliminate) these dangers and bring comparative advantage to traders in the market. They do so because traders who share an identity have greater trust, and trust lowers the risks of doing business in all economies, whether legal or illegal.

Finally, many organized crime groups are based squarely on rational business principles. For example, the Medellín and Cali organizations of Colombia are described widely and correctly as drug cartels because they sought to monopolize every stage of the production, manufacture, shipping, and sale of cocaine during the 1980s (Shelley 1995). By controlling all of the economic inputs and outputs of an industry, a cartel can determine the availability of the product and set the market price for it. The Organization of Petroleum Exporting Countries (OPEC) represents a successful cartel of the oil industry. Its Arab offshoot, the Organization of Arab Petroleum Exporting Countries (OAPEC), flexed its muscles in 1973 by announcing an oil embargo on NATO countries, particularly the United States, for their support of Israel during the Yom Kippur War.

In contrast to this unity of purpose, the Mexican drug "cartels" currently in the throes of a bloody internecine war over control of trafficking routes near the U.S. border are not literally cartels. Although the media routinely refers to them as such – hence, the Tijuana *Cartel*, the Sinaloa *Cartel*, the Gulf *Cartel*, and the Beltrán Leyva *Cartel* – the rivalry and bloodletting among some of these groups signals an inability to reach the level of consensus and cooperation that the concept of a cartel suggests (Lacey 2009). It is entirely possible, of course, that the current gang war will serve as an elimination contest, lead to a concentration in the industry, and therefore promote cartel-like conditions. Until then, however, the continued use of the term "cartel" by the mass media to designate Mexican drug organizations is best framed as an instance of concept stretching (see Chapter 2).

Globalization has had an enormous impact on organized crime, expanding its opportunities while at the same time compelling it to adapt and innovate. Revolutions in telecommunications and transportation, the erosion of national barriers to trade, the explosion of unregulated money markets, and the unprecedented movements of peoples around the globe have made for a transformed opportunity structure for organized crime. Criminals have been handed new opportunities to exploit this increased openness, while states have come to face more constraints in controlling both their open and shadow economies. In an ironic twist of fate, the push of states for free trade, privatization, and deregulation has undercut their very ability to control illegal activities. In this new environment, organized crime groups have increasingly adopted business models and entrepreneurial styles pioneered in the legal free market, absorbing sophisticated intelligence on financial markets, information technology, logistics, and law enforcement innovations. Merely to participate in organized criminal ventures in today's globalized economy implies that one is technically competent in such diverse fields as banking, customs, shipping, and communications. As Alison Jamieson explains, "like a legitimate business, a criminal organization wishing to compete in the international market of illicit goods and services must have a network of marketing, sales, and distribution agents; transportation facilities; and financial services in locations around the world where elements of different nationalities contribute specific skills to the efficiency of the global operation" (Jamieson 2001, 378; see also Etges and Suttcliffe 2008).

Globalization has fundamentally altered the basic ethos of organized crime groups, transforming men of honor into criminal entrepreneurs. Many of today's criminal organizations are decentralized, fluid, and flexible in comparison to the rigidly hierarchical honor societies of the past. Studies on people smuggling, the marijuana trade, and the car theft industry find such activities are more often than not run by small groups of entrepreneurs who are linked by loosely affiliated and ever-changing social networks (Finckenauer 2005; Glenny 2009). Decentralization allows greater operational freedom to the sundry branches of a criminal network and also makes it easier to avoid total disruption by police who may pull down one branch of activity but cannot fell the entire tree. Furthermore, the glue of shared identity is less attractive today in market terms than the availability of specialized skills for which precise criminal tasks can be outsourced. Again a quote from Alison Jamieson is instructive:

> The single, pyramid-shaped structure of the traditional organized crime group has tended to make way for less visible criminal networks in which national identity is subordinate to function or skill. . . . Services such as money laundering or high-technology crime are outsourced to specialized agencies. Transnational organized crime today is characterized by multiservice agencies based on fluid networks and functional cooperation. Transnational criminals are "sovereign-free" actors in that they trail their activities across several jurisdictions to minimize law enforcement risks, with no single jurisdiction having effective "ownership" of a particular criminal case. (Jamieson 2001, 378).

Not even the Cosa Nostra of Sicily has remained untouched by the broad changes in the global economy. Mafia scholars in Italy note that since the mid-1960s, the classic honor-based organizations have undergone an "entrepreneurial transformation." Two factors account for this change. The first is that economic modernization finally reached the impoverished and neglected Italian south. The introduction of massive public-works projects, as well as cars, television, and other modern amenities, have completely altered the cultural landscape. The precipitous decline of blood feuds and honor crimes is but one sign of this change. A second factor prompting the rise of an "entrepreneurial mafia" is the considerable expansion of the global drug market in the 1970s and the Sicilian mafia's rapid attainment of a preeminent position in it. The infusion of new wealth forced a redefinition of what it meant to be a man of respect. In essence, the cult of honor was replaced by the "cult of accumulation" (Arlacchi 1979; Catanzaro 1985).

■ CONTOURS OF THE POLITICAL-CRIMINAL NEXUS

In this section, we trace common links between criminals and the state. Our hope is to introduce a number of concepts and empirical patterns that demonstrate the close relationship that can develop between crime and politics, or what is commonly called the political-criminal nexus. These patterns and concepts can then be used to guide the comparative case analysis that follows. Let us start by defining one of the very oldest types of political crime: corruption.

Corruption is a fundamental modus operandi of organized crime and it is the primary means by which it penetrates the state. Corruption occurs when a public agent violates the formal rules of office by trading the resources of that office (decisional power, privileged information, economic goods) for personal gain. In Robert Klitgaard's succinct formulation, corruption equals "monopoly plus discretion minus accountability" (Klitgaard 1988, 75). State agents control goods and services-like licenses, permits, official seals, stamps and signatures, public tenders (or offers for business), the right to grant concessions (or special privileges), information, jobs, and monies, and often have decision-making authority over their use. When the public accountability of such offices is weak, conditions are favorable for the entry of corrupt actors.

To be sure, corruption is not solely the province of organized crime. Politicians are certainly capable of producing corruption scandals without any assistance from the mafia. Helmut Kohl, the sixteen-year chancellor who unified East and West Germany, was ousted in 1999 for accepting illegal campaign contributions. In that same year, the entire twenty-member European Commission, the executive body of the European Union, resigned after an independent investigation revealed widespread fraud, nepotism, and mismanagement (BBC 1999; Livingston 2000). Corrupt exchanges between businessmen, lobbyists, and wealthy citizens on the one hand and politicians, bureaucrats, and party leaders on the other are commonplace in democracies and may have nothing to do with organized crime or vast criminal conspiracies.

It is only when criminal organizations and the state develop durable collaborative relationships for illegal ends that we can say a political-criminal nexus (PCN) is in place. The PCN denotes systematic, ongoing, surreptitious exchange relationships between the criminal underworld and the formal political establishment (Godson 2003). One side or the other may initiate the relationship, and one or the other may have the upper hand in it at any given time. The PCN construct is therefore more flexible than other terms that convey the corruption of a state. For example, the World Bank has articulated and developed the notion of "state capture," which means the degree to which private actors or businesses use corrupt payments to influence the formation and implementation of public policy (Hellman et al. 2000). In this scenario, the impetus to subvert the rule of law comes from outside the state. Conversely, terms like "predatory state" or "kleptocracy" indicate that the state is the primary corrupt institution and that its representatives take the initiative in seeking personal enrichment at public expense (Pei 2003). The PCN concept, in contrast, casts a wider net by not presupposing in advance which side is primarily responsible for corruption. Rather, it stipulates more generally that criminal and state actors interact and collude for mutual gain. Which side holds the balance of power at any given time is context-dependent. What then, does each get from the transaction?

Criminal organizations need, above all else, immunity. The freedom to break the law with impunity is the key to longevity in the criminal world. Every long-standing organized crime group in the world has utilized corruption to secure its existence and livelihood. By corrupting state officials, organized criminals "neutralize" the application of the law in their domain of activity (Geffray 2002). Corrupt state agents may deliver sensitive intelligence information to criminals regarding police crackdowns, or they may be employed to intervene in judicial cases and secure court delays, reduced sentences, acquittals, and the application of maximum penalties to criminal competitors (Porta and Vannucci 1999). In this way, corruption brings an organized crime group advantages vis-à-vis its rivals.

A system of corrupt exchanges between criminals and politicians also lends an air of legitimacy to the former, particularly if prominent national politicians are placed on the payroll. Invitations to important state functions, public ceremonies, and philanthropic events can alter public perceptions and rehabilitate the reputation of a powerful crime figure, making him appear the very model of an upstanding citizen. As Godson (2003, 9) notes, "successful criminal elites often want to be accepted by the upper world and seek social mobility for themselves and their families. They often want to mix with celebrities, be seen in fashionable places, and have their families blessed by senior religious authorities." Furthermore, a PCN provides criminals with access to the authoritative decision-making processes of the state. From this vantage point, they can obtain a lucrative claim of priority in the distribution of public-works projects, insider information on economic policy, bids for public contracts, and the privatization of state assets, as well as a multitude of "small favors" (Della Porta and Vannucci, 1999).

State actors, in turn, receive their fair share of benefits. In weak states, where the rule of law, political parties, the civil service, and civil society are underdeveloped, organized crime groups can often deliver votes. Such settings are typically marked by a system of informal patron-client relationships. If organized crime groups function as patrons and control de facto specific territorial jurisdictions of a state, they can use intimidation to direct the political choices of the entire voting-age population. In Sicily, for instance, the investigations of the Parliamentary Anti-Mafia Committee in 1993 discovered that

> The Mafia makes it known in the environment in which it operates that it is able to control the vote and it thus makes voters fear reprisals. Intimidation of this type is rather widespread and so also is the surveillance of polling places. In various cases elections have been rigged. More often no outright intimidation is needed. Advice is sufficient. (Della Porta and Vannucci 1999, 226)

Politicians receive numerous other benefits from association with criminal syndicates. Election campaigns are costly affairs, and crime groups are happy to deliver needed funds because it helps to place politicians under the obligation to reciprocate with favorable legislation. Personal enrichment is also a major incentive for politicians to get entangled in the web of organized crime. In addition to such pecuniary motives, organized crime provides politicians with a concealed and coercive approach to dispute resolution that can conveniently make some problems and political opponents simply "go away." The ability to mobilize subterranean sources of physical violence is a critical asset for politicians in many parts of the world. In Italy, for instance, politicians in the south would often work the campaign trail with "men of honor" in their entourage, for this produced a powerful chilling effect on opponents and likewise informed voters that they alone are supported by "men who count." An untimely demise awaited aspiring, assertive, and/or independent-minded politicians who failed to receive the message (Della Porta and Vannucci 1999). If criminals gain respectability when publicly associating with politicians, then in return, politicians get the aura of invincibility.

The precise nature of a PCN will vary from case to case. In some instances, only some branches of government or ministries will be involved; in others, the PCN will be confined to the head of state and his or her closest allies and cronies; in still other situations, the entire state may be compromised. In all of these cases, however, the PCN is an invisible structure of power located behind the legal, constitutionally mandated offices and functions of the state. It thereby constitutes another example of the hidden, secret structures that Linz and Stepan (1996) label "reserve domains" of power.

There are generally three political conditions that give rise to PCNs: (1) strong states and weak societies; (2) weak states and strong societies; and (3) states in transition (Godson 2003, 9–11). In the first case, some states have hypercentralized and overbureaucratized governance mechanisms, which historically worked to stifle the development of robust civic organizations that can petition, monitor, and pressure the state into some semblance of accountability. Long-standing one-party dominance in both Russia and Mexico are excellent examples. Weak states and strong societies furnish the exact opposite conditions. In these instances, the state has never fully established a monopoly of violence, extended its rule over its entire territory, or even attained legitimacy in the eyes of its whole citizenry. There thus remain autonomous, politically significant social forces that are suspicious of the state and outside its operational control. These are perfect conditions for the growth of organized crime groups that act as an ersatz state in the territories under their control. Italy falls into this category, as do many states in the developing world. In the final case, transitioning states replicate conditions of anarchy, for the old constitutional order is dying and the new one has yet to fully congeal. Law enforcement and security agencies in particular are often set adrift during these times, underpaid and uncertain as to which laws to enforce. In such *tabula rasa* circumstances, criminal groups proliferate. This is the largely the story of postcommunist countries in Eastern Europe and the successor states of the Soviet Union.

Let us now take these insights and explore actual instances in which a PCN has developed.

Italy's Men of Honor

We start with Italy not only because this country provides the classic model of organized crime, but also because "there has been no more striking a case of interaction between politics and organized crime in any Western democracy" (Della Porta and Vannucci 1999, 217). Extraordinary details of the PCN in Italy is public knowledge today because of the breakdown of *omertà* in the 1990s when the government began a full-scale assault on mafia operations and offered witness protection and relocation programs. Consequently, more than 1,000 mafia members became *pentiti* (literally, "those who have repented") and provided the government with inside information on the inner workings of this hitherto secretive and shadowy criminal structure (Paoli 1999).

There are four basic criminal groupings in Italy, all of which are located in the southern part of the country, known as the Mezzogiorno. The Cosa Nostra of Sicily is certainly the most powerful historically and the best known. But since the 1990s, the `Ndrangheta (which means, in the local dialect, "men of honor") has become the country's most formidable criminal organization. Its base of operations is southern Calabria. Less powerful, but nonetheless significant, are the *Camorra* of Campania (around Naples) and the *Sacra Corona Unita* ("United Sacred Crown") in Apulia. Approximately ninety families form the foundation of both Cosa Nostra and the `Ndrangheta, with the former having (in the 1990s) 3,000 initiated members and the latter 6,000 (Paoli 1999). Italy's Mezzogiorno is home to such an impressive array of criminal organizations because historically the region has been characterized by profound economic underdevelopment and the near-absence of any central state presence. In these circumstances, mafia families provided a governance mechanism for conflict management and the protection of private property, all of which was made possible by the inability of the state to deliver these public goods. When the Rome-centered state began, in the late nineteenth century, to impose national obligations on the south, such as military conscription and taxation, it was met with massive resistance.

Perceived as an alien and untrustworthy entity throughout the Mezzogiorno, the central state was simply not powerful enough to subdue the local informal power structure and therefore had to accommodate it. This was the beginning of the PCN in Italy.

"State within a state," "dual regime," "duopoly," "pacts" – these are but a sample of the terms used to describe the symbiotic relationships that developed between the state and mafia families over the course of the post–World War II period. During this time, the Christian Democrats (*Democrazia Cristiana*, or DC) were the dominant party in Italy and the lynchpin of every governing coalition from 1944 to 1994. The DC developed very intimate ties with Cosa Nostra. Seven-time prime minister and one of the most powerful politicians in all of Italy, Giulio Andreotti, allegedly attended mafia meetings and even received the "kiss of honor" from Cosa Nostra "boss of bosses," Salvatore (Totò) Riina, otherwise known as "the Beast." Andreotti's political allies in the Sicilian DC granted Cosa Nostra members exclusive tax collection rights and integrated many more such privileges into local political institutions. The DC and Cosa Nostra were so intertwined in Sicily that factions and disagreements in one were directly echoed in the other (Della Porta and Vannucci 1999). The `Ndrangheta, in contrast, built a more variegated set of political connections, sometimes affiliating with the DC, sometimes with the Liberal Party, and occasionally even with the neo-fascist Italian Social Movement *and* the Communist Party of Italy. When the government in Rome turned against the mafia clans in the 1990s, a wholesale cleansing of local governments commenced that was aimed at purging all politicians with mafia links. Just how deeply the mafia penetrated the formal political institutions is evidenced by the dismissal and/or arrest of more than half of the deputies in the Sicilian Regional Parliament, 17 Sicilian deputies in the national parliament, 12 town councils in Calabria, 110 communal councils in Campania, Calabria, and Sicily, and 400 Calabrian public administrators (Paoli 1999).

The form that Italy's PCN took has much to do with its feeble and feckless state and the entrenched culture of suspicion toward outside authority in the Mezzogiorno, but the evolution of the Italian party system also played an important role. What started in the 1950s as clearly delineated ideological competition between the DC on the one hand and the Socialist and Communist parties on the other gradually mutated into a catch-all party system (see Chapter 5). Hereafter, ideology was de-emphasized as the party leaderships became content with the instrumental goal of capturing and controlling the distribution of spoils that power brings. Moreover, the Left parties began to shed their working-class base and courted a new generation of middle-class professionals (referred to as the *rampanti*, or fast-rising, unscrupulous politicians) who saw their parties as convenient avenues for upward social mobility. The advent of modern political competition – mass media advertising, the use of computers, faxes, and photocopiers, and the need for paid professional (and therefore not volunteer) staff – added to party expenses at the same time that membership rolls and party dues began to decline. Party collusion with crime syndicates could mitigate these costs as well as deliver needed votes. The parties were thus driven, hat in hand, into the arms of the mafia. As one *pentito* confessed: "I do not solicit politicians. They solicit me at election time. They need me, I don't need them" (Della Porta and Vannucci 1999, 225).

Mafiosi supplied numerous benefits to the political establishment. The dense patron-client networks maintained by the mafia families in Sicily enabled them to mobilize hundreds of thousands of votes for favored candidates. In addition, mafia figures played a key role in stabilizing and guaranteeing political coalitions. For example, if there were ever challenges to local intra- or inter-party agreements governing the division of power and economic resources, men of honor would intervene, eliminate the troublemakers, and guarantee the continuation of the pact. They also played a vital role in securing corrupt exchanges between the business community and political parties. As the enforcer of the "iron triangle" linking parties, businesses, and their own interests, the mafia ensured that bribes would be paid, contracts awarded, promises honored, businesses protected, and offices occupied by the "right" people. According to the testimony of one mafia repentant, "there is an agreement between politicians and businessmen, then between businessmen and the *Cosa Nostra*, and finally between politicians and *Cosa Nostra*. The function of the *Cosa Nostra* is to control everything, every step of the way" (Della Porta and Vannucci 1999, 233).

In return for such "services," mafia families gained dominion over key sectors of the southern economy, such as construction, credit, labor, and the wholesale distribution industry. They were granted tax collection authority and they controlled public-works contracts. Politically, they placed their "friends" in local office and selected and promoted candidates to the national parliament. In the 1970s, the mafia infiltrated the Freemason secret society, giving them access to an even broader cross-section of the Italian political and military establishment, for Masonic members included seventeen army generals, four air force generals, nine

Carabinieri (special police force) generals, eight admirals, the directors of the three secret service bureaus, thirty-eight parliamentarians, fourteen judges, three cabinet ministers, and five prefects (Sterling 1994, 74). With this move, they extended their tentacles into the entire Italian state apparatus. It is no wonder then that mafiosi accused of crimes enjoyed such a degree of immunity that for them to flee the country or go underground was hardly necessary. When the boss of bosses, Totò Riina, was arrested in 1993 after thirty years of evading police warrants, many Italians were surprised to discover that he had been residing in Palermo the whole time. His underboss and replacement, Bernardo "the Tractor" Provenzano, was on the lam for forty-three years, but continued to live near his native Corleone until his arrest in 2006.

The PCN in Italy began to fracture, however, in the 1990s. There are many reasons for this. First of all, in the early 1980s, a power struggle over control of the lucrative heroin trade broke out among the mafia families, producing a considerable amount of carnage and resulting in the victory of the Corleone clan led by Riina and Provenzano. Known as the Great Mafia War, more than 1,000 mafiosi were murdered between 1981 and 1983; 400 were killed in Palermo alone. Scores of politicians, judges, prosecutors, police, and journalists were targeted as well. In response, special anti-mafia prosecutors, Giovanni Falcone and Paolo Borsellino (both native sons of Palermo), led a campaign to disrupt and dismantle the activities of organized crime. The La Torre law, named after a popular Sicilian communist leader slain in 1982, made association with the mafia a crime, and this empowered Falcone and Borsellino to orchestrate the "maxi-trial" at which hundreds of men of honor were brought to justice.

Incensed by the state crackdown and unable to alter the verdicts of the maxi-trial, Riina retaliated by ordering the liquidation of both Falcone and Borsellino in 1992. Both were eliminated, less than two months apart, in spectacular bomb attacks that shocked and revolted Italian society. Mafia retribution, however, was only just beginning. In 1993, Cosa Nostra unleashed, for the first time, a terrorist bombing campaign throughout Italy, including targets in Rome, Milan, and Florence. Plans were even developed for blowing up the Leaning Tower of Pisa. But such wanton violence was a severe miscalculation for it underestimated the degree to which Italian civil society, including that in the Mezzogiorno, had quietly modernized in the preceding decades and was now able and willing to express its "voice" against this illegal and rogue "state within a state."

In Sicily, the killing of favorite sons Falcone and Borsellino produced a wave of angry protests against Cosa Nostra that effectively broke its hitherto hegemonic status; in June 1992, 500,000 demonstrators marched through the streets in what has been dubbed the "Palermo Spring" (Lo Dato 2000). Consequently, the political class came under enormous popular pressure and could no longer offer protection to its mafia partners. Additionally, the uncovering of a bribery scandal in Milan (dubbed *tangentopoli*, or Bribe City) in February 1992 led to the revelation of massive, system-wide corruption in which all the major political parties were implicated. This further tied the hands of those politicians affiliated with organized crime.

The national government seized the moment, sending 7,000 Carabinieri to Sicily and passing a series of laws for witness protection, wiretapping, and the forfeiture of mafiosi property. As thousands of *pentiti* came forward, *omertà* was broken, and the upper echelon in many of the mafia families were arrested and placed in high-security prisons. The Italian state thus made great strides in the 1990s by extricating itself from the once invincible and invisible Cosa Nostra–anchored PCN. Nonetheless, the job is far from over in the Mezzogiorno. Rather than completely eradicating organized crime, the state's anti-mafia campaign merely shifted power from diminished Sicilian clans to the `Ndrangheta and the Camorra, who continue to ply their trade in Calabria, Naples, and beyond (Donadio 2010; Fisher 2007).

*W*AIT A MINUTE. **CONSIDER THIS.** A 2007 study in Italy, commissioned by a consortium of businesses, found that organized crime accounts for 7 percent of the country's GDP, making it the single biggest sector of the Italian economy (Kiefer 2007). After the Italian state made so much progress fighting Cosa Nostra in Sicily, how can organized crime continue to be such a problem in Italy? Does this say something about the continued weakness of that specific state, or does this say something more generally about the limits of all states to punish, deter, and eliminate crime and criminals?

Russia's Violent Entrepreneurs

When organized crime became a significant problem in Russia in the 1990s, several scholars observed parallels with the PCN in Italy. Federico Varese, for example, provocatively entitled an essay "Is Sicily the Future of Russia?" (Varese 1994). Similarly, Diego Gambetta, who applied an economic approach to his study of the Cosa Nostra, wrote that Russia "bears a striking resemblance to nineteenth century Sicily" (Gambetta 1993, 252). What is similar across these two cases, specifically, is the rise and development of organized crime as an institution that provides protection for private property and economic transactions when the state is unable to do so. In both cases, mafia groups arose as the state disappeared and they essentially substituted for it.

The story in Russia starts in 1986 when the seventh, and ultimately last, General Secretary of the Communist Party of the Soviet Union, Mikhail Gorbachev, launched his reform agenda based on the principles of *perestroika* (economic restructuring), *glasnost* (openness), *demokratizatsiya* (democratization), and *novoye mishleniye* (new thinking) in foreign policy. Gorbachev's hope was to inject a new dynamism into the stagnant communist system so that it could better compete with the West. At first, small steps were made in allowing small-scale private enterprise, liberalizing the media, and reforming the political system. After close to seventy years of one-party rule, however, Soviet society was beset with serious problems and grievances that could not be managed or contained as easily as Gorbachev had naively imagined. The media, dissidents, intellectuals, and everyday citizens used the new liberalized atmosphere to air their complaints publicly, while *perestroika* created an unworkable economic halfway house that was no longer socialist but had not yet become capitalist.

Stunned by the unfolding of events in the USSR, the East European ruling communist parties, which had previously been coerced into slavish adherence to the Soviet line, wondered what Gorbachev's reforms meant for them. Their answer came with the announcement of "the Sinatra Doctrine" (a reference to Frank Sinatra's song, "My Way"), which suggested that just as Gorbachev "did it his way," so East European states should reform "their way." The unintended consequence of this policy was to give a green light to the roiling undercurrent of democratic social forces that subsequently swept across Eastern Europe in 1989 and ended one-party communist rule. By 1991, the combination of widespread economic misery and the newfound voice of ethnic nationalism across the fifteen republics that comprised the Soviet Union brought about the disintegration of the once mighty USSR.

What happens when the state collapses? In Russia, the demise of the state meant that no longer was there a central institution that monopolized law enforcement, tax collection, adjudication, and general social coordination. To say it differently, the vertical state was replaced by horizontal anarchy, and social life approached the miserable condition that Hobbes described as the "state of nature." The dilemma for the reformers was that at the very moment the state was withering away, market capitalism was beginning to blossom. This is a dilemma, because classical economic thinking, as represented by Adam Smith, held that the state was not all that necessary for a system in which the "propensity to truck, barter, and exchange come from the womb and do not leave until death" (Smith 1976). Smith and the classical liberals asserted that capitalist behavior was as natural as breathing air, and is replicated in the daily activities of humans all over the world, even if shipwrecked on a deserted island like Robinson Crusoe. Directly contrary to this simplistic description of the origin and practice of free markets, however, capitalism is actually dependent on an effective state for its functioning. Gorbachev had legalized private property in 1990, but how could property be bought and sold without a working legal infrastructure that provides third-party authorization and arbitration of contracts? How can investment take place if there are no credible commitments to guarantee a return when profits are made? Who would police market transactions so that swindlers and predators are deterred and punished? Where could small shop owners turn if their premises are vandalized or robbed? In short, Russia's first steps toward capitalism were weighed down by enormous transaction costs.

The solution to this institutional problem was found in the growth of organized criminal groups who supplied "protection" at a time when the state was found wanting. The scholar Vadim Volkov (2002) calls these groups "violent entrepreneurs" because, as owners of the means of coercion, they were called to life by the very same market forces that created owners of capital. What they offered to businesses were "enforcement partnerships" whereby they "sold" a package of private goods, such as protecting property, monitoring transactions, gathering information, enforcing contracts, ensuring payment, settling disputes, guaranteeing deliveries, and generally "solving problems." While there is no doubt that the selling of such services often took the classic mafia form of "the offer one cannot refuse," business enterprises in Russia's emerging market economy genuinely needed help because of the widespread flouting of contracts, the shirking of debt obligations, the poor efficacy of the courts, the opaqueness of the legal code, and the unreliability of the police. For this reason, Russian enforcement partnerships cannot be reduced to the cruder forms of confiscatory predation that the American mafia historically employed with its protection rackets. Instead, "enforcement partnership is a more sophisticated relationship that involves risk control, supervision of contracts as well as creation of competitive advantages by violent entrepreneurs for the client enterprises" (Volkov 2002, 53).

Enforcement partnerships sprouted with the first seedlings of capitalism. In 1986, the number of reported extortion cases in Russia was 1,122; by 1996, it had reached 17,169, which was more than 15 times the 1986 number. The growth of organized crime groups shows a similar surge. Thus, in 1991, there were only 952 crime groups known to the police. By 1995, there were 14,050. Legal private security agencies also multiplied to meet market demands. In 1993, the state registered 4,000 such groups; by 1996, that figure doubled to 8,000 (Volkov 2002). From what social ranks did all these violent entrepreneurs come? Many came from the sporting world. As a heavily subsidized and prized showcase of the Soviet state, athletics fell on hard times with the end of communism. Deprived of their status and means of livelihood, athletes – particularly in the fields that rewarded physical strength, such as wrestling, boxing, weight lifting, and the martial arts – gravitated toward another field that valued might and muscle: organized crime. It is therefore not much of an exaggeration to conclude, as Volkov (2002, 6–11, 15) does, that "the gym and the street market" were the twin pillars of early capitalism in Russia.

Veterans from the 1979–1989 Soviet war in Afghanistan also played a large role in filling the criminal ranks. Trained in the use of violence, socially ostracized for fighting in an unpopular and losing war, and without any economic prospects, they embraced a new career in the shadow economy. Another source of recruitment for organized crime came from police and law enforcement employees of all types. Suffering from low salaries, poor morale, and massive layoffs, they discovered their skills could be more handsomely remunerated and appreciated on the other side of the law. Over the course of the 1990s, 25,000 policemen were dismissed annually and another 15,000 were arrested every year for criminal activities (Volkov 2002, 13). Finally, *vory v zakone*, Russia's traditional underground of thieves, jumped on the capitalist bandwagon, but their old-world criminal values were ill-fitted to the new milieu, and their relationship with the new violent entrepreneurs was competitive and often bloody. Whereas the world of thieves was the historical product of a harsh Soviet communism that no longer existed, violent entrepreneurs sprang from the contemporary reality of weak-state capitalism.

Eventually, the state made a comeback in Russia. After a decade of its deterioration and a tremendous growth in the economy of private protection, a new momentum for law and order took hold in the late 1990s. This new drive had both bottom-up and top-down sources. From below, businessmen began to clamor for a more efficient regulatory environment that offered predictability, transparency, and efficiency. Violent entrepreneurs themselves were undergoing profound transformations that stemmed from their very success in the marketplace. The steady of accumulation of wealth altered the decision calculus of many, steering them away from violence (which is typically costly to use) and toward ownership. Rather than employ a coterie of thugs, it started to make more business sense to hire lawyers, accountants, managers, and PR specialists. As Volkov (2002, 122–25) explains, "the more criminal groups strive to control the emerging markets, the more the markets control and transform these groups." From the ranks of plunderers, therefore, arose a new generation of capitalists.

From above, Vladimir Putin became president on the last day of 1999, and this substantially changed the direction of the state. Decrying state degeneration in his August 2000 presidential address, Putin vowed to end the "vacuum of authority" that allowed "shadowy groups" and "dubious security services" to profit from disorder. He declared the "dictatorship of the law" as his main slogan and moved accordingly to liquidate the various criminal structures that fed off business activities. While "racketeers, bandits, and bribe takers" continued to remain a problem, Putin was confident enough in April 2001 to announce that he had halted the degeneration of the state and had returned to it the monopoly of the means of violence. The history books will undoubtedly record Putin as an important state builder in Russian history, but, as Volkov (2002, 191) reminds us, "violent entrepreneurs did much of the preliminary dirty work."

*W*AIT A MINUTE. **CONSIDER THIS.** The case of Russia reveals a complex interaction between the building of capitalism and the (re)building of the state. Conditions are similar to Italy in that organized crime groups in both countries capitalized on the absence of a state for their own economic gain. But they are different in the sense that criminals in Russia did not initially have a much of a stationary state to have a "nexus" with. Rather than corrupting the state, they supplanted it and, ultimately and unwittingly, facilitated its recovery.

Why was Russia able to rebuild its state within ten years of the collapse of the Soviet Union, whereas Italy has still not subdued all of the criminal clans of the Mezzogiorno? How come Russia's violent entrepreneurs served as a springboard for the recovery of the Russian state, whereas Italy's men of honor serve to block the full development of the Italian state? What makes these two cases so different? Can the historical distinction between strong state/weak society (Russia within the USSR) and weak state/strong society (Italy) provide an explanation?

Mexico's Narcotraficantes

In Italy, the power of autonomous social groups in the Mezzorgiorno forced a weak state to accommodate a consortium of organized crime families. Together, state and criminal actors constructed a political-criminal nexus that defined the trajectory of much of Italy's political development from unification to today. In Mexico, the exact opposite conditions prevailed. There, rather than a weak-state-versus-strong-society dynamic, the pattern is one of a strong state confronting a weak society. The legacy of Spanish authoritarianism and centralization bequeathed to the Mexican state, independent since 1821, a governance framework marked by presidentialism and the spread of patron-client networks, both of which worked to keep society docile and dependent on state largesse. For more than seventy years, from 1929 to 2000, the PRI (*Partido Revolucionario Institucional*, or Institutional Revolutionary Party) dominated politics in Mexico. Its monopoly of all state institutions enabled it to act in a predatory fashion toward criminal groups, and so it did, regulating, taxing, directing, protecting, and/or eliminating criminal syndicates at will. The Italian state never had this level of control over its shadow economy.

Mexico also exhibits similarities to the Russian case in that both have recently experienced power transitions. PRI hegemony began to slip in 1997, when it lost its parliamentary majority, and then came to an end in 2000, when it also lost the presidency. Mexico is thus currently in the throes of a democratic transition, and this has brought considerable disorder and confusion to the institutionalized relationships of its PCN. The gruesome internecine war currently raging among the country's major drug-trafficking organizations (DTOs) is, in part, a response to this transitional uncertainty. Whereas Russia's transition occurred at the state level (i.e., the disintegration of the USSR), Mexico's transition remains, for the moment, confined to the regime level, or the movement from authoritarianism to democracy. Many commentators, politicians, and think tanks warn, however, that the current drug war could result in a failed Mexican state. To understand this dire prediction, let us first consider the origins and evolution of Mexico's PCN.

Mexico's economy has long served as a source of contraband for American markets. It has played this role since the 1920s, when Prohibition provided incentives for Mexicans clandestinely to ship alcohol northward. The 2,000-mile border between the two countries has always been porous, allowing first alcohol, then marijuana, heroin, cocaine, and methamphetamines to travel north, while cars, cash, and guns travel south. During its reign, the PRI managed illegal trafficking just as it managed all of Mexico's politics. The PRI was able to direct political developments because power was concentrated in the office of the president, who distributed offices, business contracts, jobs, and favors down the hierarchy while receiving, in return, obedience, acquiescence, and votes. Often called "the perfect dictatorship," political institutions were structured in such a way that "everyone except the president is both boss and servant," creating multiple levels of dependence among "political cliques" that are "loyal to the president but fiercely compete with each" (O'Neil 2009; Pimentel 1999). In short, the president controlled a vast patron-client network that purchased the loyalty of the multiple interests of civil society – business, labor, professionals, and peasants – which, in turn, facilitated their integration into the system. The political opposition, in contrast, was excluded and silenced. The same approach of selective integration and exclusion was applied to the *narcotraficantes* (drug traffickers).

Responding to the new market opened by America's counterculture revolution in the 1960s, Mexican drug trafficking started to become big business. The PRI controlled the industry by issuing "licenses" through the "plazas," or local governments situated along trafficking routes. Successful DTOs hoping to expand could purchase operating "franchises" from *judiciales* (state-level police) or *federales* (national-level police). A portion of the money government agents earned from these "concessions" would then be kicked back up the PRI hierarchy. Because plaza positions were lucrative for their holders, they too came at a high price. For example, the cost to a district attorney of taking over a plaza ran as high as $3 million, payment of which was expected in advance; thereafter, the district attorney was charged a monthly rent of $1 million (Pimentel 1999).

A major factor conditioning the buying and selling of public offices in Mexico was the meager budgets allocated by the state to ministries, law enforcement agencies, and local governments. It was thus a cultural expectation that civil servants, police, and local officials would supplement their income by way of rent-seeking behavior (or using the authority of public office to make personal profit by charging for services).

The PCN in Mexico was thus a top-down, state-controlled set of institutionalized relationships. This makes it quite different from the PCN in Italy, where Cosa Nostra often had the upper hand over politicians. The PRI treated *narcotraficantes* as "cash cows" who could be "milked" for party funds and personal enrichment. If DTOs ever ran afoul of their political patrons, they faced arrest and the seizure of their contraband, which would then be distributed to more pliant narco-syndicates. Troublesome *narcotraficantes* could also be abandoned during the certification process imposed by the United States. Starting in 1986, the Reagan administration subjected states around the globe to a "certification process" to determine their compliance in the international war on drugs. Financial and diplomatic penalties would be meted out to those that failed the test. It was normal in the run-up to certification for Mexican authorities to make a few sensational drug busts and hand over to the Americans a couple of *narcotraficantes* as "sacrificial lambs." Such "dog-and-pony show" arrests benefited all sides – the Mexican government appeared to be doing something about the drug trade, the U.S. government would be elated, and the larger drug industry would remain untouched (Chabat 2002; Pimentel 1999).

By the 1990s, the involvement of the state apparatus in the drug trade deepened with the provision of "limousine services," whereby the police and military would essentially escort the movement of drugs to the U.S. border. During this time, police roadblocks would be erected for the ostensible purpose of drug searches, but in actuality they were decoy operations designed to protect shipments of contraband cargo that passed plazas at prearranged times (Pimentel 1999). In short, the PRI in Mexico ran a PCN marked by asymmetrical power relationships between the state and drug syndicates, with the former decisively controlling the latter.

The democratic transition changed all this. With the electoral dismissal of the PRI from state governments (beginning in the late 1980s) and ultimately the presidency (in 2000), the elaborate system of political protection and patronage was broken. *Narcotraficantes* were now forced to negotiate with a new set of political actors. The demise of once closed corruption networks opened up the market and provided opportunities to nascent DTOs ready and willing to shoot their way to the top. Consequently, a horrific drug war over market share commenced and continues to this day. Essentially, the downfall of the PRI created a political vacuum that was filled by *narcrotraficantes* who gained autonomy but have yet to be either quelled or integrated into a new and stable PCN (O'Neil 2009).

Mexico's current president, Felipe Calderón of the conservative National Action Party, took office in 2006. Since then, he has presided over a major offensive against the DTOs, mobilizing 45,000 military troops and 5,000 *federales* to patrol the streets in the hottest conflict and trafficking zones. He has arrested top *narcotraficantes*, killed many others, and extradited a record number to the United States. Furthermore, law enforcement agencies are in the process of being restructured, purged of their old corrupt guard, and replenished with graduates fresh from a new police academy. Additional reforms include the implementation of drug testing, bank audits, pay increases for the forces of law and order, and polygraph tests to ensure police force integrity (Lawson 2009; McKinley 2008).

What has been the result of this new surge in the war against drugs? For starters, more than 30,000 people have been killed since Calderón took office and launched his military campaign. The violence is so bad that some cities have even registered a higher murder rate than Baghdad. Politicians, soldiers, police officers, and journalists (who dare to write about the *narcotraficantes*) have all been targeted for retribution by the DTOs. For example, more than 2,000 of the 30,000-plus murdered since 2006 are policemen. Much of the mayhem is quite grisly, including torture, beheadings, and dropping victims in vats of acid. In one particularly heartbreaking episode, hitmen working for the Beltrán Leyva syndicate carried out a revenge attack for the murder of their crime boss by massacring nearly the entire family of a navy ensign who was involved in the raid. As one journalist concluded from all this carnage, "Calderón took a stick and whacked the beehive" (Kellner and Pipitone 2010; Lacey 2009).

Calderón's war has also revealed how deeply corruption runs in the Mexican state. Scores of top security officials entrusted to lead the crackdown have been arrested for collusion with the DTOs, including the commissioner of the *federales*, the Mexican head of Interpol, the director and senior heads of the Special Investigation of Organized Crime (or SIEDO), the founder of the State Police Intelligence Corps, and, in the state of Michoacan alone, ten mayors, two police chiefs, the police academy director, and the governor's advisor. In addition, a special investigation of 400 *federales* revealed that 90 percent of them were linked to DTOs, whereas another estimates that over the last seven years, 100,000 soldiers have left the service to join the drug syndicates. Prisons also have been infiltrated by the DTOs. Not only have there been spectacular escapes of high-profile detainees, but corrupt wardens have also been caught releasing prisoners at night who then serve as hitmen against rival syndicates. A final indicator of the challenges facing the Calderón government is that despite a great reduction in the number of "zones of impunity" across the state since the military mobilization (there were over 2,000 in 2008), there still remain 233 locales where law enforcement is powerless. The noted Mexican expert on drug trafficking, Jorge Chabat, sums up the war on drugs in the following way: "Calderón said he would be the worst nightmare of the narcos. But it's the opposite – the narcos are the worst nightmare for him" (Kellner and Pipitone 2010; Lacey 2009; Lawson 2009).

Finally, no account of Mexico's PCN would be complete without mentioning the special role of the United States. There are essentially three levels at which the U.S. influences conditions in Mexico: (1) as primary consumer of illegal drugs; (2) as chief enforcer of the war on drugs; and (3) as main supplier of weapons. Although the last point is not emphasized much in the American media, Mexican DTOs purchase the bulk of their weapons from the 6,600 gun dealers located along the U.S. side of the border. Unlike in the United States, guns in Mexico are actually hard to purchase, and this is why 90 percent of the weapons seized by Mexican authorities are of U.S. origin (McKinley 2009). In terms of drug consumption, Americans spent a reported $62.9 billion on drugs in 2000, while the Mexican DTOs rake in between $6 and $15 billion annually (Chabat 2002). And yet the Mérida Initiative – a Bush- and now Obama-sponsored plan to help Mexico continue the war – promises only $1.6 billion in funds for equipment, training, and intelligence over a three-year period. The math of the drug war simply does not add up. As long as American consumers provide the world's biggest market demand for illicit substances, Mexico's war against DTOs appears futile. Short of legalization, which will undercut drug prices and thus the economic incentives of the drug syndicates, the best that can be hoped for is a reduction in violence either through a market concentration among competing DTOs or a new peace pact that halts their gruesome turf wars.

WAIT A MINUTE. **CONSIDER THIS.** Despite decades of fighting the war on drugs, the flow of illicit drugs from Mexico to America continues unabated. In the 2010 National Drug Threat Assessment issued by the U.S. Department of Justice, it was disclosed that the production and flow of heroin, marijuana, and amphetamines from Mexico to the United States had all increased (National Drug Intelligence Center 2010). In fact, Mexico is now the third-biggest producer of opium in the world. Many scholars, commentators, and politicians are slowly coming to the conclusion that the war on drugs does not work and has been far more costly in terms of wrecking human lives than the drugs themselves. For example, in August 2010, former Mexican presidents Vicente Fox (2000–2006) and Ernesto Zedillo (1994–2000), along with former presidents Fernando Enrique Cardoso of Brazil and Cesar Gaviria of Colombia, announced their support for the legalization of drugs as a better and more humane strategy to combat organized crime. Although personally against drug use, Vicente Fox argues "we should see legalization . . . as a strategy to . . . break the economic structure that allows mafias to reap enormous earnings . . . which in turn are used to corrupt and to increase their share of power" (Guillermoprieto 2010). In perhaps a telling shift in Mexico's drug war, President Calderón himself convened a forum on August 17 at which the legalization of drugs (specifically marijuana) was discussed. What do you think about this policy option?

CONCLUSION

If states did not exist, neither would crime, because it is states that establish the laws delineating legal from illegal behavior. An important *raison d'être* of states is to provide domestic tranquility, which means, among other things, enforcing laws aimed at deterring and punishing crime. Criminals are entrepreneurs who search for opportunities in the shadow economy. The pursuit of fantastic rewards typically involves high risks. This combination of huge profits and high risks attracts tenacious individuals who have the will to adapt, innovate, and introduce countermoves to deflect actions of the state. Globalization has raised the prospects for criminal adventures, providing a much bigger economic "haystack" within which the "needles" of crime can be concealed. Some states have grown stronger in this new era, employing ever more sophisticated technologies to eradicate crime, whereas others have faltered, unable to deter or diminish the equally sophisticated forms of crime undertaken by criminal enterprises. In many places in the world, the interests of state actors and criminals collude in mutually beneficial networks. We have seen two distinct types of PCNs in Italy and Mexico and a complex relationship among capitalism, organized crime, and state building in Russia. In short, states and criminal organizations exhibit relationships that are simultaneously antagonistic, symbiotic, and evolving.

10 Conclusion

The state stands at the apex of political power in the modern world. States are the primary actors in global affairs, and the system of state sovereignty forms the foundation of the international order. International organizations like the UN, the EU, the World Bank, NATO, and Interpol are organized and run by, and for, states. No other institution in any society claims and maintains a concentrated near-monopoly of the means of violence like the state. Of all the forms of social organization created by humankind, none has done so much good for so many people. Equally, none has repressed and murdered more people than the state. Military competition drove the historical evolution of the state, and this pattern continues today. In fact, even though states already possess enough firepower to destroy the world several times over, the global arms trade is a thriving $50–60 billion dollar industry. Military expenditures of states amounted to more than $1.5 trillion in 2009, with sixteen of the nineteen states in the G20 increasing their spending in real terms in that year. The accumulation of military power by one state, the United States, is a wholly unprecedented phenomenon in world history. With its 700-plus military installations in more than 130 countries, there is no place on the planet where the United States cannot project its military power.

Of course, not all states are equal. There is considerable variation across them in terms of wealth, military prowess, regulatory capacity, legitimacy, and general effectiveness. Still, even weak states enjoy a seat at the UN and the rights, privileges, and obligations associated with the internationally recognized claim of supreme sovereignty over a given territory. This means, above all, legal equality with other states and the right to claim noninterference from others in domestic affairs.

Generally speaking, states have at their command an impressive range of the resources of power. They regulate, coordinate, and administer myriad details of the economic and social activities of their citizens. They deploy extensive domestic police systems to ensure law and order. Powerful bureaucracies monitor and extract tax revenues from the income and consumer spending of all citizens. State actors have easy access to the mass media and therefore can communicate state interests and mobilize citizens in pursuit of the ends they define. Moreover, the capacities for control that states have at their disposal have steadily accumulated over time, shifting power decisively in favor of the state at the expense of the citizen, even in democratic regimes. For all of these reasons, the state is the preeminent political institution in the modern world.

For comparative politics, the state offers a rich field of scholarly investigation. As an object of study, it is a complex entity to come to terms with for it is both empirical and theoretical, cause and effect, and fact and value. State institutions like the bureaucracy and the police are empirically concrete, and yet the state as a concept is more abstract and difficult to grasp than semantically related terms like the regime, the government, the executive, or even the nation. To put it simply, the state is greater than the sum of its parts. Historically, it gets invested with moral purpose; from the limited property defender of John Locke to the infallible sovereign of Jean-Jacques Rousseau, the state has been accorded many and varied historical missions. For many contemporary scholars, the state is an organizing device that helps frame and contextualize politics. The multiplication of state types in the literature – for example, Westphalian state, postcolonial state, postmodern state, developmental state, petrostate, narcostate, rogue state, and strong, weak, and failed states, to name but a few – demonstrates the continued heuristic and explanatory value of the construct.

Perhaps the most intriguing aspect of the state is its persistence and adaptability over time. Numerous social forces have declared their intention to eliminate the state, or to circumscribe severely its sphere of action. In the nineteenth and twentieth centuries, anarchists and Marxists both framed the state as a repressive force that should be overthrown and abolished. Whereas anarchism never gained a critical mass of popular support, the Bolsheviks in Russia faced squarely the issue of how to reconcile governance and stateness. In his *State and Revolution*, written while in hiding and on the eve of the 1917 Russian revolution, Lenin announced the communists would disaggregate the state into workers' soviets (councils), which would allow the masses to take part in the "everyday administration of the State." In other words, Lenin advocated, just prior to seizing power, a democratic, participatory, noncoercive form of self-governing. But of course what Lenin and later Stalin produced in practice was a frighteningly invasive, violent, and paranoid totalitarian state that easily surpassed the traditional authoritarianism of the czars. The encounter between Marxism and the state offers students of comparative politics a classic lesson in unintended consequences.

Classical liberals have been no more successful at curbing the growth and expansion of the state. American presidents Ronald Reagan (1980–1988) and George W. Bush (2000–2008) both rose to power as free-market conservatives bent on taming and rolling back the federal government. Neither succeeded. Upon entering office, Reagan explained that "only by reducing the growth of government can we increase the growth of the economy." When he left, federal government spending had increased at an annual average rate of 6.8 percent, 61,000 workers had been added to the federal payroll, and the federal debt had grown by $1.9 trillion, from 33.3 to 50.1 percent of GDP. President Bush had an impact on the state even more profound than Reagan's. In response to the 9/11 terrorist attacks, Bush created the Department of Homeland Security, a massive bureaucracy employing 230,000 people. Two hundred and sixty-three government agencies were either created or redirected to fight the war on terror. Thirty thousand people were employed to eavesdrop on domestic communications. The intelligence budget was increased by 250 percent (to $75 billion), amounting to more than the rest of the world's intelligence budgets combined. One observer holds that "the assertion and expansion of presidential power is arguably the defining feature of the Bush years. . . . A vast infrastructure for electronic surveillance, secret sites for detention and interrogation and a sheaf of legal opinions empowering the executive to do whatever he feels necessary to protect the country" will be handed off to his successor who "will enter office as the most powerful president who has ever sat in the White House" (Mahler 2010; Zakaria 2010). As we noted in Chapter 3, the growth of executive power, and the corresponding decline of legislatures, is a trend observable across Western democracies.

Undoubtedly one of the most significant challenges to the modern state in the past thirty years has been the onset of globalization (see Chapter 6). Scores of scholars, pundits, and journalists have argued that the forces of globalization will undermine the modern state. The proliferation of IGOs (the UN, the EU, NATO, the WTO, the ICC), NGOs (Amnesty International, Human Rights Watch, the International Crisis Group, Doctors without Borders), transnational corporations, and transnational social movements means that states increasingly have to share authority through a process of leakage that is "upwards, sideways, and downwards" – that is, upward to IGOs and private, commercial interests; sideways to NGOs, corporations, and social movements; and downward to regional and ethnic groups within some states (Strange 1999).

All of the elements associated with globalization have made governing a more difficult proposition for states. The movement toward free markets has led to growing inequality within states as well as between them. This, together with the increasing immigration that goes hand in hand with globalization, has created a perfect storm of conditions for the rise of right-wing populist movements. Working and middle classes are fearful for their economic and cultural futures, and many have been seduced by the rhetoric of parties preaching patriotism, hostility to immigrants, and a return to a more ethnically and religiously homogeneous nation-state image. "Give us our country back" is how the right-wing "Tea Party" in the United States expressed their anger during the 2010 congressional elections. In Europe, right-wing parties in the Netherlands, Sweden, Norway, Finland, Switzerland, Austria, Belgium, and Denmark have been steadily gaining popularity and power. In both the United States and Europe, the rise of the radical right threatens to change the basic rules of the political game.

Revolutions in technology have brought new challenges to the state. Mobile phones, the Internet, Twitter, and Skype present new contested spaces between state and citizen. The global diffusion of ideas, images, and information means authoritarian regimes and dictatorships have a more difficult time sealing off their societies from outside cultural influences. China's effort in 2010 to censor and control Google, which led to the search engine company leaving the country, is a case in point. In other places, popular movements exploit the new modes of communication to raise awareness, money, and membership in their struggle with state authority. Both Moldovan and Iranian protesters used Twitter in 2009 to organize, inform, and mobilize thousands of supporters and to communicate their cause to the world. Egyptians used Facebook to launch their uprising against Mubarak in 2011. The Web-based whistle-blowing group, Wikileaks, provoked the wrath of the American and other governments in 2010 for publicly releasing a portion of the 250,000 classified diplomatic cables it had surreptitiously obtained. In cyberspace, the battle between political activists and state censors, as well as between "hacktivists" and the guardians of state secrets, is very much "on."

Global commerce and especially the growth of international financial markets have eroded the state's traditional power of the purse. If a state cannot control capital mobility, then it is very difficult to provide for the general welfare and to shape the economy so as to achieve national ends. The American sociologist Fred Block calls this phenomenon the "dictatorship of international financial markets," for it imposes on states significant policy constraints and painful adjustments when economic troubles occur (quoted in Evans 1997). It is increasingly the case that influential actors other than states are involved in the making of decisions that affect domestic patterns of economic growth, employment, and trade. Prior to globalization, markets were embedded in states that possessed a variety of levers, such as tariffs, subsidies, fixed exchange rates, and monetary and fiscal policy, to regulate the national economy. Now states are embedded in markets, and it is incontrovertible that their sovereignty has been compromised in this new game.

As always, the distribution of vulnerabilities to market perturbations is uneven across states. Globalization impacts them differently, such that state autonomy (or conversely, state dependence) is variable across the international system. In this sense, the autonomy of the Irish state, which currently owes approximately 100 billion euros to international creditors, appears substantially more restricted than that of Brazil, which growing at an annual rate of 5 percent, is both energy independent and a net external creditor, enjoys "investment grade" status by market ratings agencies, and can look forward to enhanced voting power within the IMF (Banville 2010; Economist 2010). Essentially, globalization does not constrain all states in the same way or to the same degree.

Just as the emergence of globalization in the 1980s and 1990s led scholars and journalists to stress state erosion and decline, so the terrorist attacks on the United States on 9/11 shifted resources, labor power, and momentum back toward a state renewed in the means of surveillance, intelligence, interrogation, policing, detention, and militarization. In Chapter 8 on terrorism, we labeled this the hard security state, noting that France, the United States, and Great Britain in particular have adopted this model of counterterrorism. Israel offers another example. Terrorism strikes at the heart of the state's ability to provide security and protection for its citizens, two public goods that comprise the core of the state's *raison d'être*. With the threat of terrorism ever present in today's political discourse, it is not surprising to find that the model of the hard security state is gaining ground around the globe. Between 2001 and 2007, thirty-three countries adopted counterterrorism measures patterned after the USA PATRIOT Act (Whitaker 2007). At the opposite end of the scale, a handful of states – Yemen, Somalia, and Pakistan – have virtually succumbed to terrorist organizations, de facto ceding territory and the right to govern to Al Qaeda-affiliated groups.

The events of 9/11 thus mark a critical juncture, after which the state has generally asserted itself to become more intrusive and coercive. The fight against terrorism has had spillover effects in the areas of crime prevention and the state regulation of immigration, border crossings, air travel, and international shipping. Heightened border security after 9/11, for example, led to a 325 percent increase in drug seizures along the Canadian border. Likewise, the Department of Justice (DOJ) has used its augmented "sneak and peak" surveillance powers mostly to go after drug dealers. In 2008, of the DOJ's 763 spying cases, only 3 dealt with terrorist suspects; all the others were related to drug trafficking (Butterfield 2001; Grim 2009). In America, there are currently 40 million surveillance cameras, and the average American is filmed 300 times a day. The average Briton is filmed at the same rate. Will the new forms of intensive surveillance and eavesdropping deployed in some Western democracies become a regular part of the state apparatus? What will happen to personal privacy, liberty, and democracy if the hard security state becomes permanent?

According to a recent study on the state, "it is impossible to look at the modern world and not recognize the overwhelming significance of the state as an institutional force. At present, and especially post-9/11, the notion of growing statelessness in the international system and the global economy has evaporated. Gone are the days when analysts could prophesy, champions could celebrate, and skeptics could anguish over the eventual withering away of the state in face of the onward march of globalization" (King and Lieberman 2009). In a word, proclamations on the death of the state have been grossly overstated.

The state does, nonetheless, continue to face serious challenges to its role and purpose in society. Chapter 9 shows that transnational organized crime has come to pose special problems for the state. Like terrorism, organized crime challenges the state's very *raison d`être*, which is to provide domestic tranquility by enforcing laws and punishing criminals. The emergence of globalization has provided a plethora of new opportunities for criminal entrepreneurs. In the fight against them, some states have grown stronger and more formidable in the area of law enforcement, whereas others have faltered and colluded in relationships we identified as the "political-criminal nexus." States, like Mexico, that supply the international market with illegal drugs face a very real threat of internal subversion by organized crime syndicates, whereas Western states like the United States are locked in the paradoxical position of promoting a war on drugs that creates more human carnage than the drugs themselves. As we look to the future, new generations will have to ask whether the war on drugs is worth so much blood and treasure and whether there is not a more humane path forward.

In Chapter 6 on globalization and Chapter 7 on ethnic nationalism, the demographic crisis percolating within many Western countries is identified as another serious challenge for the state over the next half century. In Western Europe, for example, the native Caucasian population has experienced a sharp decline in both birth and mortality rates. Taken together, this means Europe's population is shrinking and aging. To resupply its declining workforce, Europe will need to import another 47 million new immigrants by the year 2020. This is seven times the number that entered over the period between 1985 and 1995 (Berend 2010). The unprecedented levels of immigration to Europe from the Middle East and Africa have already generated cultural clashes between communities and have triggered the rise of right-wing populist parties in many countries. Immigration challenges states everywhere with fundamental and intractable issues of identity, religion, language, and culture. Whether and how the developed European state can manage the cultural and demographic challenges it faces remains very much an open question.

It is a fundamental truism, however, that states can and do adapt and change. Think for a moment of the across-the-board transformations involved in the movement from France's long-established monarchy to the republic of 1789, from the czarist state of Russia to the Union of Soviet Socialist Republics, from the laissez faire American republic to the New Deal Keynesian welfare state that prevailed in the post-WWII era, and from monarchical Iran under the Shah to the Islamic Republic. In each case, the purpose, scope, and reach of the state were completely altered. Ideologies, institutions, strategic objectives, forms of legitimation, and the modes, styles, and values of governing all changed fundamentally.

States today are in flux. A fiscal crisis is looming for many states, and it is questionable whether they can continue to provide the same types and levels of services given their mounting public debt. Both Europe and America face a fiscal crisis. The fall of 2010 witnessed a wave of strikes and protests across Europe as citizens mobilized against various types of state spending cutbacks, from the raising of the retirement age in France, to the raising of tuition at Britain's universities, to the imposition of austerity measures in economically troubled Greece, Ireland, and Portugal. In the United States, vocal protests have come recently from both the right and the left. The Tea Party emerged in 2009 to protest against new government spending programs, like national health care; the Occupy Wall Street protest and its Occupy offshoots sprang to life in the fall of 2011 to protest rising inequality, unemployment, and corporate influence in Washington DC. Will states be compelled by fiscal crises to redefine their traditional roles and functions in the future?

Some political forces indeed hope the state can be further reduced via privatization. During Margaret Thatcher's premiership in Britain, the "New Public Management" (see Chapter 3) movement took hold. Thatcher privatized state assets, selling off state-owned industries and cutting the state sector by half between 1979 and 1989. In the United States, the military, prisons, and state schools have all seen an expanded use of the private sector in the execution of public functions. Over the course of the American occupation of Iraq, the U.S. government has employed more than 30,000 private armed guards and more than 100,000 private contractors. The state of Arizona is the U.S. leader in prison privatization, having invited bids for the privatization of nine of ten of its state prisons. And the push to promote private, nonunionized, charter schools across America has come at the expense of reinvesting in the public school system.

What happens to the public interest when private profit is introduced? Will private contractors be willing and able to provide for security and the general welfare of the citizenry on an efficient, impartial, and fair basis? What kind of state would you like to see develop? By all indications, the state will face even more dire crises in the future. Is it up to the task? Which types of frameworks and institutions of governance (see Chapters 3 and 4) can make the state more effective in the delivery of public goods and services and more subservient to the needs and interests of the population?

We conclude this book with a few thoughts on these issues from the recently deceased writer, Tony Judt (2010):

> All change is disruptive. We have seen that the specter of terrorism is enough to cast stable democracies into turmoil. Climate change will have even more dramatic consequences. Men and women will be thrown back

upon the resources of the state. They will look to their political leaders and representatives to protect them: open societies will once again be urged to close in upon themselves, sacrificing freedom for "security." The choice will no longer be between the state and the market, but between two sorts of state. It is thus incumbent upon us to reconceive the role of government. If we do not, others will.

REFERENCES

Alesina, Alberto, Edward Glaeser, and Bruce Sacerdote. 2001. "Why Doesn't the United States Have a European-Style Welfare System?" *Brookings Papers on Economic Activity* 2001: 187–254.

Alter, Peter. 1989. *Nationalism*. London: Edward Arnold.

Amster, Randall. 2006. "Perspectives on Ecoterrorism: Catalysts, Conflations, and Casualties." *Contemporary Justice Review* 9: 287–301.

Anderson, Benedict. 1983. *Imagined Communities: Reflections on the Origin and Spread of Nationalism*. London: Verso.

Aristotle. 1958. *The Politics of Aristotle*. New York: Oxford University Press.

Arlacchi, Pino. 1979. "The Mafioso: From Man of Honor to Entrepreneur." *New Left Review* 118: 53–72.

Ash, Timothy Garton. 2001. "Is There A Good Terrorist?" *The New York Review of Books* (November 29).

Augustine. 1998. *The City of God against the Pagans*. Cambridge: Cambridge University Press.

Baker, Al. 2011. "When the Police Go Military," *The New York Times* (December 3).

Banville, John. 2010. "The Debtor of the Western World." *The New York Times* (November 18).

Barnes, Samuel H. and Max Kaase. 1979. *Political Action: Mass Participation in Five Western Democracies*. London: Sage.

Bartolini, Stefano and Peter Mair. 1990. *Identity, Competition and Electoral Availability: The Stabilization of European Electorates*. New York: Cambridge University Press.

BBC. 1999. "Why They Had to Go." (March 16).

Bean, Richard. 1973. "War and the Birth of the Nation State." *The Journal of Economic History* 33: 203–21.

Bednar, Jenna. 2009. *The Robust Federation*. Cambridge: Cambridge University Press.

Berend, Iván T. 2010. *Europe since 1980*. Cambridge: Cambridge University Press.

Berger, Suzanne. 2000. "Globalization and Politics." *Annual Review of Political Science* 3: 43–62.

Bergner, Daniel. 2005. "The Other Army." *The New York Times* (August 14).

Berlin, Isaiah. 2000. *The Power of Ideas*. Princeton, NJ: Princeton University Press.

Binder, David and Barbara Crossette. 1993. "As Ethnic Wars Multiply, U.S. Strives for a Policy." *The New York Times* (February 7).

Bodin, Jean. 1955. *Six Books of the Commonwealth*. Oxford: Basil Blackwell.

Boehmer, Elleke. 2005. "Postcolonial Terrorist: The Example of Nelson Mandela." *Parallax* 11: 46–55.

Bookman, Milica Z. 1994. "War and Peace: The Divergent Breakups of Yugoslavia and Czechoslovakia." *Journal of Peace Research* 31: 175–87.

Bordo, Michael D., Alan M. Taylor and Jeffrey G. Williamson, eds. 2003. *Globalization in Historical Perspective*. Chicago: University of Chicago Press.

Bovenkerk, Frank. 1998. "Organized Crime and Ethnic Minorities: Is There a Link?" *Transnational Organized Crime* 4: 109–26.

Bowen, John R. 1996. "The Myth of Global Ethnic Conflict." *Journal of Democracy* 7: 3–14.

Bremmer, Ian. 2010. *The End of the Free Market: Who Wins the War Between States and Corporations?* New York: Portfolio.

Broad, William J. 2008. "Russia's Claim under Polar Ice Irks America." *The New York Times* (February 19).

Brownlee, Jason. 2007. *Authoritarianism in an Age of Democratization*. New York: Cambridge University Press.

Bryce, James. 1893. *The American Commonwealth*. 2 vols. 3rd ed. New York: Macmillan.

Bryce, Lord. 1921. *Modern Democracies*. London: Macmillan.

Budge, Ian and Denis J. Farlie. 1983. *Explaining and Predicting Elections: Issue Effects and Party Strategies in Twenty-Three Democracies*. London: Allen & Unwin.

Bunce, Valerie. 1990. "The Struggle for Liberal Democracy in Eastern Europe." *World Policy Journal* 7: 390–430.

Burg, Steven L. 1983. *Conflict and Cohesion in Socialist Yugoslavia: Political Decision Making since 1966*. Princeton, NJ: Princeton University Press.

Burns, Edward McNall, Philip Lee Ralph, Robert E. Lerner, and Standish Meacham. 1982. *World Civilizations: Their History and Their Culture*. 6th ed. New York: Norton.

Burns, John F. 2011. "Basque Separatists Declare Halt to Violence." *The New York Times* (October 20).

Butterfield, Fox. 2001. "Drug Seizures Have Surged at the Borders." *The New York Times* (December 16).

Caramani, Daniele. 2004. *The Nationalization of Politics: The Formation of National Electorates and Party Systems in Western Europe*. New York: Cambridge University Press.

Carnoy, Martin. 1984. *The State and Political Theory*. Princeton, NJ: Princeton University Press.

Carothers, Thomas. 2002. "The End of the Transition Paradigm." *Journal of Democracy* 13: 5–21.

Catanzaro, Raimondo. 1985. "Enforcers, Entrepreneurs, and Survivors: How the Mafia Has Adapted to Change." *The British Journal of Sociology* 36: 34–57.

Chabat, Jorge. 2002. "Mexico's War on Drugs: No Margin for Maneuver." *The Annals of the American Academy of Political and Social Sciences* 582: 134–48.

Chalk, Peter. 1998. "The Response to Terrorism as a Threat to Liberal Democracy." *Australian Journal of Politics and History* 44: 373–88.

Chanda, Nayan. 2007. *Bound Together: How Traders, Preachers, Adventurers, and Warriors Shaped Globalization*. New Haven, CT: Yale University Press.

Chandra, Kanchan. 2004. *Why Ethnic Parties Succeed: Patronage and Ethnic Head Counts in India*. New York: Cambridge University Press.

Cheibub, Jose. 2007. *Presidentialism, Parliamentarism and Democracy*. New York: Cambridge University Press.

Chhibber, Pradeep K. and Ken Kollman. 2004. *The Formation of National Party Systems: Federalism and Party Competition in Canada, Great Britain, India, and the United States*. New York: Cambridge University Press.

Chomsky, Noam and Edward Herman. 1979. *The Washington Connection and Third World Fascism*. Boston: South End Press.

CIA World Factbook <www.cia.gov/library/publications/the-world-factbook/>.

Clausewitz, Karl von. 1943. *On War*. New York: Random House.

Clayton, Richard and Jonas Pontusson. 1998. "Welfare-State Retrenchment Revisited: Entitlement Cuts, Public Sector Restructuring, and Inegalitarian Trends in Advanced Capitalist Societies." *World Politics* 51: 67–98.

Cole, David. 2009. "What to Do About the Torturers?" *The New York Review of Books* (January 15).

Conquest, Robert. 1986. *The Harvest of Sorrow: Soviet Collectivization and the Terror-Famine*. Oxford: Oxford University Press.

Cook, Robin. 2001. "Robin Cook's Chicken Tikka Masala Speech." *The Guardian* (April 19).

Cornelius, Wayne, Takeyuki Tsuda, Philip Martin, and James Hollifield. eds. 2004. *Controlling Immigration: A Global Perspective*, 2nd ed. Stanford, CA: Stanford University Press.

Croft, Stuart. 2007. "British Jihadis and the British War on Terrorism." *Defense Studies* 7: 317–37.

Dallas, Gregor. 1989. "An Exercise in Terror? The Paris Commune. 1871." *History Today* 39: 38–44.

Danner, Mark. 2005. "The Secret Way to War." *The New York Review of Books* (June 9).

Danner, Mark. 2009. "The Red Cross Torture Report: What It Means?" *The New York Review of Books* (April 30).

Democracy Now! 2008. <http://www.democracynow.org>.

De Tocqueville, Alexis. 1990. *Democracy in America*. New York: Vintage Books.

DePalma, Anthony. 2001. "NAFTA's Powerful Little Secret," *The New York Times* (March 11).

Diamond, Larry. 1996. "Is the Third Wave Over?" *Journal of Democracy* 7: 20–37.

Dogan, Mattei and Dominique Pelassy. 1984. *How to Compare Nations: Strategies in Comparative Politics*. Chatham, NJ: Chatham House Publishers.

Donadio, Rachel. 2010. "Race Riots Grip Italian Town, and Mafia Is Suspected." *The New York Times* (January 11).

Downs, Anthony. 1957. *An Economic Theory of Democracy*. New York: Harper & Row.

Drew, Elizabeth. 2006. "Power Grab." *The New York Review of Books* (June 22).

Duverger, Maurice. 1954. *Political Parties*. New York: Wiley.

Easton, David. 1965. *A Framework for Political Analysis*. Englewood Cliffs, NJ: Prentice-Hall.

Eckstein, Harry. 1960. *Pressure Group Politics: The Case of the British Medical Association*. Stanford, CA: Stanford University Press.

Economist, The. 2010. "Brazil Takes Off." (November 12).

Eddy, Melissa. 2010. "Angela Merkel: German Multicultural Society Has 'Utterly Failed'." *The Huffington Post* (October 17).

Egan, Timothy. 2010. "Building a Nation of Know-Nothings." *The New York Times* (August 25).

Epstein, Leon D. 1967. *Political Parties in Western Democracies*. New York: Praeger.

Erlanger, Steven. 2010. "Chaos in Yemen Aids Qaeda Cell's Growth." *The New York Times* (January 3).

Esposito, John L. and John O. Voll. 1996. *Islam and Democracy*. Oxford: Oxford University Press.

Etges, Rafael and Emma Suttcliffe. 2008. "An Overview of Transnational Organized Cyber Crime." *Information Security Journal: A Global Perspective* 17: 87–94.

Etheridge, Eric. 2009. "Does Bin Laden Still Matter?" *The New York Times* (September 15).

Evans, Peter. 1997. "The Eclipse of the State? Reflections on Stateness in an Era of Globalization." *World Politics* 50: 62–87.

Fatton, Robert. 1988. "Bringing the Ruling Class Back In: Class, State, and Hegemony in Africa." *Comparative Politics* 20: 253–64.

Fay, Brian. 1975. *Social Theory and Political Practice*. London: George Allen and Unwin.

Fearon, James D. and David D. Laitin. 1996. "Explaining Interethnic Cooperation." *The American Political Science Review* 90: 715–35.

Feldman, Noah. 2006. "Our Presidential Era: Who Can Check the President?" *The New York Times* (January 8).

Ferrera, Maurizio. 2008. "The European Welfare State: Golden Achievements, Silver Prospects." *West European Politics* 31: 82–107.

Finckenauer, James O. 2005. "Problems of Definition: What Is Organized Crime?" *Trends in Organized Crime* 8: 63–83.

Fish, M. Steven Fish and Matthew Kroenig. 2009. *The Handbook of National Legislatures*. Cambridge: Cambridge University Press.

Fisher, Ian. 2007. "In Mire of Politics and the Mafia, Garbage Reigns." *The New York Times* (May 31).

Foreign Broadcast Information Service. 2004. "Compilation of Usama bin Laden Statements, 1994–January 2004." FBIS report, January.

Foster, Kenneth W. 2001. "Associations in the Embrace of an Authoritarian State: State Domination of Society?" *Studies in Comparative International Development* 35: 84–109.

Friedman, Milton and Rose Friedman. 1980. *Free to Choose: A Personal Statement*. New York: Avon Books.

Frye, Timothy. 2002. "Private Protection in Russia and Poland." *American Journal of Political Science* 46: 572–84.

Fukuyama, Francis. 1989. "The End of History?" *The National Interest* 22: 3–18.

Fukuyama, Francis. 2004. "The Imperative of State-Building." *Journal of Democracy* 15: 17–31.

Fukuyama, Francis. 2006. "Identity, Immigration, and Liberal Democracy." *Journal of Democracy* 17: 5–20.

Gagnon, V.P. 2004. *The Myth of Ethnic War: Serbia and Croatia in the 1990s*. Ithaca, NY: Cornell University Press.

Gall, Carlotta and Ismail Khan. 2006. "Taliban and Allies Tighten Grip in North of Pakistan." *The New York Times* (December 11).

Gambetta, Diego. 1993. *The Sicilian Mafia: The Business of Private Protection*. Cambridge, MA: Harvard University Press.

Gandhi, Jennifer. 2008. *Political Institutions under Dictatorship*. New York: Cambridge University Press.

Gandhi, Jennifer and Ellen Lust-Okar. 2009. "Elections under Authoritarianism." *Annual Review of Political Science* 12: 403–22.

Geddes, Barbara. 1999. "What Do We Know about Democratization after Twenty Years?" *Annual Review of Political Science* 2: 115–44.

Geertz, Clifford. 1963. "The Integrative Revolution: Primordial Sentiments and Civil Politics in the New States," in *idem*. ed., *Old Societies and New States: The Quest for Modernity in Asia and Africa*. New York: Free Press.

Geertz, Clifford. 1987. "'From the Native's Point of View': On the Nature of Anthropological Understanding," in Michael T. Gibbons, ed., *Interpreting Politics*. New York: New York University Press.

Geffray, Christian. 2002. "State, Wealth, and Criminals." *Lusotopie* 1: 83–106.

Gehler, Michael and Wolfram Kaiser, eds. 2004. *Christian Democracy in Europe since 1945*. London: Routledge.

Gellner, Ernest. 1983. *Nations and Nationalism*. Ithaca, NY: Cornell University Press.

Gerth, H.H. and C. Wright Mills. 1946. *From Max Weber: Essays in Sociology*. New York: Oxford University Press.

Giddens, Anthony. 1998. *The Third Way*. Cambridge: Polity Press.

Ginsburg, Tom. 2008. "The Global Spread of Judicial Review," in Keith E. Whittington, R. Daniel Kelemen, and Gregory A. Caldeira, eds., *The Oxford Handbook of Law and Politics*. Oxford: Oxford University Press.

Ginsburg, Tom and Tamir Mosustafa. eds. 2008. *Rule by Law: The Politics of Courts in Authoritarian Regimes*. Cambridge: Cambridge University Press.

Glenny, Misha. 1996. *The Fall of Yugoslavia: The Third Balkan War*, 3rd ed. New York: Penguin.

Glenny, Misha. 2000. *The Balkans: Nationalism, War, and the Great Powers, 1804–1999*. New York: Viking.

Glenny, Misha. 2009. *McMafia*. New York: Vintage Books,

Global Policy Forum. 2008. <http://www.globalpolicy.org/security/issues/iraq/pollindex.htm>.

Godson, Roy. 2003. "The Political-Criminal Nexus and Global Security," in *idem*. ed., *Menace to Society: Political-Criminal Collaboration around the World*. New Brunswick, NJ: Transaction Publishers.

Golder, Matt. 2005. "Democratic Electoral Systems around the World, 1946–2000." *Electoral Studies* 24: 103–21.

Gonzalez, Francisco E. and Desmond King. 2004. "The State and Democratization: The United States in Comparative Perspective." *British Journal of Political Science* 34: 193–210.

Goodwin, Jeff. 2006. "A Theory of Categorical Terrorism." *Social Forces* 84: 2027–46.

Gray, Mitchell. 2003. "Urban Surveillance and Panopticism: Will We Recognize the Facial Recognition Society?" *Surveillance & Society* 1: 314–30.

Greenfeld, Liah. 1992. *Nationalism: Five Roads to Modernity*. Cambridge, MA: Harvard University Press.

Grim, Ryan. 2009. "DOJ Official Blows Cover off Patriot Act." *The Huffington Post* (September 23).

Guillermoprieto, Alma. 2010. "A Quiet Shift in Mexico's Drug War." *The New York Review of Books* (August 12).

Gunther, Richard and Anthony Mughan. 1993. "Political Institutions and Cleavage Management," in R. Kent Weaver and Bert A. Rockman, eds., *Do Institutions Matter?* Washington, DC: Brookings.

Gurr, Ted Robert. 1994. "Peoples against States: Ethnopolitical Conflict and the Changing World System." *International Studies Quarterly* 38: 347–77.

Gurr, Ted Robert. 2000. "Ethnic Warfare on the Wane." *Foreign Affairs* 79: 52–64.

Haddad, Yvonne Yazbeck and Michael J. Balz. 2008. "Taming the Imams: European Governments and Islamic Preachers since 9/11." *Islam and Christian-Muslim Relations* 19: 215–35.

Hadenius, Axel and Jan Teorell. 2007. "Pathways from Authoritarianism." *Journal of Democracy* 18: 143–56.

Hagan, Frank E. 2006. "'ORGANIZED CRIME' and 'Organized Crime': Indeterminate Problems of Definition." *Trends in Organized Crime* 9: 127–37.

Hardt, Michael. 2002. "Today's Bandung?" *New Left Review* 14: 112–18.

Harold Pinter Interview. 2008. *Democracy Now!* (December 31). <http://www.democracynow.org>.

Haubrich, Dirk. 2006. "Modern Politics in an Age of Global Terrorism: New Challenges for Domestic Policy." *Political Studies* 54: 399–423.

Held, David, Anthony McGrew, David Goldblatt, and Jonathan Perraton. 1999. *Global Transformations: Politics, Economic and Culture.* Stanford, CA: Stanford University Press.

Hellman, Joel S., Geraint Jones, and Daniel Kaufman. 2000. "'Seize the Day, Seize the State': State Capture, Corruption, and Influence in Transition." *Policy Research Working Paper* no. 2444. Washington, DC: The World Bank.

Higham, John. 1955. *Strangers in the Land: Patterns of American Nativism, 1860-1925.* New Brunswick, NJ: Rutgers University Press.

Hirschl, Ran. 2008. "The Judicialization of Mega-Politics and the Rise of Political Courts." *Annual Review of Political Science* 11: 93–118.

Hislope, Robert. 1995. *Nationalism, Ethnic Politics, and Democratic Consolidation: A Comparative Study of Croatia, Serbia, and Bosnia-Hercegovina.* PhD dissertation, The Ohio State University.

Hislope, Robert. 1996. "Intra-Ethnic Conflict in Croatia and Serbia: Flanking and the Consequences for Democracy." *East European Quarterly* 30: 471–94.

Hislope, Robert. 2003. "Between a Bad Peace and a Good War: Insights and Lessons from the Almost-War in Macedonia." *Ethnic and Racial Studies* 26: 129–51.

Hislope, Robert. 2004. "Crime and Honor in a Weak State: Paramilitary Forces and Violence in Macedonia." *Problems of Post–Communism* 51: 18–26.

Hislope, Robert. 2007. "From Expressive to Actionable Hatred: Ethnic Divisions and Riots in Macedonia," in J. Craig Jenkins and Esther E. Gottlieb, eds., *Identity Conflicts: Can Violence Be Regulated?* New Brunswick, NJ: Transaction Publishers.

Hitchens, Christopher. 1994. "Letter from Macedonia." *New Statesman and Society* (April 15).

Hobbes, Thomas. 1958. *Leviathan: Parts 1 & 2.* Indianapolis, IN: Bobbs-Merrill Educational Publishing.

Hobsbawm, Eric. 1990. *Nations and Nationalism since 1780: Programme, Myth, Reality.* New York: Cambridge University Press.

Hobsbawm, Eric. 2000. *Bandits.* New York: The New Press.

Horowitz, Donald L. 1985. *Ethnic Groups in Conflict.* Berkeley, CA: University of California Press.

Horowitz, Donald L. 1990. "Making Moderation Pay: The Comparative Politics of Ethnic Conflict Management," in Joseph V. Montville, ed., *Conflict and Peacemaking in Multiethnic Societies.* Lexington, KY: Lexington Books.

Hroch, Miroslav. 2000. *Social Preconditions of National Revival in Europe: A Comparative Analysis of the Social Composition of Patriotic Groups among the Smaller European Nations.* New York: Columbia University Press.

Huntington, Samuel P. 1968. *Political Order in Changing Societies.* New Haven, CT: Yale University Press.

Huntington, Samuel P. 1991. *The Third Wave: Democratization in the Late Twentieth Century*. Norman: University of Oklahoma Press.

Huntington, Samuel P. 1993a. "The Clash of Civilizations?" *Foreign Affairs* 72: 22–49.

Huntington, Samuel P. 1993b. "If Not Civilizations, What? Paradigms and the Post–Cold War World." *Foreign Affairs* 72: 186–94.

Huntington, Samuel P. 1996. *The Clash of Civilizations and the Remaking of World Order*. New York: Simon & Schuster.

Huntington, Samuel P. 1997. "After Twenty Years: The Future of the Third Wave." *Journal of Democracy* 8: 3–12.

Hutchcroft, Paul D, 1997. "The Politics of Privilege: Assessing the Impact of Rents, Corruption, and Clientelism on Third World Development." *Political Studies* 45: 639–58.

International Crisis Group. 2006. *Pakistan's Tribal Areas: Appeasing the Militants*. Asia Report no. 125. Islamabad/Brussels: ICG.

International Social Survey Program. 2004. *Citizenship Study*.

Isaak, Robert A. 1995. *Managing World Economic Change*, 2nd ed. Englewood Cliffs, NJ: Prentice-Hall.

Jackson, Robert H. 1982. Why Africa's Weak States Persist: The Empirical and the Juridical in Statehood. *World Politics* 35: 1–24.

Jackson, Robert H. 1990. *Quasi-States: Sovereignty, International Relations, and the Third World*. New York: Cambridge University Press.

Jackson, Robert H. and Carl G. Rosberg. 1982. *Personal Rule in Black Africa: Prince, Autocrat, Prophet, Tyrant*. Berkeley, CA: University of California Press.

James, William. 1931. *The Principles of Psychology*. New York: Holt.

Jamieson, Alison. 2001. "Transnational Organized Crime: A European Perspective." *Studies in Conflict and Terrorism* 24: 377–87.

Johnson, Larry C. 2001. "The Future of Terrorism." *The American Behavioral Scientist* 44: 894–913.

Judt, Tony. 2005. "Europe vs. America." *The New York Review of Books* (February 10).

Judt, Tony. 2010. "Ill Fares the Land," *The New York Review of Books* (April 29).

Kaldor, Mary. 2001. *New and Old Wars: Organized Violence in a Global Era*. Stanford, CA: Stanford University Press.

Kaldor, Mary and Ivan Vejvoda. 1997. "Democratization in Central and East European Countries." *International Affairs* 73: 59–82.

Kaplan, Robert D. 1994. "The Coming Anarchy." *The Atlantic Monthly* 273: 44–75.

Kass, Jeff. 1998. "Violence Escalates in the Name of Environmentalism." *The Christian Science Monitor* (October 26).

Kasza, Gregory J. 1995. *The Conscription Society: Administered Mass Organizations*. New Haven, CT: Yale University Press.

Keck, Margaret E. and Kathryn Sikkink. 1998. *Activists beyond Borders: Advocacy Networks in International Politics*. Ithaca, NY: Cornell University Press.

Kellner, Tomas and Francesco Pipitone. 2010. "Inside Mexico's Drug War." *World Policy Journal* 27: 29–37.

Ketcham, Ralph L. 1958. "James Madison and the Nature of Man." *Journal of the History of Ideas* 19: 62–76.

Kiefer, Peter. 2007. "Mafia Crime is 7% of GDP in Italy, Group Reports." *The New York Times* (October 22).

Kieh, Jr., George Klay and Pita Ogaba Agbese, eds. 2004. *The Military and Politics in Africa: From Engagement to Democratic and Constitutional Control.* Burlington, IN: Ashgate Publishing.

King, Desmond and Robert C. Lieberman. 2009. "Ironies of State Building: A Comparative Perspective on the American State." *World Politics* 61: 547–88.

Kinzer, Stephen. 2006. *Overthrow: America's Century of Regime Change from Hawaii to Iraq.* New York: Times Books.

Kircheimer, Otto. 1966. "The Transformation of the Western European Party System," in Joseph LaPalombara and Myron Weiner, eds., *Political Parties and Political Development.* Princeton, NJ: Princeton University Press.

Klein, Naomi. 2008. *The Shock Doctrine: The Rise of Disaster Capitalism.* New York: Picador.

Klitgaard, Robert. 1988. *Controlling Corruption.* Berkeley, CA: University of California Press.

Kocieniewski, David. 2010. "A Rum Battle, a Tax Hangover." *The New York Times* (October 16).

Kolakowski, Leszek. 2005. *Main Currents of Marxism: The Founders, The Golden Age, The Breakdown.* New York: Norton.

Krasner, Stephen. 1993. "Westphalia and All That," in Judith Goldstein and Robert O. Keohane, eds., *Ideas and Foreign Policy.* Ithaca, NY: Cornell University Press.

Krasner, Stephen D. 2001. *Rethinking the Sovereign State Model.* New York: Cambridge University Press.

Krauss, Clifford. 2004. "Canada Reinforces its Disputed Claims in the Arctic." *The New York Times* (August 29).

Lacey, Marc. 2009. "In Drug War, Mexico Fights Cartel and Itself." *The New York Times* (March 30).

Lacey, Marc. 2009. "Drug Wars: When A Cartel Really Isn't." *The New York Times* (September 21).

Landler, Mark. 2005. "Where to Be Jobless in Europe." *The New York Times* (October 9).

Lane, Frederic. 1979. *Profits from Power: Readings in Protection Rent and Violence-Controlling Enterprises.* Albany, NY: State University of New York Press.

LaPalombara, Joseph and Myron Weiner. 1966. "The Origin and Development of Political Parties," in *idem*, eds., *Political Parties and Political Development.* Princeton, NJ: Princeton University Press.

Laqueur, Walter. 1986. "Reflections on Terrorism." *Foreign Affairs* 65: 86–100.

Lasswell, Harold D. 1936. *Politics: Who Gets What, When, How.* New York: McGraw-Hill.

Lawson, Guy. 2009. "The Making of a Narco State." *Rolling Stone* (March 9).

Lechner, Frank J. 2009. *Globalization: The Making of World Society*. New York: Wiley-Blackwell.

Lenin, Vladimir. 1932. *State and Revolution*. New York: International Publishers.

Lentner, Howard. 2005. "Hegemony and Autonomy." *Political Studies* 53: 735–52.

Levack, Brian, Edward Muir, Michael Mass, and Meredith Veldman. 2007. *The West: Encounters & Transformations, volume II (since 1550)*. 2nd ed. London: Longman.

Levitsky, Steven and Lucan A. Way. 2002. "The Rise of Competitive Authoritarianism." *Journal of Democracy* 13: 51–65.

Lichbach, Mark Irving. 2005. "Information, Trust, and Power: The Impact of Conflict Histories, Policy Regimes, and Political Institutions on Terrorism." *International Studies Review* 7: 162–65.

Lijphart, Arend. 1977. *Democracy in Plural Societies: A Comparative Exploration*. New Haven, CT: Yale University Press.

Lijphart, Arend. 1979. "Religious vs. Linguistic vs. Class Voting: The Crucial Experiment of Comparing Belgium, Canada, South Africa and Switzerland." *American Political Science Review* 73: 442–58.

Lijphart, Arend. 1999. *Patterns of Democracy: Government Forms and Performance in Thirty-Six Countries*. New Haven, CT: Yale University Press.

Lindblom, Charles. 1977. *Politics and Markets: The World's Political-Economic Systems*. New York: Basic Books.

Linton, Marisa. 2006. "Robespierre and the Terror." *History Today* 56: 23–27.

Linz, Juan J. and Alfred Stepan. 1996. *Problems of Democratic Transition and Consolidation: Southern Europe, South America, and Post-Communist Europe*. Baltimore, MD: Johns Hopkins University Press.

Lipset Seymour Martin and Stein Rokkan. 1967. "Cleavage Structures, Party Systems, and Voter Alignments: An Introduction," in *idem*. eds., *Party Systems and Voter Alignments*. New York: Free Press.

Liptak, Adam. 2008. "Inmate Count in US Dwarfs Other Nations." *The New York Times* (April 23).

Livingston, Robert Gerald. 2000. "The Party's Over: Kohl's Disservice to German Democracy." *Foreign Affairs* (May–June): 13–17.

Locke, John. 1980. *Second Treatise of Government*. Indianapolis, IN: Hackett Publishing Co.

Lo Dato, Enzo. 2000. "Palermo's Cultural Revolution and the Renewal Project of the City Administration." *Trends in Organized Crime* 5: 10–34.

Loewenberg, Gerhard, ed. 1971. *Modern Parliaments: Change or Decline?* Chicago: Atherton.

Lustick, Ian. 1997. "Lijphart, Lakatos, and Consociationalism." *World Politics* 50: 88–117.

Machiavelli, Niccolò. 1979. *The Portable Machiavelli*. New York: Penguin Books.

Madison, James. 1893. *Journal of the Constitutional Convention*. E. H. Scott, ed. Chicago: Scott, Foresman.

Mahler, Jonathan. 2010. "After the Imperial Presidency." *The New York Times* (November 9).

Mandela, Nelson. 1994. *Long Walk to Freedom*. Boston: Little, Brown.

Mann, Michael. 2003. *Incoherent Empire*. London: Verso.

Mann, Michael. 2005. *The Dark Side of Democracy: Explaining Ethnic Cleansing*. Cambridge: Cambridge University Press.

Manor, James. 1998. "Making Federalism Work." *Journal of Democracy* 9: 21–35.

Mansbach, Richard W. 2000. *The Global Puzzle: Issues and Actors in World Politics*. 3rd ed. Boston: Houghton Mifflin.

Marcuse, Herbert. 1964. *One-Dimensional Man: Studies in the Ideology of Advanced Industrial Society*. Boston: Beacon Press.

Marongiu, Antonio. 1968. *Medieval Parliaments: A Comparative Study*. London: Eyre & Spottiswoode.

Marx, Karl. 1967. *Capital: A Critique of Political Economy*. vol.1, Frederick Engels, ed. New York: International Publishers.

McCormick, John P. 2007. "Irrational Choice and Mortal Combat as Political Destiny: The Essential Carl Schmitt." *Annual Review of Political Science* 10: 315–39.

McEldowney, John F. 2005. "Political Security and Democratic Rights." *Democratization* 12: 766–82.

McKinley, James C. 2008. "Mexico's War against Drugs Kills Its Police." *The New York Times* (May 26).

McKinley, James C. 2009. "U.S. Is a Vast Arms Bazaar for Mexican Cartels." *The New York Times* (February 26).

McPherson, James M. 2003. "A Confederate Guerrilla." *The New York Review of Books* (February 27).

Merrill, Tim. ed. 1993. *Nicaragua: A Country Study*. Washington, DC: GPO for the Library of Congress.

Mershon, Carol. 1996. "The Costs of Coalition: Coalition Theories and Italian Governments." *The American Political Science Review* 90: 534–54.

Midlarsky, Manus I., Martha Crenshaw, and Fumihiko Yoshida. 1980. "Why Violence Spreads: The Contagion of International Terrorism." *International Studies Quarterly* 24: 262–98.

Mill, John Stuart. 1861. *Considerations on Representative Government*. London: Parker, Son and Bourn.

Mill, John Stuart. 1910. *Representative Government*. London: Dent.

Miller, Gregory D. 2007. "Confronting Terrorisms: Group Motivation and Successful Policies." *Terrorism and Political Violence* 19: 331–51.

Mitchell, Paul. 1995. "Party Competition in an Ethnic Dual Party System." *Ethnic and Racial Studies* 18: 773–96.

Moghadam, Valentine M. 2005. *Globalizing Women: Transnational Feminist Networks*. Baltimore, MD: The Johns Hopkins University Press.

Moore, Jr., Barrington. 1966. *Social Origins of Dictatorship and Democracy: Lord and Peasant in the Making of the Modern World*. Boston: Beacon Press.

Mudde, Cas. 2007. *Populist Radical Right Parties in Europe.* New York: Cambridge University Press.

Mughan, Anthony. 2000. *Media and the Presidentialization of Parliamentary Elections.* New York: Palgrave.

Mughan, Anthony and Pamela Paxton. 2006. "Anti-Immigrant Sentiment, Policy Preferences and Populist Party Voting in Australia." *British Journal of Political Science* 36: 341–58.

Mydans, Seth. 2007. "Across Cultures, English Is the Word." *The New York Times* (April 9).

Nash, Nathaniel C. (1992). "Army Unrest Stirs Bolivia, the Land of Coups." *The New York Times* (June 3).

National Drug Intelligence Center. 2010. *National Drug Threat Assessment 2010.* Washington, DC: U.S. Department of Justice.

Nematt. Salameh. 2011. "Arab Pundits Cheer the Tunisia, Egypt Protests." *Newsweek* (January 28).

Neustadt, Richard E. 1960. *Presidential Power.* New York: Wiley.

Norris, Pippa. 2004. *Electoral Engineering: Voting Rules and Political Behavior.* New York: Cambridge University Press.

Norris, Pippa. 2005. *Radical Right: Voters and Parties in the Electoral Market.* New York: Cambridge University Press.

Nye, Jr., Joseph. S. 2008. *The Powers to Lead.* New York: Oxford University Press.

Oberschall, Anthony. 1996. "Opportunities and Framing in the East European Revolts of 1989," in Doug McAdam, John D. McCarthy, and Mayer N. Zald, eds., *Comparative Perspectives on Social Movements: Political Opportunities, Mobilizing Structures, and Cultural Framings.* New York: Cambridge University Press.

O'Brien, Kevin. 1988. "China's National People's Congress: Reform and Its Limits." *Legislative Studies Quarterly* 13: 343–74.

O'Donnell, Guillermo, Philippe C. Schmitter, and Laurence Whitehead, eds. 1986. *Transitions from Authoritarian Rule: Prospects for Democracy.* Baltimore, MD: Johns Hopkins University Press.

O'Neil, Shannon. 2009. "The Real War in Mexico." *Foreign Affairs* 88: 63–77.

O'Neill, William L. 2001. *The New Left: A History.* Wheeling, IL: Harlan Davidson.

Olson, Mancur. 1982. *The Rise and Decline of Nations: Economic Growth, Stagflation and Social Rigidities.* New Haven, CT: Yale University Press.

Olson, Mancur. 1993. "Dictatorship, Democracy, and Development." *American Political Science Review* 87: 567–76.

Osborne, David and Ted Gaebler. 1992. *Reinventing Government: How the Entrepreneurial Spirit Is Transforming the Public Sector.* New York: Penguin.

Osiander, Andreas. 2001. "Sovereignty, International Relations, and the Westphalian Myth." *International Organization* 55: 251–87.

Owolabi, Kunle. 2007. "Politics, Institutions and Ethnic Voting in Plural Democracies: Comparative Lessons from Trinidad and Tobago, Guyana, and

Mauritius." Paper presented at Midwest Political Science Association Conference, Chicago, April 12–15.

Paoli, Letizia. 1999. "The Political-Criminal Nexus in Italy." *Trends in Organized Crime* 5: 15–58.

Paoli, Letizia and Marvin E. Wolfgang. 2001. "Crime, Italian Style." *Daedalus* 130: 157–85.

Parris, Carl. 1990. "Trinidad and Tobago, 1956–86: Has the Political Elite Changed?" *Round Table* 79: 147–56.

Patterson, Samuel C. and Anthony Mughan, eds. 1999. *Senates: Bicameralism in the Contemporary World*. Columbus, OH: The Ohio State University Press.

Pei, Minxin. 2003. "Rotten From Within: Decentralized Predation and Incapacitated State," in T.V. Paul, G. John Ikenberry, and John A. Hall, eds., *The Nation-State in Question*. Princeton, NJ: Princeton University Press.

Perlez, Jane. 2009. "Pakistan Rebuffs U.S. on Taliban Crackdown." *The New York Times* (December 15).

Petersen, Roger. 2002. *Understanding Ethnic Violence: Fear, Hatred, and Resentment in Twentieth Century Eastern Europe*. New York: Cambridge University Press.

Peterson, Jon E. 2001. "Succession in the States of the Gulf Cooperation Council." *The Washington Quarterly* 24: 173–86.

Pierson, Paul. 1996. "The New Politics of the Welfare State." *World Politics* 48: 143–79.

Pimentel, Stanley A. 1999. "The Nexus of Organized Crime and Politics in Mexico." *Trends in Organized Crime* 4: 9–28.

Plato. 1982. *Plato's Republic*. New York: Modern Library.

Porta, Donatella Della and Alberto Vannucci. 1997. "The 'Perverse Effects' of Political Corruption." *Political Studies* 45: 516–38.

Porta, Donatella Della and Alberto Vannucci. 1999. *Corrupt Exchanges: Actors, Resources, and Mechanisms of Political Corruption*. New York: Aldine de Gruyter.

Posen, Barry R. 1993. "The Security Dilemma and Ethnic Conflict." *Survival* 5: 27–47.

Premdas, Ralph R. and Bishnu Ragoonth. 1998. "Ethnicity, Elections, and Democracy in Trinidad and Tobago: Analysing the 1995 and 1996 Elections." *Commonwealth and Comparative Politics* 36: 30–53.

Proudhon, Pierre Joseph. 1923. *General Idea of the Revolution in the Nineteenth Century*. London: Freedom Press.

Prunckun, Jr., Henry W. and Philip B. Mohr. 1997. "Military Deterrence of International Terrorism: An Evaluation of Operation El Dorado Canyon." *Studies in Conflict and Terrorism* 20: 267–80.

Przeworski, Adam. 1986. "Some Problems in the Study of the Transition to Democracy," in Guillermo O'Donnell, Philippe C. Schmitter, and Laurence Whitehead, eds., *Transitions from Authoritarian Rule: Prospects for Democracy*. Baltimore: Johns Hopkins University Press.

Pulzer, Peter. 1967. *Political Representation and Elections in Britain*. London: Allen and Unwin.

Rao, Parsa Venkateshwar. 2010. "Email and Web Nationalism Are the Latest Forms: Benedict Anderson." *Daily News and Analysis* (February 7).

Rapoport, David C. 2004. "The Four Waves of Modern Terrorism," in Audrey Kurth Cronin and James Ludes, eds., *Attacking Terrorism: Elements of a Grand Strategy*. Washington, DC: Georgetown University Press.

Reif, Linda, ed. *International Ombudsman Anthology*. The Hague: Kluwer

Ripley, Tim. 2001. "Waging War by Terrorvision." *The Scotsman* (September 17).

Ritzer, George F. 2007. *The McDonaldization of Society*, 5th ed. Thousand Oaks, CA: Pine Forge Press.

Roberts, Sam. 2008. "In a Generation, Minorities May Be the U.S. Majority." *The New York Times* (August 14).

Roeder, Philip G. 1999. "People and States after 1989: The Political Costs of Incomplete National Revolutions." *Slavic Review* 58: 854–82.

Roosevelt, Kermit. 2006. *The Myth of Judicial Activism: Making Sense of Supreme Court Decisions*. New Haven, CT: Yale University Press.

Rose, Richard. 1989. *Politics in England: Change and Persistence*. Boston: Little, Brown.

Rossiter, Clinton. 1956. *The American Presidency*. New York: Harcourt, Brace.

Rothschild, Joseph. 1974. *East Central Europe between the Two World Wars*. Seattle, WA: University of Washington Press.

Rothschild, Joseph. 1981. *Ethnopolitics: A Conceptual Framework*. New York: Columbia University Press.

Rousseau, Jean-Jacques. 1983. *On the Social Contract and Discourses*. Indianapolis, IN: Hackett Publishing Co.

Rudra, Nita. 2008. *Globalization and the Race to the Bottom in Developing Countries: Who Really Gets Hurt?* New York: Cambridge: Cambridge University Press.

Sartori, Giovanni. 1966. "European Political Parties: The Case of Polarized Pluralism," in Joseph LaPalombara and Myron Weiner, eds., *Political Parties and Political Development*. Princeton: Princeton University Press.

Sartori, Giovanni. 1970. "Concept Misformation in Comparative Politics." *American Political Science Review* 64: 1033–53.

Sartori, Giovanni. 1973. "What Is 'Politics?'" *Political Theory* 1: 5–26.

Sartori, Giovanni. 1987. *The Theory of Democracy Revisited. Parts 1 & 2*. Chatham, NJ: Chatham House.

Sartori, Giovanni. 1994. *Comparative Constitutional Engineering: An Inquiry into Structures, Incentives and Outcomes*. New York: New York University Press.

Schattschneider, Elmer E. 1942. *Party Government*. New York: Holt, Rinehart & Winston.

Schattschneider, Elmer E. 1960. *The Semisovereign People: A Realist's View of Democracy in America*. New York: Holt, Rinehart & Winston.

Schedler, Andreas, ed. 2006. *Electoral Authoritarianism: The Dynamics of Unfree Competition*. Boulder, CO: Lynne Reiner.

Schmid, Alex. 1984. *Political Terrorism: A Research Guide*. New Brunswick, NJ: Transaction Books.

Scholte, Jan Aart. 2005. *Globalization: A Critical Introduction*. New York: St. Martin's Press.

Schwarz, Benjamin. 1995. "The Diversity Myth: America's Leading Export." *The Atlantic Monthly* (May).

Shabad, Goldie. 1986. "After Autonomy," in Stanley G. Payne, ed., *The Politics of Democratic Spain*. Chicago: The Chicago Council on Foreign Relations.

Shane, Scott. 2009. "The War in Pashtunistan." *The New York Times* (December 5).

Shapiro, Jeremy and Bénédicte Suzan. 2003. "The French Experience of Counter-Terrorism," *Survival* 45: 67–98.

Shelley, Louise I. 1995. "Transnational Organized Crime: An Imminent Threat to the Nation-State?" *Journal of International Affairs* 48: 463–89.

Sibley, Mulford Q. 1970. *Political Ideas and Ideologies: A History of Political Thought*. New York: Harper and Row.

Sidel, John T. 1999. *Capital, Coercion, and Crime: Bossism in the Philippines*. Stanford, CA: Stanford University Press.

Simons, Marise. 2010. "Supermodel Called to Testify at War Crimes Trial." *The New York Times* (July 1).

Sitter, Nick. 2002. "Cleavages, Party Strategy and Party System Change in Europe, East and West." *Perspectives on European Politics and Society* 3: 425–51.

Skilling, H. Gordon, ed. 1971. *Interest Groups in Soviet Politics*. Princeton, NJ: Princeton University Press.

Small Arms Survey. 2007. *Completing the Count: Civilian Firearms*. Oxford: Oxford University Press.

Smith, Adam. 1976. *An Inquiry into the Nature and Causes of the Wealth of Nations*. Chicago: University of Chicago Press.

Smith, Anthony. 2000. *The Nation in History: Historiographical Debates about Ethnicity and Nationalism*. Cambridge: Polity Press.

Smith, Benjamin. 2006. "The Wrong Kind of Crisis: Why Oil Booms and Busts Rarely Lead to Authoritarian Breakdown." *Studies in Comparative International Development* 40: 55–76.

Snyder, Jack. 2000. *From Voting to Violence: Democratization and Nationalist Conflict*. New York: Norton.

Sombart, Werner. 1976. *Why Is There No Socialism in the United States?* White Plains, NY: International Arts and Sciences Press.

Spruyt, Hendrick. 2002. "The Origins, Development, and Possible Decline of the Modern State." *Annual Review of Political Science* 5: 127–49.

Steen, Michael. 2010. "Intolerant Kingmaker Defies Dutch Clichés." *Financial Times* (February 27/28).

Sterling, Claire. 1994. *Thieves' World: The Threat of the New Global Network of Organized Crime*. New York: Simon and Schuster.

Stigler, George. 1971. "The Theory of Economic Regulation." *Bell Journal of Economics and Management Science* 3: 3–18.

Strange, Susan. 1999. "The Westfailure System." *Review of International Studies* 25: 345–54.

Sweet, Alec Stone. 2008. "*Constitutions and Judicial Power,*" in Daniele Caramani, ed., *Comparative Politics*. Oxford: Oxford University Press.

The Failed States Index 2011. *Foreign Policy*. <www.foreignpolicy.com/failed states>.

Thomas, Clive S., ed. 1993. *First World Interest Groups: A Comparative Perspective*. Westport, CT: Greenwood Press.

Thompson, Alexander and Duncan Snidal. 2012. "International Organization: Institutions and Order in World Politics," in Boudewijn Bouckaert and Gerrit De Geest, eds., *Encyclopedia of Law and Economics*. 2nd ed. Cheltenham: Edward Elgar.

Tilly, Charles. 1985. "War Making and State Making as Organized Crime," in Peter B. Evans, Dietrich Rueschemeyer, and Theda Skocpol, eds., *Bringing the State Back In*. New York: Cambridge University Press.

Transparency International. 2011. *Corruption Perceptions Index 2011*. Berlin.

Trotsky, Leon. 1920. *In Defense of Terrorism*. <http://www.marxists.org/archive>.

Tsebelis, George and Jeannette Money. 1997. *Bicameralism*. New York: Cambridge University Press.

Ungar, Sanford J. and Peter Vale.1985. "South Africa: Why Constructive Engagement Failed." *Foreign Affairs* 64: 234–58.

United Nations Development Program. 2011. *Human Development Report 2011*. New York: UNDP.

United Nations Office on Drugs and Crime. 2010. *World Drug Report 2010*. New York: United Nations Publications.

United States Department of State. 2010. *International Narcotics Control Strategy Report*, vol. 1. Washington, DC.

Urquhart, Cornal. 2006. "Hamas in Call to End Suicide Bombings." *The Observer* (April 9).

Uvin, Peter. 1997. "Prejudice, Crisis, and Genocide in Rwanda." *African Studies Review* 40: 91–115.

Van Dijk, Jan. 2007. "Mafia Markers: Assessing Organized Crime and Its Impact upon Societies." *Trends in Organized Crime* 10: 39–56.

Varese, Federico. 1994. "Is Sicily the Future of Russia? Private Protection and the Rise of the Russian Mafia." *Archives Européennes de Sociologie* 35: 224–58.

Vestal, Theodore M. 2001. "*A Peace Corps History*." Speech delivered at the 40th Anniversary of the Founding of the Peace Corps (April 28), Tulsa, Oklahoma. <http://fp.okstate.edu/vestal/InternationalStudy/Peace_Corps_History.htm>.

Volkov, Vadim. 2002. *Violent Entrepreneurs: The Use of Force in the Making of Russian Capitalism*. Ithaca, NY: Cornell University Press.

Wallechinsky, David. 2006. *Tyrants: The World's 20 Worst Living Dictators*. New York: Regan.

Wheare, K.C. 1967. *Legislatures*. 2nd ed. Oxford: Oxford University Press.

Whitaker, Beth Elise. 2007. "Exporting the Patriot Act? Democracy and the 'War on Terror' in the Third World." *Third World Quarterly* 28: 1017–32.

White, Richard. 1981. "Outlaw Gangs of the Middle Border: American Social Bandits." *The Western Historical Quarterly* 12: 387–408.

Whittington, Keith E. 2008. "Constitutionalism," in Keith E. Whittington, R. Daniel Kelemen, and Gregory A. Caldeira, eds., *The Oxford Handbook of Law and Politics*. Oxford: Oxford University Press.

Wiseman, Paul. 2010. "Not Extending Unemployment Benefits Would Lower Economic Growth." *The Huffington Post* (November 30), <http://www.huffingtonpost.com>.

Wood, Gordon S. 1969. *The Creation of the American Republic, 1776–1787*. New York: W. W. Norton.

Woodward, Susan L. 1995. *Balkan Tragedy: Chaos and Dissolution after the Cold War*. Washington, DC: Brookings Institution.

Wolff, Robert Paul. 1970. *In Defense of Anarchism*. New York: Harper Torchbooks.

World Public Opinion.Org. 2006. "The Iraqi Public on the U.S. Presence and the Future of Iraq," Program on International Policy Attitudes, Center for International and Security Studies at Maryland, the University of Maryland's School for Public Policy, (September 27).

Yardley, Welliam. 2008. "Ecoterrorism Suspected in House Fires in Seattle Suburb." *The New York Times* (March 4).

Zacher, Mark W. 2001. "The Territorial Integrity Norm: International Boundaries and the Use of Force." *International Organization* 55: 215–50.

Zakaria, Fareed. 2010. "What America Has Lost." *Newsweek* (September 4).

Ziblatt, Daniel. 2004. "Rethinking the Origins of Federalism: Puzzles, Theories and Evidence from Nineteenth-Century Europe." *World Politics* 57: 70–98.

Zick, Andreas, Thomas F. Pettigrew, and Ulrich Wagner. 2008. "Ethnic Prejudice and Discrimination in Europe." *Journal of Social Issues* 64: 233–51.

Zolberg, Aristide. 1966. *Creating Political Order: The Party-States of West Africa*. Chicago: Rand McNally.

INDEX